I0328077

PENTECOSTAL
and
HOLINESS STATEMENTS
on WAR *and* PEACE

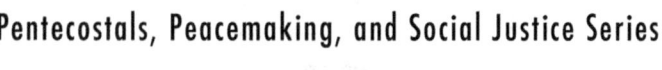

Pentecostals, Peacemaking, and Social Justice Series

PAUL ALEXANDER AND JAY BEAMAN, SERIES EDITORS

Volumes in the Series:

Pentecostal Pacifism: The Origin, Development, and Rejection of Pacific Belief among the Pentecostals
by Jay Beaman

A Liberating Spirit: Pentecostals and Social Action in North America
edited by Michael Wilkinson and Steven M. Studebaker

Forgiveness, Reconciliation, and Restoration: Mulitdisciplinary Studies from a Pentecostal Perspective
edited by Martin W. Mittelstadt and Geoffrey W. Sutton

The Liberating Mission of Jesus: The Message of the Gospel of Luke
by Dario Lopez Rodriguez

Christ at the Checkpoint: Theology in the Service of Justice and Peace
edited by Paul Nathan Alexander

Pentecostal and Holiness Statements on War and Peace

EDITED BY

JAY BEAMAN and BRIAN K. PIPKIN

FOREWORD BY

TITUS PEACHY

PICKWICK *Publications* • Eugene, Oregon

PENTECOSTAL AND HOLINESS STATEMENTS ON WAR AND PEACE

Pentecostals, Peacemaking, and Social Justice 6

Copyright © 2013 Wipf and Stock Publishers. All rights reserved. Except for brief quotations in critical publications or reviews, no part of this book may be reproduced in any manner without prior written permission from the publisher. Write: Permissions. Wipf and Stock Publishers, 199 W. 8th Ave., Suite 3, Eugene, OR 97401.

Pickwick Publications
An Imprint of Wipf and Stock Publishers
199 W. 8th Ave., Suite 3
Eugene, OR 97401

www.wipfandstock.com

ISBN 13: 978-1-61097-908-5

Cataloguing-in-Publication Data

Pentecostal and holiness statements on war and peace / edited by Jay Beaman and Brian K. Pipkin

Pentecostals, Peacemaking, and Social Justice 6

xx + 292 p. ; 23 cm. Includes bibliographical references.

ISBN 13: 978-1-61097-908-5

1. Peace—Religious aspects—Pentecostal churches. 2. Peace—Religious aspects—Holiness churches. 3. Nonviolence—Religious aspects—Christianity. I. Beaman, Jay. II. Pipkin, Brian K. III. Series. IV. Title.

BX8765.5 B213 2013

Manufactured in the U.S.A.

Contents

Foreword by Titus Peachy / ix

Acknowledgments / xix

1 Introduction / 1
Jay Beaman

2 Anabaptist Peace as Context / 40
Introduction
Mennonites (Anabaptists) / 43
Church of God in Christ, Mennonite / 43

3 Antebellum Holiness Statements / 46
Introduction
Amos Dresser / 49
Churches of God in North America (Winebrenner) / 50
John Wesley / 51
Methodism and War / 52
Thomas C. Upham / 52

4 Radical Holiness Statements / 56
Introduction
Allegheny Wesleyan Methodist Connection / 63
Brethren in Christ [Formerly River Brethren] / 64
Calvary Holiness Church / 68
Christian Catholic Apostolic Church / 68
Church of God (Fort Scott, Kansas) / 70
Church of the Living God / 71
Christ's Sanctified Holy Church / 72
Christian Nation Church / 74

Church of God (Anderson, Indiana) / 74
Church of God Apostolic, Inc. / 84
Church of God (Guthrie, Oklahoma) / 84
Church of the Gospel / 93
Church of the Nazarene / 93
Churches of God in North America [Winebrenner] / 95
Congregational: Broadway Tabernacle / 97
Emmanuel Holiness Church / 98
Emmanuel Association / 98
Emmanuel's Fellowship / 99
Free Methodist Church / 100
God's Missionary Church / 106
Gospel Mission Corps, Inc. / 106
Holiness Christian Church / 107
Kentucky Mountain Holiness Association / 108
Mennonite Brethren in Christ, later Missionary Church Association / United
   Missionary Church / 108
Pilgrim Holiness Church (San Diego, California) / 109
Pillar of Fire / 110
Religious Society of Friends / 111
The Fire Baptized Holiness Church / 116
The Missionary Church Association / The United Missionary Church / 116
The New Testament Church (Los Angeles, California) / 118
The Salvation Army / 118
The Wesleyan Church / 124
United Holiness Church of North America / 125

5 Pentecostal Statements / 126
Introduction
Apostolic Church (Bay City, Texas) / 133
Apostolic Faith (Baxter Springs, Kansas) / 134
Apostolic Faith Mission / 137
Apostolic Faith (Portland, Oregon) / 141
Apostolic Faith or Church of God (Mulberry, Kansas / Tulsa, Oklahoma) / 143
Assemblies of God / 143
Assemblies of the Lord Jesus Christ / 147
Bethel Baptist Assembly, Inc. / 148
California Evangelistic Association / 149
Calvary Pentecostal Church / 149
Church of God (Cleveland, Tennessee) / 150
Church of God (Huntsville, Alabama) / 153
Church of God in Christ / 153
Church of God in Christ, Congregational / 158
Church of God (Stanberry, Missouri) / 159
Church of the Living God (Berkeley, California) / 160
Church of the Lord Jesus Christ of the Apostolic Faith / 160
Churches of God of the Original Mountain Assembly Incorporated / 162

Congregational Holiness Church / 164
Filipino Assemblies of the First-Born, Incorporated / 164
Homestead Heritage / 165
Iglesia Cristiana Evangelica Mexicana / 167
International Church of the Foursquare Gospel / 167
International Pentecostal Assemblies / 179
La Iglesia De Dios Pentecostal, Incorporada / 179
Mount Sinai Holy Church of America, Inc. / 180
Olazabal Council of Latin-American Churches / 180
Open Bible Standard Churches, Inc. / 181
Original Pentecostal Church of God / 183
Pentecostal Assemblies of the World / 183
Pentecostals and Charismatics for Peace and Justice / 186
Pentecostal Evangelical Church / 191
Pentecostal Fire-Baptized Holiness Church / 191
Pentecostal Holiness Church / 191
Romanian Apostolic Pentecostal Church of God / 197
Seventh Day Pentecostal Church of the Living God / 197
The Comeouter [Pentecostal Periodical] / 198
The Full Gospel Church Association / 201
The General Assembly and Church of the Firstborn / 202
The Pentecostal Church of God of America / 203
Triumph The Church / 203
United Pentecostal Church / 204
Westgate Chapel / 216

6 **International Holiness and Pentecostal Statements / 217**
Introduction
Australia / 223
Britain / 223
Canada / 246
Palestine / 247
Peru / 254
Russia / 256
South Africa / 263
Switzerland / 264

Appendix: Pentecostal Assemblies of the World Statement of Faith (1917) / 265

Bibliography / 271
Name Index / 287
Group Index / 289

vii

Foreword

Titus Peachey

This book is an invitation to think deeply about the beliefs that shape our lives and our actions. In a world where wars and terror have become our daily bread, how does Jesus call us to live? Are we living by the faith and hope that we find in the Spirit of Christ, or has the spirit of a violent and fear–filled culture seeped into our souls?

The statements in this book spring from the lived experiences of Pentecostal and Holiness communities of faith during a century of struggle to be faithful disciples of Jesus. The question is not if these communities were faithful, or if we would have been faithful in their setting. These statements are a mirror, helping us to reflect on the challenges before us in our day.

The year was 1918 and the world was at war. On July 26 of that year my great-uncle, Ed Beitzel, was drafted into the U.S. Army. A conservative Mennonite farm boy who grew up in the relative isolation of western Maryland's hill country, he declared himself a conscientious objector to war, and was sent off to Camp Meade to serve his time. Little is known within the family about great-uncle Ed's experiences in the military. However a response to a post-World War I survey of conscientious objectors revealed this response to a question about mistreatment in his own handwriting:

What mistreatment, if any, did you receive in the first camp? "I once was taken out by two men with guns. I think an officer went along. There was a Dunkard boy with me too. I was ordered to turn my back. The gun's

ix

x   Foreword

hammer snapped but no harm was done. I had no fear. The Bible says not to fear them that can kill the body, but should rather fear God."[1]

I am struck by the simple faith and spiritual power packed into this short account of my great uncle's experience nearly 100 years ago. There is a calm and unquestioning resolve built on a bedrock of faith and biblicism that no gun could shake. It is indeed remarkable that a young farm hand with grade school education could say no to his military commander in the midst of a nation at war when pressure to conform was intense.

This clarity and resolve is found in many of the early statements from the Pentecostal and Holiness groups that appear in this collection. They reflect the strength of communities of faith that nurture these commitments to peace as a separate people, called to live holy and peaceful lives distinct from the ways of the world.

Opposition to war was a part of the identity of many of these faith communities represented and was often a test of membership. A 1917 statement by a Church of God in Missouri states: "We are forever opposed to war, . . . we are opposed to our members training or in any way preparing to kill, we refuse to be trained or drilled for combatant military service in any nation, Heartily Approved."

Similarly, a 1918 court statement by Elder C. H. Mason of the Church of God in Christ, states that their members are "not allowed to carry arms or to shed the blood of any man and still be members . . ."

In the context of World War I, these early statements represent a minority position held by people on the fringes of society. Yet the statements found in this book have their roots in a deep reservoir of Christian faith and experience dating back to the early church. In the first three centuries it was assumed that followers of Jesus did not become soldiers. Further, if soldiers already in the army converted to Christianity, they normally ended their military service, sometimes by way of martyrdom.[2]

Many young Pentecostal conscientious objectors during World War I were separated from their families and communities of faith and sent to military camps. There they endured the dilemmas of living out the meaning of their convictions under the sometimes harsh authority of military commanders. Indeed, a World War I database of conscientious objectors

1. *World War I Conscientious Objector Questionnaires A–B.*
2. *The American Flag.*

Foreword   xi

lists a number of Pentecostal, Holiness, and Apostolic men with prison sentences at Ft. Leavenworth, KS or Camp Meade, MD.[3]

During that era there were no provisions for alternative service, so each conscientious objector had to work out their own arrangements with their commander. While some commanders were understanding, many sought to "break" the conscientious objectors into submission. Joseph and Michael Hofer, Hutterite brothers from South Dakota, died from extreme mistreatment at Ft. Leavenworth in 1918.[4] Emanuel Swartzendruber, a Mennonite from Michigan, was lowered head first into a latrine pit for refusing to wear a military uniform.[5]

Oscar Wheeler, a Pentecostal from West Virginia was imprisoned at Ft. Leavenworth. On October 18, 1917, he was dragged into a shack, smothered with a blanket, assaulted, and robbed.[6] Edward Hein of the Holiness Church of God in Chancey, Oklahoma, was court martialed for refusing to wear the military uniform and imprisoned at Ft. Leavenworth.[7] With stories like these in circulation, how would individual conscientious objectors remain true to their faith and the convictions of their faith community? What would guide them through decisions about wearing a military uniform, standing in formation or holding a gun? What level of compliance with military authority was acceptable while remaining true to the "Prince of Peace" so often referenced in the statements of their communities?

In a story from the record of George S. Miller, a conscientious objector at Camp Dodge during World War I, we learn how a group of conscientious objectors tried to apply their peacemaking convictions and skills with the officers in charge. This was no small matter. George's nose had been crushed by the fist of an officer, and the camp's group of five conscientious objectors had been stripped and scrubbed down with firm brushes and brooms till their skin had become raw.

> One day a small box of apples came through for the Pentecostal boy, and the officer that mistreated us saw it and felt bad that he did not get a hold of it. The Pentecostal boy picked out the biggest and shining one and brought it to this officer. It was in-

3. *World War I Conscientious Objectors Database.*

4. Peachey, *Christ or Country*, 21.

5. Ibid., 182.

6. *Record Detail from World War I Conscientious Objectors Database.*

7. Ibid.

teresting to watch him. First he hesitated to take it. Next tears came to his eyes and he finally reached out his hand and took it. After this he always treated us fine. Now we have tried to put that scripture into practice (If a man's ways please the Lord, He maketh even his enemies to be at peace with him). (Proverbs 16:7). In other words we have tried to return good for evil and it nearly always worked.[8]

I read these stories and statements against the backdrop of my own life experiences. I grew up in a Mennonite community which valued peace, discipleship, and separation from the world. Our theology called us to live counter-culturally, out of sync with the values of this world because Jesus' way was the way of service and love, even for our enemies. Conscientious objection to war was only one of the many ways we tried to live out the meaning of Rom 12:2: "Do not be conformed to this world, but be transformed by the renewing of your minds . . ." We lived this out very imperfectly. We were often judgmental of others and at times were much too rigid with one another; but the call to follow Jesus in faithful living was clear.

So in 1970, fifty-two years after my great uncle Ed was sent to Camp Meade, I got on a plane in Columbus, Ohio and flew to Vietnam to do my alternative service as a conscientious objector. While there were many stateside opportunities to do my alternative service, my particular skills and interests led me to a three-year assignment with the Mennonite Mission, teaching English to high school and university students in Saigon. I also worked for several months in the Central Highlands on a public health project in a tribal village near Pleiku.

I do not remember this as something unusual. I was simply following in the footsteps of many who had gone before me. I had been nurtured in an alternative community, and was finding my own path to live out its values. Some years later my wife Linda and I worked with Mennonite Central Committee in Laos, a country bordering Vietnam that had suffered a nine-year secret U.S. air war that left behind approximately 80 million unexploded bombs which continue to maim and kill villagers today. From my life experience I resonate with many of the themes present in these statements. The themes are highly relevant to all who would follow Christ's call to live as peacemakers in our world today.

---

8. *World War I Conscientious Objector Questionnaires, G Miller–J Plank.*

Foreword   xiii

ALLEGIANCE

Allegiance and identity are central issues for Christians, especially in times of war. When the nation calls on its youth to submit to military command and learn to kill, Christians often wonder if this is compatible with loving God with heart, soul, mind, and strength and loving neighbor as self. A common refrain in many of the statements in this collection is that, "Our first duty is to God," and we "must obey God rather than man."[9] In so doing, these statements are rooted in a tradition that goes back to the earliest days of the Christian community.

Marcellus, a centurion in the Roman army, addressed the issue of allegiance when required to venerate Caesar at his birthday festivities. Throwing down his belt and weapons in front of his troops he declared, "I am a soldier of Jesus Christ the eternal king. From now on I cease to serve your emperors. . . . For it is not fitting that a Christian, who fights for Christ his Lord, should fight for the armies of this world." Marcellus was tried and executed on October 30, 298 A.D.[10] An 1892 document from this collection follows in the tradition of Marcellus, stating: "All so called 'Christian testimony against war' which does not definitely encourage every christian [sic] soldier to lay down his arms even if he be imprisoned or shot for it . . . is either false and hypocritical or else culpably ignorant."[11]

Richard Davis, a former chaplain in the U.S. Army who became a conscientious objector to war in the 1990s contrasts allegiance to God and allegiance to country in very clear terms: "I realized that the type of allegiance that the military calls from young people is an idolatrous type of allegiance. It calls you to a different God . . . to the god of war. Ultimately, I just had to say I have given my allegiance incorrectly to the United States of America. I need to retract that . . . and then give it back to Jesus Christ because He is the only one that has the right . . . to call from us this kind of allegiance."[12]

There are broader issues than the individual decisions of soldiers or individuals facing conscription. A stirring statement from the pastor of the Apostolic Faith Church in England during World War I raises a troubling set of questions: "Ecclesiastics on both sides have made the vindication of the national cause identical with triumph of the kingdom of God!"

9. See statement by the Church of God, Guthrie, OK, 1961.

10. *The American Flag.*

11. See chapter 6, Booth–Clibborn, *War and the Gospel: Forward!*

12. *Change of Command.*

xiv   Foreword

How do we pray for our leaders in time of war? What message is sent to Christians in another country when U.S. presidents who profess Christian faith use spiritual language to describe the other nation as evil? Can we Christians announce our allegiance to our own country in pledges and songs while our nation's bombs fall on others created and loved by God? How do we love our neighbor, the soldier who returns from combat with the demons of war still stirring within? How do our lives and consumption patterns contribute to the U.S.'s projection of military power to protect our access to oil and other economic interests? Can we expect to give our full allegiance to God and experience no discomfort in the social and political context in which we live? These are hard questions. God and nation are not two equal powers vying for our allegiance. These early statements urge us to keep our allegiance to God primary.

THE INTERNATIONAL CHURCH

The Pentecost event in Acts speaks to Christian unity in a powerful way, as the Holy Spirit enabled people from "every nation under heaven" (Acts 2:5) to hear the good news in their native tongue. The barriers of race, nation, and language were overcome as the Spirit led the hearers to repent of their sins, become baptized, and share all things. It was a powerful movement of the Spirit that brought unity and peace to a very diverse human family.

Perhaps the strongest statement that references the international body of Christ comes from the Church of God in Guthrie, Oklahoma. This statement notes that a misinterpretation of Romans 13 "would require the true Christians of all nations engaged in war to fight for their respective governments, with the result that brethren in Christ would meet on the battlefield, seeking to kill and destroy one another. Such a course is unthinkable, for it would violate every cardinal teaching of Christ." A statement by Pentecostals and Charismatics for Peace and Justice (PCPJ) states this concern more positively, noting that many "early twentieth century Pentecostals recognized that the missionary message of the Good News necessitated nonviolence and racial reconciliation at local, national, and international levels of society."

Glen Guyton, a U.S. Air Force veteran from the 1990s notes the incompatibility of war with the spread of the gospel. "The Great Commission says, 'go ye therefore and teach all nations.' I can't teach anyone with an

M-16 [semi-automatic rifle] pointed to their head. I'm not going to be welcomed enough in a foreign nation if I'm coming in there to destroy that nation."[13]

Pentecostal leader Arthur Booth Clibborn makes the point eloquently in *Blood Against Blood*, published in 1914: "Those persons who died out yonder belonged, after all, to no empire, to no church, to no organization or sect. They belonged to God, to humanity, to each of us, as we belong to them . . ." This, he wrote, "will settle the question of war forever."[14]

We may well ask ourselves, is our identity as a member of the worldwide body of Christ as strong as our identity as U.S. citizens? What are the markers that would help us know? Can we imagine bonds with sisters and brothers around the world so strong and so true that no U.S. President would dare launch a war?

The worldwide family of faith, from Pentecost to Revelation, is at the heart of Christian life and identity in the New Testament. The vision of John in the book of Revelation includes a "great multitude that no one could count, from every nation, from all tribes and peoples and languages, standing before the throne and before the lamb . . ." (Rev 7:9). This vision is a sign of the unity we are called to live out in our world, and helps to loosen the divisive grip of nationalism and race on the life of the Christian community.

THE REALITY OF WAR AND MORAL INJURY

A Church of God Anderson statement addresses the reality of war directly. It begins with: "It is wrong to kill people . . . War is cruel . . ." It then describes war in graphic terms, referring to devastation, murder, disease, destruction of property, breaking-up of homes, dead bodies, starving widows, and fatherless children; and, in a precursor to a popular bumper sticker of our day, the statement continues: "Jesus Christ said, 'Love your enemies,' He did not say shoot them."[15] Surely the destruction of war is hard to reconcile with Jesus' call to become peacemakers. Increasingly, we are becoming more aware of the woundedness of our soldiers and veterans.

Several years ago I met Mr. Y, an Iraq war veteran who had returned to the U.S., and was having great difficulty adjusting. On his computer, he

13. Ibid.

14. Schlabach and Hughes, *Proclaim Peace*, 44.

15. See chapter 4, *On the Sacredness of Human Life*, Church of God (Anderson).

xvi Foreword

had collected photos of dead Iraqis. He told me that he got pleasure from looking at the photos. However, he wondered aloud, "What has happened to me? Why can't I feel any compassion for them and their families?"[16]

Mr. Y is just one of many combat veterans whose wartime experiences come home with them, haunting their sleep and troubling their relationships. For Mr. Y, the emotional shut down that was likely a survival skill in Iraq had robbed him, at least temporarily, of the important human quality of empathy.

In response to the experiences of U.S. Iraq and Afghanistan war veterans, the Veterans Administration has identified a new category of harm known as moral injury. "In the context of war, moral injuries may stem from direct participation in acts of combat, such as killing or harming others, or indirect acts, such as witnessing death or dying, failing to prevent immoral acts of others, or giving or receiving orders that are perceived as gross moral violations."[17]

Moral injury is not limited to soldiers who have become conscientious objectors or who have had training about peace from a religious perspective. Moral injury can happen to any soldier, including those without religious upbringings. Combat frequently raises questions about responsibility, morality, guilt, and human suffering that soldiers have not confronted before. In battle, and subject to a strong chain of command, they are not always able to avoid violating their conscience. Some soldiers describe the experience as losing their soul, or "soul sickness."[18]

In the aftermath of the Vietnam War, our nation has experienced the collective trauma of war in the lives of our veterans, many of them wounded in body and soul. With the wars in Iraq and Afghanistan, yet another wave of trauma to soldiers and their families is returning to our shores. Will our veterans find our churches a place of healing? If veterans are able to speak the truth about the spiritual costs of war and its trauma, what will be the impact on youth who are thinking about military enlistment? How can we help our congregations create a sacred space, where veterans can find healing, where truth can be spoken, and we can grow in our identity as people of Christ's peace?

16. Interview by Titus Peachey, 2006. Name withheld.

17. Maguen and Litz, *Moral Injury*; *The GI Rights Hotline*.

18. *Soldier's Heart*.

A COLLECTIVE WITNESS

There is a contrast in these statements between communities that make conscientious objection to war a clear test of membership, and communities that present it as a matter of individual conscience. There are some dangers that lurk behind both approaches. Perhaps the common ground between these two is for faith communities to assume their pastoral role in nurturing the conscience of individuals and shaping our collective commitment to peacemaking.

As a counselor on the GI Rights Hotline, I have often talked to soldiers who are already in the military before they discover that deep within, they have a conscience against killing. These soldiers often face a very lonely and difficult road, even if they use the official procedures to seek an honorable discharge from the military as conscientious objectors to war.

Any serious commitment to following Christ's way of peace in our world is a deeply spiritual and communal task. I long for all churches, whether peace church or just war in perspective, to nurture this peacemaking identity in creative and engaging ways. I long for all churches to help young people understand the moral and spiritual issues that surround killing before they ever speak with a military recruiter. The gospel message and the integrity of our relationship with the young people in our pews and in our communities require it.

FIRE FROM HEAVEN

There is a fascinating sequence in the Gospel of Luke. Jesus and the disciples have just come from the Mount of Transfiguration (Luke 9:28–36) where they were blessed by the presence of Moses and Elijah. On their way to Jerusalem, they stop at a Samaritan village (Luke 9:51–56) for rest and hospitality. The Samaritans reject them. James and John are furious, and rush to Jesus to ask, "Lord, do you want us to command fire to come down from heaven and consume them?" Fire from heaven was used by Elijah to destroy false prophets on more than one occasion, so the disciples may have thought this to be a normal response to the insult they had received from the hated Samaritans.

Jesus rebuked them, and they moved on to another village. It is several days later that Jesus tells a story that must have grated on the ears of his disciples. It is the story we all know as the good Samaritan (Luke

xviii   Foreword

10:30–37). It is almost as if Jesus reaches back several days to the village his disciples wanted to turn into a smoldering pile of rubble and dramatically sets their hated social enemy down in the story as the hero—the one who brings grace and healing to the wounded traveler. Not only does Jesus reject fire from heaven, his story asserts that our enemies whom we presume to be outside the circle of grace, may be the ones to offer grace.

Fire from heaven is in the air we breathe. It is in our comic strips and cartoons, our video games and films and the six o'clock evening news. It is in our homes when domestic violence strikes, and in the fights on the school playgrounds. Writ large, fire from heaven is in the attacks of September 11, 2001, the car bombs in Baghdad and roadside bombs in Afghanistan. Fire from heaven is in the drone attacks in Pakistan, our nation's invasion of Iraq and Afghanistan and their continued occupation. As a people, we have been gripped by the same passion to call down fire on our enemies as James and John.

Midst the fire from heaven in our day, I wonder, what story Jesus longs to tell us. Who might show up in this story as the unlikely hero? Are our hearts open to receive this story? As we listen for the voice and movement of the Spirit in this book of statements, let us prayerfully consider the statements we will make with the way we live our lives today.

Titus Peachey
Peace Education Coordinator
Mennonite Central Committee U.S.
December, 2012

Acknowledgments

This project is a part of a much larger project of research into the roots of Pentecostal and Holiness Pacifism. It turns out, it is no longer measured in years or decades but in computer operating systems and storage devices which no longer communicate with one another. It is measured in how many computer crashes and lost emails the project endures. I (Jay) had two hard-drive crashes during this project. Unfortunately, with the loss of emails comes a loss of memory as to specific kind deeds on the parts of various college librarians, archivists, and administrators from every imaginable Holiness and Pentecostal institutions. Such college administrators often responded to requests for any information or sources they could help us locate.

Our most productive sources for much of this volume came from two archives in particular. First, the truly amazing archive at the Assemblies of God headquarters in Springfield, Missouri, the Flower Pentecostal Heritage Center or iFPHC.org. Darrin Rogers, director, overcame whatever obstacles to help get some of the arcane pamphlets of out-of-the-way Pentecostal groups, only some of which still exist. Glenn Gohr searched out early congregational records and in the process located a "form letter" sent to many early Pentecostal congregations at the time of World War I, and some letters back and forth between the denomination and the local churches. That became the basis of much of the introductory chapter in this volume. A few of the sources in this volume were shared as early as 1981 when I visited the same archive and was helped by Wayne Warner.

Acknowledgments

A second archive, The Arthur C. Piepkorn Research Collection for "Profiles in Belief," the Religious Bodies of the United States and Canada, is housed at the library of the Graduate Theological Union in Berkeley, California. Lucinda Glenn, archivist, and the staff at GTU Library were very helpful.

Several good friends were called upon to read the introductory chapter to help bring it to the point of publication. First was Megan Kimmelshue, at the time, an undergraduate at Portland State University and a very generous and insightful first reader. Next, Matthew Westbrook, a Ph.D. candidate at Drew University and friend from Portland Mennonite Church read, corrected, and shared a variety of very important insights. My former supervisor at Lewis & Clark College, colleague, and dear friend, Mervin Brockett, tried valiantly to push me, wherever possible, to both clarity and charity.

There were so many more, but let me mention three in passing. Duane Funk, retired military man and member of Rivergate Community Church in Portland, Oregon gave me some ideas from his genealogical research which led among other things to early and "original" Pentecostal Assemblies of the World denominational statement of belief as well as Apostolic Faith, Portland, Oregon, documents. Wendy Washburn, from the Provost's office at Lewis & Clark College gave encouragement in finding online documents. Jenny Bornstein, Lewis & Clark College interlibrary loan specialist was a cheerful and an apparently indefatigable professional.

Brian Pipkin has been for me a delightful and thoughtful colleague and has done some truly heavy lifting on this project. It would not have happened without him.

My family, especially my wife Rockie, have bore with me, through what must seem like the "Jaundice and Jaundice" of academic careers all of which seemed to circle around and return to "Pentecostal Pacifism." As Rockie has more than once reminded me, I don't deserve her. All these years, and I couldn't agree more.

Introduction

By Jay Beaman

I have a recurring experience. I send an email to someone on Ancestry. com, the genealogy site, and tell the person that I have found a relative of theirs who claimed religious objection on their World War I draft card as a member of a religious denomination opposed to going to war. The relative—a granddaughter, a nephew, and a son—writes back and says, in so many words, that I must be mistaken, and where did I get the idea that their relative was against going to war. Let me share two examples.

One retired Pentecostal minister was sure I must be mistaken because he knew that his father had served in World War I. He also told me that after the United States entered World War II, his father who was also his pastor, had not discouraged him on the day he graduated from high school from joining up and fighting as a soldier. He also had no recollection that his own denomination had changed its original statement against going to war while he himself was serving as an official of the denomination and as a pastor of one of its large churches.

Many years before this conversation, I had interviewed another elderly Pentecostal minister who told me that he remembered this man's father as a young friend who had been a pacifist during World War I.

2   PENTECOSTAL AND HOLINESS STATEMENTS ON WAR AND PEACE

So, here I was with a friend of his father who testified to his pacifism, and an official draft card claiming religious objection on the basis of his Pentecostal faith, and a surviving son who had fought in World War II and was astonished to hear me claim his father had been a pacifist during World War I.

The son, who is now an old man himself, told me he had photographs of his dad in uniform during the war. I asked if there was any chance his father served as a medical orderly, cook, or a member of the Quartermaster Corps in supply, transport, or engineering? I explained that the only option the government gave religious objectors drafted in World War I was to serve in some noncombatant capacity in one of these roles. Then he told me that this explained something he had never understood—why his dad had been a cook in World War I. He sent me photographs of his dad in a cook's outfit taken while he was at a military camp during the war. Apparently, the father came home from the war and became a Pentecostal minister, but never preached against World War II and never told his son that he had been a religious objector and a noncombatant in World War I, based upon his Pentecostal denomination's official stance against fighting in war. The son was both surprised and enlightened by this forgotten episode from in his father's early life. I could repeat many similar instances where later generations are totally unaware that their forebears had been pacifist.

A second example comes from the opportunity I had a few years ago to visit the archive of a very small Pentecostal denomination. I was graciously received, even though the gentleman escorting me assured me that his denomination had never expressed pacifism. I told him that I thought I had seen a paragraph on pacifism in the doctrinal statement printed in their publication. He said that he knew the doctrinal statement, and was quite sure that it had never changed, and quite sure that it did not include pacifism among its core beliefs. I asked if I could browse through the publications. Soon enough, I came across the doctrinal statement I had seen before, and it contained no reference to pacifism. I continued to browse through the archives until I found publications dating to the timeframe of World War I. And there it was, their statement of pacifism. The denomination had forgotten, but the government vigilantes from World War I had found this statement and used it as evidence of the group's seditious activities. That is how I knew about the doctrinal statement. When I showed my host the document in his own denomination's publication,

Introduction   3

he was shocked. A forgotten legacy. However, he quickly recovered. He
told me that he did not think I would find any individuals from his denomination who had been objectors to war. I asked him if there were any
early records of names of members. There were such records. From these
I was able to find draft cards for quite a number of men. A clear majority
listed their religious objection to war, and many did so citing the name
of their Pentecostal denominational membership as the reason. So, a core
belief of the denomination a century earlier had been against going to
war and members of the denomination had followed that teaching and
resisted going to war. But today the denomination had completely forgotten its early doctrinal history. Even those who had access to the historical
records were unaware. The memory of pacifism had been completely lost.

It is for this reason that we have compiled this book of statements by
Holiness and Pentecostal groups advocating resistance to warfare, many
made during or immediately prior to World War I. Living as we do, nearly
a hundred years after *The Great War* as it is also known, these statements
of faith are particularly surprising because the denominations, taken together, represent a large cross-section of what is often referred to today
as the American Christian Right. Given that the Christian Right has been
known to champion many of our nation's wars in recent years, we are
led to wonder how these denominations produced statements, which on
their face, read as pacifist tracts, and which are numerous enough to fill
a small book. More curious still, why are these statements unknown to
most of us, even to the most well-informed of us among these groups?

Most of the statements in this book are official denominational
statements taken from pamphlets, often called "Disciplines," representing
the denomination's most basic beliefs and identifying features. They were
named thus because they were seen as manuals for Christian discipleship. In this book we are using the term pacifism to identify denominations that once upheld Christian nonviolence as official doctrine. In
some cases, we quote a leader associated with a particular group, when
we have no such official denominational statement or when the leader
sees themselves as representing the group. While many of these groups
did not self-identify with the term pacifist, they did fall within a common
definition of pacifist in their attitudes on war and peace, as later historians recognized. We should not be surprised that they did not use the
term "pacifist" since World War I propaganda and "war hysteria" could

4   PENTECOSTAL AND HOLINESS STATEMENTS ON WAR AND PEACE

result in imprisonment for being associated with words such as pacifist, yellowback, slacker, conchie, and the like.

How and why a book like ours has come about is sometimes as much accident as divine appointment. In 1979, Professor Carl Piepkorn published a four-volume collection titled, *Profiles in Belief*.[1] About the same time, Robert Mapes Anderson had just written a new interpretation of Pentecostal origins, *Vision of the Disinherited*, in which he mentioned the pacifism of some early leaders.[2]

I was a seminary student at the time and one of the questions that I was trying to answer was how widespread pacifism had been in the early Pentecostal movement. Piepkorn's, *Profiles* provided brief summaries of each denominational group. Piepkorn, a military chaplain, communicated his findings about denominations to the government, perhaps so the military could apportion the appropriate number of chaplains to serve the beliefs of drafted men. He noted groups that had taken a position relative to members going to war. This information allowed me to draw up a brief list of denominations opposed to war, and in turn convinced me that the pacifism referred to in Anderson's book was just the tip of the iceberg. Having been raised in the Assemblies of God and having trained for pastoral ministry at one of their colleges, I was shocked that almost all awareness of this heritage had been lost by the time of the Vietnam War, when the evening news almost every day carried stories about my peers at state universities who were protesting the war. Most Pentecostals I knew either did not remember or did not want to remember their pacifist roots. So in 1982 I wrote my master's thesis on the subject which was published later in book form.[3] While studying for my thesis, I came across the paper by Donald Dayton and Lucille Sider-Dayton on "Holiness and Attitudes toward War." This paper has charted the rough outlines of all my subsequent work. I am constantly making fresh "discoveries" only to find when I reread their paper, that I should have been pointed there a generation ago. It was also apparent that the Holiness and Pentecostal movements had parallel legacies of war resistance; indeed, closer examination showed it to be more than parallel. Many of the Holiness leaders who advocated

---

1. Piepkorn, *Profiles in Belief*.

2. Anderson, *Vision of the Disinherited*.

3. Beaman, *Pentecostal Pacifism*.

Introduction 5

pacifism subsequently became Pentecostals and continued their peace witness. It was not two movements but one.[4]

In an attempt to partially rectify this loss of memory, we have collected the official statements from these many groups and placed them together into one compilation, which you have before you. It is a recollection of a lost peace movement, from the nineteenth and twentieth centuries. A part of recollection is recollection of what has been lost, or in many cases misplaced—even occasionally deliberately forgotten. Some of these documents are now housed in the International Flower Pentecostal Heritage Center in Springfield, Missouri, at the headquarters of the Assemblies of God. Many more were found by returning to Piepkorn, whose archival collection is now held by the Graduate Theological Union Library in Berkeley, California.

In cases where we could not locate official denominational statements in disciplines or manuals, we were sometimes able to find credal equivalents in magazines, some of which are now available digitally from the various Pentecostal archives. In our re-collecting, we have tried to identify the earliest possible date associated with each submission. Sometimes we knew the piece was early, but the publication we got it from was not dated or was a later date. These have been included in the footnote and the early date has been provided with the submission. The purpose is to reconstruct for the reader a time and chronology where the reader can see when pacifism was more clearly stated. Although it has taken years to accomplish, the result is that we now have access to many more of the original documents. In my previous attempts, relying largely on Piepkorn, two-thirds of early Pentecostal groups were identified as pacifist. Now, however, there is evidence of pacifism in almost every early Pentecostal group, as well as in many Holiness groups. This represents something of sea-change in the findings.

However, recollection is more than just assembling documents in one place. It can also be an attempt to "revivify" or bring to life again. It is to remember. We do not wish this book to be an act of nostalgia for the "glory days" of the early Pentecostal movement. It is more important

4. Vinson Synan and Donald Dayton treat these movements as one larger movement even if they divided over speaking in tongues. I am suggesting that their commonality on aversion to participation in war is one of the best clues to their actual unitary nature as one movement. See Synan, *The Holiness-Pentecostal Movement in the United States*; Dayton, *Theological Roots of Pentecostalism*; Dayton and Lucille S. Dayton, "An Historical Survey of Attitudes Towards War and Peace."

6 PENTECOSTAL AND HOLINESS STATEMENTS ON WAR AND PEACE

to focus on the present, and as we examine how pacifist beliefs deeply influenced the larger worldview of these groups, to ask the hard question of why these beliefs disappeared.

We have also included a few "Antebellum" Holiness documents. Reading these statements written before the Civil War is very poignant and troubling considering the long travail of wars that have followed. Early Holiness writers were full of hope that they were on the cusp of millennial peace; that things were improving—that history was moving toward a more promising future of righteousness. Even their spiritual descendants in the Holiness and Pentecostal movements of the late nineteenth century and early twentieth century, despite their pre-millennial pessimism, were able to hold on to the dream of millennial peace. Ironically, it was in better times of prosperity and power, in the latter half of the twentieth century, that many of these groups abandoned their millennial hope for peace in this age. That hope had been forged in an era when they were marginal and consciously standing outside the organized religion of the traditional churches. The story of how these unorganized war resisters themselves became organized and assimilated within the mainstream is to be found in the run-up to the First World War.

THE STRUCTURAL DEMANDS OF WAR AND RESISTANCE TO WAR

In the Great War, we can observe a process that is so often repeated as to become a commonplace, whereby modern war provides the impetus for the bureaucratization or the organizing of society. Max Weber, the most eminent sociologist of bureaucracy, drew the connection between military organizing for war and the organization of society as its byproduct. For Americans, already experiencing the transition to industrialization, the Great War had the effect of imposing bureaucratic regulation on everyone and all of life.

The creation of the Selective Service System (SSS) in 1917 forced rural populations, immigrants, the uneducated, and the religious, all to conform to uniform standards of organization. The first national draft registration day, June 5, 1917, and its draft registration cards, many signed by men who neither knew their exact date of birth, nor how to write their names, gave new meaning to the word "mobilize." The draft board became a local outpost and the human face of the federal government. Its work would ultimately remove millions of men from their homes and communities. The most rural communities, especially in the South, did not yet have a universal register for births, and family Bibles were often the only record of births. Sometimes the draft board required these family Bibles to provide evidence for the age of a young man. Many families stopped using the Bible to record births after they saw the use to which this holy registry was put.[5] Two-weeks following the June 5, 1917 draft registration, the Dallas Morning News reported wryly, "It used to be the fashion to register births in the family Bible, a formality that was attended by some ceremony, but in recent years as a general custom it is said to have been dropped."[6]

Sociologists use the term "societalization" to describe the process by which larger communities, such as the nation, displace the close-knit structures of the local community. Bureaucratic organization is the main form of connection to this larger society. The Great War, and the greatly increased bureaucratization which accompanied it, ushered in a period of major transition to the contemporary world. Most males between the ages of eighteen and forty in 1917 and 1918 were entered into a system of record keeping, monitoring, and control that was as unprecedented as it was impersonal. Jeanette Keith, in, *Rich Man's War, Poor Man's Fight*, notes,

> Censuses and statistical compilations are hallmarks of the modern state, tools through which the populace can be seen and worked upon. However, seeing into the South, and particularly the rural South, was well-nigh as difficult in 1917 as it had been in 1800. Consider what was not there: no requirements for birth registration; no driver's licenses; no uniform compulsory education laws, so no really usable school records; and no death certificates. There were no parish records, as in England, because (except in Louisiana) there were no parishes. For southern men, the draft card of 1917 must have been their first piece of official identification. One wonders if they even had wallets to stow it in, given the propensity of rural southern men to carry their money (when they had it) in rolls secured by rubber bands.[7]

In the documents presented in this book, you see a snapshot of one set of responses from people of deep religious faith to World War I and, to some

5. Keith, *Rich Man's War*, 158–9.
6. Ibid., citing *Dallas Morning News*, June 17, 1917.
7. Ibid.

8   PENTECOSTAL AND HOLINESS STATEMENTS ON WAR AND PEACE

extent, World War II. Both voluntary associations and social-religious movements were forced to organize in response to war. If the war was to be resisted, even in some small way, these associations and movements needed a form of bureaucratic structure able to comply with the policies and regulatory demands of the SSS.[8] And so, a new and diverse set of social groups were compelled to organize for the war by adopting the traditional form of organization found among religious groups in a pluralistic society: the denomination. The denomination—with its basic statement of beliefs, its list of official ministers eligible for ministerial exemption from military service, its list of members, its definition of eligibility for membership, and its publications where instructions about draft registration could be disseminated—became more important than ever.

In this sense, World War I served to mobilize religion. When you read the denominational statements of faith in this book, you are reading statements that were directed as much to the government and to draft boards as they were to members of the faith. These statements, like so many religious statements throughout history, conform to the pattern of an "apologia" or argument made to the larger society. They are written Janus-like, with one head facing forward toward the faithful, and one head looking back over the shoulder to see who is in pursuit. Because many of the groups included in this collection were still very young at the time of the Great War, their documents provide a series of successive images that chronicle their response to the requirements of the larger society; at first naïve and hurried, and later more deliberate, elaborated, and compromised.

The loss of life during World War I was staggering. Most Americans who died were soldiers that had been drafted under the SSS, and their surviving family members were often bitter towards CO's. Why had some men been allowed to take exemption because of conscience? Their numbers may have been small, but their reputation in the public consciousness was disproportionately large. Only seven-tenths of 1 percent of the draft pool for World War I claimed religious objection or conscientious objection. By contrast, about two-thirds of the draft-pool were granted an exemption to support their family.[9] However, the conscientious objector, deemed slackers or "conchies," received most of the public wrath. The

8. Ibid.

9. Keith, 10. Keith shows that almost 90 percent of the 4.9 million married men in the first draft received deferments.

United States government was called upon publicly to justify letting the tiny percentage of those who could not kill in good conscience be excused from war duty. Walter Guest Kellogg, Judge Advocate Major, published a defense of the government's policy in 1919 called, *The Conscientious Objector*. Kellogg had been in charge of examining the conscientious objectors in the military camps after they had been drafted to make sure that only "worthy" objectors were allowed to become noncombatants.

Kellogg interviewed an unnamed early Pentecostal objector and presented his case as his primary example of the Pentecostal conscientious objector. I was able to discover from Pentecostal records that the unnamed individual was Mike Laleff from near Spokane, Washington, who was one of the more unusual objectors. Kellogg was not a particularly sympathetic observer, but his account of the interrogation is worth repeating.

> One objector testified that nine years ago he had immigrated to this country from Bulgaria and five years ago had taken out his first papers. He was a laborer and seemed in his wanderings to have acquired many of the characteristics of the tramp. He was of the Pentecostal faith. The Bible was the only book he read. He said he had attended many different churches but "could not agree with them, so he went into the woods and lived as a wild man." The woods were about twenty miles south of Spokane; he built a log hut and lived in it nearly a year on fruit and nuts. He said. "I don't know why I went—God knows all. I suffered because God wanted me to. God talks to me but it is not for me to tell what he says. He says, 'I give you courage and will be by your side through to the end.' I try as far as possible to follow God and live close to God and to seek peace with all mankind. Christ says it is wrong to fight. If you find I am not sincere in my life you can do whatever you please. I had rather obey God than man."[10]

---

10. Kellogg, *The Conscientious Objector*, 85.

10   PENTECOSTAL AND HOLINESS STATEMENTS ON WAR AND PEACE

Mike Laleff, early Pentecostal pacifist.[11]

Shortly after his conversion from atheism to belief in Christ in 1914, Laleff
was deeply challenged by socialist colleagues at work on the railroad who
mocked the larger Christian support of the European War. "What kind
of a Christ have you," they asked, "who always thirsts for human blood?"
Laleff wrote: ". . . I began to examine myself. Could a Christian kill a human being for whom Christ had died? Could a follower of the Nazarene
do this? In examining my heart I found that I had love for everybody,
regardless of nationality. I heard my pastor preach against the slaughter in
Europe, and saw the inconsistency in the ranks of Christendom."[12]

Through reading the Sermon on the Mount and Rev 13:10, "He that
killeth with the sword must be killed with the sword," Laleff came to see
that peacemaking was required of followers of Jesus. He was at this time

11. Laleff, *From Atheism to Christ*, 47.

12. Ibid., 38.

Introduction   11

part of a Holiness mission in Spokane, Washington, the Brown Street Mission, affiliated with the Volunteers of America, a Salvation Army off-shoot.[13] In short order, he became a part of a 'full gospel' or Pentecostal church. Like other Holiness and Pentecostal adherents, when he filled out his draft registration in 1917, he requested exemption as a religious objector, answering the question why he was requesting exemption, he wrote: "Pentecostal—Christ."

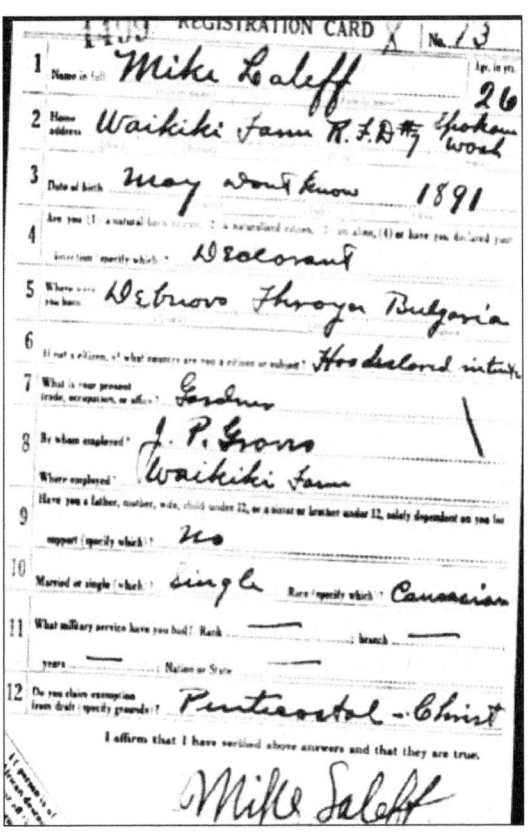

Laleff's account of how he came to embrace Jesus' teaching of peace while he was a Holiness follower and moments later when he became a Pentecostal, is a supplement to the documentary evidence we present in this book. Members of Holiness and Pentecostal groups fought over the details of their various doctrines, especially speaking in tongues, at the time these statements were hammered out. They never came to agree on

13. Ibid., 38–39, 49.

speaking in tongues and are often considered to be two different movements as a result. They were two different movements as to their timing and their trajectory from sect to the mainstream of society. Nevertheless, they shared the belief that Jesus was calling His followers to promote peace and reject war. More than almost anything else, they agreed upon this.

As should be apparent in the following pages, those who crafted these statements saw themselves as people who waited upon and were empowered by the coming of the Spirit; they were prophetic, and prophecy looked forward to God's reign of peace. Thus, they began to practice peace in their time, in faith and hope. Moreover, the story of how Pentecostals formed into organized denominations is not simply that of people who were "kicked out" of other congregations forming together to promote mission, although it was that, it was also specifically coming together to promote pacifism at the time of World War I in response to the demands of the SSS.

In the statements collected in this book, we attempt to document the widespread adoption of various models of pacifism before and at the time of the Great War. With the passage of the *Selective Service Act of 1917*, churches wishing to help members resist going to war on grounds of conscientious objection had to be well-established churches before the draft and to be officially on record as opposed to their members participating in war. Every doctrinal statement is a mode of expression and a cultural artifact that resonates with a specific place and time. Today, many of us are less prone to cite lists of proof texts when we make a case for our beliefs. Not so in the early twentieth century. Sometimes doctrinal statements consisted only of scriptural quotations, believed to be self-explanatory. Reading over the variety of statements, one gets the sense that these groups believed that God's government here on earth had already begun, and they looked forward to an even more dramatic future unfolding. For a variety of reasons, some of them theological, they held less tightly to the reins of earthly government and were more skeptical than their immediate forebears in the nineteenth century about human achievements.

The statements were written for the flock, but also for the government. In most cases, they were answers to the demands made by the Great War. They were often hastily constructed and sometimes greatly oversimplified. Most of them are audacious for their time: they request the right to decide on grounds of moral conscience against killing, even

Introduction   13

when their government has declared war. They knew that such a claim carried the seeds of anarchy within it. Quite a few were uncomfortable swallowing that pill and required it to be buffered or encapsulated in affirmations of "obedience to authority, or loyalty." We all live with degrees of ambivalence, inconsistency, and even contradiction; and some of these statements embody these kinds of contradiction.

A resolution passed by the General Council of the Assemblies of God in 1917 provides a lens into the process by which denominations included such statements against War in their creed. The full text is as follows:

> Resolution Concerning the Attitude of the General Council of the Assemblies of God Toward any Military Service which Involves the Actual Participation in the Destruction of Human Life.
> While recognizing Human Government as of Divine ordination and affirming our unswerving loyalty to the Government of the United States, nevertheless we are constrained to define our position with reference to the taking of human life.
>
> WHEREAS, in the Constitutional Resolution adopted at the Hot Springs General Council, April 1–10, 1914, we plainly declare the Holy Inspired Scriptures to be the all-sufficient rule of faith and practice, and
> WHEREAS the Scriptures deal plainly with the obligations and relations of humanity, setting forth the principles of "Peace on earth, good will toward men." (Luke 2:14); and
> WHEREAS we, as followers of the Lord Jesus Christ, the Prince of Peace, believe in implicit obedience to the Divine commands and precepts which instruct us to "Follow peace with all men," (Heb. 12:14); "Thou shall not kill," (Exod. 20:13); "Resist not evil," (Matt. 5:39); "Love your enemies," (Matt.5:44): etc. and
> WHEREAS these and other Scriptures have always been accepted and interpreted by our churches as prohibiting Christians from shedding blood or taking human life;
> THEREFORE we, as a body of Christians, while purposing to fulfill all the obligations of loyal citizenship, are nevertheless constrained to declare we cannot conscientiously participate in war and armed resistance which involves the actual destruction of human life, since this is contrary to our view of

14 PENTECOSTAL AND HOLINESS STATEMENTS ON WAR AND PEACE

the clear teachings of the inspired Word of God, which is the sole basis of our faith.[14]

It appears that the central portion of the statement was written first. It presented a reasoned statement with proof-texts about why one could not kill and remain a Christian. It was absolute. It was pacifist; it was all for making peace and all against war or participation in war. The law given by Moses commanded no killing. Jesus reiterated as much. The statement affirmed that following both peace and holiness was a requirement to see God (Heb 12:14). It then pointed to the universal and unchanging understanding among Pentecostals that this is a prohibition against shedding blood or taking human life. That much was clear. Perhaps as a conciliatory gesture, it was moderated by being sandwiched between two iterations of loyalty to the secular authorities.

Loyalty clauses were placed before and after the pacifist center of the statement, without the scriptural references which the pacifist center had required. The first of these iterations acknowledged the Divine ordination of human government—an apparent reference to Romans 13, though the verse is not cited—and immediately transitioned to "unswerving loyalty to the government of the U.S." The second, following the pacifist core of the resolution, could be assumed to be based on the teaching of Romans 13, contextually applied, but was a complete gloss. Then the title was added, "Resolution Concerning the Attitude of the General Council of the Assemblies of God Toward Military Service Which Involves the Actual Participation in the Destruction of Human Life." Some Mennonites would ask, "What other kind of military service is there?" The statement was making a compromise which even some Mennonites made, by offering the option of noncombatant service. The title to the Assemblies of God statement had the effect of naming the sandwich. We might try to be humorous, "One pacifist sandwich on a Kaiser bun, coming right up!" But, the Assemblies of God was not alone in this concession, and it was a recognition that the United States government was not going to give an absolute exemption from military service, that pacifists by law were going to be forced to do noncombatant service under military command.

While a few thousand draftees absolutely refused noncombatant service to the end, the government also remained resolute. Many of the statements in the collection illustrate something of the resulting

14. "The Pentecostal Movement and the Conscription Law," 6. Emphasis in original.

compromise. One could argue that the seeds of pacifism's demise were in this compromise, but the compromise would not have required the affirmation of loyalty. One could argue that Romans 13 might lead in a direction attributing legitimacy to human government and some of its limited demands, but that hardly "requires" loyalty. The assertion of unquestioned loyalty was problematic and set a trajectory which would bear fruit sooner rather than later. In their defense, the leaders of the Assemblies of God had reason to compromise. The public mood was one that required loyalty oaths from various groups labeled as "pro-German." These included any that openly questioned the government's assumptions about the war.

The specific timing of this compromise was no accident. During World War I, the government required all individuals who objected to war to do so on religious grounds through membership in an officially recognized denomination with evidence of a preexisting stance against members going to war. The Assemblies of God was using the requirements of the SSS to recruit unaffiliated congregations to join the denomination and sent a form-letter to independent congregations warning them of the consequences of not officially joining the organization: their young men would not be eligible for exemption from the draft according to the SSS requirements for obtaining exemption.

The letter was sent with a complete statement of the position that the Assemblies of God held toward war. Chairman J. W. Welch wrote to congregations urging immediate action on this issue of "great importance," with the U.S. now involved in the war. Welch pointedly referred to recently established hierarchy of authority within the denomination by saying that the statement had been crafted by the "Executive Presbytery and endorsed by the General Presbytery," and submitted to the congregational government, "for your careful and prayerful perusal."[15] The specific occasion was the activation of the SSS, the imminent military draft, and the importance for pacifist denominations of being able to document their opposition to participation in war, and at the level of the local

15. J. W. Welch to various congregations, which internal evidence suggests was at the time of preparation for draft registration on June 5, 1917. Many of the churches responded directly to the letter by early May 1917. I have only page one of the letter which refers to the attached statement of the Assemblies of God on war. Return letters from congregations in New York City, Tulsa, San Francisco, and Spokane, all add to knowledge of the contents of the letter by specific references. This particular original was attached to communication from Welch to John T. Wilson, pastor of Thayer, Missouri.

16 PENTECOSTAL AND HOLINESS STATEMENTS ON WAR AND PEACE

congregation, the importance of being connected to such a denomination through "a tie which will be recognized by law." Welch had already sent a letter to President Wilson to highlight the denomination's compliance with the law. He detailed the process to the congregations. "In order to take advantage of the protection afforded by the General Council of the Assemblies of God, through this statement of its position, it is necessary that the local assemblies have such connection with the General Council as will give them recognition as such by the law and Government. To say that you are a part of the General Council is not sufficient, you must have documentary proof that you are actually a part of the Council."[16]

Welch then recommended each congregation have a formal business meeting to vote on joining the denomination and that minutes of such a meeting, with documentation, be sent to the denomination and kept locally as a legal reference. Welch also warned that some congregations had lost property by not keeping careful records and copies of deeds. The letter included an appeal for funds for publishing, for missions, and for the support of the denomination's central offices. Clearly the Great War created the exigency which made necessary a more formal organization of the denomination, along with the need for more financial support to operate the burgeoning denomination.

The letter was a clear example of how bureaucratic pressure from the government as it sought to execute the war and the response of a social movement as it sought to organize against participation in the war led in turn, to pressure on local congregations to formalize their loose connections to the denomination. Of necessity, congregations had to affiliate, so the argument went, with the organization that was assuming the formal role in relationship with the government.

We can look at the way this statement from the Assemblies of God was received at the level of the local congregation by following how the Spokane Pentecostal congregation, where Mike Laleff was a member, processed the request from the denominational leaders.[17] The denomination had asked them to hold a business meeting and set up a formal governance structure—if they had not yet done so—and to make a formal

16. Ibid.

17. Charter member list and related letters between the Spokane, Washington (Pentecostal) Assemblies of God and J. W. Welch, General Secretary of the Assemblies of God. I owe a great debt to Glenn Gohr and Darren Rogers of the Flower Pentecostal Heritage Center (iFPHC.org) for their extraordinary work to find a host of World War I founding documents for Assemblies of God congregations.

Introduction   17

application to join the denomination. Would they adopt the denomination's position on war? Would they join the denomination, or would pacifism be a stumbling block? Would the denominational sanction of conscientious objection presented to the government be an incentive to join the denomination in a formal way? Here was a little congregation of some twenty adults. They would decide either to join the denomination or not based upon their previous ideas about the Assemblies of God and their current understanding of the responsibilities of Christians in time of war.

On May 8, 1917, the Spokane (Pentecostal) Assembly of God met for business. The pastor read the letter from J. W. Welch, General Secretary of the Assemblies of God, including the official position of the Assemblies of God on participation in war. The pastor proposed that the letter from the denomination to President Wilson should be significantly altered, and the congregation voted in favor of his proposal. The leaders in the Spokane congregation had serious objections to the loyalty statement at the beginning of the Assemblies of God position on participation in War. The official record of the meeting by the secretary, George W. Ruch, did not mention the main reason the denomination had called upon churches to meet: namely, to formally join the denomination. Instead, the minutes provide detailed instructions about the way they wished the denomination to edit the statement to nullify the promise of loyalty to President Wilson, with a qualification "so far as our Christian principles permit." In the loyalty statement in the official position on participation in war, they suggested that, "after the words, 'our unswerving loyalty' . . . insert 'as children of God,' and in the last paragraph insert the word 'Christian' just before the word 'citizenship.'"[18]

A week later the pastor, H. R. Bursell, followed up with a letter to J. W. Welch of the denomination, explaining that unanimity at the meeting had been conditional on amending the denomination's position, both in the letter to President Wilson and in the official statement on participation in war. Only after such amendments was the vote unanimous in favor. "I suppose it unnecessary to impose these minutes upon you, but I have caused a copy to be written for you, and I want you to know just how we stand on this question—that the disposition on the part of some amongst us is *so strong* against war that the clauses in your letter and

18. Ruch, "Minutes of Business Meeting of the Pentecostal Assembly of God, Spokane."

18   PENTECOSTAL AND HOLINESS STATEMENTS ON WAR AND PEACE

resolutions expressing willingness to 'support' President Wilson were unacceptable. Hence the change, for the sake of unanimity."[19]

Looking back on the path that Pentecostalism followed from being a social movement to becoming a bureaucratic organization makes one wonder how a denomination trying to promote pacifism as its official belief—a belief that was in direct contradiction to any requirement for a universal draft into the military—could try to affirm both its pacifism and its loyalty to the government. Already, we can see an example of the tension that existed between the objectives of the denomination, for organization and control, and the priority for the local congregation of assuring freedom—to obey the dictates of individual conscience.

After receiving this letter, J. W. Welch wrote back to the Spokane congregation to remind them of the original intent of the circular letter: to invite them to establish formal membership in the denomination, and to suggest the amendments were inappropriate. How could the congregation have passed an unanimous vote to amend the letter to President Wilson and to amend the denomination's stated position on participation in war, before voting to join the denomination? The denominational leader decided to accept the unanimous vote as an affirmation of their desire to join the organization " . . . we thank you for the hearty response of the saints there."[20]

> We feel that a little explanation is necessary in the matter of your uniting with the General Council, and are therefore enclosing a circular letter. You will see that the matter is not so much one of endorsing the letter sent to the President, or the Resolutions adopted by the General Council presbytery, as it is a matter of creating organic union with the General Council itself through the carrying out of the program given in the enclosed letter. Whatever amendments made will have no bearing upon the Resolutions which have already been submitted to the President, and the letter which accompanied them. The purpose is of having all the Assemblies that desire to do so, identify themselves with the General Council in such a vital way that whatever concessions are granted to the General Council will extend to the local assemblies. Kindly look over the letter enclosed and see if you can arrange for another meeting which will result in the necessary steps toward organic union. This copy of the Minutes

19. H. R. Bursell to J. W. Welch, May 13, 1917. Emphasis in the original.
20. J. W. Welch to Brother Bursell, May 23, 1917.

is quite incomplete since it states nothing as to your identifying yourself with the General Council of the Assemblies of God, Incorporate, etc. etc. We will be glad to send you the regular official letter upon receipt of sufficient identification with us.[21]

The following week the congregation met in a business meeting to reaffirm in total the earlier motions to amend, and even describe them more clearly. They continued to officially unite with the denomination. These minutes were sent to J. W. Welch by pastor Bursell on May 30, 1917. However the business was unfinished and the congregation had some misapprehensions of their role in this relationship. Pastor Bursell also let Welch know that while the vote to strengthen the statement on pacifism had been unanimous, the vote to join the denomination had been divided. "Herewith are amended minutes, of further steps we have taken toward a stronger union with you, for purposes already set forth and understood. There is a good deal of indifference on the part of some (in our midst) in regard to this matter, and this is the best we can do. I trust enough have signed to secure our recognition on your part."[22]

Ten of twenty members signed the letter to join the denomination, among them, both Agnes Ozman LaBerge and Philemon Laberge. Agnes Ozman figures prominently in the Pentecostal birth myth of the outpouring of the latter rain in Topeka, Kansas on New Year's Eve of 1900–1901. Of the ten Spokane signatories, four were women, four were ministers and beyond draft age, and one man was a ranch cook but too old for this draft. Only one man, Mike Laleff, was young enough for the draft when he signed the charter members list.[23] On June 5, 1917, only one week later, was the first national registration day. When Mike Laleff filled out his draft registration card, on line 12, (where the request and reason for an exemption was recorded), he wrote cryptically, "Pentecostal—Christ." The Assemblies of God had organized against war and had been organized by war.

However, not all Pentecostal groups qualified their pacifism with expressions of loyalty. Some statements like that of the Church of God,

21. Ibid.

22. H. R. Bursell to J. W. Welch, May 30, 1917, including amended minutes to (post-dated) May 8, 1917 business meeting for Spokane, WA, Pentecostal Assemblies of God, including the list of Charter member signatories.

23. The charter member list of signatories is in the May 30, 1917 letter from H. R. Bursell to J. W. Welch.

20   PENTECOSTAL AND HOLINESS STATEMENTS ON WAR AND PEACE

Cleveland, Tennessee, perhaps reflecting the injunction of Jesus to be plain-spoken, were crafted for parsimony, "Against members going to war—Ex. 20:13, 1 Chron. 28:3, Psalm 120:7, Math. 5:38–48; 6:14, 15; 26:50–56, Luke 22:49–52, John 18:10, 11, 36; Rom. 12:19." That was the entire statement; short enough to fit on a bumper sticker!

Other statements worked at setting out the principles of the legitimacy of a limited human government, which at times would have to be overridden by requirements of the rule of Jesus Christ, especially regarding biblical commands to love peace and to pursue it. The following confessions, taken from the longer statement of the Pentecostal Assemblies of the World (see Appendix), is instructive in this regard. Unlike the Assemblies of God which had framed their statement within an affirmation of loyalty to government, the Pentecostal Assemblies of the World (PAW) statement started out with a declaration of religious purpose much like the Westminster Confession. Then the statement transitioned to the Holiness commitment to being a separate people, but part of this separation for purity and worship included shining the light of nonviolence in a dark society to guide it from the way of death "into the way of peace."

The statement then laid out the duty of PAW members to serve those who are outsiders and downtrodden. This was to take place in the context of the priestly function to pray for the governing authorities, that members be allowed to live "a quiet and peaceable life in all godliness and honesty." They were to submit to government rule unless it interfered with service to God. That service had already been defined to include worship, service to the downtrodden, and shining the light of nonviolence and peace. This statement charted out considerable scope for the believing community to do good deeds—"their liberty of service towards God." At times, however, the rule of human government would be trumped by the rule of God. The statement asserted that any conflict between the rule of men and the rule of God would be determined by the individual conscience, and implied that conscience would prevail over governmental decree.

MAIN BIBLICAL THEMES AND SCRIPTURAL REFERENTS
The Role of the Millennium

From early in the nineteenth century, Holiness advocates, like Thomas Upham, professor at Bowdoin College, were looking for God's government in a millennial reign of peace. Before the American Civil War, the Holiness movement believed that this reign of peace would result from efforts to educate and reform society. After the painful realities of that war, late nineteenth-century holiness advocates became more pessimistic about reforming society, and opted for a premillennialist vision which saw peace coming only after the second coming of Christ and his inauguration of the millennial kingdom. Early nineteenth-century millennialists, reacting against the predestination of Calvinism, had emphasized human freedom and responsibility, and were more optimistic and forward-looking. Both groups understood the peace-vision of the millennium as a call to live hopefully in the present and pursue peace in their actions. Both groups began to reflect on ways that the ethic of the coming millennium with its unmediated rule of Jesus might cross the boundary into their own time.

We can detect elements of the millennial hope in these peace statements. Sometimes groups had a formal statement about the millennium, some which are not reproduced in this book, since we have selected out peace statements and not reproduced doctrinal statements in their entirety. When statements use terminology like, "Prince of Peace" (twelve cases), "heraldic angels," "Peace on Earth Good Will to Men," "reigning king," "King of kings" (two each) "coming king" (one), "kingdom" (seventeen) as in "my Kingdom is, not of this world," these were intended, given their context, to associate current peace behavior with God's millennial kingdom.

Reciprocal Movement from Holiness to Peace, from Peace to Holiness

Some traditional peace churches joined the Holiness movement. In a couple of cases Mennonite groups became Holiness groups advocating the experience of sanctification or Baptism in the Spirit as a second work of grace following conversion. The Church of God in Christ-Mennonite Church and Missionary Church Association are two examples.

The Brethren in Christ (BIC) was a traditional peace church that came into the orbit of the Holiness movement after it had been a peace church for generations. One can also see that at times this kind of cultural merger was attended by struggles to maintain the original peace witness. So the BIC experienced a similar erosion of pacifism as the Holiness and Pentecostal groups during or after World War II.

The same can be said of Quakers. We include the statements of two Quaker groups, The Northwest Yearly Meeting and the Indiana Yearly Meeting because both were among the most influenced by the Holiness movement. This influence was mutual, with the Holiness and Pentecostal movements being influenced by Quaker pacifism and the Quakers being influence to downplay their peace witness by the Holiness movement. Causation is more difficult to establish, but the timing at least suggests that as Quakers moved into the larger evangelical milieu they tended to lose some of their uniqueness, one facet of which was pacifism, at a time when the pacifism was being undermined in Holiness circles.

Several early peace church leaders such as Menno Simons, George Fox, and other Quakers, are included to show commonalities and possible sources of Holiness and Pentecostal pacifism, as well as to demonstrate how peace was framed in much earlier times. Some of these are segregated in their own chapter to show that they are distinct from the main purpose of this book, which is to document the pacifism in the early Holiness and Pentecostal movements. However, there can be no doubt that the groups they founded—the Mennonites and the Quakers—had some influence upon the later Holiness and Pentecostal believers. At the very least they provided a context and model for pacifism as members moved between these groups. Sometimes peace church members became part of the Holiness and Pentecostal movements and brought their pacifist beliefs with them. In other cases, peace church denominations were drawn into the orbit of the Holiness movement.

INTENDED AUDIENCES AND PURPOSE OF THIS BOOK

This book is foremost a book of remembering. My adult life has been spent remembering a lost narrative of religion: religion as empowerment to see the world and its greatest troubles in fresh, hopeful and Spirit-filled ways. I hope I have no illusions that any of us can go back and live in the early twentieth century. However, conversations with our forebears can sometimes help us see them in a more sympathetic and honorable light. The Holiness and Pentecostal movements could probably benefit from honoring their parents afresh, by seeing them for the people they really were and for what they tried to stand for.

Most of the groups named in this book are now widely considered to be stalwarts of the religious right, or at least to be at the core of the evangelical subculture. Contemporary detractors on the political left would be totally surprised by how critical these groups in earlier generations were of wars to spread democracy around the world. The left would also be challenged to learn that some of the most deeply committed social justice movements were (and are) prophetic first because they were movements of the Spirit. Similarly, the findings in this book should give pause to members of the contemporary religious right as they reflect on how far they have gone to accommodate to the principles of the kingdoms of this world.

Another purpose of this book is to provide the documentary evidence for contemporary war resisters of their strong and relatively recent heritage of peacemaking. Sometimes when our contemporaries cannot or will not encourage us, our religious forebears can. There are young men and women who even now are facing agonizing personal questions of conscience regarding war. In a day when impersonal military technologies such as missiles and drones sometime mask the human actors in war, this book offers examples of dedicated folk who wanted to draw a line in the sand against killing. We may quibble at where they drew that line, but they call upon us personally to decide where we will make our stand.

Another group for whom we hope this book will be useful is those scholars whose interests lie in the area of religion and society. Here is a collection of primary documents and original texts that are diverse, unknown, and perhaps alien to the very groups that used to espouse such beliefs. Some scholars will differ with the conclusions reached here, but the exercise of dealing with primary sources and deducing authorial intent within the real historical context will be eminently worthwhile in itself.

We recognize that the organization of this book is less than ideal. Compromise is inevitable when compiling and ordering lists. We have followed the conventional division between Holiness and Pentecostal movements and listed them alphabetically. My personal inclination would not be to make this distinction because I see them as the same thing, and I believe that what has been collected in this volume provides more evidence that they are one prophetic movement. Certainly, since the time of Donald Dayton's and Vinson Synan's writings there has been a growing body of evidence of the continuity between the two groups. When we look at what they profess today it is difficult to discern much difference, except that the Holiness groups were the earliest to organize and the first to make the transition to the middle-class mainstream. Yet, that difference in timing alone might be enough to present them in separate chapters.

The Holiness movement preceded and then became an established contemporary of the Pentecostal movement. Chronology is significant. Some of the Holiness groups were already in place and concerned over the Spanish-American War at the turn of the twentieth century just as the Pentecostal movement was being born. That Holiness experience with war had already matured across nearly a generation by the time the Pentecostals had to deal with the Great War. Some of the Holiness groups presented here were well on their way to denominational respectability by the time of the Great War whereas none of the Pentecostal groups were.

Dividing the two chapters between Holiness and Pentecostal also creates confusing separations where one Holiness group later became "Pentecostalized." Each respective group would be assigned to a separate chapter with a different name. A case in point is the Fire-Baptized Holiness Church and the later Pentecostal Holiness Church. They were the same group with different names at different times. Another troubling compromise was the decision to list groups alphabetically within the two main chapters. This was done for those who simply wish to look up groups by name and in this case it will be useful; however, it masks the fact that some statements, separated by many pages, are almost identical to other statements to which they are historically related. In some cases we have tried to compensate for this by footnoting the similarity between statements.

However, dividing the Holiness and Pentecostal groups, and further dividing the Holiness into Antebellum and later Holiness groups has its uses. First, the Holiness movement covers the better part of two centuries and during this time developed fairly dramatic differences regarding postmillennial and later premillennial eschatologies, as well as changing their status from a sect to a mainstream denomination that was becoming institutionalized. Moreover, many of the Holiness groups represented in this volume were very small and later merged with other more "successful" groups. If their pacifist or partially pacifist stance seems anachronistic, there is also much more about them that seems so.

In many cases, these groups were adapting rapidly to the changing role of the U.S. in the world with the Spanish-American War and World War I. Their credal statements reflect their attempts to respond to these new realities. Pentecostalism was born between those two wars and the one helped to frame the movement's response to the other. World War I initiated the universal draft at the time when Pentecostalism was beginning to organize, and I will show elsewhere that World War I was a contributing factor to this need to organize. In this collection of documents early Pentecostalism showed evidence of forms of pacifism in almost every group.

FROM SECT TO DENOMINATION; FROM PACIFISM TO ACCOMMODATION

In some ways, our catalog is a reminder that timing is everything. If we think of pacifism as, at least in part, the purview of a sectarian movement, we must remember that many Holiness and Pentecostal groups from those like the Church of God (Winebrenner) in the first half of the nineteenth century that refused to participate in the war with Mexico to the Holiness groups that resisted at the time of the Spanish-American War (1898–1902) such as John Alexander Dowie's Christian Catholic Church in Zion, Illinois, to the new Pentecostal Groups who almost universally objected at the time of World War I. By World War II, pacifism had declined among the same groups as they had joined the ranks of established religion, and it was left to the breakaway, marginal, groups to preach and practice pacifism. The latter were starting out on their sectarian phase.

WHENCE PACIFISM?

The Legacy of Biblicism

Because Holiness and Pentecostal leaders attempted to use the Bible to frame their beliefs, they created the potential for serious divergence rather than consistency or uniformity of belief. Christian Smith defines biblicism as a "theory about the Bible that emphasizes together its exclusive authority, infallibility, perspicuity, self-sufficiency, internal consistency, self-evident meaning, and universal applicability.[24] The notion of consistency is particularly important. From the time of the earliest Holiness advocates of pacifism before the American Civil War, such as Oberlin graduate Amos Dresser who wrote, *The Bible Against War*, there had

---

24. Smith, *The Bible Made Impossible*, viii.

been an attempt to harmonize apparently inconsistent passages across the Bible.

There is a striking diversity among the statements collected in this book regarding pacifism. They range from early absolutist pacifism to later statements originating from the same groups where pacifism is entirely absent. They are all ostensibly based upon the Bible. As a cultural product, they all reflect a deep-seated biblicism. Some of the statements are a stringing together of quotes from various scriptures with the assumption that they are self-explanatory. This is not surprising, given that many of the groups despite their doctrinal statements, held the Bible to be their only rule of faith.

Smith also pointed to the way that biblicism assumes the notion of congruence the harmony of all passages within the Bible into one coherent whole. He notes that, "All related passages of the Bible on any given subject fit together almost like puzzle pieces into single unified, internally consistent bodies of instruction about right and wrong beliefs and behaviors."[25] In the case of Holiness and Pentecostal pacifists, biblicism led to efforts to harmonize all passages about war and peace across the Bible. Initially this created the sense that all passages were accounted for but it also codified internal contradictions within movements into continuing antagonisms that in time would almost certainly require adjustments. When the groups found themselves moving up in social status, they could use the same biblical passages, shifting the interpretive center, to argue a modified pacifism or no pacifism at all.

Wilma Bailey refers to the process whereby biblical scholars and denominational leaders changed the translation of Exodus 20:13, the sixth command in the Decalogue, from "Thou shalt not kill," to "Thou shalt not murder," as "The Assault on the Biblical Text." Bailey argues that the translation of the word is broadly "kill" in the rest of the Old Testament and that the use of the specific translation "murder," popularized by American evangelicals in the 1960s, reflected political predispositions imposed upon the text from the outside.[26] In addition, Holiness pacifists from as early as the 1830s championed the use of the sixth command to preclude killing in war. Holiness leader, John Alexander Dowie, during the Boer War, in 1900, argued:

25. Ibid., 5.
26. Bailey, *You Shall Not Kill.*

We feel that all War is wrong, and that without exceptions. It is sinful for Christian men to fight and destroy life. We read that the command of God is: "Thou shalt not kill." No human or demoniacal sophistry can ever justify murder in any form especially for the members of the Christian Catholic Church who stand on each side, whom we have earnestly exhorted not to fight. We are willing that our people should go, if need be, on the firing line to remove the wounded and dying, and to minister to them.[27]

T. C. Upham, nineteenth-century Holiness professor at Bowdoin College, argued the sacredness of human life based upon the sixth commandment. At least eighteen times in the present volume you can find the sixth commandment used to teach against killing. However, the entries in this volume for the Assemblies of God illustrate that by 1917, they were arguing that the sixth command taught not killing in war, and by 1953 and 1967 they understood it to teach only against individual murder but not killing in war. This change may have been anticipated by such leaders as E. N. Bell in 1918 arguing for capital punishment, and echoed by Ernest Williams in 1935.[28]

By including earlier and later statements of groups, we can see the way that accommodations were made over time, and how Scripture was reinterpreted in the process. I performed a rough content analysis of the early and late Holiness and Pentecostal belief statements about war and government from the 1890s to the present, using 1930 as the dividing line.[29] The number of post-1930 statements (seventy-three) was approximately equal to pre-1930 statements (seventy-two), so we might expect to see similar counts of referents before and after 1930, if the groups were unchanged. We already know that many of these groups had ceased to officially believe in pacifism. More of the early groups (fifty-three) were pacifist or resistant to war than later groups (forty-four). Explicit ap-

27. *Leaves of Healing VI*, 722. See also Healing Evangelists, 1881–1957.

28. E. N. Bell, writing in 1918, supported capital punishment as long as the "sheriff who hangs the criminal as commanded by law need have no hatred in his heart." Bell, "Questions and Answers," 5. Likewise, in 1935, E. S. Williams, who, supporting capital punishment, noted when God said, "Thou shalt not kill," he was referring to murder not to "executing the sentence of the law of the land." Williams, "Questions and Answers," 5.

29. I did not include the PCPJ.org (Pentecostals and Charismatics for Peace and Justice) since this group was formed as a peace social action group in recent years and is not a denomination or church.

28 PENTECOSTAL AND HOLINESS STATEMENTS ON WAR AND PEACE

proval of non-combat service in the military was less common in early statements (ten) than in later statements (thirty-three). Noncombatant service in the military was the only government-sanctioned choice for religious objectors in World War I, with few exceptions, and it was apparently allowed in most of these Holiness and Pentecostal groups, even if not sanctioned or encouraged.[30] Full combat duty was almost never allowed in early documents (four) and much more likely in later ones (sixteen). However, one large difference in how decisions were argued in early and late groups is significant. Before 1930, fewer groups argued the right of individual conscience to choose (twenty) than after 1930 (thirty-six). Moreover, the earlier use of conscience was typically an argument to follow one's conscience against going to war whereas later conscience became the freedom to serve as a combatant if one so believed. The magnitude of these differences is easy to understate, especially the later use of the idea of individual conscience.

So how does it happen that a Spirit-led movement that argued the Bible provided the only rule of faith, would later argue for individual choice? One suspects that scriptural arguments had stronger appeal to working class people and that conscience was more appealing to the middle class. Latter-day Holiness and Pentecostal advocates are like pro-choice advocates for the right to abortion. Both move the center of the debate from the actual ethics of a specific act of life-taking, and focus on freedom of individual choice in such matters. However, Holiness and Pentecostal advocates now tend to hold on to a formal biblicism and in the case of pacifism, have replaced it with individual choice or conscience.

Group-forming Functions Tending toward Authority and Loyalty

Indeed, this book, which catalogs official denominational statements, is testament to the tendency of groups to stake out official territory. These statements are examples of highly routinized ways of creating boundaries between groups, by ruling some beliefs acceptable for members and other beliefs as characterizing those who do not believe.

---

30. I will analyze this further in another publication. I do not wish to overstate noncombatant service here, as many Holiness and Pentecostal followers asked for and appear to have received exemption of some kind from service. However, there seems to not have been much negative consequence if they served noncombatant in most of these groups.

Introduction   29

Jonathan Haidt, a moral psychologist, has recently highlighted the differences in the way that liberals and conservatives come to quite different moral sensibilities. Haidt defines six foundations underlying "intuitive ethics" or taken-for-granted ways of acting ethically, and claims that emphasizing some of the six rather than others is at the root of our culture wars. He describes six pairings or vectors underlying competing moral systems: care/harm, fairness/cheating, liberty/oppression, loyalty/betrayal, authority/subversion, and sanctity/degradation.[31] Within this architecture liberals emphasize the first three vectors and conservatives attempt to emphasize all six vectors. Although Haidt does not draw this conclusion, it appears that conservatives try to live with contradictions, while liberals essentially avoid them. The fact is that the last three vectors are useful in building social groups and "in-group" cohesion, but often at the expense of the concerns for caring, fairness, and civil liberties that define the first three vectors. Conservatives point out that liberals emphasize the first three ideals but undermine social cohesion by failing to recognize the importance of group-bonding and structure-maintaining activities in the last three.

Regarding pacifism, the first three vectors are conducive to a liberal or individualistic approach to pacifism, whereas the hierarchical and authoritarian tendencies implicit in the last three vectors probably contributed to the shift from social movement to formal organization but also had the effect of moderating the element of social protest in favor of obedience to governing authorities. Such a shift could obviously serve to undercut thoroughgoing pacifism.

We can quibble with Haidt over his assumptions, but his findings are relevant to this narrative. The statements about war and government from the groups represented in this volume are often just short extracts from their much longer statements of belief and practice. Many of these longer statements included prohibitions on drinking, dancing, sexual practices, dress, eating, entertainment, and the like; all of which are designed to create a sense of disgust toward those who fail to abide by the standards. Some second and third generation Pentecostals have in conversation referred to these earlier prohibitions as a way of explaining the shift away from pacifism: "Early day Pentecostals had all kinds of rules of what you couldn't do. You couldn't drink a coke or wear a tie or you would get kicked out of the church. Conscientious objection was one of

31. *Moral Foundations.*

those rules which over time Pentecostals gave up following, just like not drinking coke or wearing a tie."[32]

One prominent Holiness reformer was so adamant against alcohol use that he would not allow an alcohol fueled hair curler in the home.[33] That places the locus of moral decisiveness at the level of disgust or repulsion. Whether, as Haidt suggests, these six tendencies *represent* predispositions or they *become* dispositions, they function as framing devices that might lead to a kind of disgust with others not in the group. Depending on which of the six vectors were emphasized, at a given time, it might be that the authoritarian vectors, which incidentally can contribute to group cohesion and growth, were the ones that won the day at the expense of the altruistic and enemy-loving (outgroup-embracing?) tendencies.

Moreover, if those who followed proscriptions against going to war did so as an almost automatic response to submit to their group's authority, such as preacher or Bible, the process of transferring allegiance to a governmental authority may have been done with little discussion, especially if the latter position was positively sanctioned in the larger society. Denominational statements of pacifism that at the same time require loyalty and other markers of patriotism provide evidence that these groups were concerned about loyalty and authority of the nation state too.[34]

---

32. Sorrow, phone interview with Jay Beaman, April 3, 2012. My quotation is not exact, but I have attempted to give an accurate representation. Norman Sorrow was the son of a World War I conscientious objector, Fletcher Dolphus Sorrow, who helped found the Congregational Holiness Church. His uncle, Watson Sorrow, was one of the main founders. Norman's comments were not alone among sons of World War I Pentecostals whom I have interviewed or corresponded with. Lest we get too exercised about the moral equivalence of drinking coke, wearing a necktie, and killing in war, we should remember that Mennonites, Quakers, and Brethren, the mainstays of the peace churches, argued to the point of division about appropriate clothing, including neckties. Rules, such as these, no matter how tedious they may seem today, gave a sense of cohesion, group identity, and clearly defined boundaries.

33. Lindsay, *John Alexander Dowie*, 217. When Dowie, famous healing evangelist and founder of Zion City, IL, and the Christian Catholic Church, had his daughter die from burns caused by an overturned alcohol lamp used to heat her hair-curling iron, he considered her alcohol use a sin. "The only act of disobedience, willful or direct, that I ever knew her to commit was this one. She only once stepped aside from the path of obedience, and then the devil struck her with that 'liquid fire and distilled damnation,' which I have fought against all my life, and which I forbade her ever to use."

34. Wacker, *Heaven Below*, 217–39. Although I sometimes think Wacker mistakes flag-waving and love of homeland as willingness to support all war, he is no doubt partially right, and some Pentecostals probably did do both.

Signposts to the Millennium Replaced Ethics of the Millennium

To some extent, the pacifism that originated in postmillennialist eschatology was immediately replanted in the premillennialism that replaced it. Optimism leading to action was replaced with pessimism. Postmillennialists had been more likely to believe that action and education could end wars. Arbitration and education had been important activities. A part of that education was to preach against war. However, the premillenialist was torn between viewing warfare as an inevitable sign of the movement of history on one hand, and warfare as evil to be avoided on the other. Premillennialism, at the time of World War I, became associated with the belief that Jesus' return was imminent. For many, World War I had apocalyptic overtones and seemed to be leading up to the war of Armageddon. Two World Wars, both with apocalyptic qualities, eroded optimism, but surviving them and achieving a kind of normalcy tended to undermine the claims that the second coming would be the immediate outcome to this "Armageddon." To the degree that pacifism became associated not with the ethics of the millennium, but with the imminence of the millennium, it was vulnerable to reinterpretation when the millennium failed to develop from the ashes of World War II. One might say that the ideals captured by the millennium of the imagination were displaced by a reliance upon the imminent features of a literal millennium. Where postmillennialism had focused more on ethics, premillennialism was preoccupied with signs of the times. Could the focus on signifier supplant the thing signified? Could warfare as a sign of the end time supplant the end of all warfare in history as the promise of the millennium?

Social Mobility Moves Groups to the Mainstream

The eminent German social scientist Max Weber found that groups which practice self-denying lifestyles characterized by discipline and asceticism (what he termed the "Protestant Ethic") experience upward social mobility in capitalist societies. This social mobility tends to have an ironic outcome because succeeding generations have greater financial opportunity, are better educated, and adopt a more worldly approach to their faith; in general they become less sectarian in their religious practice. To the degree that the refusal to fight had been based upon a sense of alienation from the mainstream goals of society and an unwillingness to defend an ungodly social order, their commitment to pacifism was vulnerable to the worldly success that drew them to a new feeling of belonging to the larger society. Paraphrasing Jesus' answer to Pilate, "their kingdom was now of this world . . . and then would their servants fight "(John 18:36).

Tension with Society is Difficult to Sustain

Countercultural groups find that a continuing state of tension with the larger society to be untenable over time. Resolution of that conflict is important if the group is to survive. This is a special problem for groups where peacemaking is a core value. Children of pacifists sometimes serve in wars. If they are not negatively sanctioned within the group, or if the sanctions are tolerable, they can continue to be part of the group. A lot depends on the ability of the religious group and the government to negotiate a compromise position to reduce the friction between them.

Pacifist Mennonite and Quaker groups were less interested in proselytizing in World War I, for example, than Pentecostals and Holiness groups. Some Quaker groups went on record that they would not take in new members during the war, lest some join for the benefit of exemption from military duty.[35] In one sense, this was a survival tactic, because they represented less of a threat to the government in time of a universal draft. They might be questioning authority, but they weren't growing. Pentecostals were all about growth and evangelism. To accomplish these, they had to make deals.

The growth of Pentecostal groups during and after World War I came, to some degree, at the cost of holding the line on conscientious objection, since many of the new adherents would be men who had served in the war or had not been opposed to doing so. Signs of the Spirit could be given more emphasis than behavioral proscriptions. After the war was over, other behavioral proscriptions such as those related to drinking and dress could be emphasized and these had favorable outcomes for church growth.

DEGREES OF PACIFISM

The terms "pacifism" and "pacifist" are not clear and straightforward. Certainly, most of the earlier documents and many of the later documents in this book affirm a pacifist, or pro-peacemaking stance. Recently

35. "Quakers Pledge Aid to a Nation in War," 3.

people have asked where the line is to be drawn on conscientious objection? Where do you draw the line against war? Some resist complicity with any law or policy or program that is coercive or that benefits from coercion. Some draw the line at state-organized warfare and any actions that might support it, such as paying war taxes, doing military service, or working for war-related industries. Some draw the line at killing or "direct support" for killing. Others wish to distinguish between just and unjust wars. For the early twentieth-century Holiness and Pentecostal groups, there was also a question about God's involvement in war. Was Jesus a pacifist? How about God the Father?

Is the expectation of a literal Armageddon, with the armies on one side being led by Jesus, a contradiction of pacifism? In one notable case, Frank W. Sandford, a prominent Holiness leader in Shiloh, Maine, reversed the commitment to pacifism he had taught for twenty years, to call for believers to fight on the side of the U.S. in World War I. Sandford came to this change in point of view through a new revelation in which he came to see World War I as leading to Armageddon. Presumably, he saw Jesus as leading the charge. The tendency among dispensationalists to view specific ethics as associated with specific historical times implied that pacifism could be appropriate for one dispensation and not for another. These questions are not explored in this volume, but they suggest that there are still unresolved issues for those who take these documents seriously.

A few groups advocated what might be termed "personal nonresistance." The scriptural references they used in their doctrinal statements begged further application to war, but the connection was not made in the documents we have. Five Holiness groups, the Allegheny Wesleyan Methodist Connection, Christian Nation Church, Kentucky Mountain Holiness Association, The Fire-Baptized Holiness Church, and the group named the New Testament Church are examples of personal nonresistance. Likely, these groups knew of other Holiness groups which went further and made the connection to refusal to go to war, and they were not making that point, but their approach may have contributed to a larger willingness to make the further application to war. Moreover, the explicit statements of other groups forced them to make statements in the same vein, if much less widely applied.

PENTECOSTAL AND HOLINESS STATEMENTS ON WAR AND PEACE

Absolute Pacifism and Nonresistance

Some of these groups recognized that governments would sometimes draft men who refused to do military service. Initially, they did not propose the legitimacy of serving noncombatant roles in the military, but rather that if an individual was forced into the military, he should refuse to obey commands to kill. Dowie advised believers, that if they were drafted into infantry, they should intentionally aim above the heads of the enemy when firing their weapons. Leaders in the Church of God, Anderson, Indiana, advocated disobeying orders to kill an enemy. In both of these cases, the assumption was that the individual had done all he could to avoid military service, had been conscripted against his will, and that noncombatant status in the military was not a stated option but an adaptation.

During World War I, when most Pentecostal groups had to make their position explicit, the only official alternative the U.S. government offered to pacifists was to serve as a noncombatant in the military. A number of groups conceded to this demand, but for many it was a tenuous compromise. In time, however, they got used to the idea.

Pacifism and Civic Involvement

Another related ethical question concerns civic involvement. Where is the line to be drawn on civic involvement? Many of the statements in this collection quote Jesus' words disavowing earthly fighting: "If my kingdom were of this world, then would my servants fight." How one understands that statement and others like it will be determined by one's involvement in the larger society.

Those at the bottom of the social ladder, who have been socialized to their outsider status, are more likely to understand that their involvement is limited to service, while those with higher status will desire their involvement to include decision making. This crucial difference gets expressed theologically in terms of what involvement is appropriate. These questions were part of what motivated some of the credal statements in this book, and many of them differ over time according to social location and social mobility. They reflect a more fundamental question: What is the legitimate role of human government, and how does this differ from or equate with the role of Jesus' government? Most of these questions are beyond the scope of this volume, but to show how both pacifism and civic involvement intersected with attitudes toward secular authority we have located different doctrinal positions along two axes in the tables below:

Pacifism

Attitude Toward Government	Absolute Pacifism (Fairly)	Against Killing (Non-Combatant O.K.)	Individual Choice (Conscience)	Militaristic
High mistrust / distance	Church of God, Cleveland, TN, 1917			
Legitimacy but limited authority		Pentecostal Assemblies of the World, 1918		
Legitimate and loyal		Assemblies of God, 1917	Assemblies of God, 1967	

Civic Involvement

Attitude Toward Government	Non-Resistants / Comeouters	Voting and Taxes	Lobby and Chaplaincy	Run Government and Sanction War
High mistrust / distance	Brethren in Christ, 1900	Church of God, Cleveland, TN		Sarah Palin (Assemblies of God), 2008
Legitimacy but limited authority		Pentecostal Assemblies of the World, 1917		
Legitimate and loyal		Assemblies of God, 1917	Assemblies of God, 1940	Assemblies of God, 2003 / Elton Trueblood (Quaker)

Commitment to pacifism and engagement in society vary across a continuum from absolute commitment to pacifism and complete separation from secular society at one end, to total rejection of pacifism (i.e., militarism) and full participation in secular institutions at the other end. For example, credal statements articulated by Holiness and Pentecostal

36 PENTECOSTAL AND HOLINESS STATEMENTS ON WAR AND PEACE

churches concerning obedience to governments in time of war can be categorized along a range that extends from absolute resistance to moderate compliance.

The other dimension of the dilemma regarding the legitimacy of human government authority is the public stance of churches, and the attitudes of members within these churches to civic and political involvement. The second table illustrates how new positions have evolved, because paradoxically, high levels of political involvement can be associated either with high levels of mistrust of human government or with high levels of support for the legitimacy of government.

One of these polar positions (extreme distrust of government) would be represented by Sarah Palin, who belonged to an Assembly of God church in Wasilla, Alaska, whereas the opposite pole (extreme commitment to the legitimacy of government) would be represented by John Ashcroft, a member of the Assembly of God church in Springfield, Missouri. The terminology used by these movements has been incorporated into the tables where possible. Thus the rubric on the left column, "Non-resistants and Comeouters," is quite foreign to most of us now, but both terms were prominent among mid-nineteenth-century abolitionists who were initially pacifist and opposed to war, including some who were a part of the early Holiness movement. Nonresistants took their cue from the teachings of Jesus and the Apostle Paul not to resist evil with force but to allow God to exercise rule in such cases. "Comeouter" was the term for those who had tried to reform civil institutions from within but had found institutionalized structures such as slavery to be so entrenched that they had to forsake all association with them just as the children of Israel had been exhorted to come out of Babylon, the symbol of all evil governments.

Some believers viewed government and institutions as inherently coercive and corrupt. William Lloyd Garrison is perhaps one of the more famous examples of this view. For a time, he embraced both Nonresistance and the Comeouter stance as viable political positions.[36] By the end of the nineteenth century, Comeouters were often Holiness independents who saw themselves as radical reformers. Most of them had probably been expelled from some church or denomination they tried to reform.

We include portions of a little magazine from 1917 published in Highland Park, Kentucky, called *The Comeouter*, with an article titled

36. Ziegler, *The Advocates of Peace*, 48–75.

"The Patriotic Harlot." The masthead for the magazine quoted 2 Cor 6:17: "Come out of her, my people, that ye be not partakers of her sins, and that ye receive not of her plagues." The magazine may have had the lifespan of only one issue, because it quickly came to the attention of the federal government, and its writers were jailed. Fortunately, for us, the government preserved a copy of the incriminating document.

As to consistency, there is a reason why one might expect groups to cluster along an axis from upper left to lower right in both tables, and for the most part they do. So, for example, in 1917, the Church of God, Cleveland, Tennessee, was logically consistent in holding to both a fairly absolute pacifism and a high degree of mistrust of governmental involvement from Christians. In similar fashion, the PAW were consistent in holding a limited view of governmental authority over Christians and allowing members limited involvement in military as noncombatants, but not allowing members to kill in war.

The Assemblies of God in 1917 were less consistent in limiting members to noncombatants while expressing their complete loyalty to the government. By 1967 they had resolved this inconsistency by expressing complete loyalty and by allowing members the full range of options up to and including combat service. Examples are absent from the right hand column because Christians, generally speaking, and Holiness-pacifist groups, have difficulty in becoming overtly militaristic. Their biblicism makes overt militarism problematic. So, if they are supportive of war, it will be tacitly or in an unarticulated way. The move by the Assemblies of God in 1967 to put conscience and not the Bible or the words of Jesus at the center of articulation, certainly paved the way.

One might look at the cells in the second table in a similar way, expecting groups to cluster on the axis from upper left to lower right. While it is more difficult for Christian groups to adopt full-blown militarism, it is sometimes rhetorically more acceptable for them to do so for civic and political involvement. Sarah Palin and John Ashcroft are prominent members of Assemblies of God congregations and well-known modern examples from the political right. They show just how far Pentecostals have come in terms of being accepted in the mainstream of their society and of representing political viewpoints widely held in that society. They are particularly interesting in their different attitudes to civic involvement, with one evincing a high level of mistrust in government and the other willing to become completely immersed in its exercise of power. He

38   PENTECOSTAL AND HOLINESS STATEMENTS ON WAR AND PEACE

is not unusual—even later day mid-twentieth-century Holiness Quakers like Elton Trueblood were able to affirm a high degree of civic and political involvement and loyalty to the government at the height of the Cold War.

Of course, consistency can be the "hobgoblin of little minds," and sometimes groups were forced into seemingly inconsistent statements either by a sense that all parts of the Bible had to be reconciled, or more likely by accusations that resistance to war or governmental coercive authority might be a kind of disloyalty. The very accusation was enough to cause some groups to try to express their loyalty alongside of their resistance. Often, the government and other secular vigilante groups pushed the religious groups to the point of expressing inconsistencies. Still the tables indicate that groups tended to cluster along the diagonal. They believed in the logic of their position.

John Ashcroft, for example, composer of "Let the Eagle Soar," might be considered quite logically consistent.[37] It is more difficult to claim that the Assemblies of God in 1917, with their requirements of loyalty and conscientious objection or noncombat duty, were being consistent. Sarah Palin, on the other hand, illustrates the contradictory tendency to emphasize the evils of government and the call to take over its coercive instruments of power for ostensibly righteous ends. Her celebrated tag line, "Lock and load," simultaneously expressed her willingness to countenance violence against political leaders with whom she disagreed, while she was running for official office herself.

We have included statements from the historic peace churches like the Quakers, the Brethren in Christ, and the Mennonites, whose commitment to peacemaking predates the nineteenth-century Holiness revival, for at least two reasons. First, their peace witness clearly had an influence on the Holiness movement that they joined. Second, by including changes in the text of their statements over time we can see that cultural accommodation affected them as much as did the Holiness and Pentecostals, even though they have remained among the groups we still consider to be peace churches. The latter point is important for a couple of reasons.

First, there is a tendency to hold up the historic peace churches as groups that have a pristine form of pacifism that does not change, whereas the Holiness and Pentecostal movement had an imperfect form of pacifism that was not really pacifism, which is why it no longer exists.

---

37. Ashcroft, "Let the Eagle Soar."

By a similar logic we could explain away the earlier pacifism of these peace churches, because at later times it has been seriously compromised. Also, by including these groups and tracing their changes we provide the opportunity to compare their evolution with that of the Holiness and Pentecostal groups over a similar timeline. In this comparison, we should not forget that some of the historic peace churches listed here, notably the Brethren in Christ and some yearly meetings of Quakers, were also Holiness churches in the early twentieth century.

In summary, this volume offers these historical statements, issued by denominations and their leaders from across the Holiness and Pentecostal movements, and in a few cases by individual members, for your examination and discussion. Our hope is that they will lead to a reexamination of how these movements helped to shape the social ethic of evangelicalism in America and contribute to its missionary outreach around the world. In a time when we continue to hear that we are waging war to extend democracy, just as the young were told to join the Great War to end all wars, these many courageous voices from our Christian past might serve to reveal that the contemporary leaders' calls to war are merely "sounding brass and clanging symbol[s]."

2

Anabaptist Peace as Context

INTRODUCTION

In this chapter we include an Anabaptist peace testimony by quoting Menno Simons. This is for context, since later Holiness and Pentecostal statements do not originate in a vacuum, and the statement by Simons is perhaps one of the prototype statements of the sort we are documenting from the nineteenth and twentieth centuries. Furthermore, the statement from the Church of God in Christ, Mennonite, illustrates that Mennonites were indeed influenced by revivalism and the Holiness movement of the nineteenth century. Some of that influence stayed within Mennonite groups, and some spilled into new Holiness-influenced denominations. These brief statements, then, illustrate a reciprocal influence; most notably, that Holiness and Pentecostal leaders were influenced by Anabaptist groups.

Today, the Anabaptist peace testimony continues to influence Pentecostals committed to social justice and peacemaking. In his book, *The Naked Anabaptist*, Stuart Murray notes that people of diverse theological backgrounds are attracted to Anabaptism, not because they want to join a new denomination, but because they are seeking to enrich their lives. In our post-denominational era, Christians rarely draw from one source of spirituality, and since Anabaptism is a tradition rather than a denomination, individuals can experience Anabaptism without leaving their denominations. "They can explore it and learn from it without feeling disloyal to their own community." The Anabaptist commitment to peace, Murray writes, is one of the gifts the Anabaptist tradition brings to the wider church. "[Anabaptism] represents a recovery of the practice of the early churches, a natural expression of what it means to be followers of Jesus in a post-Christendom culture where the church is no longer compromised by its partnership with wealth, power, status, and control."[1]

Pentecostal denominations today have abandoned pacifism, like a parent abandoning a child. Consequently, many Pentecostal denominations no longer speak the language of class struggle, peace, and nonviolence. The Anabaptist tradition serves as a step-parent—a role model and supporter—for Pentecostal pacifists who cannot look to their denominations for support. Darío A. López Rodríguez, Church of God pastor, activist, and teacher in Peru, reminds us that Pentecostals do not need other institutions to lend them "theological crutches" to sustain peace and fight injustice. This is true. However, while Pentecostal history has a rich peace and justice tradition, contemporary peacemakers need more than history to sustain their convictions. They need day-to-day community, especially living in a nation that depends so much on war. Social pressure to conform to nationalism and war requires a strong community dedicated to peace. Because some Pentecostals cannot find support within the U.S. Pentecostal subculture, many migrate to Mennonite communities. This is not to say that all Mennonite churches oppose war. That is not true. Not all Mennonite churches are pacifist churches and not all Pentecostal churches are war churches.[2] Mennonite communities are, however, providing Pentecostals with a contemporary language of nonviolent resistance, peacemaking, and antiwar activism—a language needed to sustain peace.

Pentecostal denominations that have (1) abandoned pacifism or (2) do not tolerate pacifist members, have created an unmet need for their pacifists-oriented constituents. Anabaptist-related churches are filling

1. Murray, *The Naked Anabaptist*, 35–36, 41. For a complete analysis of Anabaptist hermeneutics, see Murray's, *Biblical Interpretation in the Anabaptist Tradition*.

2. We realize individuals and groups that support war do not prefer the label "pro-war." No matter how militaristic and nationalistic their rhetoric, most people and institutions do not see themselves as being "pro-war." Everyone, including Hitler, believes they are "pro-peace." Even the worst criminals claim noble intentions. Titles are not transparent. They typically do not convey reality, especially those sanctioning violence. War supporters prefer "pro-peace" like abortion advocates prefer "pro-choice." Both groups, however, sanction killing.

the void created by Pentecostal denominations who have abandoned Christian nonviolence. Many Pentecostal peacemakers have some connection to Anabaptist churches. Although having roots in Assemblies of God and Foursquare churches and colleges, I (Brian) attend an Anabaptist congregation in Pennsylvania while remaining licensed with The Foursquare Church.[3] Jay Beaman is a member of a Mennonite church and has been influenced by Mennonites since young adulthood, even teaching at Tabor College. Paul N. Alexander, co-founder of Pentecostals and Charismatics for Peace and Justice, and licensed minister with the Assemblies of God, attended Pasadena Mennonite Church.[4]

To illustrate the Anabaptist influence on Pentecostal pacifists, Martin Mittelstadt, professor of New Testament at Evangel University, refers to himself as a "Mennocostal,"—the blending of Mennonite and Pentecostal faith and tradition. In his article, "My Life as a Mennocostal: A Personal and Theological Narrative," Mittelstadt, who grew up Pentecostal, recounts how the Mennonite tradition influenced his faith. His inspiration is John Howard Yoder, a Mennonite scholar, who wrote that Pentecostalism is the "closest parallel to what Anabaptism was in the sixteenth [century]." Mittelstadt documents the convergence of Mennonite and Pentecostal traditions, noting they are both counter-cultural, primitive and pragmatic movements that share a similar Spirit-led, story-based hermeneutic. Both movements, Mittelstadt says, rejected nationalism and embraced pacifism. "The shared pacifist heritage of Mennonites and Pentecostals flows out of a rejection of nationalism."[5]

We also include in this brief chapter two other sets of statements from the Historic Peace Churches: Religious Society of Friends (Quakers) and Brethren in Christ. However, we include them in the alphabetical listing of Holiness statements. We do not mean to imply that either of these groups originated in the Holiness movement, or were simply expressions

3. I first stumbled across Anabaptism in the most unexpected place—a Pentecostal seminary in the Philippines. My class, theology of missions, was assigned a book, *The Upside Down Kingdom*, by the Anabaptist scholar Donald B. Kraybill. The book was unrelated to anything we discussed, and oddly felt mistakenly assigned. Nevertheless, I read cover to cover. Kraybill's work introduced me to the Anabaptist peace theology while attending a Pentecostal seminary. Shortly after, I learned it is not always easy to take what you learn from the Mennonites and apply it in a Pentecostal community.

4. I met Paul Alexander when he taught at Azusa Pacific University in California. I had to pinch myself when I heard him speak on Pentecostal pacifism and peacemaking. He was the first living Pentecostal peacemaker I met. I will never forget that day.

5. Mittelstadt, "My Life as a Mennocostal," 10–17.

of the Holiness movement. Their inclusion in the Holiness movement does two things: it adds weight and context from two sources of pacifism to the Holiness movement from groups that contributed members and leaders, and from groups that were reciprocally influenced by the Holiness movement through revivalism.

MENNONITES (ANABAPTISTS)

Menno Simons on War and Nonresistance, 1496–1561

The Scriptures teach that there are two opposing princes and two opposing kingdoms: the one is the Prince of peace; the other the prince of strife. Each of these princes has his particular kingdom and as the prince is so is also the kingdom. The Prince of peace is Christ Jesus; His kingdom is the kingdom of peace, which is His church; His messengers are the messengers of peace; His Word is the word of peace; His body is the body of peace; His children are the seed of peace.[6]

Peter was commanded to sheathe his sword. All Christians are commanded to love their enemies; to do good until those who abuse and persecute them; to give the mantle when the cloak is taken, the other cheek when one is struck. Tell me, how can a Christian defend Scripturally retaliation, rebellion, war, striking, slaying, torturing, stealing, robbing and plundering and burning cities, and conquering countries?[7]

The regenerated do not go to war, nor engage in strife. They are the children of peace who have beaten their swords into plowshares and their spears into pruninghooks, and know of no war. . . . Since we are to be conformed to the image of Christ, how can we then fight our enemies with the sword? . . . Spears and swords of iron we leave to those who, alas, consider human blood and swine's blood of well-nigh equal value.[8]

CHURCH OF GOD IN CHRIST, MENNONITE,[9] 1859

Because of persecution and their desire for religious freedom, Mennonites began to immigrate to America beginning in 1683 and continuing until

6. Simons, "Reply to False Accusations," 554.

7. Simons, "Reply to Gellius Faber," 554–56.

8. Hershberger, Crous, and Burkholder, "Nonresistance."

9. This Mennonite church was influenced by the Holiness movement.

the late 1800s. They braved the dangers of frontier life and became known as quiet, God-fearing people; sober and devout in faith and industrious and temperate in everyday life. They steadfastly refused to participate in war, which earned them the reputation of being a peace-loving church.

However, times of test and prosperity brought a spiritual decline. During the nineteenth century it appeared to some Mennonites that not all the historic practices were being upheld. Among those who contended for the historic faith was John Holdeman (1832–1900), of Wayne County, Ohio. He increasingly felt that the Mennonite Church no longer was practicing the true doctrine in many areas. He appealed to church leaders for spiritual revival. Although some agreed with his evaluation, little action was taken to bring reform. In 1859, he and others began worshiping separately. Eventually, this small group organized as the Church of God in Christ, Mennonite.

[Peace], n.d.

We believe in baptism for believers, nonresistance, and a simple, modest lifestyle. The Bible teaches that Christians are to be separate (nonconformed) from the world in spirit (attitude and outlook) and manner of life. Since Christians belong to the kingdom of God, Christ teaches us to live peacefully with others. We do not take any part in politics, elected government offices, or the military. We teach that men should wear a beard and that Christian women should wear a devotional head covering.[10]

From *What We Believe*, n.d.

The Church and the World
The church and the world are distinctly separate institutions with different desires, goals, and accomplishments. Christians are not to be conformed to the world. God has set forth a clear standard of righteousness, which must not be compromised by worldly dress, amusements, or other worldly attractions. Entertainment provided by movies, musical instruments, radio, television, and the improper use of the internet detract from the sanctity and simplicity of one's spiritual life in Christ and should be avoided. Matthew 6:24; Romans 12:1–2; 2 Corinthians 6:14–18; 1 John 2:15–16; Titus 2:11–14; Ephesians 5:11.

10. "Who We Are."

Anabaptist Peace as Context 45

The Sacredness of Human Life

Human life is a sacred gift from God. He has created and sustains life according to His will and purpose. It is man's obligation to treat the whole of human life as existing for the honor and glory of God. The Christian refuses to inflict harm on anyone or take human life, which would include abortion or euthanasia. Genesis 2:7; Genesis 9:6; Exodus 20:13; Psalm 139:13; Psalm 139:15–16; Acts 17:29; 1 Peter 2:17.

Nonresistance

The gospel emphatically teaches against strife, contention, and war. Therefore, no believer should take part in any strife, whether between individuals, in lawsuits, or in conflicts among nations. The doctrine of nonresistance was taught and exemplified by Christ and the apostles. It has been practiced by true Christians until the present time. Matthew 5:38–45; Matthew 26:52; John 18:36; 1 Corinthians 6:1–8; Romans 12:17–21; 2 Corinthians 10:4.

Miracles and Divine Healing

The miracles of the Bible were extraordinary events and are literally true. They are wonderful manifestations of the divine power of God. Divine healing lies within the realm of miracles. Those who are sick and who ask in faith should be anointed with oil and prayed for by the "elders" of the church. Matthew 12:40; Acts 1:3; Acts 2:22; Acts 4:16; James 5:14–15; Mark 6:13; Mark 16:18.

Church and State

The Scriptures teach that the authority of secular governments is ordained of God. However, there should be complete separation between church and state. Although we should be subject unto authorities, Christians owe their first allegiance to God. We believe Christians should not sere in secular government, or in positions that require the use of force. John 18:36; Acts 5:29; Romans 13:1–5; Hebrews 11:13.[11]

---

11. *What We Believe.* While some aspects of this movement are controversial, they are included here to show that the Holiness and Anabaptist movements were mutually influencing each other in the nineteenth century. While this church is not formally a part of the Holiness movement, their origin was from the same influences shaping the Holiness movement. John Holdeman appears to have been converted through a revival in a Church of God (Winebrenner) congregation, one of the earliest Holiness groups, under the leadership of John Funk, a former Mennonite. See Hiebert, *The Holdeman People*, 167–75.

3

Antebellum Holiness Statements

INTRODUCTION

If we are going to ponder the roots of pacifism which ran deep in the Holiness movement, we are wise to consider John Wesley as one of the likely sources. Most of the late nineteenth-century Holiness movement considered him the proximate headwaters. In Wesley, we see someone who almost talked his movement into nonresistance, by almost talking himself into it. His approach is both highly theological and pastoral. By starting with the unlimited love of God and love for all humankind, war was an example of the incomplete outworking of the consequences of that love by confining it to kinship and societal bounds. Where love remained confined in his own society, it was an experiential evidence of the incompleteness of the gospel work in transforming the nation.

In Wesley's reference to war as contradictory to the example of Jesus, the love of God and man, and contrary to "reason, virtue, and humanity," we almost arrive at an example of Wesley's quadrilateral of Scripture, tradition, reason, and experience as guides to faith. Francis Asberry and Jesse Lee provide early Methodist leaders who applied nonresistance to the life of a Christian minister, but did not universalize it. Back then, nonresistance was channeled into various forms of Christian ministry and missionary activity. Many Holiness revivalists were nonresistant to war,

46

but were interpreted as simply more religious and following a manner of holiness not available to most people. This dualism has existed for most of Christian history, and has siphoned off some of the pacifism in revivalism into a separated clergy.[1] Nevertheless, the Holiness movement pushed back on all forms of dualisms that suggested that holiness was only for a separated clergy. Such "push-back" often took forms that encouraged pacifism among the laity.

By the late 1820s, John Winebrenner, founder of the Church of God, would cast a much more focused and intense shadow of pacifism. Winebrenner, influenced by the Holiness Revivals associated with Charles G. Finney, but unlike Finney, adopted and promoted Christian pacifism and nonresistance to war. Winebrenner was influential both in being a founding member of the Church of God sector of the Holiness movement, which, although a small church, cast a very long shadow. A part of that shadow must have been pacifist. It seemed directly influenced by the Mennonites, but it broke completely out of those bounds and influenced the larger evangelical movement and the later Holiness and Pentecostal groups under the name of Church of God, and even those by much more diverse names.

One way that influence was carried forward was by Daniel S. Warner, a Civil War veteran who converted to Winebrenner's church after the war and after Winebrenner had died. After Warner's death, Warner's followers in the Church of God, Anderson, Indiana, were for a time the foremost promoters of pacifism among the early twentieth-century Holiness movement. Early Pentecostals were also influenced by the Church of God, Anderson. For its part, the original Church of God, Winebrenner, directly resisted the Mexican-American War in the 1840s.

Perhaps the largest Holiness-pacifist footprint in the nineteenth century was that of Thomas C. Upham, professor of moral philosophy at Bowdoin College in Maine from the late 1830s to the early 1870s. Upham was brought to sanctification when he attended Phoebe Palmer's Tuesday meetings for the promotion of holiness at the encouragement of his wife. This Holiness-pacifist was also one of the "founding generation" of American psychology, contributed to the popularity of the Catholic spirituality of Madame Guyon and Fenelon in America, and promoted

---

1. See Yoder, *Christian Attitudes to War, Peace, and Revolution*, 54–5.

48   PENTECOSTAL AND HOLINESS STATEMENTS ON WAR AND PEACE

understanding of human agency and free will. He became a favorite long after his death of thoughtful later Holiness advocates.[2]

Upham was an early advocate of nonresistance to evil, and found himself challenged by those who assumed that Romans 13 justified the violent rule of leaders and our requirement to obey them in execution of war. He took pains to extricate a Christian's submission to governing authority from any notion of righteous participation in violence, especially based upon Romans 13. Writing as he was a little over a generation after the American Revolution, Upham's critique is a reminder of the temptation of post-revolutionary Christians to baptize their own (now conservative) government's use of violence, in part because government is supposedly ordained of God in whatever form, moments after finding it necessary to overthrow the previous government with violence. Upham did so by reminding readers that Romans 13 had to be understood in the context of Romans 12, and arguing that it is inconceivable that early Christians could ever believe that the government's use of the sword was an expression of God's justice, when they were personally often the unjust recipients of such violence.

A similar argument about Romans 13 was made by Amos Dresser in a personal testimony. Dresser, one of the first students of Oberlin College, Ohio, and advocate of what became called Oberlin Holiness, was also an early Oberlin peace student leader. In this he differed strongly with Charles G. Finney, whose brand of Holiness revivalism had been one of the formative contexts for the founding of Oberlin College.

Dresser tells of being an abolitionist Bible salesman in the South and being publicly beaten by Nashville governmental authorities, whose own testimony was that Dresser was innocent of any wrongdoing. How, Dresser asked, was that an expression of how governing authorities always reward good behavior and punish wrongdoing? Dresser who served his whole career as a Congregational pastor, is a reminder that many Congregationalists were deeply sympathetic to holiness social causes such as temperance, abolitionism, and peace.

Significantly, Amos Dresser's son, Amos Jr., became a follower of Holiness evangelist and advocate of peace, John Alexander Dowie. Amos Dresser Sr. spoke to Dowie's followers in Zion, Illinois, in his old age, at a time when Dowie was promoting pacifism among his followers in Zion. Zion was one of the early sources of Pentecostal leaders, and in this way

2. Salter, *Spirit and Intellect*; Bundy, "Thomas Cogswell Upham," 23–40.

we can see that an early holiness-peace advocate was directly influential upon early Pentecostal leaders in their pacifist beliefs.

No doubt, nineteenth-century Holiness pacifists were predominantly postmillennialists who believed in the efficacy of improvements in human society through education and social reform. The transformation of Holiness and Pentecostal pacifism in the early twentieth century to a more pessimistic-tending premillennialism pulled in most of the tendencies of the postmillennial variety. The contradictions inherent in these two varieties must have had something to do with the later diminished pacifist footprint among Holiness and Pentecostal adherents in the late twentieth century. However, this should not be overstated. These nineteenth-century Holiness pacifists were not just expressing a kind of optimism fueled by the early successes of American democracy. Amos Dresser was a case in point. He bore in his own body the marks of being tortured by that democracy. Dresser, Upham, and others, saw their pacifism as continuous with Mennonites, Quakers, and even early Christian communities.

AMOS DRESSER (1812–1904)
[Old Testament Wars], 1848

So it was "because of the hardness of their hearts" that God even used them as instruments of destruction.

Their exodus from Egypt, their whole history, *their being carried away captives into Babylon*, shows that it was not with God's approval that they waged war. Of their own choice, and *according to their own plan* "they took the sword," and they finally *"perished by the sword."* True, for his own name's sake among the heathen, He often blessed them, but much more would his name have been honored and revered had they been willing to hold their peace, stand still and see the salvation of Jehovah.[3]

[Romans 13], 1848

Against those who argued that Romans 13 taught that rulers only punish those who do evil, Dresser gave his own experience as an abolitionist in the South before the Civil War:

3. Dresser, *The Bible Against War*, 52. Dresser was a missionary, pastor, and abolitionist, among other things. Emphasis in original.

The mayor of Nashville, in acquainting the mob with the decision of the committee of vigilance against me, prefaced his sentence of condemnation by saying, "Mr. Dresser appears to be a fine young man; he has evidently designed no evil," etc. And the secretary afterwards in defending the action of the committee, said, "Dresser had broken no law;" and then went on to show that it was necessary for the public good to resort to lynch law. And though there was no form of law in my trial; yet I was tried by the "rulers" of the city. Members of the committee who passed sentence upon me, with whom I had sat at the communion table three weeks before, said they believed me to be a Christian, etc. Yet their praise did not protect my naked back from the cow-skin.[4]

Such governments are not the creatures of God's approval. We are not to pray that they may be sustained, but that they may be broken to pieces by the "stone cut out without hands," and the righteous kingdom of Jesus Christ established on the ruins, "that the kingdoms of this world may become the kingdoms of our Lord and his Christ, and that He may reign forever and ever," that the thrones may be cast down, and the ancient of days may sit.[5]

CHURCHES OF GOD IN NORTH AMERICA [WINEBRENNER]

From *The Faith and Practice of the Church of God,* 1829

[WAR]

She [the Church] believes that all civil wars are unholy and sinful, and in which the saints of the Most High ought never to participate. 2 Cor. X. 4. For the weapons of our warfare are not carnal, but mighty through God to the pulling down of strongholds. Heb. Xii. 14. Follow peace with all men, and holiness, without which no man shall see the Lord. Matt. Vii. 12. Therefore all things whatsoever ye would that men should do to you, do ye even so to them: for this is the law and the prophets. Chap, xxvi. 52. Then said Jesus to him, Put up again thy sword into his place: for all they that take the sword, shall perish with

4. Ibid., 83.
5. Ibid., 67.

the sword. Chap. V. 39. But I say to you, That ye resist not evil: but whosoever shall smite thee on thy right cheek, turn to him the other also. 44 But I say to you. Love your enemies, bless them that curse you, do good to them that hate you, and pray for them which despitefully use you, and persecute you.[6]

[Civil Government]

She believes that civil governments are ordained of God for the general good; that Christians ought to be subject to the same in all things, except what is manifestly unscriptural; and that appeals to the law, out of the church, for justice, and the adjustments of civil rights, are not inconsistent with the principles and duties of the Christian religion.[7]

JOHN WESLEY (1703–1791)
[On War], n.d.

[The peacemaker is one who] being willed with the love of God and of mankind, cannot confine the expressions of it to his own family, or friends, or acquaintance, or party, or to those of his own opinions,—no, nor to those who are partakers of like precious faith; but steps over all these narrow bounds, that he may do good to every man, that he may, some way or other, manifest his love to neighbors and strangers, friends and enemies.[8]

[Christians should be] lovers of God and man, who utterly detest and abhor all strife and debate, all variance and contention; and accordingly labor with all their might to prevent this fire of hell from being kindled . . .[9]

War [proves that] the very foundations of all things . . . are utterly out of course in the Christian . . . world.[10]

---

6. Winebrenner, *History of all the Religious Denominations in the United States*, 179. Unlike many pacifists, Winebrenner was willing to use the court system.

7. Ibid., 180.

8. Wesley, Sermon 203, quoted in Alexander, *Peace to War*, 98. Wesley was a Church of England pastor and theologian.

9. Ibid.

10. Ibid.

PENTECOSTAL AND HOLINESS STATEMENTS ON WAR AND PEACE

[He made clear that a person could not reconcile war with any attempt to] "walk also as [Jesus] walked."

War was a "horrid reproach to the Christian name," that defied reason, virtue, and humanity.[11]

METHODISM AND WAR

Francis Asberry (1745–1816), n.d.

[Refused to sign Maryland's oath of loyalty because he believed that] "he as a minister should not bear arms."[12]

Jesse Lee (b. 1758), n.d.

As a Christian and as a preacher of the gospel I could not fight. I could not reconcile it to myself to bear arms, or to kill one of my fellow creatures.[13]

THOMAS C. UPHAM (1799–1872)

Practical Efficacy of the Principle of Peace, 1842

It may be said, with some degree of plausibility, that the principles of peace are not the principles of protection, and that, if we throw off the aspect and attitude of war, we shall not only be insecure against hostility, but shall invite it. Whether this objection involves a fallacy or not, it is beyond all question that it is cordially received as an undoubted truth by many persons, who invest themselves with it as with a shield, and avail themselves of its aid to throw back, to a measureless distance, whatever is addressed either to their understandings or to their hearts, on the stand upon this simple proposition alone—that no nation is safe without military preparation. They assert, with as much confidence as if they were pleading the authority of a mathematical axiom, that there is no security, and no peace, except on the con-

---

11. Ibid.

12. Richard Cameron, *Methodism and Society*, 89. Francis Asbury quote, as well as brief summary, was quoted from Alexander, 99. Asberry was the first superintendent of the Methodist Episcopal Church, USA.

13. Quoted in Alexander, 101. Jesse Lee was an early Methodist leader.

Antebellum Holiness Statements   53

dition of bloodshed,—that he who will not fight must make up
his mind to become the prey of every species of depredation. . . .
And yet we feel, in some degree, prepared to maintain . . . that,
amid all the belligerent elements existing either in individuals
or communities, pacific principles are the surest safeguard. We
verily believe that in these principles there is a secret power, a
hidden, but most effective energy, which is but imperfectly understood. If men had the faith to receive it, they would not fail
to find that the panoply of love is more impenetrable to the attacks of adversaries than that of steel. . . . The security which is
to be found in pacific principles, is based in the constitution of
the human mind itself. We are so constituted by our Maker, that
we naturally feel an interest in innocence and weakness; and it
excites in every man, whose feelings have not been greatly per-
verted, the deepest disapprobation and abhorrence, when they
are made to suffer. Why is it that little children, and women, and
feeble old men, are, in a vast majority of cases, fully protected
amid the wide-spread and deepest horrors or war? Will it be said
that they find their protection in force? But they exhibit nothing
of this kind; they have no arms; they present no organization
and array of battle: on the contrary, they make their appeal to
the penetralia of the soul; they look for protection to the great
principles of humanity alone.[14]

[War], 1842

Every belligerent nation, with scarcely a single exception, scorn-
fully rejects the imputation of being the original aggressor, and
professes to prosecute its warlike measures for purposes of
self-protection. And so long as we admit that defensive wars
are allowable on Christian principles, so long we grant, for all
practical purposes, every thing which the advocates of war wish.
The true doctrine is, that human life, both in its individual and
corporate state, as one and as many, is inviolable; that it cannot be taken away for any purpose whatever, except by explicit
divine permission; and that war, in every shape, and for every
purpose, is *wrong*, absolutely *wrong*, wholly *wrong*. Any doctrine

14. Upham, *The Manual of Peace*, 199–200. Upham was the professor of moral philosophy at Bowdoin College, ME, one of the founders of American psychology, and
a Holiness movement advocate who frequented Phoebe Palmer's Tuesday meetings
for the promotion of holiness in the late 1830s. See Salter, *Spirit and Intellect: Thomas
Upham's Holiness Theology*.

54   PENTECOSTAL AND HOLINESS STATEMENTS ON WAR AND PEACE

short of this will fall altogether powerless and useless upon the broad surface of the world's crimes and miseries; it will dim the light of no sword; it will wipe the tear of no widow and orphan.[15]

In proceeding now to examine the subject of War in the light of the New Testament, we remark, in the first place, that war, in all its forms, is opposed by those numerous passages which require men to love their fellow men.—Matt. xxii. 37, 8, 9: "Jesus said unto him, Thou shalt love the Lord thy God with all thy heart, and with all thy soul, and with all thy mind. This is the first and great commandment. And the second is like unto it,—Thou shalt love thy neighbor as thyself." The Savior himself, in the parable of the good Samaritan, has explained whom we are to understand by our neighbor. The commentary of the Savior authorizes us to understand the term as including all mankind, every class and condition of men; however they may be separated from us by difference of language, by distance of country, by diversities of opinion, religion, customs, government, and political interests; however they be, from some unpropitious circumstances, arrayed even in actual or supposed hostility. There is not, even under these circumstances, a release from the law of love.[16]

[Romans 13], 1842

The following passage, in the 13th of Romans, where the apostle is speaking of the duty of obedience to rulers, is often brought up, in opposition to the doctrine of non-resistance. "For he is the minister of God to thee for good. But if thou do that which is evil, be afraid; *for he beareth not the sword in vain*; for he is the minister of God, a revenger to execute wrath upon him that doeth evil."—The reader is requested, if he wishes to have a right understanding of this passage, to read carefully this whole chapter, taken in connection with the latter part of the 12th chapter. If he will do this, he will find that this exceedingly interesting portion of Scripture teaches something very different from a spirit of strife and contention. The leading ideas contained in it are evidently these: (1.) We are to exercise love and forgiveness towards all men, and under all circumstances, whatever their conduct may be towards us. (2.) In the exercise of this spirit of

15. Ibid., 89. Emphasis in original.
16. Ibid., 108.

Antebellum Holiness Statements 55

love and forgiveness, it is incumbent upon Christians to render entire submission to the civil and political administration of the country where they reside. Now, when we consider that the primitive Christians lived, in any instances, at least, under administrators of government which were exceedingly unjust, perverse, and cruel, the explicit and urgent directions, contained in the 13th of Romans, to be submissive and obedient to those in authority, must be regarded as any thing rather than contentious and belligerent. Such directors are obviously the natural and true result of those doctrines of love and peace which the Savior himself had so earnestly inculcated. If any people in the world ever had occasion for complaint against those in authority, and strong motives for resistance to them, it was the primitive Christians, at certain periods and in certain countries; but they were required not to resist, not to return evil for evil, to endure every indignity and suffering, even to death itself, rather than lift the hand against the civil rulers.[17]

17. Ibid., 127–28. Emphasis in original.

4

Radical Holiness Statements

INTRODUCTION

As you read these statements about government, citizenship, and warfare, pay attention to the two kingdom distinction between the kingdom of God and earthly kingdoms. Notice the priority given to the lordship of Jesus Christ and the rule of God. The two kingdoms have differing modes of rule, and to fight with "carnal" weapons transgresses the kingdom of God. Moreover, in some cases, membership in the military with its oath of allegiance is a transgression of membership in the kingdom of God.

Sometimes, early Holiness and Pentecostals, who promoted nonresistance to war, have been analyzed exclusively as believing the end of the world was imminent, and therefore one should not fight to preserve its kingdoms, which would take precedence before the kingdom of God. While they held this conviction, they also believed that the in-breaking reality created a present rule of God that had to be obeyed. The coming kingdom did, in some sense, compete with and delegitimize contemporary governments. They said as much when they promoted the lordship of Jesus Christ and his teachings in the Sermon on the Mount. This can be seen clearly in this chapter with groups such as the Brethren in Christ, who not only precluded military service, but also oath-taking and even police work. However, it was also the common language of many of the

56

other groups. For instance, there are at least twenty-seven referents to the Sermon on the Mount in this volume. There were thirty-nine referents to the kingdom of God having priority over the kingdoms of this world. Most significantly, over eighty times, reference is made to Jesus Christ and his teaching or leadership in peacemaking, nonresistance, leading alternative battles, and the like—all regarding Christian peacemaking.

The Holiness movement covers almost two hundred years of history by now, but came to prominence in the 1870s for its emphasis on Wesley's teaching of sanctification, as they understood it as a second work of grace, sought for as an experience of God's dramatic presence which removed the root or tendency to be governed by sin. Holiness followers were therefore known for being different, in ways they understood to count as separation from the world and to God. Such signs of separation included markers such as plain dress, abstaining from alcohol, sexual purity, food prohibitions, no swearing or oaths, and the like. This much is known. Less known, perhaps forgotten, is that holiness also often meant separation from military service and warfare, a veritable laying-down of sword and shield and "studying war no more."

Like historic peace churches, the Holiness movement saw living differently as what the Apostle Paul termed nonconformity (Rom 12:1), and they suggested this was the result of repentance, a turning from the ways of the world toward God. To Holiness advocates, it was not possible without the cleansing experience of sanctification and becoming disciplined or discipled. A favorite scripture for Holiness believers was Hebrews 12:14, "Follow peace with all men, and holiness, without which no man shall see the Lord" (KJV). As a result, peacemaking was part of early Holiness theology and practice. In the case of two Holiness groups in this volume, Calvary Holiness and the New Testament Church, you can see the explicit connection to Hebrews 12:14.

Furthermore, nine Pentecostal groups followed suit, considering themselves to be Holiness groups as well. One group, Alma White's Pillar of Fire, took the high ground from just war Christians who championed the "two-swords" passage about Jesus and his disciples in the garden of Gethsemane, where Jesus instructed them to buy two swords (Luke 22). Just war advocates had argued that this showed that Jesus, contrary to the Sermon on the Mount, taught the use of fighting with weapons of war. However A. F. Wolfram of the Pillar of Fire argued simultaneously that the passage could not mean swords for fighting a battle with Roman

58   PENTECOSTAL AND HOLINESS STATEMENTS ON WAR AND PEACE

governing authorities, as two swords would not be enough for twelve disciples and their Lord. Jesus had remarked on the two swords that "it is enough." Instead, Wolfram argued the two swords were metaphorical of separate experiences—conversion and sanctification; a singularly Holiness interpretation.

Timing sets a powerful context. Statements that originated around the time of World War I were constrained by extreme curtailment of freedom of speech by the passage of the Espionage and Sedition Acts in 1917. The U.S. government required groups to go on record against participation in war. But if going on record could be construed as interference with the prosecution of the war, preachers and leaders could be imprisoned. This happened to Holiness folks. Their sentiments were clearer during the Spanish-American War.

Two groups spoke out against the government's war policy: The Church of God, Anderson, Indiana, and John Alexander Dowie's Christian Catholic Apostolic Church. Dowie, considered by followers to be a modern-day apostle, made his name preaching against doctors, drugs, and devils, and was absolute in his prohibition against alcohol in the utopian healing community, Zion, Illinois, which his followers built. Dowie could say without equivocation, "All War is wrong, and that without exceptions. It is sinful for Christian men to fight and destroy life." It is unusual to have a prayer such as we have been able to include here from him praying for his followers to be spared from war, if necessary to have the courage to die rather than fight, and for forgiveness for soldiers and our country for the injustices of that war. The prayer includes scathing rebukes for official government policy during the Spanish-American War in the Philippines. One wonders how a Holiness preacher today would be received who prayed these words in relation to the U.S. involvement in Afghanistan and Iraq. "O God, keep thy people from war. Grant unto us that if war should come to us we may be willing to die rather than kill any one else. God help us! Now we pray Thee, for Jesus' sake, to look upon this nation that is engaged in such a bloody, detestable war, thrusting its government upon the Philippine islanders who do not want our rule."

The Church of God (Anderson) leaders used the same sacredness of human life terminology that today's evangelicals use for an unborn child. They also argued for civil disobedience and argued the immorality of capital punishment. Their official publication, *The Gospel Trumpet*, used satire to argue against war stating, "Jesus Christ said 'love your enemies.' He did not say shoot them."

Lawrence D. Pruitt of the Church of God, Guthrie, Oklahoma, made an argument against participation in war based upon a Holiness understanding of sanctification. He argued that in the garden of Gethsemane, Peter pulled a sword as an expression of his carnal nature, but that Jesus told him to put away his sword. However, after Pentecost, and one presumes Peter was sanctified, Peter went to enemies with the gospel and not with the sword. Pruitt also argued from early church history that early Christian pacifism provided a model for Holiness pacifists in the twentieth century. Pruitt also argues against those who would serve the military in noncombatant positions. He used the scripture in Acts where Saul of Tarsus held the coats of those who killed Stephen while Stephen was martyred. He argued that Saul was guilty of blood, and by analogy that noncombatants are guilty of bloodshed in war. In a similar way he argued against buying war bonds and doing defense-plant work.

The Church of God, based in Ft. Scott, Kansas, warned followers of the dangers of patriotism and pointed out the passions involved in patriotism led one to do great evils. Imagine an evangelical leader today using the economic argument they used: "War is for greed—BUSINESS."

Some of the conferences of the Free Methodist Church, a church founded out of concern of the poor being turned away from worship, railed against capitalism and war early in World War I. "The world has long been cursed by an economic system that has stood as a bulwark against human progress, and for the sake of sordid gain has fostered well nigh every vice known to man." They pledged themselves to its overthrow. They believed that through Christian activity society would be improved and the millennium would arrive. World War I and the travails of capitalism both convinced them that the millennium was further away than they had anticipated. "Has Civilization perished from the earth? Have the ideals of Christianity, introduced two thousand years ago by the PRINCE OF PEACE [emphasis in original], utterly failed? The appeal to the god of brute force is founded upon the basest elements in the nature of men. We are far short of the millennium, rather are we come to the fulfillment of prophecy in reference to the conditions preceding the coming of the Son of Man. We commend the efforts of the little nuclei of men who are endeavoring to bring about peaceful arbitration in the nations of the earth."

60   PENTECOSTAL AND HOLINESS STATEMENTS ON WAR AND PEACE

Still, the passage and enforcement of the Espionage and Sedition Acts made it difficult for Christians to express their opposition to war. Many groups, therefore, couched their indifference to War in some kind of acknowledgement of submission to governing authorities. The context in World War I was much more repressive of free speech than during the Spanish American War or in the 1930s. Still, the U.S. government forced Holiness and Pentecostal denominations out in the open because without officially going on record with a statement of belief, members could not exercise their beliefs against killing in war.

The Church of God (Anderson), was forthright in arguing civil disobedience in 1902 in the Spanish-American War. What is more astounding was their republication of those arguments verbatim in 1917 in a much more dangerous context. The Church of God cast a long shadow in this argument, which also influenced some Pentecostals. The Church of God also shows us a link to an early nineteenth-century Holiness leader, T. C. Upham, who argued that the Mosaic prohibition against killing still stands and exhibits a principle of the sacredness of human life, especially in relation to warfare. Dowie made the same argument, and was likely also influenced by Upham. By 1971, however, the moral center of the Church of God's argument had shifted to freedom of conscience or individual choice. Ironically, this choice argument is parallel to the one used in the abortion controversy in the larger society and reflecting the expansion of market metaphors to the heart of religion. In the materials on the Churches of God (Winebrenner), one can track an example of a church that changed dramatically over time from 1829 to 1959.

A. M. Kiergan, Church of God (Ft. Scott, KS), warned against the dangers of "godless enthusiasm for flags, patriotism and business." He was not alone in this argument among Holiness folks. He turned mainstream thinking on its head when he equated war to anarchy. Popular press constantly highlighted anarchists who were (sometimes violently) opposed to World War I. For Kiergan, the very spirit of war was opposed to the very core of good governing, in that it destroyed life and was destructive of the social fabric. War was not opposed by anarchists, but those who supported war were, in fact, anarchists. The Church of God Apostolic (Beckley, West Virginia) made a similar argument, substituting the word "confusion" for anarchy. "We do not believe in war, nor going to war, for God is not the author of confusion, but of peace."

The two kingdoms, the governments of this world and the government of God, was a salient theme at the time of World War I. The Holiness movement in the early nineteenth century had been fired by images of millennial peace associated with the rule of Jesus. Early nineteenth-century Holiness millennialism focused on social transformation, including democratizing race relations by ending slavery, democratizing gender relations by experimenting with variations in the nuclear family and questioning patriarchy, democratizing the economy with communistic or communal experiments, and democratizing governing by calling for an end to war as a mechanism for international conflict resolution. It is this configuration of this-worldly transformations, based upon an imagination fired by the millennium and the presence of the prophetic spirit, that was the radical holiness wing. There were elements of the holiness movement more focused upon the internal subjective experience of the Spirit in sanctification, with less societal transformation directly in mind. Radical holiness set about to practice the kingdom of God, the millennium, in an anticipatory way. In this, we are in concert with the way the term radical holiness has been used by Randall Stephens and William Kostlevy. Stephens used the term without defining it, but giving numerous examples. Generally it referred to a movement originating in Holiness abolitionists who became poor, persecuted, and radicalized by participating a movement that identified with social justice for slaves, women, poor, and outsiders. Kostlevy found that the movement became radicalized especially by its competition with socialists, for the religious imaginations of followers, since both movements were proclaiming a path to the millennium. Both groups questioned the capitalist's vision of millennium which they saw unfolding around them.[1] In our presentation, we want to highlight texts that remind us that, especially in the early twentieth century, radical holiness included a tendency to pacifism. Because of the timing of the founding of each group, groups that formed early in the twentieth century were more likely to still be in a sectarian phase by the time of World War I, and therefore have the social distance necessary to practice radical critique and resistance to governmental demands. Some of the groups included in this chapter had already entered the mainstream and found it impossible to embrace pacifism as a movement, but we can find the tendency among their adherents.

---

1. See Stephens, *The Fire Spreads* and Kostlevy, *Holy Jumpers*.

62   PENTECOSTAL AND HOLINESS STATEMENTS ON WAR AND PEACE

Later in the nineteenth century the tide began to turn on the millennium. The wave hit shore during World War I. For many in the premillennial camp, innovators for their time, the possibility that Jerusalem might be "liberated" from Arab control, opened the possibility that Jesus might be returning to rule from Zion. Some Holiness leaders had already been poised. Dowie had died more than ten years before Jerusalem changed hands, but he had named his utopian healing community Zion in anticipation of just such an event. Leaders in Zion, during World War I, were against participating in killing. However, liberating Jerusalem, even by force, fired their imagination in new ways. In a parallel healing utopia, Shiloh (Main), headed by Holiness evangelist, Frank Sandford, we can see a snapshot of the moment for many Holiness and Pentecostal folks when they began to wonder about the efficacy of violence in a righteous cause. Frank Sandford, turned his back on twenty years of teaching pacifism and told his followers to join the battle of Armageddon, which he had come to believe World War I was becoming. Some Holiness folks were able to make the transition to premillennialism and retain pacifism, and the more well known of these became Pentecostals and took their pacifism into that movement. The Holiness movement had more folks who never stopped being Mennonites, Anabaptists, and Quakers and they perceived their emphasis on sanctification and revival did not completely change that past. After all, Quaker and Anabaptist churches were holding camp meetings and revival meetings too, and both groups had a history of emphasizing both holiness and separation from the world. It may also be that premillennialsim, was associated with a critique of holiness groups that were becoming mainstream, and losing their ability to critique either capitalism or militarism. Thus, holiness premillennialists could be radical holiness proponents. So, it was more from the radical edge of the holiness movement in the early twentieth century that promotion of pacifism found its center.

Some Holiness groups came to pacifism or became focused on peacemaking after World War I. The Salvation Amy was one such group, and one can surmise almost became pacifist during the Boer War. However, while the founder of the Salvation Army, General William Booth, refused to let pacifism take center stage within his movement, other Salvation Army pacifist-oriented members took their pacifism to the Pentecostals. The pacifist element centered in Sydney H. Booth-Clibborn, and his wife, Kate Booth-Clibborn, the son-in-law and daughter of the founders and the leaders of the Salvation Army in Continental Europe. When the General refused to allow pacifist preaching and organizing, the Booth-Clibborn's followed Dowie into Zion and later became influential in the Pentecostal movement with pacifism. When the General died, his wife Catherine and son, Herbert, both promoted pacifism. However, it never became the predominant position in the Salvation Army. A number of other established Holiness groups, the Free Methodists, the Nazarenes, and the Wesleyans, were not officially pacifist and were not generally predominated by pacifists, but had large pockets of ardent pacifism within them from various sources at different times. The Nazarenes and Wesleyans both merged with other groups which had been officially pacifist in their past, and retained some of that emphasis for a time. On the other hand, some holiness groups that were unapologetically pacifist migrated their way into Pentecostal groups.

ALLEGHENY WESLEYAN METHODIST CONNECTION, FOUNDED 1966
What We Believe, n.d.

(Must avoid) fighting, quarreling, brawling, brother going to law with brother, returning evil for evil, or railing for railing. The Bible: "Let all bitterness, and wrath, and anger, and clamor, and evil speaking be put away from you, with all malice: and be ye kind one to another, tender-hearted, forgiving one another, even as God for Christ's sake hath forgiven you." (Eph. 4:31, 32.)

(Must avoid) the buying or selling of men, women or children, with an intention to enslave them, or holding them as slaves, or claiming that it is right so to do. Comments: For more than a century this was a burning question in America and other countries. In English domains slaves were freed by national purchase and emancipation laws, in America their liberty was authorized as a war measure during the Civil War. In brief, the evils of slavery are: it interferes with the supreme claims of God upon humanity, including all races (Deut. 6:5); interferes with freedom to work out human destiny by education, Bible-reading and freedom of choice, (John 5:39; John 8:32); it interferes with marriage and the duties of parents (1 Cor. 7:2; Eph, 5:31); it originated in man-stealing, which is to be condemned (Exod. 21:16); it is involuntary servitude, which is wrong except as a legal punishment for crime (Deut. 23:15, 16); and demands work without wages. (Jer. 22:13, 14)[2]

BRETHREN IN CHRIST [FORMERLY RIVER BRETHREN]
Oath and Nonresistance, 1779–1782

We also learn from the doctrine of the Lord Jesus that swearing of pledge is forbidden, therefore it shall be forbidden to us also. Matt. 5:34. Therefore it is also completely forbidden to bear the sword for revenge or defense. Verses 39, 40.[3]

"Government," 1779–1782

From the doctrine of the Lord Jesus and his apostles we learn that it is forbidden to any member or follower of Jesus Christ to occupy authoritative offices; therefore it is and shall be forbidden to us. We shall, however, not oppose authority, but be obedient in everything good, paying taxes or for protection, because Paul calls it God's servant. Rom. 13. We also see that God rules all Nature and has also servants—men who are to rule Nature; and that is also for the benefit of God's children, otherwise it would be still more difficult to live in this world. Therefore Paul bids us pray for them, so that they accomplish their duty faith-

2. *What We Believe: Doctrine and General Rules*, 6–7.

3. Schrag, *Oath and Nonresistance*. The confessions were signed in the name of the fellowship by Johannes Meyer, Johannes Funk, Samuel Bentzner, Jacob Engle, Stofel Hollinger, Philip Stern, Johannes Greider, Benjamin Beyer. Six of the eight men whose names appear lived in Donegal Township in the years 1779–1782. All Brethren in Christ historical documents were provided to us by Glen Pierce, Director of the Brethren in Christ Historical Library and Archives of Messiah College, PA. The Brethren in Christ, like other peace churches, seldom used the term "pacifism" to define their peace convictions. The early Brethren in Christ preferred words like nonresistance, nonviolence, and conscientious objection to pacifism. Morris Sherk, researcher at Messiah College, searched the term pacifism between 1887 and 2004. He found eighty-six file cards with the heading "nonresistance" or "nonviolence" and only seven file cards with the heading "pacifism." Sherk concluded that "it appears the term pacifism was used infrequently in the Brethren in Christ literature." Email correspondence with Glen Pierce, director of the BIC historical library and archives, February 8, 2012, personal files of Brian Pipkin. Donald Kraybill, Anabaptist scholar, confirms that all traditional and older Anabaptist communities in North America—Amish, Mennonites, Hutterites, and Brethren—used nonresistance rather than pacifism. Email correspondence with Donald Kraybill, February 13, 2012, personal files of Brian Pipkin.

fully, that children under them may lead a quiet life, pleasing to God, but may not need them for force.[4]

[Prohibition of Alcohol], 1889

Whereas, The Pennsylvania brethren petition General Conference for an expression of its attitude on the prohibition question. Resolved, That inasmuch as the Brethren in Christ do not believe it consistent with their faith as non-resistant people, to take part in political elections, but since the prohibition question is a moral and not a political one, General Conference submits the question to the conscientious consideration of each brother, but positively forbids any brother, either in sentiment or vote, to give any encouragement to the regular traffic.[5]

"Non-Resistant Doctrine," 1909

The Brethren in Christ have not accepted any historical creed or confession; but have certain generally recognized doctrines to which they adhere.

They believe that the Church is built on faith in an Almighty, Triune, External, Self-Existing God, Father, Son and Holy Spirit. They accept the doctrines of the immortality of the soul: redemption through Jesus Christ as the Son of God, who was delivered for our offences, and was raised again for our justification, and who has, and does, by His shed blood, make atonement for the sin of sins to God and man, by regeneration through the influence and operations of the Holy Spirit, resulting in holy living. The observance of the ordinances of baptism by triune immersion as the proper mode, the sacrament of the Eucharist accompanied by the ceremony of feet washing, in anticipation of the second coming of Christ as the glorious hope of the Church. The recognition of Christ not only as Saviour but as Lord and Master and coming King, involves in their view, the acceptance of the tenets and principles of His government; accordingly, they believe that inasmuch as He is Prince of Peace, His Kingdom is of peace; and that, as His subjects, they should abstain from the employment of carnal forces which involve the taking of human

4. Ibid.
5. "Article 7," 55.

66 PENTECOSTAL AND HOLINESS STATEMENTS ON WAR AND PEACE

life. For this reason, the doctrine of non-resistance is a prominent feature of their belief.[6]

"Petition Concerning the Consistency of Brethren Joining the Police Force," 1913

Resolved, that since the Brotherhood, both in doctrine and practice,[7] seeks to adhere to the principles of non-resistance, it is deemed unadvisable for any member of the body to engage in police or military service.[8]

"Article XXIII," 1948

Section I

Whereas, our brotherhood has been released from the war hysteria which we experienced during the recent years; and,

Whereas, it has become apparent that the church does not have a united testimony in respect to non-resistance; and,

Whereas, there is a conflicting declaration of our stand by the action of the Conference of 1942 and 1943, Article 13, Section 9, and Article 42, Section 2, respectively; and,

Whereas, we need a definite basis for action in the future, therefore,

Resolved, that this Conference reconsider the declaration of her position as a non-resistant church relative to military service.

Section II

Whereas, the accepted and declared position of the Church from its earliest history has been that of non-resistance and abstinence from all forms of military service and all means of support of war; and,

Whereas, this position has been officially recorded with, and recognized by the governments of both Canada and the United States; and,

Whereas, it is evident that for any member of the Brethren in Christ Church to accept military service, is a betrayal of her doctrine, and evidence of lack of harmony with her principles, and a violation of her practice; therefore,

6. *Minutes of General Conference of The Brethren in Christ*, 13–14.
7. Changed "pracitse" to "practice."
8. "Article 32," 55. Emphasis in original.

Resolved, that the Brethren in Christ Church declares that membership cannot be continued for one who participates in military service, combatant or non-combatant, and be it further, Resolved, that membership of such transgressors, be terminated by Constitution and By-Laws procedure, (Rituals, Art. III, pages 95, 96) can be regained only upon satisfactory acknowledgement of his error, a declaration of his acceptance of the Bible teaching on this doctrine of non-resistance, and subscription to the tenets of the church.

Section III
Whereas, participation in defense work and War Industry partakes of the same spirit as does military service, and since such participation reveals a lack of conformity to the principles and practices of the Church; and

Whereas, participation in defense work and War Industries shall be defined as any work or industry which directly supports the war through the manufacture, production, or construction of equipment which is used for destruction; therefore,

Resolved, that members who compromise the principles of the gospel and loyalty to the doctrine of the Church by accepting such employment be considered as being in like transgression with those who enter into military service.

Section IV
Whereas, church members are largely a product of church leaders; and,

Whereas, such leaders are responsible for teaching a standard basis for church faith and practice; and,

Whereas, evidence is apparent that such responsible people have not been unified in faith and teaching; and,

Whereas, indoctrination needs to be the technique of securing our desired end rather than by remedial measures; and,

Whereas, much of indoctrination is directly or indirectly influenced by our church schools; therefore,

Resolved, that no Bishop, Minister, Licensed Minister, Deacon, Home or Foreign Missionary, or faculty members of our church schools, can serve in their capacities if they are not in harmony with the declared stand of the Church on Non-Resistance in respect to military service and war work.

Section V
Whereas, a church is what its members are as individuals; and,

Whereas, lack of unity on our conformity to this doctrine on the part of the lay members as well as the officials, is clearly inconsistent, as well as subversive; therefore,

Resolved, that espousal of the Church's declaration of the doctrine and principles of Non-Resistance be an unavoidable requirement for church membership, hereafter.

Henry Schneider, Sec'y.[9]

CALVARY HOLINESS CHURCH

[Non-Resistance], 1963

We are called with a holy calling to a life of separation from the world, its follies, sinful practices and methods; and yet, that the believer should demonstrate the spirit of non-resistance in all maters according to Christ's Sermon on the Mount, even though the Christian has a prior commitment of loyalty to God and His Will as revealed in His Word, he is enjoined to obey the rulers of government under which he lives.[10]

CHRISTIAN CATHOLIC APOSTOLIC CHURCH[11] (1847—1907)

John Alexander Dowie on the Boer War, 1900

We feel that all War is wrong, and that without exceptions. It is sinful for Christian men to fight and destroy life. We read that the command of God is: "Thou shalt not kill." No human or demoniacal sophistry can ever justify murder in any form especially for the members of the Christian Catholic Church who stand on each side, whom we have earnestly exhorted not to fight. We are willing that our people should go, if need be, on the firing line to remove the wounded and dying, and to minister to them. We are sure that no one will accuse us for a moment of desiring that our people shall be other than helpful to the utmost

9. "Article XXIII Examining Board Report," 56–57.

10. *Manual of the Calvary Holiness Church*, n.p.

11. John Alexander Dowie, prominent forerunner of Pentecostal pacifism, was a leading evangelist and advocate of divine healing, and founder of the religious community called the Christian Catholic Apostolic Church in Zion City, IL.

extent of their power in relieving the sufferings, both physical and spiritual, of those who fall beneath the bayonet, the bullet, or the shell.[12]

Dowie on Civil Government, 1901

Zion loyalty renders unto Caesar, whether he be President, Czar, Emperor, or King, that which belongs unto Caesar; and yet Zion absolutely refuses to recognize the right of Caesar to enter the domain of the conscience or to interfere with the actions of those who offend no righteous law, but live quiet, peaceable and good lives.[13]

"Prayer for Deliverance of Mankind from Wars" by Dowie, 1902

Help men everywhere to see that War is hateful to Thee, War is needless; that the wrath of man can never work the righteousness of God, and that Thy Word is true, "All they that take the sword shall perish with the sword." O God, keep thy people from war. Grant unto us that if war should come to us we may be willing to die rather than kill any one else. God help us! Now we pray Thee, for Jesus' sake, to look upon this nation that is engaged in such a bloody, and such a mean and detestable war, thrusting its government upon the Philippine islanders who do not want our rule. This nation bought their islands for twenty million dollars from an accursed power that had destroyed all liberty. O God, make this nation to see that they bought human beings in the market, and now they are paying for them in blood. They thought they could pay for them in dollars and they cannot. Their armies are killing in some places everybody over ten years old. Have mercy, O God, upon the brutal soldiers of America who have been doing this in the Philippine islands [sic]. Deliver this nation from the awful, shameful blot upon its flag.[14]

---

12. *Leaves of Healing VI*, 722. See also *Healing Evangelists, 1881–1957*.
13. *Leaves of Healing VIII*, 66–68. See also *Healing Evangelists, 1881–1957*.
14. *Leaves of Healing XI*, 122. See also *Healing Evangelists, 1881–1957*.

CHURCH OF GOD (FORT SCOTT, KANSAS)

"Convention Minutes," 1914

Resolved that we, the Churches of God, represented in this convention deplore the war now raging in Europe, that we are anti-war and we pray that the war may be brought to a speedy close and that our homeland be continually blessed with peace.[15]

From "War—What For?" by A. M. Kiergan, 1915

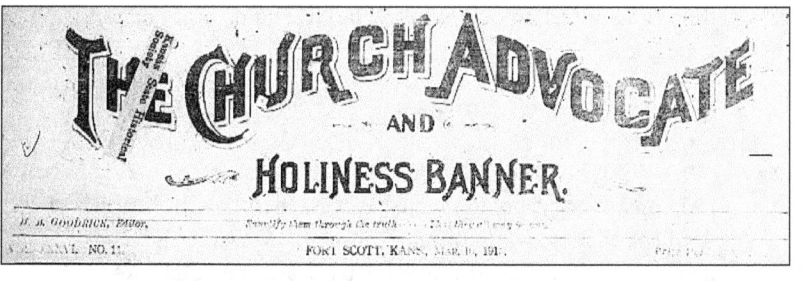

Just now and hence, those who love God and their fellowman should pray, take heed and be on our guard lest we be carried away by a godless enthusiasm for flags, patriotism and business. The largest element of such enthusiasm is the rankest fanaticism—War is fanaticism, and anarchy. A false idea of duty will be fatal and plunge us into bloody conflict, when our hands will be red with the blood of our fellow-man. There is a higher duty than anything proposed or maintained by war—duty to God and our felow-man [sic]. And this first and higher duty, if the other be a duty at all, is anti-war, is forever at war with war. If you look a little deeper you will likely discover that the glorification of flags, the beating of drums and cheers to patriotism is but to inflame the baser heart with a bloody sentiment, while the real intent, not seen by the excited multitude who are expected to expose their breasts to the crash of cold steel, is adroitly concealed. War is for greed—BUSINESS. At the bottom of all wars is the love of power, greed, business, gain, all of which is absolutely unworthy, and unChristian.

In the Scriptures cited [sic] James says in the 2nd verse: "You fight, and war, and kill." Plainly stated, you MURDER.

---

15. "Convention Minutes," n.p.

Radical Holiness Statements   71

Any attempt to smooth murder out of killing in war, is futile if James is to be accepted as authority. If what he says is to be scouted, then let us be sincere and throw the whole New Testament away. John Sherman said, "War is hell;" James said: "War is murder;" Christ said, "Put up thy sword;" John said, "If any one kills with the sword, with the sword he must be killed."

If War is right, if it is a good thing to be indulged in, if killing men is good for men, and glorifying to God, if it conduces to the advancement of morality, and civilization, then what is to be thought of the mission of Jesus Christ? At his advent at Bethlehem the angels sang, "Peace on earth, good will among men." What becomes of the commandment to "love our neighbor as ourselves," and what becomes of the "golden rule"—"all things whatsoever ye would that men should do to you, do ye even so to them?" Mark you, it is to apply IN ALL THINGS. Do you want men to shoot you down in battle? thrust cold steel through your bowels? blow you to atoms with dynamite? make your wife a widow and your babies orphans and send them to starvation and the pottersfield [sic]? Do you want men to make a hell on earth for you? Well, no, not exactly; your better sense and feeling justify the angel song and the "golden rule." Can we set at naught the "golden rule" and lay any claims to be ["] Christians?" It must be a strange infatuation, that under any pretext whatsoever any one would volunteer to shoot down his fellowman in war; and stranger still, that any follower of the Christ of peace, and any one whose heart is touched with the spirit of peace over whom the dove of peace should hover evermore, could ever bring himself to such forgetful, fanatical frenzy as to do it—strange![16]

CHURCH OF THE LIVING GOD
Frank Sandford on War, before 1907

Sometime before 1907, Frank Sandford wrote *Revelation*. In it, he taught pacifism, which was the rule for the kingdom.

16. Kiergan, "War—What For?," 1. Emphasis in original.

Here is the faith and patience of the saints, "He that takes the sword must perish with the sword." In other words, every man that takes worldly weapons to defend himself must in that manner perish. What have I always taught you? Not to resist evil. He says, "If my kingdom were of this world, then would my people fight." He that takes the sword in the troublesome times that are coming are going to perish, and he that does not is going to suffer. To suffer rather than fight men with carnal weapons is where the faith and patience of the saints comes in.[17]

[1917] During World War I, with Shiloh in serious decline, and Sandford in Atlanta Penitentiary, Sandford had a new revelation in which God revealed that World War I was the war of Armageddon and the U.S. would come to the aid of Israel and be on the winning side. He called upon all young men in the movement to join the military. One follower, August Frank Marsteller, was pacifist on his draft card, giving witness to the earlier view.[18]

CHRIST'S SANCTIFIED HOLY CHURCH
"Concerning War," 1893

It is the faith, and belief, of Christ's Sanctified Holy Church, that its members should take no part in war. But indorse [sic] the peace treaty, and believe that all controversies and difficulties between nations should be settled by counsel and arbitration.[19]

---

17. Sandford, *Revelation*. Sandford (1862–1948) an author, publisher, pastor, evangelist, and Bible school founder who provided training to Holiness folks, many of whom later became affiliated with the Pentecostal tradition. See Robeck, "Frank Sandford," 1037–38.

18. Shirley, *Fair, Clear, and Terrible*, 359–63.

19. Lynch and Collins, *Doctrines and Disciplines*. When the U.S. entered World War I, Christ's Sanctified Holiness Church was gathered for months in Louisville, KY, for a large camp meeting. Leaders, "advised all young men to take their families to the seaport towns and enter the shipyards to work, whereby they could be exempt from bearing arms in time of war. Dan [Bonner] moved with his family to Mobile, Ala., to work in the shipyard. The family was still in Mobile at the end of the war when the armistice was signed in November 11, 1918." See Collins and Hagan, *History of Christ's Sanctified Holy Church*, 36.

"Statement of Christ's Sanctified Holy Church Concerning War," 1968

Under no circumstances should one of our members take up arms or train with same. The teachings of the Holy Scriptures, together with the Holy Spirit, has caused us to take this position. Jesus himself says in Matthew 5th chapter, verses 38 and 39, "Ye have heard it hath been said an eye for an eye and a tooth for a tooth; but I say unto you that ye resist not evil, but whosoever shall smite thee on thy right cheek, turn to him the other also." Now again in Ephesians 6th chapter, verses 11 and 12, "Put on the whole armour of God, that ye may be able to stand against the wiles of the devil; for we wrestle not against flesh and blood, but against principalities, against powers, against the rulers of darkness of this world, against spiritual wickedness in high places." Romans 12th chapter, 19th verse, "Dearly beloved, avenge not yourselves but rather give place unto wrath; for it is written, vengeance is mine, I will repay, saith the Lord." II Corinthians, 3rd and 4th verses: "For though we walk in the flesh we do not war after the flesh; for the weapons of our warfare are not carnal, but mighty though God to the pulling down of strongholds." St. John 18th chapter, 36th verse: "Jesus answered, my kingdom is not of this world; if my kingdom were of this world then would my servants fight, that I should not be delivered to the Jews. But now is my kingdom not from hence."

Under the first covenant, before Christ's time, the people of God fought army against army with carnal weapons, but Christ came to do away with the thing that causes war on the inside. "For what the law could not do in that it was weak through the flesh, God sending his own Son in the likeness of sinful flesh, and for sin, condemned sin in the flesh."—Romans 8:3.

Christ's Sanctified Holy Church believes that because of the transgression of our first fathers in the Garden of Eden right after He made man, sin entered into the world. All are sinners in the sight of God until they are regenerated, which we believe takes place instantaneously, as the Apostle Paul was when he was converted on his way to Damascus.

Of course, environment and training educates or teaches the conscience what is right or what is wrong. We do teach and train our people on this doctrine concerning opposition to War in any form.

But, we feel in early life as young people start out in life, they may deviate from the warning they have been trained and taught because of the nature of sin in their heart and life. We believe that they may become convicted of sin and repent and have a change of life take place and cause them to "walk in newness of life." We feel this should be given much consideration, as the desire to conform to the Divine will comes only when we become a Christian.[20]

CHRISTIAN NATION CHURCH

"Resisting Evil, Faultfinding," 1896

We believe in a brotherly love for all men, even our enemies, and under no circumstances should we resist an injury done us, even of the grossest kind, but should simply let the law of the land punish the offender, and God to avenge the wrong; that all fault-finding, to others, about anyone, in their absence, must not be done, as such proceeds from a heart of evil. All faultfinding and complaints must first be brought to the one considered faulty. Matt. 5:39–45; 18:12–17; Gal. 6:2; Rom. 12:17–21.[21]

CHURCH OF GOD (ANDERSON, INDIANA)

"On Our Attitude toward War," 1898–1916

"Should We Go to War?"

"Please answer through the Gospel Trumpet: Providing there should be War in the United States, would it be right for a holy man of God to go as a soldier?"

—Francis Brown.

We answer no. Emphatically no. There is no place in the New Testament wherein Christ gave instruction to his followers to take the life of a fellowman. In olden times it was 'an eye for an eye and a tooth for a tooth.' 'Love your neighbor and hate your enemy.' In this gospel dispensation it is quite different. Jesus says: 'But I say

20. "Statement of Christ's Sanctified Holy Church Concerning War."
21. *Short History and Polity of the Christian Nation Church*, 15.

unto you, Love your enemies, bless them that curse you, do good to them that hate you, and pray for them that despitefully use you,' etc. (Matt. 5:44). 'Avenge not yourselves.' 'If thine enemy hunger, feed him; if he thirst, give him drink'—not shoot him.

—The Gospel Trumpet, Apr. 14, 1898.

"Is it wrong . . . to go to war when called on to do so by the government?["]

As to going to war and fighting, there is one text that ought to settle this question for every spiritually minded person. It is in Rom. 13:10. "Love worketh no ill to his neighbor; therefore love is the fulfilling of the law."

—The Gospel Trumpet, May 30, 1907.

"If I were called to war, should I go, and at the officers' command shoot down my brothers or friends?"

[—]One Seeking Light.

I should refuse to go to war or to obey an officer's command to shoot any one. We are followers of the "Prince of peace" and "the weapons of our warfare are not carnal."

—The Gospel Trumpet, Apr. 1, 1909.

It is evident that the destruction of human life is not in accordance with the spiritual precepts of the gospel.

—Evolution of Christianity (1911), 269.

"Is it Wrong to be a Soldier?"

. . . It is wrong to kill people . . . War is cruel, and devastation, with foul murder, disease, destruction of property, breaking-up of homes, follows its track, leaving the land strewn with the dead bodies of the best talent the country can afford; and starving widows and fatherless children continue to partake of the miseries that follow in the wake of war. There are no humane bullets.

Jesus Christ said, "Love your enemies." He did not say shoot them. He set forth the spirit of arbitration in Matt. 5:23–26, which principle will apply to nations as well to individuals.

—The Gospel Trumpet, Apr. 27, 1916.

76 PENTECOSTAL AND HOLINESS STATEMENTS ON WAR AND PEACE

A Declaration signed by the ministers of the Church, on file in our Office, states:

"As minister of the church of God, I, in agreement with my fellow ministers, hereby declare: That I believe in being a loyal citizen and servant of the Government under which I live in so far as its requirements do not conflict with my duty to God as enforced by the law of my conscience. That . . . it is contrary to my religious convictions as a follower of Christ for me to take human life. My religion and my conscience forbid my taking up arms for the slaughter of my fellowmen.

Signed_____"
We hereby certify that the foregoing quotations are correct.
Executive Committee of the Missionary Board of the Church of
God, Anderson, Indiana, U.S.A.
F. G. Smith
President of the Board and Editor of The Gospel Trumpet.
E. E. Byrum
Vice-President.
J. W. Phelps
Secretary-Treasurer.[22]

On The Relationship of the Church to Government, 1899

I am constrained to reverence the political powers and to uphold them because they are instituted by God, but I can not [sic] be induced to believe that all their laws are made by divine inspiration. . . . We should be subject to the laws although they may be erroneous and unjust, when they do not interfere with our duty to God; but there is no just reason why we should not feel ourselves at liberty to . . . (decline to obey) a law enacted by men that is contrary to the sentiments of that perfect law revealed unto us by our Savior.

—*The Better Testament* (1899), 341, 342.

"Where does the Bible teach we shall abide by the laws of our country?["]

22. *Teaching of the Church of God Concerning Civil Government, the Sacredness of Human Life, and War.*

Tit. 3:1; 1 Pet. 2:13; Rom. 13:1. We are not, however, to obey the civil law should it conflict with the divine law.

—*The Gospel Trumpet*, July 17, 1902.[23]

"On The Sacredness of Human Life," 1899

The law of Moses upheld capital punishment, but this is not sufficient proof that it should be practised in this glorious gospel age. . . . The statute of Moses, which commanded the taking of eye for eye, and tooth for tooth, is the same that enjoined capital punishment, in the expression "life for life." If Jesus abolished this statute, he abolished it as a whole, and men should no longer be punished according to the rule of "eye for eye, tooth for tooth," nor "life for life." Modern civilization sets aside this statute of Moses completely, except that little clause in it which requires the taking of life for life. It would be considered inhuman to punish one who has destroyed an eye or a hand of a fellow man by depriving him of the same member; but to take life for life, a thing which is a thousand times more wicked, is thought to be in perfect harmony with the gospel. . . . "The Lord set a mark upon Cain, lest any finding him should kill him" (Gen. 4:12–15). According to this scripture the Lord placed as great a value upon the life of Cain as upon the life of others, and declared that if any man should slay Cain, vengeance should be taken upon him sevenfold. This surely shows the mind of God regarding murderers; and if we follow his sublime example, we shall consider all human life a sacred thing."

—*The Better Testament*, 342–48.

The more true Christianity spreads, the greater will be the humane sentiment, and the greater the regard for human life. These principles have so far pervaded society already that in a number of countries and in several States of the Union capital punishment has been abolished entirely.

—*Evolution of Christianity* (1911), 269.[24]

23. Ibid.
24. Ibid.

78 PENTECOSTAL AND HOLINESS STATEMENTS ON WAR AND PEACE

[Statement on Conscientious Objection to War], 1971

Like all true Americans, we as members of the General Assembly of the Church of God meeting in regular session in Anderson, Indiana, this 16th day of June, 1971, view with deep concern the military involvement and the conscription of our youth for military service. We believe that war represents our moral failures. We abhor war and the causes that lead to it. We stand by the teaching and example of our Lord who taught us and showed us the way of radical, sacrificial love.

We are thankful to God that we live in a land of basic freedoms whose law makes provision for alternative service by those "who, by reason of religious training and belief, are conscientiously opposed to participation in War in any form." We encourage our young men who conscientiously object to war and participation in it to engage in such civilian work which contributes "to the maintenance of the national health, safety or interest."

We respect the right of each person to arrive at his own convictions. We believe in the principle of freedom of worship and freedom of conscience. We respect the rights of the individual conscience within our fellowship. We have not set up an authoritative creed. Instead, we accept the entire New Testament as our rule of faith and practice. We seek to lead every member of our fellowship to full comprehension and full acceptance of the Spirit of Christ as the guide for all conduct. What we seek for ourselves we seek for every citizen of our land—the right of individual conscience which no governmental authority can abrogate or violate.

We believe that the cause of Christ is best served when the Christian of draft age responds freely to his own conscience. Because we believe this, we support those who take the position of the conscientious objector, at the same time we insist that the conscientious military person has similar privileges and responsibilities before God. We also support that person who differs with our position regarding conscientious objectors and participates in military service. We seek to follow all persons with a ministry of help and guidance, but this is not to be construed as approval of war.

We fervently pray for the leaders of our nation and of other nations, many of whom we believe to be sincerely striving for peace. We pray that efforts by negotiation among countries, through the United Nations, and every possible channel may succeed in bringing peace to our troubled world. We pray for the Church all over the world to continue her rightful role in peacemaking.

Let this statement of conviction be construed by any and all to mean that we fully support young men of the Church of God who sincerely and conscientiously are opposed to participation in military service. We encourage them to seek constructive alternatives intended to bring health, healing, and understanding, and which serve the highest interests of our beloved country and of the whole world.[25]

From "The Church of God and Military Service: Questions and Answers," 2004

"If the draft is reinstated, will my special circumstances be taken into account?"

There is a classification system that allows for deferments and exemptions for physical and mental health conditions, extreme hardship to dependents, ministerial students and ministers, and surviving sons whose father, brother, or sister was killed in action or died as a result of injury or illness incurred while on active duty. If you are the only child in your family, you are still subject to the draft. A special service category is provided for persons with moral, ethical, and religious objections to participation in the war. There are no student deferments, but your induction can be postponed until you complete the term or until you graduate if you are in the last year of school. There would be no classification before the induction orders would be issued. At that time, there would be an opportunity to claim all the classifications to which one is entitled.

"Do you have any suggestions for making a responsible Christian decision about military service?"

Prayer, study, reflection, sharing, and testing under the guidance of God's Spirit will lead you to faithful decisions. Begin to pray for guidance from God as you make your decision. Read the Bible to help you discern how your decision will lead you to doing God's will and to being a part of the Kingdom that Jesus describes. Talk with others about their experiences in military

25. Perry, *Words of Conscience*, 39–40.

service and with those who oppose it; ask them about their decisions, their beliefs, and how they relate their decisions to faith in Jesus Christ.

Talk with your minister, a counselor, your parents, or someone else that you trust who will listen carefully, help you consider the options, and help you to make a decision that is consistent with your faith.

"What if I want to enlist in the armed forces? Will the Church of God be supportive?"

Yes, the Church of God recognizes that Christians can and do, in good conscience, enlist and serve in the military. Further, the church helps recruit, train, and support chaplains who provide for worship and pastoral care for members of the armed forces. The church also advocates that local congregations should support those in the armed forces with prayer and regular communication. If you are considering enlisting, you may wish to talk with a minister, counselor, family, or trusted friend about why you want to join the military in order to be clear with yourself about your reasons.

Talk to recruiters from each of the services. Examine the options they give you and choose the one that meets your skills, interest, and needs for joining the military. Get every promise of training confirmed in writing and signed by the recruiter.

If you are or will be a college student, you may wish to examine the Reserve Officer Training Corps (ROTC) programs available on some campuses. Large universities often offer ROTC programs from each branch of the armed forces. These programs provide officer training while you are in college. Many provide financial aid for schooling. Once you graduate, ROTC requirements completed, you will be commissioned as an officer (second lieutenant or the equivalent) and serve active duty for several years and then in the reserves. This approach may suit your style and schedule.

Whichever approach to military service you decide to take, do not be afraid to live out and share your faith convictions while serving within the military. As a Church of God military service member, you are expected to refrain from consuming alcohol, tobacco, or illicit drugs. If you feel you are ever being asked or ordered to compromise any generally accepted practice, standard, or element of your Church of God faith beliefs, seek out the counsel and support of your chaplain or of individuals higher up in your chain of command. If these avenues fail to help resolve the issue, then seek the assistance of the coordinator of Chaplain Ministries within Church of God Ministries.

While serving in the military, you are encouraged to continue to grow spiritually, and to maintain and carry out the practices and generally accepted holiness standards and beliefs of the Church of God reformation movement. You are encouraged to continue to maintain close ties with your family and your home Church of God congregation through regular correspondence and contact, a mutual covenant of prayer support, and financial support. Whenever you are stationed near a Church of God (Anderson, Indiana) congregation, you are encouraged to contact its pastor, attend its worship services and other related activities, become involved, and invite others to join you.

You are also encouraged to seek out the other Christians within your unit or command, offer them your friendship and encouragement, join with them in Bible studies and prayer fellowships, and offer your aid with various command humanitarian assistance projects.

If you are enlisted, connect with Christian Military Fellowship (CMF), PO Box 1207, Englewood, CO 80150–1207, 303–761–1959, or www.cmf.com. CMF supports military personnel and their families, worldwide, with prayer, Bible studies, local fellowships, conferences, referrals, free literature, correspondence, hospitality, and Christian resources.

If you are an officer, try to join or start a local Officers' Christian Fellowship (OCF) group. Further information on how to join or start an OCF group, the purpose and vision of OCF, its statement of faith, spiritual pillars, etc. can be found by writing to OCF, 3784 South Inca, Englewood, CO 80110, calling 800–424–1984, or visiting ocfusa.org.

If you become involved in any form of the military service, seek out a chaplain. Tell them that you are a Christian and ask for a schedule of worship services and other church-related activities. Indicate that you want to be involved.

"What is a military chaplain?"

Military chaplains are non-combatant commissioned officers endorsed by their particular religious bodies to perform ministry within the military. They provide for the religious needs of people within their faith tradition serving in the military in the same manner as they would as a pastor, priest, or rabbi ministering within their respective civilian communities. They develop and implement religious programs and activities, help facilitate the faith needs of others, and provide pastoral care and confidential counseling to all individuals and their dependents within the military. Chaplains also serve as advisors to military commanders on matters of religion, morals, and morale.

"What if I am a conscientious objector to war?"

The Church of God has a significant tradition as a peace church, and therefore, it supports individuals who register as conscientious objectors. Early documents of the church make strong statements regarding opposition to war and to participation in military service.

The present draft law limits the provision for conscientious objection to those who are opposed to participation in War in any form. This conviction must be based on religious training and belief; the Supreme Court has ruled that this includes deeply held moral or ethical beliefs as well.

Individuals who are opposed only to their personal use of weapons in war but would be willing to serve in the armed forces would be inducted and assigned to non-combatant service.

Those who are conscientiously opposed to any military service would be, instead of being inducted, ordered to alternative service. Such service would perhaps be in church-sponsored programs that meet the legal requirements of service in the "national health, safety, and interest." In current rules and regulations, alternative-service workers would serve just as long as those drafted into the armed forces, and rates of pay are recommended to be at the prevailing rates for such work. It is important to know that the special benefits afforded to those who complete military service are not available to those who complete alternative service.

"What should I do if I believe I am a conscientious objector?"

Be clear in your own mind of your reasons for being a conscientious objector. Talk with your family, minister, counselor, or concerned friends about your beliefs and feelings. Contact a counseling organization for the latest materials on qualifying as a conscientious objector (see the list of organizations at end of this document).

Radical Holiness Statements   83

"What if I object to some wars but not to others?"

Selective conscientious objection is objection to participation in a particular war or wars. Many Christians who claim selective objection base their claim on an understanding of the just war tradition. This term should never be construed as meaning "righteous war" but should be understood closer in meaning to "justifiable war" in the sense that armed conflict may be determined as the most responsible of various moral options in a given situation, such as:

Exhausting all other means to resolve conflict before resorting to violence.

A declaration of reasons for going to war (as in the Declaration of Independence).

Having proportionality: that things should turn out better than if a nation did not go to war.

Having morally just purposes (self defense).

The actual declaration and conduct of the war must be subject to the restraint of legitimate political leadership.

These statements, adopted by and incorporated in international law, have been considered guidelines determining a nation's participation in war. Many Christians see them also as traditional teaching of the church. The restrictions of the traditional teaching about justifiable war are broad. Many others believe that few, if any wars, ever qualified, and virtually no future war as presently imagined would. While the law specifically excludes from CO status those who want to "choose their wars," the "selective objector" may qualify as a legal conscientious objector under present law. Such a person should keep a record of beliefs. Even if denied CO classification by a local board and having lost all appeals, the evidence of conscience and sincerity in the file might be a mitigating factor in any subsequent court case.

"What if, in addition to being a conscientious objector, I decide that I cannot in good conscience even register for the draft?"

Failure to comply with the law and regulations of the Selective Service System is a felony if convicted. Nevertheless, people are aware that their opposition to war may also include opposition to participating in preparation for war, and they feel that registration has those political and military purposes.

At present, only the most vocal or self-reporting non-registrants are being prosecuted, but if this is your stance, begin to

84 PENTECOSTAL AND HOLINESS STATEMENTS ON WAR AND PEACE

prepare yourself spiritually and psychologically for possible trial and imprisonment. Gather support around you. Contact one of the groups listed in the back for referral to an attorney knowledgeable about current draft law. As described earlier, keep a record of your convictions and behavior accessible.[26]

CHURCH OF GOD APOSTOLIC, INC.

"Laws of the Land," after 1943

We believe the magistrates are ordered for peace, safety, and welfare of all people. Therefore under these conditions our duty is to be in obedience to all of the laws of the land so long as they are not contrary to the word of God. We do not believe in war, nor going to war, for God is not the author of confusion, but of peace.[27]

CHURCH OF GOD (GUTHRIE, OKLAHOMA)

26. "Church of God and Military Service."

27. *Discipline of the Church of God (Apostolic, Inc.)*, 21. Piepkorn notes that this group does not consider itself Pentecostal, but does share "Oneness" theology with that part of the Pentecostal faith. See Piepkorn, *Profiles in Belief*, 36.

Ex-slave, George and Carrie Winn were founding leaders in the Church of God (Guthrie, OK) congregation. They had two sons who were religious objectors during World War I. The older son, Stafford Silas Winn, was held in Ft. Leavenworth, Kansas, military detention for religious objection to war. The younger brother, Edward Winn, asked for religious objection as a member of the Church of God.[28]

World War I draft registration card of son of ex-slave Edward Winn.[29] In answering if he claimed exemption from the draft on line 12, he wrote, "Yes, member of the Church of God."

[Resolution on Christian Participation in War], 1948

> The ministers of the Church of God assembled at the Annual National Campmeeting (July 21–30, 1961) of the Church of God at Neosho (Monark Springs), Mo., being aware of the present critical world situation and the urgent need for the Church to re-affirm its position in regard to participation in war, approved and

28. Photo courtesy of Faith Publishing House. Used by permission.

29. This image reprinted by permission of Ancestry.com. To view additional family history records, please visit www.ancestry.com.

adopted the resolution which had been approved by the ministers of the Church of God at the Oklahoma State Campmeeting, Guthrie, Okla., on August 13, 1948, which reads as follows:

Whereas: The Holy Scriptures teach us that our first duty is to God, namely, "Thou shalt love the Lord thy God with all thy heart, soul, mind, and strength," and the second is like unto this, "Thou shalt love thy neighbor as thyself." Furthermore, Jesus taught His followers to love their enemies, do good to them that hate you and pray for them which despitefully use you and persecute you that you may be the children your Father which is in heaven (Matt. 5:39, 44–48);

And Whereas: There are many other scriptures such as John 18:36; Matt. 26:52; Rom. 12:14, 17, 19–21; Luke 6:31, which definitely forbid us to take up arms to fight or defend ourselves; and whereas, because of the teaching of such Scriptures, we are conscientiously opposed to accept noncombatant service in warfare or to work in any factory or plant which is directly engaged in producing instruments and / or munitions for the destruction of human life and happiness;

And Whereas: We are conscientiously opposed to participation in War in any form at any time, whether civil, political, or religious;

And Whereas: We are conscientiously opposed to the purchase of defense or war bonds and stamps for the prosecution of war;

And Whereas: We are citizens of the U.S. of America in all things willing to live honestly, believing that our Government is ordained of God and praying for our President and for all that are in authority, that we may lead a quiet and peaceful life in all godliness; Now, Therefore Be It Resolved: That the above statement be adopted as a uniform teaching and practice of the Church of God, a copy of which is on file with the Secretary of the National Campmeeting.

The foregoing resolution was concurred in and approved by the ministers of the Church of God at the National Campmeeting on July 25, 1961.[30]

---

30. Perry, *Words of Conscience*, 40–41.

Radical Holiness Statements   87

From *The Christian Versus War* by Lawrence D. Pruitt, 1940

Let us accept as our authority the teachings and example of Jesus Christ, the Founder of the Church and the Prince of peace, and consider the teachings and practices of the apostles and saints of the early morning Church. Many may want to take an easier way, the way of least resistance, the way the majority are going, and the way which shuns the reproach of the cross of Christ, but it is certain that all who "live godly in Christ Jesus shall suffer persecution."

Jesus' sermon on the Mount, as recorded in the 5th, 6th, and 7th chapters of Matthew, sets forth the rules of Christian conduct. Relative to the Christian doctrine of non-resistance, let us read what Jesus taught. "But I say unto you, that ye resist not evil (nonresistance); but whosoever shall smite thee on the right cheek, turn to him the other also. Love your enemies, bless them that curse you, do good to them which despitefully use you and persecute you; that ye may be the children of your Father which is in heaven; for he maketh his sun to rise on the evil and on the good, and sendeth rain on the just and on the unjust. For if ye love them which love you, what reward have ye? Be ye therefore perfect, even as your Father which is in heaven is perfect," Matt. 5:39, 44–48. "And as ye would that men should do to you, do ye also to them likewise," Luke 6:31. This might more correctly be termed the "forgotten rule" instead of the "golden rule" because of its widespread, universal violation today. When Jesus sent the disciples forth to preach the gospel, He said, "Behold I send you forth as sheep in the midst of wolves; be ye therefore wise as serpents, and harmless as doves. But when they persecute you in this city, flee [non-resistance] ye into another." Matt. 10:16, 23. When Jesus was on trial before Pilate, He answered, "My kingdom is not of the [*sic*] this world: if my kingdom were of this world, then would my servants fight, that I should not be delivered to the Jews; but now is my kingdom not from hence." John 16:36. Are you in Christ's kingdom in which His servants do not fight?

At the time Jesus was arrested, Peter, under the influence of the carnal nature, drew his sword and cut off the ear of the high priest's servant. "Then Jesus said unto him, Put [*sic*] up again thy sword into his place; for all they that take the sword shall perish [be lost] with the sword." Matt. 26:52. After Pentecost, Peter had no more use for carnal weapons. Jesus commanded the disciples,

"Go ye into all the world," and that includes other nations, even though they be enemies—not with sword or gun, but with the gospel (good news) of salvation.

Let us notice the teachings of the Apostles, for they agree with the teachings of Jesus. Paul writes, "Bless them which persecute you; bless, and curse not. Recompense to no man evil for evil. Avenge not yourselves, but rather give place unto wrath; for it is written, Vengeance is mine; I will repay, saith the Lord. Therefore, if thine enemy hunger, feed him; if he thirst, give him drink; for in doing thou shalt heap coals of fire on his head. Be not overcome of evil, but overcome evil with good," Rom. 12:14, 17, 19–21. Peter writes: "Christ also suffered for us, leaving us an example that ye should follow in his steps: who, when he was reviled, reviled not again; when he suffered, he threatened not." 1 Peter 2:21, 23. "Follow peace with all men, and holiness, without which no man shall see the Lord." Heb. 12:14.

The Practice of the Early Church
The foregoing is what Jesus and the apostles taught and practiced. Now let us notice how these truths were interpreted and practiced in the early morning Church, as recorded by the church fathers and historians.

In Cadaux' "History of the Church" is found documentary evidence from the church fathers that for the first two and one-half centuries when a soldier was converted he left the army.

We now quote from West's "World Progress" history which was the Oklahoma state-adopted text when (1928) the writer attend [sic] high school: "Clean lives marked the early Christians to a notable degree. The Christians kept apart from most public amusements. This made Christians seem unsocial. Also, because Christ had preached peace, many Christians refused to join the legions, or to fight, if drafted. These 'pacifists' and 'conscientious objectors' irritated their neighbors by even refusing to illuminate their houses or garland their portals in honor of national triumphs."

Myers' "General History" records the following: "Christianity had come into the world as a religion of peace and good will. The Master had commanded His disciples to put up the sword and had forbidden its use by them, either in the spread or in the defense of the new faith. For three centuries now His followers had obeyed literally this injunction of the Founder of the Church, so that a Quaker, non-military spirit had up to this time (A.D. 312) characterized the new sect. By many of the early Christians the profession of arms had been declared to be incompatible with the Christian life."

How Practice Changed to Those of Today

These historical records show clearly that a non-resistant, non-military spirit prevailed generally in the early Church for three centuries. Now let us notice how and who accepted the military spirit into nominal Christianity. As the Bible student well knows, the seeds of apostasy began to grow in the time of the Apostle Paul and John the Revelator. The leaven of spiritual decay spread gradually but surely. Christianity (so-called) because so popular that by A.D. 306, when Constantine the Great succeeded to the throne as emperor of the Roman Empire, he became a Christian by profession, but not by practice, and is known as the first Christian emperor. Christianity by him was made the state religion, and he also recognized the Christian Sunday, the first day of the week, as a day of rest, forbidding ordinary work on that day.

Constantine had several rivals for the imperial throne, and he fought to hold his position. One of the most important of the battles was that of Melvian Bridge, about two miles from Rome. The historian Myers says: "Constantine's standard on this celebrated battlefield was the Christian cross. He had been led to adopt this emblem through the appearance, as once he prayed to the sun-god, of a cross over the setting sun, with the inscription above it; 'In this sign conquer.' Obedient unto the celestial vision, Constantine had at once made the cross his banner, and it was beneath this new emblem that his soldiers marched to victory at the battle of the Melvian Bridge."

Myers further states: "This act of Constantine constitutes a turning point in the history of the Christian Church. The most sacred emblem of the new faith was made a battle standard, and into the new religion was infused the military spirit of the imperial government that had made that emblem the ensign of the state. From the day of the battle at the Melvian Bridge a martial spirit has animated the religion of the Prince of Peace. Since then Christian (?) warriors have often made the cross their battle standard."

From then until the present, most of Christendom, both Catholic and Protestant, participate in military service and enter into the war efforts of their respective nations. Even so-called holiness movements, some passively and some positively, glorify war from the pulpit and press, and they "whose minds are blinded by the god of this world," say that Jesus' Sermon on the Mount is not applicable to our age. Some would place loyalty to country above loyalty to God, concluding that one who dies in defense of his country has a sure passport to heaven.

What is War?

War is the enemy of all Christian ideals. War means all that Jesus did not stand for. It is the complete reversal of the Christian attitude toward life. Instead of ministering to and healing the wounds of man, experiments and research are made as to how greater and more deadly wounds can be inflicted. The Chief of Chaplains of the U.S. Army is quoted as saying that "War is a nasty, dirty, destructive, damnable business." If he is right in his description—and I think he is—then some good (?) folk have gone into a terrible business.

The Scriptures most commonly used to support participation in carnal warfare are Rom. 13:1–6 and 1 Peter 2:13–17. The argument usually presented is that the Christian must be subject "to the powers that be" and this includes taking part in carnal warfare at the command of that government of which he is a citizen. To accept this interpretation would require the true Christians of ALL THE NATIONS engaged in war to fight for their respective governments, with the result that brethren in Christ would meet on the battlefield, seeking to kill and destroy one another. Such a course is unthinkable, for it would violate every cardinal teaching of Christ. In Rom. 13:1–6 the thought that the Christian should participate in carnal warfare at the command of the "powers that be" is not under consideration by the Apostle; but the opposite is taught, as is clearly shown by reading the preceding chapter and the verses following the 6th verse of the 13th chapter. It reveals an unbroken line of truth relative to love in action to our brethren, our neighbor, our enemy, and to all men, and leaves no room for vengeance or retaliation of any kind.

However, it is the Christian's duty to faithfully obey the State in all requirements which do not involve a violation of the New Testament teachings. But he must obey God rather than man when the demands of the State conflict with his supreme loyalty to Christ. Government is ordained of God, especially for the punishment of evil doers. God's people are a called-out, holy nation, separate in spirit from the world, and whose "citizenship is in heaven."

Some try to justify fighting by the Old Testament practice of warfare, forgetting that "the times of this ignorance God winked at: but now commandeth all men everywhere to repent." Acts 17:30. The Israelites under the Old Testament were permitted to go to war only by specific Divine appointment or commission. When they went to battle out of Divine order, they were defeated. No such Divine sanction has ever been made by the Lord in the New Testament dispensation. On the contrary, the use of military force or violence as pertaining to God's people was annulled by the Lord's Sermon on the Mount, as was also the practice of polygamy.

Consenting or Aiding in the Deed

Some will say that we all help in wars—by paying taxes, etc. That is true, more or less, but the responsibility is on those who spend the tax money. Here are some points to consider relative to paying taxes. First, taxes are levied for collection—not a voluntary contribution—and, second, Jesus, by precept and example, teaches us to pay taxes, Luke 20:20–25; Matt. 17:27.

There are those who feel their conscience allows them to accept non-combatant service in the military. Saul of Tarsus, evidently in "all good conscience" thought within himself "that I ought to do many things contrary to the name of Jesus." Acts. 26:9. In this thought he persecuted the unresisting church, "and when they were put to death, I [Saul] gave my voice against them." He "kept the raiment of them who slew" Stephen, "consenting unto his death." But later, when awakened, he sensed his guilt of the blood of Stephen, and says he "obtained mercy because he did it ignorantly in unbelief."

On a large bill-board were these words: "The war bonds you hold are *fighting* bonds."[31] Perhaps you would not fight, but will loan your money to carry on the fight. War plant or defense workers are termed "soldiers on the home front," and surely they are as necessary for the prosecution of war as the soldiers who use the weapons on the battle front. However, farming and producing food for general use is not necessarily considered as directly engaged in the war effort.

In 1 John 3:8 we read, "For this purpose the Son of God was manifested, that he might destroy the works of the devil." God is not the author of war, nor the creator of any implement for wag-

31. This poster, created by the U.S. Treasury Department, "The War Bonds You Hold Are Fighting Bonds," dates to 1944. Therefore, we can date L. D. Pruitt's document to later than 1944.

ing war. Therefore, war and all things pertaining thereto, must necessarily be the works of the devil. How can professed children of God knowingly and willingly aid in and help carry on that which Christ came to destroy? "In this the children of God are manifest, and the children of the devil." 1 John 3:10.

No Hope for Permanent World Peace

Peace is derived only from a right condition of the heart and mind. War and fighting will continue as long as man possesses the carnal nature or the principle of sin in the heart. Ever since Cain slew his brother Abel, there have been fighting and killing in the course of history, and such a condition will exist as long as the world stands, regardless of the number of peace conferences held or the scope of economic and political adjustment. Not for long can peace be enforced with the threat of retaliation.

The Attitude and Hope of God's People

One may ask, "What should be the Christian's attitude toward war?" The negative attitude is to refuse to participate in military service in any form or to aid in the war effort, and on the positive side, to renounce war and work for its elimination by teaching and living the gospel of Christ which alone brings peace and good will to man. Constructive non-resistance means overcoming evil with good.

There is hope and comfort for the true children of God who face these conditions. We who are of faith know "we look for a better country, that is an [sic] heavenly," and "confess that we are strangers and pilgrims on the earth." We already enjoy the "peace that passeth understanding." We already have the "victory that overcometh the world, even our faith." The freedom we declare is "that we are made free from the law of sin and death." The liberty we share is that we are "delivered from the bondage of corruption into the glorious liberty of the children of God." Thank the Lord!—Lawrence D. Pruitt.[32]

---

32. Pruitt, *The Christian Versus War,* 2–12. Emphasis in original. Pruitt (1911–1982) was a Church of God leader and likely wrote this booklet in the late 1930s or 1940s. William C. Kostlevy notes that in 1918 Pruitt of Guthrie, Oklahoma, began publishing *Faith and Victory,* and assumed leadership of the church. See Kostlevy, "The Church of God (Guthrie, Oklahoma)," 54.

CHURCH OF THE GOSPEL

"Resolution of Convention," 1924

Be it Resolved: That it is the mind of this Holiness Convention session at Pittsfield, Massachusetts, that War is unchristian, entirely opposed and foreign to the doctrine of Jesus Christ and the principles of the gospel of peace.

Be it further Resolved: That we as Christian believers connected with the Church of God (later changed to Church of the Gospel) and gathered together in convention November 14–16, 1924, do place ourselves on record as withholding ourselves from participation in ungodly warfare.

At the annual business meeting of the church held at Pittsfield, Massachusetts, January 19, 1925, it was unanimously voted that the above resolution be placed on the church records.

At the annual business meeting of the church held at Pittsfield, Massachusetts, January 15, 1934, it was unanimously voted that this same resolution become a law of the Church of the Gospel.[33]

CHURCH OF THE NAZARENE

[Against War], 1914

During World War I in England, the Nazarene Church "declared its abhorrence of war," but fell short of requiring members to refuse military service. However, shortly after the war, they developed a strong pacific strain that lasted to the late 1960s.[34]

Charles Brougher Jernigan, 1915

. . . religion is love and that without love any and all religion is but a name; that the love of sin is destructive to Christian life; that the child of God should love him with all his heart, mind, soul, and spirit; that he should love his neighbor as himself; that he should love his enemies and sincerely pray for them; that he should love the will of God to the extent that he would say at all times, Thy will be done.[35]

33. Perry, *Words of Conscience*, 44–45.

34. Ford, *In the Steps of John Wesley*, 152–53; 209–10.

35. Redford, "History of the Church of the Nazarene," 45; Kostlevy, "Jernigan, C. B.,"

94 PENTECOSTAL AND HOLINESS STATEMENTS ON WAR AND PEACE

"Statement of the General Assemblies," 1940

We believe that the ideal world condition is that of peace and that it is the full obligation of the Christian Church to use its influence to seek such means as will enable the nations of the earth to be at peace and to devote all of its agencies for the propagation of the message of peace.

However, we realize that we are living in a world where evil forces and philosophies are actively in conflict with these Christian ideals and that there may arise such international emergencies as will require a nation to resort to War in defense of its ideals, its freedom, and its existence.

While thus committed to the cause of peace, The Church of the Nazarene recognizes that the supreme allegiance of the Christian is due to God and, therefore, it does not endeavor to bind the conscience of its members relative to participation in military service in case of war, although it does believe that the individual Christian as a citizen is bound to give service to his own nation in all ways that are compatible with the Christian faith and the Christian way of life.

We also recognize that, as an outgrowth of the Christian teaching and of the Christian desire for peace on earth, there are among our membership individuals who have conscientious objection to certain forms of military service. Therefore, the Church of the Nazarene claims for conscientious objectors within its membership the same exemptions and considerations regarding military service as are accorded members of recognized noncombatant religious organizations.

The Church of the Nazarene, through its General Church Secretary, has set up a register whereon those persons who supply evidence of being members of the Church of the Nazarene may record their convictions as conscientious objectors.[36]

---

143. Kostlevy suggests that Jernigan (1869–1930) was an evangelist and social worker who helped found the Holiness Association of Texas, and part of the Holiness Church of Christ when it merged with the Nazarene Church.

36. Perry, *Words of Conscience*, 46.

CHURCHES OF GOD IN NORTH AMERICA [WINEBRENNER] [37]

[Resolution Passed by General Conference], 1922

Whereas, There are many of the members of the Church of God who, as individuals, sincerely and earnestly believe that military service, like similar activity in private life, is, in principle, contrary to the principles of forgiveness and love as taught by Jesus, and later by His apostles, and is, therefore, unchristian; and,

Whereas, Many of said Church of God believe, as is reported to have been stated during the administration of ex-president Wilson, that "there is no non-combatant service," but that what is called non-combatant service is a necessary part and parcel of any and every military campaign; that the participant therein is a contributor to the main service, and, as such, is in harmony with common law and practice of holding one who aids and abets another in the commission of unlawful deeds, a participant and an offender with the instigator and executor of the offense; and,

Whereas, The Government of the United States has from its beginning recognized the right of every person to exalt service unto God and His Son above the service to country and to flag (and this without in any manner manifesting disrespect to one's country) in that it has provided, by its Constitution, in Amendment I, Article I—

"Congress shall make no law respecting an establishment of religion or prohibiting the free exercise thereof";—and, Article 1, Section 9, Paragraph 2,

"The privilege of the writ of habeas corpus, shall not be suspended, unless when in cases of rebellion or invasion the public safety may require it";—and, further, Article 6, Paragraph 2,

"This Constitution . . . shall be the supreme law of the land"; and,

Whereas, the Government has continuously sought to execute the spirit of these constitutionally recognized duties and provisions respecting all persons who furnish conclusive evidence that they, as avowed followers of Christ, are conscientiously opposed to military service; and,

Whereas, This Church of God does not profess a creed, other than the Bible, by or according to which it receives or controls its members, and therefore cannot declare, as a matter of de-

---

37. See the Antebellum Holiness chapter, John Winebrenner, for early [1829?] statement against war.

nominational creed, as to military service of its membership; therefore,

Be it Resolved, That this General Conference of the Church of God, in Conference assembled at Oregon, Illinois, August 17, 1922—

Urge each individual member of its number to at all times, in military and all other matters, continue true and faithful in the performance of Christian duty according to personal conviction as to what constitutes faithful and loyal service to God through His Son;

Open a book of registration for the use of each and every one of its members, male and female, who may wish to register as one religiously and conscientiously opposed to military service, combatant, non-combatant, or both;

Take steps to keep the government properly informed of those thus conscientiously opposed to military service;

Use at all times its every good office with the Government in an effort to secure to each such registrant those exemptions from military service to which such persons are Constitutionally entitled,

Cancel from the register the names of any and all persons who by habitual life prove lack of sincerity in their conscientious objection to individual military service; and,

Be It Further Resolved, That nothing in this resolution shall be construed to constitute a cause for Christian fellowship with reference to such as do, or do not, register as personally opposed to military service, either in a combatant or non-combatant manner.[38]

"The Voice of the Churches," referencing 1925

War—Our Churches do not take the position of non-resistance or conscientious objectors. The action of the General Eldership in 1925 in a strong pronouncement on world peace, said: "We are in favor of joining hands with all the great forces in America which are working for the principles that promote peace and lessen the likelihood of war." But our people believe that "civil governments are ordained of God"; that it is the right of a government to call upon its citizens for such services as may be nec-

---

38. Perry, *Words of Conscience*, 43–45. This resolution was passed on August 17, 1922, and published on September 12, 1922.

essary for its defense and preservation; and it is their duty to be subject to "powers that be."

The General session of the Eldership in 1953 opposed the system of universal military training.[39]

"A Pronouncement on War," referencing 1959

We are opposed to war because it is detrimental to the spiritual and physical welfare of man. As a Bible Church, we are subject to the higher powers, and recognize our obligation to our country. We also recognize the individual's right to choose for himself in the matter of conscientious objection to war, and our responsibility for such individual's protection. We are opposed to sending expeditionary forces away from our land, but are ready to share in the defense of our country which guarantees our religious freedom.[40]

CONGREGATIONAL: BROADWAY TABERNACLE
[War], 1930s

I have quietly considered what I would do if my nation should again be drawn into war. I am not taking a pledge, because I do not know what I would when the heat of the war mood is upon the country. But in a mood of calm consideration I do today declare that I cannot reconcile the way of Christ with the practice of war.

I do therefore set down my name to be kept in the records of my church, so that it will be for me a reminder if war should come; and will be a solemn declaration to those who hold to this conviction in time of war that I believe them to be right and I do desire with my whole mind and heart that I shall be among those who keep to this belief.[41]

39. *Teachings and Practices of the Churches of God in North America*, 23.

40. Ibid.

41. The Broadway Tabernacle was founded by Charles G. Finney in 1836. Shortly thereafter, it became Congregational. Like quite a number of Congregational churches, it was deeply influenced by the Holiness teachings of Finney, what would later be called Oberlin Holiness, for its association with the founding of Oberlin College, OH. Abolitionist Finney, could not bring himself to full pacifism at the time of the Civil

EMMANUEL HOLINESS CHURCH
"Article 8," 1963

We forbid that our members participate in actual combat service, in taking of arms in war, if their conviction is objective.[42]

EMMANUEL ASSOCIATION
"War," 1966

We feel bound explicitly to avow our unshaken persuasion that War is utterly incompatible with the plain precepts of our divine Lord and Law-giver, and with the whole spirit of the Gospel; and that no plea of necessity or policy, however urgent or peculiar, can avail to release either individuals or nations from the paramount allegiance which they owe to Him who hath said, "Love your enemies." Therefore, we cannot participate in war (Rom. 12:19), war activities, or compulsory military training.[43]

"Non-Resistance," 1966

We believe in non-resistance in a qualified sense—that war, dueling, suicide, prenatal destruction of human life, and all other

---

War, but, his student, Amos Dresser, see Antebellum Holiness chapter, was an absolute pacifist and abolitionist. In the 1930s, the heirs to Finney's legacy, the Broadway Tabernacle, now in a different location, and technically adherents of the "social gospel," were pushing pacifism, even though they had moved out of the Holiness movement orbit by that time. Significantly, this passage is secondarily quoted approvingly from the *Pentecostal Evangel* by the leader of the Assemblies of God, Ernest S. Williams (1885–1981), in an article entitled, "The Conscientious Objector." See Beaman, *Pentecostal Pacifism*, 77–81. Williams recommended that churches adopt the practice of Broadway Tabernacle in New York which: "provided a statement for its members, which, after it is signed, is preserved with the church records to show it to have been the free act of its members. It is quoted here and it would be well for other churches which believe it is not according to the spirit of Christ to take human life, to adopt a statement which meets its approval. There are other societies which have arranged statements for their followers, but the writer prefers that of the Broadway Tabernacle to others which he has read . . ." Quoted in Beaman, *Pentecostal Pacifism*, 79.

42. *Discipline of the Emmanuel Holiness Church*. Piepkorn (p. 127) notes that the Emmanuel Holiness Church came out of the Pentecostal Fire-Baptized Holiness Church after 1953.

43. *The Guidebook of the Emmanuel Association*, 14.

forms of willful human life-taking are murder. The last military command that Jesus gave was, "Put up again thy sword into his place; for all they that take the sword shall perish with the sword" (Matt. 26:52). "Ye have heard that it hath been said, An eye for an eye, and a tooth for a tooth: but I say unto you, That ye resist not evil: but whosoever shall smite thee on thy right cheek, turn to him the other also. And if any man will sue thee at the law, and take thy coat, let him have thy cloke also. And whosoever shall compel thee to go a mile, go with him twain" (Matt. 5:38–40).

There is no harm in seeking protection under a civil law that is in harmony with the Gospel, as did Paul in Jerusalem when in the hands of a violent mob, and also when transferred from Jerusalem to Caesarea (Acts 21:30–34; 22:24–30; 23:16–30). We must not, however, take the law into our own hands, and by acts of violence force an issue; but rather depend on civil authorities to execute the law.

"If any man will sue thee at the law, and take away thy coat" suggests a regular court trial. A brother has the right to appear before the court to testify truthfully in respect to his garment or property, and if the final decision is against him, through false witnesses or bribes or any other unfair influence, he must submit cheerfully, and give more rather than seek revenge. The same principle holds good in being compelled to take someone a mile, etc. Jesus says, "Take him two," and seek not revenge. God says, "Vengeance is mine, I will repay." It is the "more" that will touch the enemy's heart. "For it is better, if the will of God be so, that ye suffer for well doing, than for evil doing." (1 Peter 3:17).[44]

EMMANUEL'S FELLOWSHIP [FROM OLD RIVER BRETHREN]
Statement of Belief, 1966

We believe the law of Christ is the supreme law of love. Teaching us to love one another as He has loved us. His love was to seek and to save that which was lost.

Luke 19:10, John 13:34, 35.

We believe in the practice of nonresistance in life, in words, and in whatsoever things we do. Whether in Church [sic] mat-

---

44. Ibid., 15–16.

ters, school problems, paying taxes, occupations or taking up arms, etc. Jer. 17:5, Matt. 5:44, 22:21.

We believe in nonconformity, in not being conformed to the things of this world. Members shall not be unequally yoked with unbelievers in business and in other phases of life. They shall abstain from politics, secret societies, labor unions, life insurance, etc. We disapprove of accepting unearned government handouts. 2 Cor. 6:14, 1 John 2:15.[45]

FREE METHODIST CHURCH

From East Michigan Conference, 1914

War.—Has civilization perished from the earth? Have the ideals of Christianity, introduced two thousand years ago by the PRINCE OF PEACE, utterly failed? The shocking spectacle of the European nations rushing into war with each other without the shadow of justification, when none seem to be able to give the reason thereof, is revolting to the finer feelings of Christianity. The appeal to the god of brute force is founded upon the basest elements in the nature of men. We are far short of the millennium, rather are we come to the fulfillment of prophecy in reference to the conditions preceding the coming of the Son of Man. We commend the efforts of the little nuclei of men who are endeavoring to bring about peaceful arbitration in the nations of the earth. Lord, haste the day when Thy kingdom shall come and Thy will be done on earth as in heaven.[46]

From Genesee Conference, 1916

In addition to the foregoing we deem it proper to express our attitude as a church upon the subject of *military preparedness*. In view of the fact that all modern wars have been brought about by avarice and greed, we believe the application of the golden rule to all our dealings with other nations and acting the part of the good Samaritan toward them in their destitution and suffering will give us the best protection and the most effectual preparedness we as a nation can have.[47]

45. *Emmanuel's Fellowship Statement of Faith.*
46. *Annual Minutes, 1914.* Emphasis in original.
47. *Annual Minutes, 1916,* 189. Emphasis in original.

From Oil City Conference, 1916

War.—Possibly the greatest reform needed by the world today is a cessation of national war. The present war has cost the conflicting nations over fifty-five billion dollars. This does not include losses by destruction of property or work of industries. Millions of brilliant lives have been lost, thousands of homes have been broken up, mothers and daughters have been ravished, untold misery, suffering, want and agony have been endured by the inhabitants of the war zone. That a reform is needed there can be no doubt, but what can be done? We can beseech the mercy of the Lord on this blood-stained world. We can vote for men who stand for truth and righteousness. We can refuse to help manufacture war supplies.[48]

Economic Justice, 1917

The events of 1917 brought a response from no less than seven Free Methodist conferences on the subject of war and related themes. The Genesee Conference called military spending and training "satanic." The 1917 *Annual Minutes* reveal something of the intention of the Holiness Movement of that day by its stinging rebuke of capitalism:

> The world has long been crushed by an economic system that has stood as a bulwark against human progress, and for the sake of sordid gain has fostered well nigh every vice known to man. For ages, millions of laborers upon whom it depends for success in exploitation have seldom been free from the pinch of hunger: sties they have for homes: barred from the so-called best society, prevented from securing either a healthy body or a well-trained mind, blighted in birth and damned through life, the procession of wrong human progeny continues because of an economic system that can not be justified by either political science, moral philosophy or the Christian religion. Equality is the only rightful relation between human beings and that can never obtain so long as the masses are slaves of the classes. The capitalistic system is an economic outrage, a political fraud, and a giant leech on society. We commend the efforts of our President to cope with this great evil and pledge ourselves to the overthrow of this barrier to human progress and to the ushering in of a just regime

---

48. Ibid., 243.

PENTECOSTAL AND HOLINESS STATEMENTS ON WAR AND PEACE

when the laborer who is worthy of his hire shall receive the just reward of his toil.[49]

From *The Repairer* (Atlanta, GA), [E. E. Shelhamer's Magazine]

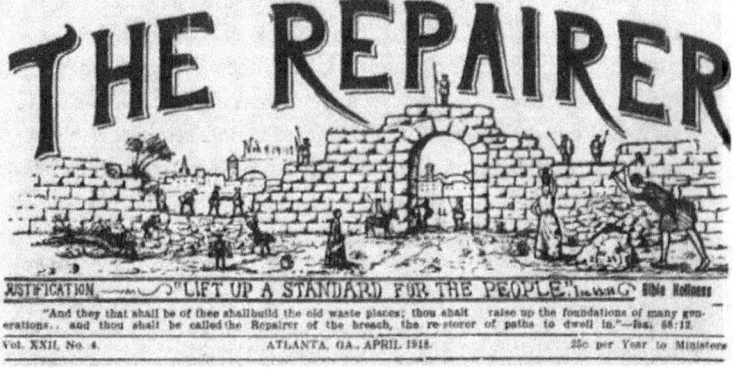

"Christians May Now Go to War" by Edgar Otis Jolley, 1918

We have manufactured some Scriptures with which we may wash the blood from our crimson hands, and that will enable us to get out of our present war dilemma without being guilty of murder (?). The following passages are taken from our latest new version, and will serve as an an-aesthetic by which to deaden the voice of conscience, permitting us to take up carnal weapons against our enemies, and at the same time feel that we are doing our Christian duty (?). At least this is what some good people as well as bad ones are telling us.

"Follow peace with all men, except with the Autocrat of militarism and his murdering dupes." Since we are afraid to trust in God for protection from autocracy, and He has left us to do our own fighting, we will simply have to do unto others as they do unto us (?).

---

49. *Annual Minutes, 1917*, 220. This year's entries also give a great deal of contrary evidence. With the U.S. entry to the war, patriotism became fashionable. The New York Conference took the lead giving America a place of cosmic significance in history, and pledging loyalty to the government. Preachers were admonished not to discuss the War Issue (p. 367). The Susquehanna Conference implied that this was a "just war" (p. 349). The Oil City Conference displayed patriotism, yet warned against "trusting alone in the arm of the flesh," (n.p.). Three other conferences, however, gave statements deploring the war (pp. 113, 186, 304–5).

"Dearly beloved, avenge not yourselves, unless it be on the wicked Germans." Saints as well as sinners will be guiltless (?) while murdering such impudent folk. Especially during war times, when murder ceases to be murder (?) and the frenzy world with its so-called democratic spirit, demands that we must preserve democracy and by all means stamp out the would be tyrants of world autocracy, even at the staggering cost of billions of money and the lives of millions of our noblest sons.

"But rather give place unto wrath (except when militarism is trying to rule), for it is written, Vengeance is mine; I will repay, saith the Lord." Unless, however, God's people usurp that prerogative, and in that event He will leave them to do so at their own charges.

"Therefore, if thine enemy hunger,"—we will have to cancel the remainder of this verse until War is over, since it condemns our present procedure. Then, perhaps, the Red Cross will comfort the widows and orphans, and administer to the maimed and suffering who may escape the bloody slaughter. The breach thus caused by ignoring God's plain commands in avenging ourselves instead of permitting Him to do so for us, will give a real opportunity at the close of the barbarous massacre to show the practical side of our Christianity, by our pretended pious actions in helping to repair the damage done (?).

Let us notice the last verse of the chapter. "Be not overcome of evil, but overcome evil with guns, bullets and swords" (?). This is the devil's emergency translation, and seems to contain just the right palliative to ease the conscience of the most devout saint among us. If the angels ever weep, it is safe to say they are doing so now, as they behold some of our leading ministers and good pilgrims advising our boys to lay aside their conscientious scruples against war and to answer the call of our country to the cruel butchery and especially since Congress has passed a supposed law whereby it is intended to compel them to go. It seems I can almost hear the sound of the fiendish jubilee that is now stirring hell. The imps must be shouting with hellish glee, as they see the multitudes stepping into the bloody whirlpool of war, and starting on their dizzy rounds down the whirling vortex ends in the center of hell.

Our title says, "Christians May Now Go to War." While it is within their power of choosing to go and of giving their means and in using their influence toward helping others to do likewise, yet I WONDER how many have seriously prayed over the matter and thouhgtfully [*sic*] considered the tremendous consequences that will inevitably follow their unscriptural course. With the teachings of Christ before us, and His reproof to the disciples at different times when they wanted to punish evil-doers, and His example of suffering at the hands of cruel militarism and wicked autocracy, without permitting His disciples to protect Him with carnal weapons; also the suffering of the disciples without fighting back, after they received their full Christian experience on the day of Pentecost; I say with these things before us, it is hard to believe that any minister or Christian should so far lose sight of the character of perfect love as to advocate war and help persuade the poor, innocent boys to step into this crafy [*sic*] snare perpetrated by the fiends of the pit. This war stratagem is so cunningly veneered with a coating of sham patriotism, as to deceive the "very elect, if it were possible." The eagle-eyed saints, however, are so enchanted with the glorious anti-war teachings of their peaceful Lord, as to be able to see the skillfully laid snare even though it is entirely hidden under the patriotic spirit of world democracy. The following plain words of Him who spake with authority, need no commentator to tell us their meaning, and should be the end of all controversy as to the Christian's duty toward war.

"Put up the sword—for all they that take the sword must perish with the sword." Jesus.

"If my kingdom were of this world, then would my servants fight."

"Jesus turned and rebuked them, and said, ye know not what manner of spirit ye are of. For the Son of man is not come to destroy men's lives, but to save them."

"Love your enemies, do good to them which hate you, bless them that curse you, and pray for them which despitefully use you."

"Behold, I send you forth as SHEEP IN THE MIDST OF WOVES [*sic*]: be ye therefore wise as serpents, and HARMLESS AS DOVES."

But why quote more since the New Testament containing scores of other passages along the same line, can be had by all wkho [*sic*] care to know. Old Testament law says, "Eye for eye, tooth for tooth, life for life," etc. But all who accept the sermon on the mount as their standard of conduct will know that it condemns the use of guns, bullets and swords, even though Prussian militarism and German autocracy is rampant. During

Christ's time, there were some conscience smitten soldiers, under deep conviction for their vindictive lives of revenge in serving as soldiers. While passing along the highway, and on hearing for the first time John the Baptist, preaching, "Do unto others as you would have others do unto you," it so condemned their military performances, that they at once "Demanded of him, saying, what shall we do then? And he said unto them, DO VIOLENCE TO NO MAN."

"He that killeth with the sword must be killed with the sword." Rev.

How sad to behold some good people and even ministers, advocating war and using their means and influence to support it, and at the same time pose as representatives of the lowly Nazarene. They come to meeting claiming to have that LOVE that suffers l-o-n-g and is KIND. They also talk fluently about, "Doing unto others as we would have them do unto us." To be consistent, they will have to change that scripture and make it read, do unto others as they do unto us.

It seems the very air is magnetized with the war spirit, until it is hardly safe to oppose it, and some are being locked behind prison bars for so doing. Professing Christians along with the vilest of sinners have altogether become inoculated with the bacteria of patriotism and democracy, combined with the hatred of autocracy and militarism, until they act just like hypnotized somnambulists, who can but do the bidding of some demoralized hypnotist. The domineering war drivers, are skillfully using the disagreeable whip of the espionage law acts passed by congress. This frightful scourge is serving well to frighten those who are opposed to war, and when they see ten years in the penitentiary, or some other hard thing awaiting them unless they cease their opposition, they at once lose courage and bow down to the merciless drivers, and jump into the mad rush for liberty bonds and war.[50]

---

50. Jolley, "Christians May Now Go to War," 2–3. Excerpt. Emphasis in original. Edgar Otis Jolley, (1875–1959), editor, was indicted for espionage for this article in July 1918. His office manager for *The Repairer* and wife, Jennie Arnold Jolley, was also accused of Espionage, but not indicted. While the Free Methodists were not at this time officially on record against going to war, E. E. Shelhamer, who published *The Repairer*, and its editors, Edgar and Jennie Jolley, actively opposed war.

106 PENTECOSTAL AND HOLINESS STATEMENTS ON WAR AND PEACE

GOD'S MISSIONARY CHURCH

"Article XXIV–War," 1971

War is at variance with the teachings of Christ and the apostles, and hence, incompatible with Christianity. Therefore, God's Missionary Church is opposed to taking up arms in time of war and to peacetime military conscription. In the event of war, if any member is drafted for military service, we advise him to enter into noncombatant service, however, this shall not infringe upon the rights of the conscientious objector (Matt. 5:9, 43, 44; Rom. 12:19–21; 1 Thess. 5:15).[51]

GOSPEL MISSION CORPS, INC., [FOUNDED EARLY 1960S]

"Articles of Doctrine," n.d.

We believe that concerning family relationships, upright business dealings, proper employment, civic affairs, and other worthy responsibilities, it is the duty of Christians to be subject to the appropriate authorities, first as faithful and obedient followers of Jesus Christ, and then as good citizens of our Country [sic]. We stress loyalty to our nation, respectful obedience to sound legislation, respectful obedience to sound legislation, responsible participation and co-operation in legitimate community, social and educational activities, and in Christ-honoring personal, family, and group living, work, and service. However, we feel that being required to swear by oath to a statement of truth, and also the taking up of arms or weapons for the intent purpose of destroying human life, are both contrary to what Christ allows for His disciples.[52]

---

51. *Discipline of God's Missionary Church*, 14. Piepkorn, *Profiles in Belief*, 48, notes that this church came out of the Pilgrim Holiness Church in 1935.

52. *Manual of the Gospel Mission Corps, Inc.*, 12–3. Piepkorn, *Profiles in Belief*, 57, notes Gospel Mission Corps was founded by ministers from Pillar of Fire, Pilgrim Holiness, and Mennonite Brethren in Christ churches.

HOLINESS CHRISTIAN CHURCH
"Conformity to the World," 1948

We as Christians are earnestly requested not to be conformed to the world, but to be transformed by the renewing of our minds, that we may prove what is the good and acceptable and perfect will of God. (Rom. 12:2). They that are conformed to the world are carnally minded. A complete separation should be manifested in our homes and houses of worship, our business, and, in short, in all manner of life and conversation. Member should keep free from oath-bound secret societies, and worldly amusements such as dancing, moving picture shows, automobile and horse racing, gambling in any form. Church suppers and festivals are prohibited. We also insist upon plainness and modesty in dress among both brethren and sisters.—Rom. 12:1, 2; John 2:13–16; I Pet. 3:3, 4.[53]

"National Reform," 1948

1. We believe it to be the duty of all Christians to use their influence in favor of a more complete recognition of the authority of Almighty God in secular and civil relations, both of society and government.

2. We believe that all civil laws should be in harmony with the laws of God as revealed in His word, and will use all our influence to have the Bible read in our public schools, and have all laws recognizing and protecting the Lord's Day faithfully enforced.

3. We believe it to be the duty of all Christians to use their influence against the manufacture and sale of intoxicating liquors.

4. We believe that all national differences should be settled by arbitration, and will not cease to pray and labor that the time may soon come when nations shall learn war no more.—Micah 4:3; Matt. 5:38–44; Prov 14:34–54.

---

53. *The Doctrines and Discipline of the Holiness Christian Church,* 16.

KENTUCKY MOUNTAIN HOLINESS ASSOCIATION
"Rules for Members," 1960

To avoid all manner of violent, unmerciful, or inconsiderate conduct, such as quarreling, hatred, brother going to law with brother, and recompensing evil for evil.[54]

MENNONITE BRETHREN IN CHRIST, 1924, LATER MISSIONARY CHURCH ASSOCIATION / UNITED MISSIONARY CHURCH[55]
"Civil Government," 1924

God ordained and instituted the civil government for the punishment of evil-doers and for the protection and defense of the good. We respect these powers with due loyalty, and are willing to be submissive, subjective and obedient to their authority, so long as not intruded upon in things which should militate against the supreme law and will of God. We pay willingly and cheerfully tribute and customs demanded of us, and pray for their protection, prosperity and welfare, "that we may lead a quiet and peaceable life, in all godliness and honesty."—Matt. 17:27; Rom. 13:1–7; I Pet. 2:14.[56]

"Self-Defense," 1924

Jesus has forbidden His disciples and followers all revenge and resistance, with the divine injunction, "Resist not evil," and, "My kingdom is not of this world; if My kingdom were of this world, then would My servants fight, but now is My kingdom not from hence."

Christ's followers are denominated His sheep, whose nature is the direct opposite of the wolf or lion. Christ, in His suffering, has given us an example, and we should follow His steps. "He is brought as a lamb to the slaughter and as a sheep before her shearers is dumb, so He openeth not His mouth." We are commanded to "recompense to no man evil for evil," and to cause

---

54. *Pastors Manual of the Kentucky Mountain Holiness Association*, 2.

55. Before 1947, Mennonite Brethren in Christ, then Missionary Church Association, and after 1947, United Missionary Church.

56. *The Doctrines and Discipline of the Mennonite Brethren in Christ Church*, 23.

grief or suffering to come upon no one; and if required, for con-science' sake, at the Lord's bidding when persecuted in one place to flee into another; and also to take the spoiling of our goods joyfully, for the Lord's sake, "knowing that there is reserved for us in heaven a better and enduring substance."—Matt. 5:39–44; I Peter 3:9.[57]

"Article XXIV Oaths," 1924

Christ has strictly forbidden the swearing of oaths, when He says, "I say unto you, Swear not at all; but let your communica-tion be, Yea, yea; Nay, nay; for whatsoever is more than these cometh of evil." It is evident that the apostles regarded it, and strictly insisted upon its careful observance. James says, "Above all things my brethren, swear not, neither by heaven, neither by earth, neither by any other oath; but let your yea be yea, and your nay, nay, lest ye fall into condemnation."

From these clear testimonies we conclude that the swearing of oaths is forbidden and not tolerated; and that anything be-yond an affirmation is violating the command of our Savior. We regard our affirmation as sacred and binding as though we had confirmed it by an oath.—Matt. 5:34–37; James 5:12.[58]

PILGRIM HOLINESS CHURCH (SAN DIEGO, CALIFORNIA)
[War], 1918

As per your request, we submit herewith a statement in brief concerning the attitude of the First Pentecost Pilgrim Church of San Diego, California, toward war and its allied associations.

We are conscientiously opposed to all war, believing it is ut-terly incompatible with the plain precepts of our divine Lord and Lawgiver, and the whole spirit of His Gospel, and that no plea of necessity or policy however urgent or peculiar, can avail to release either individuals or nations from the paramount allegiance which they owe to Him who hath said, "Love your enemies."

We are opposed to the use of alcoholic liquors, other than for medicinal and mechanical purposes; also the use of tobacco

57. Ibid., 23–24.
58. Ibid.

110   PENTECOSTAL AND HOLINESS STATEMENTS ON WAR AND PEACE

in any form believing it to be a kindred evil to the liquor, and equally condemned in the Scriptures.

We are opposed to dancing, theaters, and such classes of amusements as incompatible to holy living, and cannot conscientiously contribute funds to purchase such for the soldiers and sailors.

We are in sympathy with the humanitarian efforts, and deeds of mercy exhibited by the Red Cross, but cannot conscientiously contribute funds, either for membership in or donation to the society, when such are spent for the above purposes.

We believe in, and pledge loyalty to our government in all matters wherein it does not conflict with our paramount obligations to Him whom we worship and serve as King of Kings and Lord of Lords.

Trusting we have made our position clear, and that you will understand us, as not harboring any hostility to the government we are

Yours on behalf of the Church.[59]

PILLAR OF FIRE [ALMA WHITE, ZAREPHATH, NEW JERSEY]
"Two Swords" by A. L. Wolfram, 1917

Just before the crucifixion, Jesus said to His disciples, "When I sent you without purse, and scrip, and shoes, lacked ye anything? And they said, Nothing.

Then said he unto them, But [sic] now, he that hat a purse, let him take it, and likewise his scrip: and he that hath no sword, let him sell his garment, and buy one. For I say unto you, that this that is written must yet be accomplished in me, And [sic] he was reckoned among the transgressors: for the things concerning me have an end.

"And they said, Lord, behold, here are two swords. And he said unto them, It is enough" (Luke 22:35–38).

Commentators have been greatly puzzled over this passage, not understanding why Jesus should tell the disciples to arm themselves with swords, since theirs was a peaceful mission. Some have thought that inasmuch as they were to go out where they would be exposed to danger, they were to have weapons for self-defense.

59. "In Re: Reverend Harry Hays, German Activities."

Radical Holiness Statements   111

But if this were the meaning the Master intended to convey, why did He say that two were sufficient, for as one writer points out, that would leave nine disciples unarmed?

The mystery is such no longer when one understands the doctrine of holiness, or that of the two works of grace. A full-fledged Christian must have two swords, one against sins, or transgressions of the law, ant the other against inbred sin, or the carnal nature. The Christian has no enmity against a sinner, it is against the evil in the soul that he is fighting.[60]

RELIGIOUS SOCIETY OF FRIENDS (QUAKERS)
George Fox, 1651

I told (the Commonwealth Commissioners) I lived in the virtue of that life and power that took away the occasion of all wars and I knew from whence all wars did rise, from the lust, according to James's doctrine. . . . I told them I was come into the covenant of peace which was before wars and strifes were.[61]

George Fox to Lord Protector Oliver Cromwell, 1655

The next morning I was moved of the Lord to write a paper to the Protector, Oliver Cromwell; wherein I did, in the presence of the Lord God, declare that I denied the wearing or drawing of a carnal sword, or any other outward weapon, against him or any man; and that I was sent of God to stand a witness against all violence, and against the works of darkness; and to turn people from darkness to light; and to bring them from the causes of war and fighting, to the peaceable gospel.[62]

---

60. Wolfram, "Two Swords," 3. Excerpt. Wolfram, like Alma White, the leader of the Pillar of Fire, was not clear in promotion of pacifism. The article used a major argument of just war proponents that Jesus argued to purchase two swords, against just war adherents, by spiritualizing the passage. Antebellum Holiness Pacifists had already used his argument to say that Jesus could not mean buy swords to fight carnal war. However, Wolfram does not quite say that explicitly. He says fight with the metaphorical sword against sin in the hearts of people. Some members of this group apparently took this kind of teaching to its logical conclusion and argued as members of their church that they could not go to war.

61. Fox, "The Quaker Peace Testimony." George Fox (1624–1691).

62. Kelley, "The Quaker Peace Testimony."

Robert Barclay, 1678

Whoever can reconcile this, "Resist not evil," with "Resist violence by force," again, "Give also thy other cheek," with "Strike again"; also, "Love thine enemies," with "Spoil them, make a prey of them, pursue them with fire and the sword," or, "Pray for those that persecute you, and those that calumniate you," with "Persecute them by fines, imprisonments and death itself," whoever, I say, can find a means to reconcile these things may be supposed also to have found a way to reconcile God with the Devil, Christ with Antichrist, Light with Darkness, and good with evil. But if this be impossible, as indeed it is impossible, so will also the other be impossible, and men do but deceive both themselves and others, while they boldly adventure to establish such absurd and impossible things.[63]

John Woolman, 1898

This is like a chain in which the end of one link encloseth the end of another. The rising up of a desire to obtain wealth is the beginning; this desire being cherished, moves to action; and riches thus gotten please self; and while self has a life in them it desires to have them defended. Wealth is attended with power, by which bargains and proceedings contrary to universal righteousness are supported; and hence oppression carried on with worldly policy and order, clothes itself with the name of justice and becomes like a seed of discord in the soul. And as a spirit which wanders from the pure habitation prevails, so the seeds of war swell and sprout and grow and become strong until much fruit is ripened. Then cometh the harvest spoken of by the prophet, which "is a heap in the day of grief and desperate sorrows." Oh that we who declare against wars, and acknowledge our trust to be in God only, may walk in the light, and therein examine our foundation and motives in holding great estates! May we look upon our treasures, the furniture of our houses and our garments, and try whether the seeds of war have nourishment in these our possessions. Holding treasures in the self-pleasing spirit is a strong plant, the fruit whereof ripens fast. A day of outward distress is coming, and Divine love calls to prepare against it.[64]

63. Barclay, "The Quaker Peace Testimony." Barclay (1648–1690) was a Quaker theologian.

64. Woolman, *A Word of Remembrance* 10. Woolman (1720–1772) was a Quaker advocate.

Radical Holiness Statements   113

Indiana Yearly Meeting of Friends
"PEACE," 1887 AND 1905

We feel bound explicitly to avow our unshaken persuasion that all War is utterly incompatible with the plain precepts of our divine Lord and Law-giver, and the whole spirit of His Gospel, and that no plea of necessity or policy, however urgent or peculiar, can avail to release either individuals or nations from the paramount allegiance which they owe to Him who hath said, "Love your enemies." In enjoining this love, and the forgiveness of injuries, He who has bought us to Himself has not prescribed for man precepts which are incapable of being carried into practice, or of which the practice is to be postponed until all shall be persuaded to act upon them. We cannot doubt that they are incumbent now, and that we have in the prophetic Scriptures the distinct intimation of their direct application not only to individuals, but to nations also. When nations conform their law to this divine teaching, wars must necessarily cease.

We would, in humility, but in faithfulness to our Lord, express our firm persuasion that all the exigencies of civil government and social order may be met under the banner of the Prince of Peace, in strict conformity with His commands.[65]

---

65. "Peace" in *Declaration of Faith.* This statement was adopted by the Conference of Gurneyites in Richmond, Indiana, 1887 and 1905. Statement also found in the *Discipline of Indiana Yearly Meeting of Friends,* 66–67, 115. The 1887 Indiana statement was quoted in Hamm, Marconi, Salina, and Whitman, "The Decline of Quaker Pacifism," 50. The 1887 and 1905 Indiana Yearly Meeting of Friends statement on "Peace" is identical to the Northwest Yearly Meeting of Friends statement of 1924 with one exception, the omission of scripture references. It is possible, however, that in quoting the 1887 statement, the authors from whom we quoted, omitted scriptures references found in the 1924 version for succinctness. Interestingly, by the outset of the Vietnam War, there were serious divisions in the Quaker peace testimony, as evident within the Indiana constituency. In "The Decline of Quaker Pacifism," for example, Indiana Quaker member, D. Elton Trueblood, who served as an official in the Eisenhower administration from 1954–1955, "denounced proposals by Democratic presidential Adlai Stevenson to end both the draft and atmospheric nuclear weapons tests . . ." (p. 64). The case study documented that Trueblood, "unquestionably the yearly meeting's best-known member," valued his personal ties with Nixon and "consistently argued that Nixon's 'Peace with Honor' policies were in accord with Quaker beliefs." Although Trueblood supported the "integrity of conscientious objectors," he nevertheless "blasted the New Left elements of the antiwar movement." Trueblood's view likely represented many Indiana Quakers who, in 1967, went on official record to give "support to the United States Government in its actions to protect the free peoples of the world from Communism, at home, in Viet Nam, and elsewhere" (p. 68).

114 PENTECOSTAL AND HOLINESS STATEMENTS ON WAR AND PEACE

"Resolution No. 1," 1948

Indiana Yearly Meeting, while holding its views that the ways of love and conciliation are superior in effectiveness to the use of force in world adjustments, expresses its belief that in a world accustomed to the use of force, the so-called Fulbright Resolution which commits the United States as "favoring the creation of appropriate international machinery with power adequate to establish and to maintain a just and lasting peace among the nations, and as favoring participation by the United States . . ." is a step forward in the effort to better international relations.[66]

"Resolution No. 2," 1948

We do not censure Friends who conscientiously take part in the war effort any more than ourselves for failure to create conditions that might have done much to have avoided this war. Many a Friend could and did argue that Indiana Yearly Meeting had bravely faced the modern world with a moral realism, that the two resolutions simply put on record views which Friends have long been privately laboring with. The resolutions would enable Friends to exert a force in the postwar world commensurate with their Christian purpose . . .[67]

[Oregon] Northwest Yearly Meeting of Friends
"Liberty of Conscience in Its Relation to Civil Government," 1924

That conscience should be free, and that is matters of religious doctrine and worship man is accountable only to God, are truths which are plainly declared in the New Testament; and which are confirmed by the whole scope of the Gospel, and by the example of our Lord and His disciples. To rule over the conscience, and to command spiritual allegiance of his creature man, is the high and sacred prerogative of God alone. In religion every act ought to be free. A forced worship is plainly a contradiction in terms, under that dispensation in which the worship of the Father must be in spirit and in truth. (John iv. 24.)

---

66. "Force or Power?," 48.
67. Ibid.

Radical Holiness Statements   115

We have ever maintained that it is the duty of Christians to obey the enactments of civil government, except those which interfere with our allegiance to God. We owe much to its blessings. Through it we enjoy liberty and protection, in connection with law and order. Civil government is a divine ordinance, (Rom. xiii 1, I. Pet. ii. 13–16.) instituted to promote the best welfare of man, hence magistrates are to be regarded as God's ministers who should be a terror to evil doers and a praise to them that do well. Therefore, it is with us a matter of conscience to render them respect and obedience in the exercise of their proper functions.[68]

"Peace," 1924

We feel bound explicitly to avow our unshaken persuasion that all War is utterly incompatible with the plain precepts of our divine Lord and Law-giver, and the whole spirit of His Gospel, and that no plea of necessity or policy, however urgent or peculiar, can avail to release either individuals or nations from the paramount allegiance which they owe to Him who hath said, "Love your enemies." (Matt. v. 44, Luke vi. 27.) In enjoining this love, and the forgiveness of injuries, He who has bought us to Himself has not prescribed for man precepts which are incapable of being carried into practice, or of which the practice is to be postponed until all shall be persuaded to act upon them. We cannot doubt that they are incumbent now, and that we have in the prophetic Scriptures the distinct intimation of their direct application not only to individuals, but to nations also. (Isaiah ii. 4, Micah iv. 1.) When nations conform their law to this divine teaching, wars must necessarily cease.

We would, in humility, but in faithfulness to our Lord, express our firm persuasion that all the exigencies of civil government and social order may be met under the banner of the Prince of Peace, in strict conformity with His commands.[69]

---

68. *Discipline of Oregon Yearly Meeting of the Friends Church*, 35–7.

69. Ibid. This statement is identical to "Peace" in *Declaration of Faith* (Indiana Yearly Meeting of Friends) in 1887 and 1905. The phrase, "Quaker peace testimony," was common among early Quaker literature as shown in these primary documents. It was more common for Quakers to define their peace testimony using this terminology rather than pacifism or nonresistance. They certainly were pacifists and much more, though they did not necessarily use the term pacifism to define their position on war and peace. Earlham School of Religion, a Quaker institution, has put over 70,000 pages

116 PENTECOSTAL AND HOLINESS STATEMENTS ON WAR AND PEACE

THE FIRE BAPTIZED HOLINESS CHURCH (WESLEYAN), (LABETTE, KANSAS), ORIGIN 1890S

[War is Incompatible with the New Testament], 1963

[With] love for all, malice toward none, living peaceably with all men.[70] We believe that we should respect the government of our country and the flag that guarantees our liberties, but we feel that the principles that actuate war are utterly incompatible with the plain teaching of the New Testament, therefore, we as a Church are strictly opposed to war, and are unwilling that we or any of our children should be compelled to engage in combat service.[71]

THE MISSIONARY CHURCH ASSOCIATION / THE UNITED MISSIONARY CHURCH[72]

"Attitude Toward Civil Government," statement assumed 1960

We believe that civil government is ordained of God for the welfare of society to promote and protect the good and to restrain and punish evil (Dan. 4:17; Rom. 13:1–4; I Pet. 2:13, 14). Therefore we consider it the duty of Christians to pray for rulers and for those that are in authority over them (1 Tim. 2:1–4); to give due loyalty, respect and obedience to them (Titus 3:1); and to pay taxes and customs imposed by them (Matt.22:17–21). Where the demands of civil law would militate against the su-

---

of Quaker primary source material online. See: http://dqc.esr.earlham.edu. Most digitized manuscripts were written between 1650 and 1940. Stephen W. Angell, a Quaker scholar at Earlham, notes that in all the thousands of pages, the only use of the term "pacifism" is in a 1936 publication. Email correspondence with Stephen W. Angell, January 26, 2013, personal files of Brian Pipkin. Quaker scholar, Michael Birkel, says, "Early Quakers did not use the term pacifist, but they were opposed to war and to violence." They did not feel the need to label their peace convictions, although they frequently denounced participating in war. Today one finds Quakers using the language of "pacifism" and "peace testimony." Email correspondence with Michael Birkel, January 16, 2013, personal files of Brian Pipkin.

70. Piepkorn, 30.

71. *Articles of Faith Rules and By-Laws, The Fire Baptized Holiness Church*, 41. This church is now called the Bible Holiness Church. See Douglas and Taylor, *The History of the Bible Holiness Church.*

72. Before 1947, Mennonite Brethren in Christ, then Missionary Church Association, and after 1947, United Missionary Church.

preme law and will of God Christians should obey God rather than man (Acts 4:19; 5:29).[73]

"Attitude toward Strife and Military Service," statement assumed 1960

We believe that the teaching of Scripture enjoins believers to love their enemies, to do good to them that hate them (Matt. 5:43–45), and to overcome evil with good (Rom. 12:20, 21). They are instructed to live peaceably with all men (Rom. 12:18). The parting command of Jesus was that they should preach the gospel in all the world that men might be saved (Matt. 28:19, 20; Mark 16:15, 16). God is not willing that any should perish, but that all should come to repentance (II Peter 3:9). Therefore, the historic position of The Missionary Church Association is to oppose the bearing of arms in warfare and the gendering of strife between nations, classes, groups or individuals.

The denomination, however, respects the right of individual conscience and recognizes that various positions will be taken on war and military service. Our churches should support our Christian youth who because of faith and conscience accept the exemptions or alternatives to combat service. In any event, our churches should give spiritual aid to all of our youth in service by encouraging them to exert a positive testimony for Christ and to maintain their loyalty to Christ and the church.

Pastors are advised to instruct their churches and particularly their youth on the teaching of the Scriptures regarding war

73. *Constitution of The Missionary Church Association* [source 1956] *and The United Missionary Church* [merger 1966], 10; *Constitution and General Conference By-Laws of The Missionary Church Association*, 11, 13. The Missionary Church Association and The United Missionary Church merged in 1966 and their statements are almost identical. The Missionary Church Association was founded by Mennonites who were associates of A. B. Simpson, a Holiness movement leader. The movement had roots in a revival among Mennonites in the latter half of the nineteenth century and affirmed sanctification and divine healing, and held regular camp meetings. See Storms, *History of the United Missionary Church*, 225–27. Additionally, Piepkorn, *Profiles in Belief*, 21–23, classifies this group as Fundamentalist/Evangelical, while showing elements of Holiness. He also notes that, "in spite of its history and official opposition to war and participation in it, by the time of World War II the failure of the ministers to stress the denominational doctrine had the result that in Canada half the eligible young men of the church entered the armed services and in the United States almost all of them did so. In 1955 the General Conference gave formal approval to noncombatant service."

PENTECOSTAL AND HOLINESS STATEMENTS ON WAR AND PEACE

and its evils and to seek to give guidance in the Word to those subject to call in the service of their country.[74]

THE NEW TESTAMENT CHURCH (LOS ANGELES, CALIFORNIA)
"Holiness," 1901

The word says, "Follow peace with all men, and holiness without which no man shall see the Lord."—Heb. 12:14.

We remark: (1) That to follow peace and holiness with all men is impossible without the experiences. (2) That the injunction is for this life, for there would be no need of such an exhortation in heaven. (3) That such a life here qualifies one for the society and employment of heaven. Hence holiness is absolutely important, and all can have it if they will.[75]

"Suffer Wrong Rather Than Do Wrong," 1901

"For it is better if the will of God be so, that ye suffer for well doing than for evil doing." 1 Peter 3:17.[76]

THE SALVATION ARMY
Catherine Booth, 1887

One of the greatest employments of every Christian government and community is to train thousands of men, not to fight with their fists only, in the way of inflicting a few passing sores, but with weapons capable, it may be, of killing human beings at the rate of so many per minute. It is quite a "scientific taste" to study how to destroy a large vessel, with several hundreds of men on board, instantaneously. Talk of brutality! Is there anything half as brutal as this within the whole range of rowdyism? But against all this, modern Christianity, which professes to believe the teaching of Him Who taught us not to resist evil, but to love our enemies, and to treat with the utmost benevolence hostile na-

---

74. Ibid.
75. Teel, *The New Testament Church*, 103–4.
76. Ibid., 131.

tions, has nothing to say. All the devilish animosity, hard hearted cruelty, and harrowing consequences of modern warfare, are not only sanctioned but held up as an indispensable [*sic*] necessity of civilized life, and in times of war, patronized and prayed for in our churches and chapels, with as much impudent assurance as though Jesus Christ had taught, "But I say unto you an eye for an eye, a tooth for a tooth, and, return evil for evil, hate your enemies and pursue them with all the diabolical appliances of destruction which the Devil can enable you to invent.[77]

From *The Saint and the Sword* by Herbert Booth, 1923

As a CHRISTIAN speaking to CHRISTIANS I regard war as no subject to be dealt with in a ginger-bread, half-frightened, apologetic, may-it-not-be-possible-that-I–am-right-and-you-are-wrong fashion. That is no way for a man to deal with what he considers legalized murder. For *"pussy-foot"* pacifist literature I refer the reader elsewhere.

At a time when the Christian Church is tumbling over itself to secure the services of men who, in evangelistic campaigns, employ the most extravagant slang; breathe out denunciations little short of swearing in their attacks on dancing, theater-going and booze, one who, with General Sherman, regards war as *hell* itself, may be permitted to strike straight from the shoulder when talking about that same hell let loose. Especially so when "great Church leaders" are busy trying to prove that such ghastly hellishness finds in some way its causes, as its approval away up in heaven. If drunkenness is a crime, what shall be said of the crime which has turned half of Europe into a quagmire of youthful corpses—a shambles running with human blood— over which the bishops of the world have been holding forth holy hands in benediction!

The fact that hitting "booze," dancing, card-playing, theater-going, no longer involves, as it used to for some of us, a boy-

---

77. Booth, *Popular Christianity*, 134–35, cited in Booth, *The Saint and the Sword*, 1. This quote is cited in the foreword to Herbert Booth's, *The Saint and the Sword*, published in 1923. The book was written during World War I, but Booth could not find a publisher until after the war as all publishers' feared imprisonment for violation of the Espionage Act. The Salvation Army did not officially teach against going to war, however, there are two examples of top leader who did: (1) Catherine Booth, co-founder (1829–1890), founder of the Salvation Army, and (2) their son, Herbert Booth (1862–1926).

cotted business or a broken nose, while hitting *war* means the organized opposition of most of the forces of earth and all the powers of hell, is a pretty sure indication that, in this hour, *War is the thing to hit.*

Note carefully, however, this book is not an attack on earthly governments. It is an attack on the pugilistic Christianity of the modern Church. The governments of this age are not Christian governments. The vast majority of their subjects know nothing of the "new birth" which, Christ said, was the first essential to citizenship in His kingdom. Being under the rule of Satan, they are not subject to Christian law. It is to be expected, therefore, that these unchristian states will exercise their power to make war on each other when and where they please. They will do this as it suits their selfish ends, their imperialistic ideas, or their purely humanitarian conceptions of justice and "honor."[78]

Topsy-Turvydum

It is astounding to see how such professed Christians, just because a little clique of statesmen cry "war," will at once proceed to turn upside-down the most vital tenets of their faith and morality. Because a few "diplomats," who are supposed to have no authority of any kind in the Church of Christ, and hardly any of whom know anything of real conversion—because these announce that certain national interests must be sought, certain policies pursued or wrongs righted by an antichristian method, which involves the killing of tens of thousands of men, then bishops and divines, deacons and elders, will start in to call ghastly, dastardly crimes by plausible and even picturesque names. Premediated, wilful, and wholesale murder becomes "the conquest of the enemy;" highway and daylight robbery is "capture of treasure;" devilish pride and skilfully fostered hatred masquerades as "a commendable patriotism;" venomous, envious, red-hot rage is only "magnificent courage and fighting force;" consummate lying, that would outclass the lowest-down perjured scoundrel, is described as "brilliantly clever intelligent work;" ditches filled with gory and rotting corpses are the "quiet resting places of the heroic dead;" and hospitals full of eyeless, armless, legless, footless, ruined men are "the bases of the splendid work of Red Cross Societies."[79]

78. Booth, *The Saint and the Sword*, 9–10. Emphasis in original.
79. Ibid., 13.

Radical Holiness Statements   121

The Bayonet Versus The Ballot

If it is right for the Christian to make war with carnal weapons (which of course it never can be), there are causes which would have a far stronger claim upon the use of a sword in his hands than the aggression of a "foreign" power. . . . If it is legitimate for Christians to arm themselves and shed blood in a good cause . . . why not march through the land shooting down saloon-keepers, white-slave traffickers, boodlers, as "Christian" solders now shoot down citizens of a "foreign" land. If the "Christian" citizens of German, England and the American Republic feel justified in killing each other as the children of the Devil, it is well for them to remember that there are other armies of booze-distilling, graft-seeking, money-hunting, woman-degrading, property-swindling, negro-lynching immoral monsters whom they should also get after with their bayonets and their guns. . . . If it is right for [the Christian] to employ carnal weapons at all, he is most justified in employing them against the things that most matter. He cannot be consistently condemned as a murder because he uses a six shooter in putting a brewer out of business and then be commended for using a bayonet to stick another fellow through the bowels because he is an autocrat. In his estimation the booze scourge is every bit as bad as the scourge of Prussianism.[80]

War-Makers Who Never Fight

These [soldiers] are not the men who make the quarrels, nor those who reap any of the advantages. The diplomats-whose political schemes, whose bids for glory, whose love of power, so often invite these deluges of blood and tears—they are never those who do the fighting or suffer the loss. The princes of commerce and finance, the holders of fat stocks in great international munition plants, who pile up more millions by the innumerable bodies they break and bury with their damnable trade—these are not the gentlemen who pull up their homes by the roots, kiss their wives and children a last good-by, and go to wallow in mud and blood. If the favored few who consider themselves the only parties capable of guiding their nation's destinies would step into the battle lines and fight out the quarrels their policies involve— if the age of military service was fixed between forty-five and sixty-five, instead of eighteen, and thirty-five, there would very quickly be an end of war. Kings, princes, dukes, prime-ministers,

---

80. Ibid., 14–15.

122   PENTECOSTAL AND HOLINESS STATEMENTS ON WAR AND PEACE

chancellors, how so ever clever they may be at political intrigue, at parliamentary oratory, are not conspicuous personalities in the zones of fire, but they are predominantly in evidence among those who have everything to gain by the game of war.

The toiling multitudes who are sent to kill each other have no particular interest in national quarrels which center in such enterprises as the German railway from Berlin to Bagdad or the long coveted all British line from Cairo to the Cape. The realization of such schemes are certainly not going to increase the products of their tiny cabbage-plots or add to the scanty wages which flow into their pockets. And most decidedly such schemes can never justify Christians in going to war with each other. From the Christian standpoint, what iniquity could be more monstrous than to incite great masses of men to kill each other for a national policy which, even were it realized, could never begin to compensate for the loss of only one eternal spirit.[81]

[Patriotism]

It is not possible that worldly men should know much about [patriotism] because worldly men are essentially proud, self-centered, and nations which are, for the most part, made up of such men are even more arrogant and selfish. . . . [T]hese two qualities, pride and selfishness, are fundamental essentials of the "patriotism" of all earthly kingdoms. . . . [T]he national displays, feasting, celebrations, reviewing of troops dolled up in all kinds of gaudy and senseless uniforms; assembling of costly dreadnaughts [battleships] which emit smoke and make a ridiculous noise; inflammable speeches at national conventions full of oratorical, shallow phases, which seek to exalt the speaker's nation above all others—all this fooling and deluding of the common people, by whose permission armies and navies exist, and who endure nearly all the suffering and do most of the killing, all this has its root in pride.[82]

But selfishness is also at the root of this worldly "patriotism." The only thing to which these nations are constant, are every faithful, in their own welfare. Their "patriotism" is a persistent and consistent loyalty to themselves[;] . . . citizens will always stand for their country's interests, which of course, nine times out of ten, means a blind subservience to the dictatorship of a

81. Ibid., 198.
82. Ibid., 224.

small coterie of statesmen who preside over their "interests," sometimes create them, and always define them.[83]

We must not forget that the "patriotism" of the Christian is not confined to his own country. His sympathies go out toward all nations, for members of all nationalities are in the Kingdom of God. Most of the "patriotism" of this godless world is nothing but a thoroughly anti-Christian, narrow, selfish, greedy spirit. That spirit is responsible for nearly all wars. If it was not so wicked it would be laughable. To see people puffing themselves up with a vain imagination that their particular race and the portion of the globe which it happens to occupy is immensely superior to all other races and all other lands, is absurd enough; but to travel the world, as I have, and see every nation doing the same thing, is painfully ridiculous. . . . From the viewpoint of this world's policy, such talk[84] may be excellent "patriotism," but most certainly it is not Christianity. . . . [Patriotic speeches by our national leaders] has flooded the world with selfishness and barred off man from man by barriers of misunderstanding, envy and hatred.[85]

The Salvation Army Statement on Military Service, 1971

Many young Salvationists have served, and are serving, with distinction in the Armed Forces (some as Chaplains), and The Salvation Army has always sought to bring them a ministry of help and guidance. We owe an equal ministry to others who, by reason of conscience, are opposed to military service. We respect the right of every individual to arrive at his own decision in this matter, based on his Christian conscience.

83. Ibid., 226.

84. Booth specifically names Theodore Roosevelt in his denunciation of political patriotic rhetoric who said, in a speech given to the American public, "Don't be for me unless you are prepared to say that every citizen of this country has got to be pro-United States, first, last and all the time, and no pro-anything else at all, and that we stand for every good American everywhere, whatever his birthplace or creed, and wherever he now lives, and that in return we demand that he be an American and nothing else, with no hyphen about him. Every American citizen must be an American first and for no other country even second, and he hasn't any right to be in the United States at all if he has any divided loyalty between this and any other country. I don't care a rap for the man's creed or birthplace so long as he is straight United States, and if he isn't I'm against him" (ibid., 269).

85. Ibid., 269.

We teach respect for properly constituted civil authority and loyalty to our "nation under God." Therefore, we counsel those of our constituents who object to military service to take advantage of the legal means provided for alternative service.

We join with fellow Christians around the world in praying that all men may learn to live together in the love and power of the Lord Jesus Christ, which takes away the occasion for war and strife.[86]

THE WESLEYAN CHURCH
[The War Spirit], 1844

As early as 1844, the Wesleyan Methodists were dealing with the issue of War in their *Discipline*. They noted that the gospel was in "every way opposed to the practice of War in all its forms; and those customs which tend to foster and perpetuate the war spirit, [are] inconsistent with the benevolent designs of the Christian Religion." The St. Lawrence Annual Conference of the Wesleyan Methodists commended the Quakers for showing "that love is a more powerful defense than physical force." They also considered a resolution "to alter the denominational *Discipline* so that refusal to engage in war and military training would become a condition of membership."[87]

[Peace], 1915

The Wesleyan Methodist Church promoted peace until World War I, when they argued that, "Human War is undoubtedly the product of human sin, but it does not necessarily follow that all who engage in war are sinners."[88]

---

86. Perry, *Words of Conscience*, 96. Approved by the Commissioners' Conference, April 1971.

87. Beaman, *Pentecostal Pacifism*, 7–10, 24; "St. Lawrence Annual Conference Minutes." This paper was later published in Hostetler, *Perfect Love and War*, 132–52.

88. Dayton and Dayton, "An Historical Survey of Attitudes Toward War and Peace," 7–89; citing *Discipline of the Wesleyan Methodist Connection*, 98. For further sources, see Beaman, *Pentecostal Pacifism*, 17, footnote 24.

[The Wesleyan Church on Military Service], n.d.

The Wesleyan Church teaches respect for properly constituted civil authority and the proper loyalty to one's country. It recognizes the responsibility of the individual to answer the call of his government and to enter into military service. However, there are those within the fellowship of the Wesleyan Church who believe that military service is contrary to the teaching of the New Testament and that their consciences are violated by being compelled to take part in such. The Wesleyan Church will therefore lend moral support to any member who asks and claims exemption by legal processes from military service as a sincere conscientious objector and who asks to serve his country as a noncombatant.[89]

UNITED HOLINESS CHURCH OF NORTH AMERICA
"Militarism and War," 1969

Militarism is contrary to the spirit of the New Testament and the teachings of Jesus Christ. Even from humanitarian principles alone it is utterly indefensible. It is our profound conviction that none of our people should be required to enter military training or to bear arms except in time of national peril, and that the consciences of our individual members should be respected. Therefore we claim exemption from the bearing of arms for all members of our church who are conscientious objectors.[90]

89. Perry, *Words of Conscience*, 130.
90. *Discipline of the United Holiness Church of North America*, 12.

5

Pentecostal Statements

INTRODUCTION

This chapter begins alphabetically with the Apostolic Faith in its various forms. For most people in 1901, the age of the Apostles was long past. However, a group of small sects were making the audacious claim that their leaders might be considered modern-day apostles who were reintroducing an end time visitation of God with the same apostolic-age miracles. The Church, in essence, hit the reset button and was given a divine do-over.

The Pentecostal faith, so named after the birthday of the church—the day of Pentecost—saw itself reproducing the very church founded by the apostles. With little more than the clothes on their backs, some ephemeral miracles, and a cosmic narrative, they believed they could perhaps trigger a prophetic worldwide revival of faith that would culminate in Jesus returning to set up a millennial kingdom or reign of peace.

Charles Fox Parham considered himself one of the founders of North American Pentecostalism, although he was unable to hold the reigns for long. In retrospect, it is easy to see what a flawed leader he was; understanding it is perhaps less easy. Parham believed that one feature of the days of the apostles-returned was absolute aversion to earthly warfare, like the early church and like the coming millennial kingdom. In

126

Pentecostal Statements   127

this, he was certainly influenced by the writings of Arthur Sydney Booth-Clibborn, and Parham's writings show direct debt to his work.[1]

Pentecostals were all about revival, and every able-bodied adult had to consider if they were to be an evangelist or missionary. The enterprise of global missions and the army of evangelists and missionaries needed was already taxing every resource in people and money that the movement could expend. They were fighting a war for the hearts, minds, and souls of all people; they didn't need another war. They were already fighting for a kingdom and their allegiance was already counted.

During this time the Booth-Clibborn's were adapting the language of an army of Holiness evangelists from the Salvation Army, of which they had earlier been the European leaders. So, in borrowing their work, Parham was making an indirect appropriation of the apostolic age, through the Salvation Army. Booth-Clibborn was also a Quaker before he was a Salvationist. So, in borrowing from him, Parham was also directly dependent upon Quaker thought. Thus, during World War I, leaders of the Assemblies of God leaders declared: "We are like the Quakers."

Parham was fighting to usher a renewal of what he saw as the Apostolic Faith returned. Despite his seemingly racist views and support of racial segregation, he believed he was fighting religious and social elitism and exclusion. We hear the rebuke of working people who felt excluded from leadership of communities and institutions by the power and manipulation that wealth bought. The Apostolic Faith, however, was composed of people who had been pushed out of leadership and membership in mainstream churches when they tried to lead them in directions where any adult was a potential leader and any member could speak as a prophet and critique sin including social sin. The claim of the Apostolic Faith was that not only was the Roman Catholic Church a kind of civil religion which was aligned with powerful interests in government which oppressed people; so too were most Protestant churches. In their very forms of worship they represented the interests of wealth and power against the poor, and in the interest of maintaining their wealth and power, they led working people to war.

Parham's critique sounded vaguely familiar in the mining regions where he headquartered, and where socialists made similar claims. Though Parham was not a socialist, he was using similar arguments to

1. We included Booth-Clibborn's work in the international chapter at the end of this volume, although chronologically, he was one of the earliest.

compete for the same following in the "masses." If his message sounded anarchist, he was criticizing all earthly governments, wealth, power, and the authority they possessed; so be it. Notice, too, how Parham, like earlier Holiness postmillennialists, was not afraid to use terms vehemently rejected by fundamentalists, "Believing in the universal brotherhood of mankind and the establishment of the teachings of Jesus Christ as the foundation for all laws, whether political or social." No doubt such laws would also prohibit the sale and use of alcohol. Nonetheless, Parham must have believed that pacifism was a realistic form of human government.

We have also included an essay written by Parham's mother-in-law, Lillian Thisthlethwaite, herself a Quaker, who converted to the Pentecostal message. There is no doubt she influenced Parham as greatly as he influenced her, and she and Booth-Clibborn both illustrate the direct debt of Pentecostals to Historic Peace Churches for their early peace witness. If one has any doubt that Parham was influenced by her point of view, remember that he was publishing her in his *Apostolic Faith* magazine on the subject of pacifism. The piece is almost exclusively passages of scripture, as if they are completely self-explanatory. In this, we get a window on early twentieth century south Kansas Quaker-Pentecostal pacifism combined with perhaps antievolutionary thinking. Still, it is most clearly social evolution that she takes aim at in her essay promoting nonviolence, and not the biological arguments about evolution.

In her essay, one imagines that a thoroughgoing spirituality would free one from the temptation to view other people as competitors and enemies. Her statements were written at a time when monopolistic capitalism and eugenics initiatives were both affecting the lives of people, at the behest of social and intellectual elites who promoted forms of social evolution. One view of Pentecostalism is that it was a religion of protest against the cozy relationship of mainstream religion and local and national elites. Whatever else the Apostolic Faith was, it was also going to converse in the language of contemporary controversies. However, in Lillian Thisthlethwaite's brief article, one does not hear the fundamentalist's railing against evolution in the language of Scopes, but against unbridled capitalism and militarism as forms of modern secular belief that demean life.

If Parham gave us the Apostolic Faith and if, as J. H. Black maintained, that the "Full Gospel" was a message of peace on earth, Parham's ministry and influence was limited by scandal and racism. The Apostolic

Faith became well known through the Azusa Street revival in Los Angeles in 1906–1908, more in spite of, rather than through the good graces of Parham. The pastor of Azusa Street Mission was William J. Seymour. He published a discipline which included statements about the relationship of Christians under the rule of Christ to the state. Seymour's 1915 statements sound far less challenging to the state than that of Parham or of Seymour's colleague in the Azusa Revival, Frank Bartleman. In the context of Parham, Bartleman, and almost all the early Pentecostal groups during World War I, Seymour's teaching is undoubtedly Christian nonresistance or a form of pacifism, although his statements are decidedly non-confrontational to the state. He notes the need for submission to the state in everything where conscience and the law of Christ are not contradicted, in which case ". . . God's claims are supreme, and annihilate all claims that contradict or oppose them." This kind of dual-claim of heavenly and earthly citizenship and requirements, the latter taking precedence over the former, shows up often in documents which follow in Seymour's lead.

In Bartleman's hands, the same distinction between heavenly and earthly citizenship became stark. He took bankers, merchants, manufacturers, capitalists, and rulers all to task for selling the flesh-and-blood of the common person for profit in the execution of World War I. He attributed no good motives to any of them. His words later became the occasion where the Gospel Publishing House of the Assemblies of God was nearly shut down for marketing Bartleman's writings before they compromised and called for destroying his antiwar tract, *Present Day Conditions*. Parham and Bartleman saw their work as the hard-edge of prophecy to a degenerate state and its high priests in the mainstream religion. On the contrary, Seymour appears to have had a more pastoral focus.

The Assemblies of God were officially pacifist during World War I, although like other Pentecostals, they were generally not unwilling to compromise with government. Certainly a number went to war as noncombatants, not first choice, but also not negatively sanctioned by most Pentecostal groups. The only legitimate position in the government's eyes for a draftee from a denomination that was officially against participation in war was to serve as a noncombatant. However, we should not overstate either the inclination to go as noncombatant or the likely number who did so. Almost all Pentecostal denominations attempted to keep their men out of war.

It was not until 1967 that the leadership in the Assemblies of God crafted a new statement that suggested their position all along had not been pacifist, but freedom of conscience. Given that the justification for pacifism had been the Decalogue and Jesus' reiteration of the command not to kill in the Sermon on the Mount, the leaders in the Assemblies of God had to first work with other evangelicals to re-translate the word for "kill" in the Decalogue to murder, undercutting the force of the earlier translation.[2]

Another tradition of pacifism in Pentecostalism is the Church of God (Cleveland, Tennessee) under the leadership of A. J. Tomlinson. The Church of God had one of the shortest statements of any of the groups advocating "Against members going to war." Still, Tomlinson wrote extensively against war before the U.S. joined the War in 1917. Members knew exactly what he meant in his brief statement. The statement was justified by the Decalogue and Sermon on the Mount as well as Romans 12.

Unlike many statements of other Pentecostal groups and scriptural referents which couched the proscription against going to War in a framework of submission to governmental authority, this one did not give qualifications. The Church of God strain of pacifism was fairly productive both of adherents following the injunction, but also of splinter groups carrying on the tradition. As late as 1970, the Church of God, Huntsville, AL, was calling for something more than war-resistance. They called upon members and nations to do "exploits for Peace on Earth as risky as do men of war." They called for diversion of war budgets to social programs for the poor.

Just over one hundred years before Martin Luther King, Jr., preached his final sermon at the C. H. Mason auditorium in Memphis, Tennessee, ending with the haunting words, "I've been to the mountain," Mason, was born to former slaves. Fifty years before King died preaching nonviolent social change, Mason took a stand against fighting in World War I, as the leader of the Church of God in Christ. Mason met serious persecution for leading the pre-civil rights movement blacks against the violence of World War I. Mason argued like a holiness preacher connecting holiness and peacemaking based upon Hebrews 12:14, as the basis for "seeing God." According to Mason, "The members of said church are not allowed

2. Beaman, *Pentecostal Pacifism*, 114, 118.

to carry arms, to shed the blood of any man, and still be members of said church." The Church of God in Christ has maintained some voice against war to the present time.

In the Church of God, Stanberry, Missouri, we have one of the earliest records of Mexican-American voices against warfare. Jose M. Rodrigues and others were investigated along with writings from the denomination's paper, *The Bible Advocate*, in 1917. We also present two statements in Spanish on government and against going to war from Iglesia Cristiana Evangelica Mexicana, and La Iglesia De Dios Pentecostal, Incorporada, as well as the Filipino Assemblies of the First-Born, Inc., and Olazabal Council of Latin-American Churches (in English). The former are essentially translations of other Pentecostal denominational statements against going to war. Early on, as Pentecostalism spread across cultures, the message included peacemaking as part of its creed.

Another strain of Pentecostalism, the Oneness branch, so called for their Unitarian view of God, exhibited strong strains of interracial worship and pacifism at the time of World War I and beyond. Ironically, given the deep sense of ostracism that the oneness branch experienced, ostensibly for their view of God, they present what might be argued the most theologically grounded and nuanced pacifism at the time of World War I. This was most likely the hand of Garfield T. Haywood, African American leader of the Pentecostal Assemblies of the World (PAW), but may also have seen the input of Daniel C. O. Opperman, whose group also joined with the PAW for a time. Haywood was influenced by his time with the Church of God, Anderson, Indiana, known as the Evening Light Saints, and leaders in Holiness pacifism. Opperman had been a theological educator in Dowie's Christian Catholic Apostolic Church. The PAW document is unusual for placing a Pentecostal pacifist response to war within an overarching motif of being royal priests whose role is to bring society before God in worship and prayer, and to be a light to society and to serve society. It opens like the Westminster Catechism with the chief aim to serve God and bring glory. Only within the context of service, and bringing God's radiance to society in prophetic and priestly fashion, does pacifism make sense.

In the United Pentecostal Church International (UPCI) section we document the most recent example of a Pentecostal denomination who, after more than eighty years of maintaining a pacifist creed, and under internal pressure to conform, officially transitioned from nonviolence

132 PENTECOSTAL AND HOLINESS STATEMENTS ON WAR AND PEACE

to individual conscience. During a business session held on October 12, 2011, UPCI leaders presented *Resolution 6* which proposed amending the groups nonviolent doctrine titled *Conscientious Scruples*. Although the motive to delete pacifism was multifaceted, the resolution listed several reasons inspiring the deletion. Among them are: (1) Many members of the church are in combat positions; (2) Pacifism has mixed support, and; (3) Ministers are unwilling to sign the articles of faith because it contains a nonviolent stipulation, something many ministers now opposed. Therefore, church officials voted in favor of deleting their *Conscientious Scruples* position dating back to 1930 for a more nuanced and accommodating position. On August 29, 2012, the general superintendent reported that 79 percent of the general conference voted in favor of the amendment. The revision is now officially part of their new articles of faith.

Only slightly later in origin than other Pentecostal groups, The Foursquare Church, an evangelical Pentecostal movement, also known as International Church of the Foursquare Gospel, came to the fore as much less sectarian than their Pentecostal predecessors. Nevertheless, this social-oriented and flamboyant group, led by Aimee Semple McPherson, still had to grapple with the pacifist impulse after World War I. The Foursquare Church indeed had elements of nonhierarchical pacifism, so much so, that Foursquare ministers organized and petitioned church leaders to adopt a denomination-wide bylaw exempting all Foursquare constituents who voluntarily opposed bearing arms. This dissenting faction, though small, was vocal enough to successfully push through a pacifist clause, with McPherson's support, granting denominational support for conscientious objectors. Incidentally, the organizations patience for their pacifists quickly diminished and, by World War II, the movement chose instead the way of military force in hopes of defending and preserving "Christian America."

Furthermore, there were two groups that departed The Foursquare Church to establish their own religious organizations—the California Evangelistic Association and the Open Bible Evangelistic Association. Both groups supported nonviolence in their official creed. Oscar C. Harms, Foursquare pastor and leader, left The Foursquare Church in 1933 and established the California Evangelistic Association in 1934. Harms' group supported nonviolence, basing their position on the Decalogue, "Thou shalt not kill," and encouraged members toward noncombatant status if drafted. The other Foursquare offshoot, the Open Bible Evangelistic Association, was founded in 1932 by Foursquare leader John R. Richey. Richey, an influential leader, had roughly thirty-two Foursquare pastors follow his departure from McPherson's leadership. His group eventually merged with the Bible Standard Conference in 1935, and soon after, publicly went on record supporting Christian pacifism. (See Open Bible Standard Churches.)

A contemporary expression of Pentecostal Pacifism is found in the PCPJ.org or *Pentecostals and Charismatics for Peace and Justice.* The social activist organization, whose leader, Paul N. Alexander, has made the notion of Holy Spirit peace and justice a contemporary place for Spirit led challenges to a way of empire in the U.S. Especially unusual, is the challenge to the widespread evangelical and Pentecostal tendencies to blind militaristic support of unjust policies of the U.S./Israeli suppression of the aspirations of Palestinians, including Palestinian Christians.

Another contemporary expression is the Homestead Harvest of Waco, Texas. Originating in a Pentecostal Oneness denomination, the group is like an Amish group informed by Pentecostal norms of evangelism and a Oneness view of God. Unlike the Amish, they are not isolating from the larger society, but engaging the very economic, cultural, and communal beliefs of the larger society with an alternative model of community and family. Thus, while the main finding of this chapter is that the Pentecostal movement to begin with was widely opposed to war, we can see numerous examples of their shift away from being sectarian and world-denying to being mainstream and even very much a civil religion in support of the American State and its goals. Still, there are contemporary examples of those who are rediscovering a heritage of Holy Spirit prophetic peacemaking, and sometimes not in continuity with their immediate past, but jumping to something refreshingly new.

APOSTOLIC CHURCH (BAY CITY, TEXAS)
[Military Service], 1954

Members of the Apostolic Church, both ministers and laymen, are exhorted to request non-combatant service when they enter the service of their country. However, if an individual within

134 PENTECOSTAL AND HOLINESS STATEMENTS ON WAR AND PEACE

the church has no scruples concerning the bearing of arms, this position is not to be made a test of membership in the church.[3]

APOSTOLIC FAITH (BAXTER SPRINGS, KANSAS), FOUNDED 1906

Charles Fox Parham, American Pentecostal Pioneer

[NATIONALISM], 1911

Yet while thousands of men will volunteer and suffer the hardships and privations of an earthly war for glory, few, indeed, will volunteer and endure the slightest privations for the Master's kingdom and eternal glory.

The past order of civilization was upheld by the power of nationalism, which in turn was upheld by the spirit of patriotism, which divided the peoples of the world by geographical boundaries, over which each fought the other until they turned the world into shamble. The ruling power of this old order has always been the rich, who exploited the masses for profit or drove them in masse to war, to perpetuate their misrule. The principle teachers of patriotism maintaining nationalism were the churches, who have lost their spiritual power and been forsaken of God. Thus, on one side of the old order in the coming struggle, will be arrayed the governments, the rich, and the churches, and whatever forces they can drive or patriotically inspire to fight for them. On the other hand the new order that rises out of the sea of humanity knows no national boundaries, believing in the universal brotherhood of mankind and the establishment of the teachings of Jesus Christ as a foundation for all laws, whether political or social.[4]

3. Moore, "Handbook of Pentecostal Denominations," 274. See also *The Apostolic Church, Doctrine and Discipline*, 6.

4. Charles F. Parham, *Everlasting Gospel*, 27–28. Parham quoted in Beaman, *Pentecostal Pacifism*, 52–53. Parham (1873–1929) combined James 5 and the apocryphal vision attributed to George Washington in the American foundation myth with the speculations of socialist pamphleteers. Parham was the founder of the Apostolic Faith, Baxter, Kansas, and is recognized as one of the founders of North American classical Pentecostal theology, originating in Topeka, Kansas, in 1901. His main contribution to Pentecostalism included the doctrine of initial evidence—speaking in tongues—which served as a main distinction between Pentecostals and the Holiness movement. He also made missions a primary distinctive of Pentecostal ministry and theology. Parham "connected the basic tenets that later defined the movement: evangelical-style conversion, sanctification, divine healing, premillennialism, and the eschatological return of Holy Spirit power evidenced by glossolalia [speaking in tongues]." Quoted in Goff,

"WAR! WAR! WAR!," 1914

Recapitulation: War! War! War!—What For? To murder a fellow-creature! To receive therefore even less than thirty pieces of silver, and perhaps live to receive the plaudits and honor of a more cowardly country and imbecile nation; for that nation is imbecile which retains its existence through the struggling exploits of war. We hang our heads in shame to see Christian nations and individuals yield themselves to the embrace of the Moloch-God, Patriotism, whose principle doctrine was honor (?), there to have consumed in the death struggle the feeling of philanthropy and humanity; spending millions to build the fires for the consummation of these virtues, while the cause of Christ languishes, heaven loses, hell opens her jaws, and so-called Christian nations feed (by war) to satisfy her gluttonous appetite . . .

Yet while thousands of men will volunteer and suffer the hardships and privations of an earthly war for glory, few, indeed, will volunteer and endure the slightest privations for the Master's kingdom and eternal glory.[5]

"Victory" by Lillian Thistlethwaite, 1912

"BE NOT OVERCOME OF EVIL, BUT OVERCOME EVIL WITH GOOD." Romans 12:21.

The majority of the human race from the beginning of time to the present age, though vaguely acknowledging a Supreme Being, have practiced the law of the "survival of the fittest;" "might has been right" in personal conflict and national achievements, and the power of "brain or brawn" the mark of superiority under the general competitive systems.

At intervals during the world's history, men of humble minds, chosen of God and quickened by His spirit, have dared to stem the tide and reveal the greater law of non-resistance, picturing to

---

"Charles Fox Parham," 955–57. Additionally, in context of Parham's ethic of war, he chastised "churches for their alliance with the state and opposition to the poor" and condemned the nations of Europe for "commercial and imperialistic motivations for the war," often highlighting the obvious "contrast between the call to arms and the call to be a missionary." Quoted in Beaman, *Pentecostal Pacifism*, 52–3.

5. Parnham, "War! War! War!," 78–83. Parham quoted in Beaman, *Pentecostal Pacifism*, 53–54.

at least some degree the character and attributes of God and his requirements for humanity.

But when the fullness of time was come, God sent forth his Son, made of a woman, made under the law, "to redeem them that were under the law that we might receive the adoption of sons." In the Son was manifested the "fullness of the God-head bodily." "God was in Christ, reconciling the world unto himself," yet, as was prophesied of Him, He came to be rejected, crucified and slain, that His purposes might be fulfilled thru [sic] perfect "obedience even unto death," hence the victory over the law of sin and death thru [sic] non-resistance, and the living faith which gave him power to lay down his life and power to take it again.

. . . To the Captain of our salvation alone belongs this overcoming power, and in him we are made more than conquerors, as in obedience to Divine Law, we "resist not evil," "love our enemies," "bless and curse not," and by His spirit are we enabled to say, "Father forgive them, they know not what they do." Thus by taking up of the cross and walking under the new law of love, which is service to humanity, the self is slain, as the "ego" has lost his life for Christ's sake and the gospel's and found the "more abundant life," and the welcome of the Maker: "Inasmuch as ye have done it unto the least of one of these my brethren, ye have done it unto me," ushers us into the "joy of the Lord" as "many sons are brought unto glory."[6]

From *Apostolic Faith*, Baxter Springs, KS, [Magazine], 1912

We believe that the end of the age is so nigh that we have not time to dabble in politics, but with minds not distracted by the world we must snatch precious lives as brands from the burning. If this is fanaticism it has worked well in this town. We believe that the open saloon is an evil but so are blind pigs. The saloon keeper in many cases is human, and if everyone who believes God would fast and pray they could remove the evil sooner than by voting. Fighting by sword or ballot arouses all the carnal there is in people and they will sell and drink liquor at any cost.[7]

---

6. Thistlethwaite, "Victory," 1–3. Emphasis in original. Thistlethwaite was the mother-in-law of Charles Fox Parham, a Quaker before joining the Apostolic Faith, herself an evangelist.

7. *Apostolic Faith*, 2. This document gives a summary of Parham's teaching at meetings in Perris, Riverside, CA.

J. H. Black in *Apostolic Faith*, 1912

Black characterized Parham's message as "a man full of the Holy Spirit, bringing a message of peace on earth and good will to men; preaching the full gospel and thereby gladdening the hearts of many by leading them into the full gospel as taught by our Lord and Savior Jesus Christ."[8]

APOSTOLIC FAITH MISSION

William J. Seymour (1870–1922)

"The New Birth," 1915

Jesus told him His Kingdom was not of this world. He said, "If My Kingdom was of this world then would My servants fight, that I should not be delivered to the Jews; but now is My Kingdom not from hence." Pilate asked Him about His Kingdom and kingship, so He confessed He was a King over His people in the Holy Spirit . . .[9]

"The Character of the Church," 1915

A church constitutes a kind of spiritual kingdom in the world, but not of the world; whose King is Christ; whose law is His word; whose instructions are His ordinances; whose duty is His service; whose reward is His blessing. In all matters of faith and conscience, as well as in all matters of internal order and government, a church is "under law to Christ" (1 Cor. 9:21); but as men and citizens, its members must "submit themselves to governors" (1 Peter 2:14), like other men, so far as shall not interfere with, or contravene, the claims of the divine law and authority upon them. They must "render unto Caesar the things that are Caesar's, and unto God the things that are God's," remembering that God's claims are supreme, and annihilate all claims that contradict or oppose them (Matt. 22:21).[10]

---

8. J. H. Black, "Birthday Anniversary," 12.

9. Seymour, *The Doctrines and Discipline of Azusa Street*, 62.

10. Ibid., 93.

138   PENTECOSTAL AND HOLINESS STATEMENTS ON WAR AND PEACE

Frank Bartleman, Pastor and Participant-Reporter to the Azusa Street Revival[11]

"What Will the Harvest Be?" 1915

This War is not a holy war. It is the result of pride, greed, jealousy, hatred, hypocrisy, etc. . . . The whole thing is a game of chess, with the nations as the players. Kings and leaders, capitalists, are the chess men. They play their nations as the stake. Rulers for their private purse, bankers and financiers of the world for gain, munition manufacturers and provision merchants, all work together in this game. Flesh and blood of the common people, soldiers, are either forced or hired to do the fighting. Rev. 18:13.[12]

War and the Christian, n.d.

No Christian going into war can ever be quite the same again. He has lost the opportunity, possibly of a life-time, of standing true to Christ in a supreme test. For here is the supreme test of a Christian, to be killed rather than to kill. He can never forget his participation in the war, and his betrayal of the principles of the Christ who died for all men. A Christian must refuse to obey any spirit contrary to the Gospel. All elements of war are contrary to the teachings of the Scripture. Hate, murder, lust, etc., none of them fruits of the Spirit. No one can kill a man, and yet love him. We have got to love all men alike. War cannot be Christian. Ask the boys in camp, or on the battlefield. They will tell you it is hell, from end to end. Compare it with the Sermon on the Mount.

. . . Patriotism in most cases has been proven to spell "Graft." "Dollar" patriotism. War bonds are reduced in price until the poor man is either forced or frightened into unloading. . . . The innocent are sent to do the killing, and be killed. Those responsible for the wars are generally beyond its reach. . . . A "war church" is a Harlot church.[13]

11. This is not to suggest that Bartleman (1871–1936) was a member of the Azusa Street Mission or an official spokesperson for it. However, his name is closely associated with reporting on the Azusa Street Revival, and as such he was attempting for a time (1906–1908) to be related to that revival.

12. Bartleman, "What Will the Harvest Be?" 1.

13. Bartleman, *War and the Christian*, 3–4.

"Christian Citizenship," n.d.

He who justifies the church in going to war under the Gospel, proves he knows absolutely nothing of the nature of the Gospel. . . . In times of war we are forbidden to preach the Gospel. One must preach murder, hate and revenge. The Gospel teaches "love your enemy, do good to them that hate you, and pray for them that despitefully use you." And "resist not evil." . . . The Christian must obey the Gospel. We are bound to "obey God rather than men." Gov't is squarely up against God in its demands on Christians during war time. And Christians are squarely up against the question whether they shall obey God or man. . . .

Can we imagine Jesus or the Apostles going to war at the behest of the Roman government? Converting men by the power of the Gospel, and later killing these same converts, across some imaginary boundary line? Imagine Christian meeting Christian on the actual field of battle, and murdering one another. To a really converted man the idea is unthinkable. First Gospel, then bullets? How are the mighty fallen! War for what? Territory, commerce, etc., for the supremacy of one nation over another. Our Gospel is a Gospel of love, not hate and murder.

The Christian dare not obey even government decree when opposing the command of God to him. He must not seek to harm an enemy. He cannot engage in war under any circumstances without doing violence to the Spirit and command of Christ . . .

One of the greatest crimes of the late war was that of robbing the church of her sacred calling and "pilgrim" role, turning her aside from the saving of souls, to plunge into the vortex of world politics and patriotism, with all its fallen prejudices and preferences, avarices, cruelties, hates and murders . . .

The church is no place to flaunt flags of national preference. God's grace and Gospel are international. Christ died for all men. . . . The flags represent fallen nations, with fallen nationalistic, sectional prides, ambitions, etc., that breed strife, enmity, jealousy and war, for they are without Christ. We do not belong to them.[14]

14. Bartleman, "Christian Citizenship," 1–2. The word "Christian" is not capitalized in the original manuscript.

140   PENTECOSTAL AND HOLINESS STATEMENTS ON WAR AND PEACE

"In the Last Days," 1916

The nations at war seem gradually to be settling down to whole-sale killing as the normal order. This is terrible. The outlook is anything but assuring. There is no peace in sight. The world's conscience is being hardened. The milk of human kindness will run slowly. Great increase of cruelty is bound to follow this war. In fact violence is already greatly on the increase, even in our own land. A hardening is coming upon the people. This hardening of spirit is very evident to spiritual people. It is in the very atmosphere. . . . God's Spirit is being driven out. The Gospel of love and grace has less attraction for the masses. They are no longer greatly appealed to.

. . . Selfishness is overwhelming. There seems little interest even in the awful suffering and fate of Europe except for the dollars that can be made out of her distress. In fact there seems little feeling even for suffering in America. Monopolists are increasing prices in food stuffs, etc., against the common people. Fattening on their blood, taking advantage of their distress. They are human leeches. The rich man's dog gets more meat than the poor man's family. Great increase of crime must naturally follow increased want. Men grow desperate in their need, when their children are starving.

Our wheat is being shipped to Europe. We have not nearly enough now to feed our own people in this country until next harvest. Two percent of the people are profiting by this market, while ninety-eight per cent are paying fancy prices, or going hungry. And the worst is yet to come along this line. Jas. 5.

In a single week recently thirty-million dollars worth of ammunition and shells was shipped from New York to the allies. Millions of men have been sent suddenly to account to their Maker in hot blood through this infernal trade of ours. Oceans of hatred unto murder have been stirred up. And shall we not also account for this? Has the dollar become almighty to us? Nothing must stop reason, humanity, principle, right, love, mercy, a pitying, pleading Savior, all must be trampled under foot as long as we can make a dollar. We are creating seas of human misery, but we are gaining dollars. Is life given to make dollars, just dollars, at the expense of life and happiness, the groans and tears of outraged humanity, the murder of millions of men, and the sufferings of women and children? Must we have dollars?

This war has cost to date seventy-two-billion dollars. It is costing every hour four million dollars, to destroy men. The accumulations and savings of the entire world for fourteen years have been destroyed in two years. Fifty-billion dollar's worth of property has been destroyed. Six million women and children have been made homeless. Tens of thousands have died of starvation. Four million have been killed. Eight million have been wounded. Three million, seven hundred thousand are missing. One hundred and twenty-five thousand square miles of territory has been laid waste. What raving madness!

The U.S. Gov't Treasury and Assay Office holds to-day five hundred million dollars in gold. More than was ever gathered in one spot before since the world began. They say another year of war will free U.S. of every dollar of indebtedness to any other country. No nation has ever held such a position in the world before. And this they call prosperity. But at what cost! The jealousy of the whole world will be excited. That means war. And we are preparing. Not repenting. Nations seek God in times of adversity only. We are full of pride. Our trust is in defense, not God. We are not calling on God.[15]

APOSTOLIC FAITH (PORTLAND, OREGON)

From *The Apostolic Faith Doctrines*, 1917

War—it is our firm conviction, supported by the Word of God, our conscience bearing us witness, that we cannot take up arms against our fellow men, however great may seem the provocation or however just the cause might seem: it being the teaching of the Spirit of the Gospel presented by Christ in his sermon on the mount. Matt. 5:39–46. We maintain the highest regard for our flag and teach absolute respect for the laws and officials of our country according to Romans 13:1–7 and I Peter 2:13–14, as long as it does not violate our conscience. "For we ought to obey God rather than man." Acts 5:29. And we hold the unalienable right to worship God according to the dictates of our conscience.[16]

---

15. Bartleman, "In the Last Days," 393–94.

16. *Apostolic Faith (Portland, Oregon)*, 2. The *Apostolic Faith* magazine was not dated then. From context, we have dated it to 1917. The *Apostolic Faith* magazine collection is housed at the Apostolic Faith Headquarters, Portland, Oregon. This group, transplanted from the Azusa Street Revival, in 1906, was pacifist during World War I. See "Suspect Violation of Espionage Act," 2.

142   PENTECOSTAL AND HOLINESS STATEMENTS ON WAR AND PEACE

Baptismal photo courtesy of Apostolic Faith, Portland, OR. Used by permission.

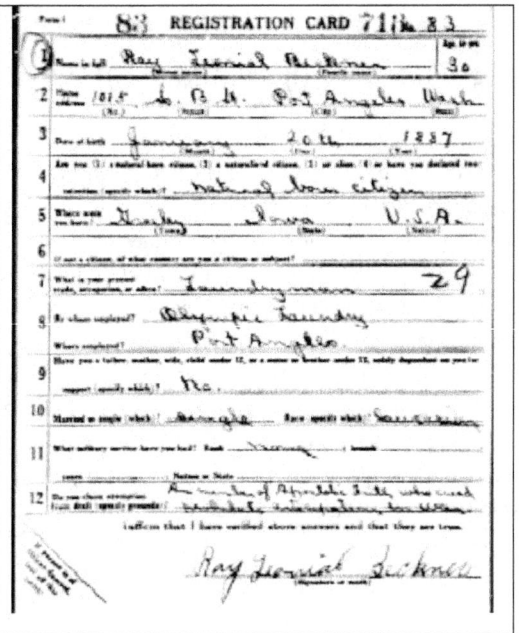

This is the WWI draft card of Ray Leonial Beckner, religious objector, and member of the Apostolic Faith, Portland, OR.[17]

17. This image reprinted by permission of Ancestry.com. To view additional family history records, please visit www.ancestry.com.

APOSTOLIC FAITH OR CHURCH OF GOD (MULBERRY, KANSAS / TULSA, OKLAHOMA) ALSO KNOWN AS CHURCH OF GOD OF THE APOSTOLIC FAITH (TULSA, OKLAHOMA)

"War," 1918 / 1966

It is our firm conviction, supported by the Word of God, our conscience also bearing us witness, that we cannot take up arms against our fellow men, however great the provocation or however just the cause might seem: it being the teaching of the spirit of the Gospel presented by Christ in His Sermon on the Mount.

Mat. 5:39–46. Also Rev. 13:10, Luke 18–18:20, [sic] Heb. 12:14.

We maintain the highest regard for our flag and teach absolute respect for the laws and officials of our country according to Romans 13:1–7 and 1 Peter 2:13–14, as far as it does not violate our conscience. "For we ought to obey God rather than man." Acts 5:29, and we hold the unalienable right to worship God according to the dictates of our own conscience.

[1966 addition] That we go as far as we conscientiously can in complying with the demands of our government in respect to war or military service has been our teaching since 1906 and as exemplified in the first and second world war [sic] draft and service.[18]

ASSEMBLIES OF GOD

"Pentecostal Saints Opposed to War," 1915

The Pentecostal people, as a whole, are uncompromisingly opposed to war, having much the same spirit as the early Quakers, who would rather be shot themselves than that they should shed the blood of their fellow-men.[19]

---

18. Titus and Buckles, *Minutes of Apostolic Faith or Church of God, Mulberry, Kansas*; *The Articles of Faith of the General Conference of The Church of God of the Apostolic Faith*, 5–6. See also *Minutes of Conference Meeting of The Apostolic Faith or Church of God*, 5.

19. "Pentecostal Saints Opposed to War," 1.

144 PENTECOSTAL AND HOLINESS STATEMENTS ON WAR AND PEACE

"Resolution Concerning the Attitude of the General Council of the Assemblies of God toward Military Service Which Involves the Actual Participation in the Destruction of Human Life," 1917

While recognizing Human Government as of Divine ordination and affirming our unswerving loyalty to the Government of the United States, nevertheless we are constrained to define our position with reference to the taking of human life.

WHEREAS, in the Constitutional Resolution adopted at the Hot Springs General Council, April 1–10, 1914, we plainly declare the Holy Inspired Scriptures to be the all-sufficient rule of faith and practice, and

WHEREAS the Scriptures deal plainly with the obligations and relations of humanity, setting forth the principles of "Peace on earth, good will toward men." (Luke 2:14); and

WHEREAS we, as followers of the Lord Jesus Christ, the Prince of Peace, believe in implicit obedience to the Divine commands and precepts which instruct us to "Follow peace with all men," (Heb. 12:14); "Thou shall not kill," (Exod. 20:13); "Resist not evil," (Matt. 5:39); "Love your enemies," (Matt.5:44): etc. and

WHEREAS these and other Scriptures have always been accepted and interpreted by our churches as prohibiting Christians from shedding blood or taking human life;

THEREFORE we, as a body of Christians, while purposing to fulfill all the obligations of loyal citizenship, are nevertheless constrained to declare we cannot conscientiously participate in war and armed resistance which involves the actual destruction of human life, since this is contrary to our view of the clear teachings of the inspired Word of God, which is the sole basis of our faith.[20]

Eudorus N. Bell, 1917

War is wrong, and no Christian should go who can honorably and lawfully keep out of it.[21]

---

20. "Resolution Concerning the Attitude of the General Council of the Assemblies of God Toward Military Service," 6. Emphasis in original.

21. Bell, "Questions and Answers," 9. Bell was the first General Chairman (title later changed to General Superintendent) of the Assemblies of God. Here he responded to the question: Does the Assemblies of God have a position on war and conscientious

"New Bylaws on Military Service," 1967

As a movement we affirm our loyalty to the government of the United States in war or peace. We shall continue to insist, as we have historically, on the right of each member to choose for himself whether to declare his position as a combatant, a non-combatant, or a conscientious objector.[22]

"War and Conscientious Objectors," 1967

The Assemblies of God position on war and conscientious objectors states: "As a Movement we affirm our loyalty to the government of the United States in war or peace. We shall continue to insist, as we have historically, on the right of each member to choose for himself whether to declare his position as a combatant [one who willingly serves in positions of violence], a noncombatant [one who serves only in nonviolent ways], or a conscientious objector [one who refuses to participate in any form of military service because of personal convictions regarding war]." (Article XXII of the Bylaws)

The implications of the above statement are clear. The Assemblies of God is committed to a position of loyalty to the government. Second, that loyalty is not imperiled by the presence of war. And third, all members are encouraged to exercise their personal convictions in how they will respond during times of war whether combatant, noncombatant, or as a conscientious objector.

What are the biblical principles which support this position? 1) The Scriptures call for civic loyalty: "Everyone must submit himself to governing authorities, for there is no authority except that which God has established" (Romans 13:1). 2) On occasion, those authorities must bear arms: "He does not bear the sword for nothing. He is God's servant, an agent of wrath to bring punishment on the wrongdoer" (Romans 13:4). 3) The Scriptures call for the employment of personal conscience in all matters. "Each of us will give an account of himself to God" (Romans 14:12).

---

objectors? Although Bell was compelled towards pacifism, his views were tempered with a strong commitment to patriotism and civil obedience. Bell ultimately led the way for Pentecostals to justify bearing arms in war. See Beaman, *Pentecostal Pacifism*, 75–77.

22. "New Bylaws on Military Service Adopted," 7.

In light of this, how are we to understand the sixth commandment: "You shall not murder" (Exodus 20:13)? The Hebrew word used here (raisach) in the ancient manuscripts is descriptive of an act of willful and personal vengeance. While the outcome may be similar to the killings of war, the motive and driving force are quite different. The language of Exodus 20:13 does not suggest that we are to disallow participation in war, even if that participation involves killing. The preservation of peace and tranquillity sometimes makes this response imperative.

The Assemblies of God as a movement deplores war. Therefore we are committed to its avoidance as much as accountability, sensibility, and responsibility allow. This will be the necessary posture, until the Prince of Peace—Jesus Christ—establishes His reign over a world that is now characterized by violence, wickedness, and war.[23]

---

23. "War and Conscientious Objectors." This 1967 statement likely had later editorial additions. The statement traces to 1967, and the explanation (most of it) is recent. The resolution, unequivocally, supports the killing-murder distinction, something previously lacking within first-generation Pentecostal arguments regarding war. In fact, Exodus 20:13 was a main scripture passage used by leaders and members to condemn the taking of human life during warfare. E. N. Bell and Ernest S. Williams, both Assemblies of God general superintendents, likely represented the group of Pentecostals who were making the theological transition arguing that the word "kill" in the Decalogue really meant "murder." Consequently, this reinterpretation rendered Exodus 20:13 irrelevant to questions pertaining to such issues as war and capital punishment. For example, by 1917, the majority of the Assemblies of God constituency supported conscientious objection to bearing arms by referencing Exodus 20:13, "You shall not kill." By 1953, however, the leadership altered their statement on military service by removing the sixth commandment. The same scripture once used to renounce killing was later used to justify its support. For an in-depth study of the sixth command and its usage within Pentecostal and other religious groups to justify taking life, see Bailey, *"You Shall Not Kill Or You Shall Not Murder?"* Bailey shows how at the very same time the Assemblies of God was promoting the kill-murder distinction, Evangelicals were retranslating the sixth command thereby lending biblical support for Christian participation in warfare. Additionally, before this new way of interpreting Exodus 20:13, many Holiness-Pentecostal groups in the early twentieth century referenced this passage and its reiteration in the Sermon on the Mount to show that one could not take human life in war. Regarding Christian participating in killing, a survey was carried out in 2001 among American Assemblies of God ministers. An astonishing 93 percent of pastors agreed with the statement: "It is appropriate for a Christian to support war." Sixty-five percent agreed that the principles of Jesus support war." Seventy-one percent affirmed they "would kill in a war." Quoted in Alexander, "Speaking in the Tongues of Nonviolence," 17.

Pentecostal Statements   147

Stanley M. Horton, AG World War II Conscientious Objector, 2009

At that time [World War II], pacifism was quite commonly taught in our Assemblies of God churches and literature. . . . Of course, you can't forget what Jesus said to Pilate, "If My kingdom were of this world, my soldiers would fight. But my kingdom is not of this world." So our primary concern needs to be for the kingdom of God and not primarily for the kingdoms of this earth. . . . We should encourage young people . . . to spread the gospel, and establish the church, and not be so quick to think that they can solve the world's problems with war and conflict, which I still don't believe we can. I think that Jesus was certainly the model[,] . . . that Jesus was here to give his life in order to save others, rather than to take life. And that there was a complete change here in the way that God was dealing with people, now that Jesus had come. . . . I think there should be room for people who, by their own conscience, feel that they should be conscientious objectors.[24]

ASSEMBLIES OF THE LORD JESUS CHRIST
"Civil Government," 1965

All civil magistrates are ordained of God for peace, safety and the welfare of all people (Rom. 13:1–10; Titus 3:1–2; I Peter 2:13–14); therefore, it is our duty to be in obedience to all requirements of the laws that are not contrary to the Word of God, and that do not force one to the violation of the sixth commandment, by bearing arms. It is our duty to honor them, pay tribute, or such taxation as may be required without murmuring (Matt. 17:24–27; 22:17–21), and show respect to them in all lawful requirements to the civil government.[25]

24. Quoted in Mittelstadt and Paugh, "The Social Conscience of Stanley Horton," 15–6. Stanley M. Horton (1916–) is a prolific Pentecostal author, educator, and theologian. Horton shared his pacifist convictions with the group Pentecostals and Charismatics for Peace and Justice (www.PCPJ.org).

25. "Articles of Faith of the Assemblies of the Lord Jesus Christ," 14.

148   PENTECOSTAL AND HOLINESS STATEMENTS ON WAR AND PEACE

"Conscientious Scruples," 1965

We propose to fulfill all the obligations of loyal citizens, but are constrained to declare against participation in combatant service in war, armed insurrection, property destruction, aiding or abetting in or the actual destruction of human life.

Furthermore, we cannot conscientiously affiliate with any union, boycott, or organization which will force or bind any of its members to perform any duties contrary to our conscience, or receive any mark, without our right to affirm or reject the same.

However, we regret the false impression created by some groups, or so-called, "conscientious objectors," that to obey the Bible is to have contempt for law or magistrates, to be disloyal to our government and in sympathy with our enemies, or to be unwilling to sacrifice for the preservation of our commonwealth. This attitude would be as contemptible to use as to any patriot. The Word of God commands us to do violence to no man. It also commands us that first of all we are to pray for rulers of our country. We therefore, exhort our members to freely and willingly respond to the call of our Government, except in the matter of bearing arms. When we say service, we mean service—no matter how hard or dangerous. The true church has no more place for cowards than has the nation. First of all, however, let us earnestly pray that we will with honor be kept out of war.

We believe that we can be consistent in service to our Government in certain noncombatant capacities, but not in the bearing of arms.[26]

BETHEL BAPTIST ASSEMBLY, INC.

Civil Government, n.d.

The Bethel Baptist Assembly Inc. hereby declares its loyalty to our government and to its Chief Executive, and hereby states its fixed purpose to assist our government in every way morally possible consistent with our faith. Romans 13:1–7.

The Bethel Baptist Assembly believes that nations can and should, whenever possible, settle their differences without going to war; however, in the event of war, if a member engages in

---

26. Ibid., 15.

combatant service, it will not affect his status with the Assembly. In case a member is called into military service who has conscientious objections to combatant service, the Assembly will support him in his constitutional rights.[27]

CALIFORNIA EVANGELISTIC ASSOCIATION
"Article XVII: Relation to War," 1939

Whereas, we believe that our government is ordained of God and whereas, we are thankful to the government of the United States of America, for the freedom to worship God according to the dictates of our own conscience, and

Whereas, our Bible teaches us, "Thou shalt not kill," therefore be it resolved that in the time of war, we shall be glad to be of service to our government in any way consistent with noncombative service.[28]

CALVARY PENTECOSTAL CHURCH
"Loyalty to the Government of the United States and Military Service," 1962

The Calvary Pentecostal Church, Inc., recognizes Human Government as of Divine ordination and affirms its unswerving loyalty to the Government of the United States and to the President of the United States, and as a body of Christians who pledge to fulfill all the obligations of loyal citizenship, nevertheless we are constrained to define our position with reference to the taking of human life.

---

27. *Articles of Faith of the Bethel Baptist Assembly Inc.*, 3.

28. *Constitution and By-Laws of the California Evangelistic Association*, 16. Oscar C. Harms, before establishing the California Evangelistic Association, served under the leadership of Aimee Semple McPherson as a Foursquare District Supervisor in the early 1930s. He pastored a Foursquare congregation in Long Beach, California, and traveled extensively around the country as an evangelist. The last reference of Harms in the *Foursquare Crusader* was in June 1933. His son, likely Raymond Harms, was a member of the board of the California Evangelistic Association. This is one of the two groups (see Open Bible Standard) that departed The Foursquare Church, and after establishing their own religious movement, went on record supporting Christian pacifism.

150   PENTECOSTAL AND HOLINESS STATEMENTS ON WAR AND PEACE

Whereas, The command of God is "Thou shalt not kill," Exodus 20:13, but "Follow peace with all men," Hebrews 12:4; and

Whereas, We as followers of the Lord Jesus Christ, believe in implicit obedience to the Divine command we cannot conscientiously participate in war and armed resistance which involves the actual taking of human life, since this is contrary to what we believe to be the clear teachings of the Bible, the inspired Word of God, which is our only basis of our faith. Therefore, Be it

Resolved, That the Calvary Pentecostal Church, Inc. restate its pledge of loyalty to our government and to our President, and our purpose to assist and support in every way morally possible, consistent with our faith.[29]

CHURCH OF GOD (CLEVELAND, TENNESSEE)

Ambrose Jessup Tomlinson (1865–1943), COG founder

"The Present Situation," 1915

Great nations are in war against each other. As nations they are doing the very thing that they forbid by their civil laws. Bloodshed and murder were forbidden by their laws and punishable by death or imprisonment, and the perpetrator was looked upon as a mean low down character, but now these same nations are engaged in a wholesale slaughter accounting human life as of no value, and the bloodshed has become an honor. If this is not vilainous [sic] then we are without expression.

Boys and men are snatched away from their homes and loved ones and rushed off to war and shot down by the thousands like cattle and hogs in the slaughter pens.

Homes are broken up never to be repaired; property destroyed by the ravages of war and people who were toiling pleasantly along a few weeks ago are reduced to poverty and starvation to-day.

Women are helpless, [comma added] little innocent children are nothing more than vagabonds on the earth.

---

29. "Scriptural Statement of Fundamentals," in *Constitution and By-Laws of the Calvary Pentecostal Church*, 16. Piepkorn, *Profiles in Belief*, 119, notes that the founders of the Calvary Pentecostal Church, Olympia, Washington, originated from the Assemblies of God in the 1920s because of what they regarded as unwarranted interference by the denominational authorities in the affairs of local congregations.

Yesterday the nations of the earth were boasting of their high state of civilization, holding their peace conferences and planning to step right into a state of millennial peacefulness; to-day they are plunged beneath the surface of a crimson sea and bathing themselves in the blood of uncivilized barbarism. So-called christian [sic] nations have lost their identity as such and fallen into their own snares.

They are proving that their profession of christianity [sic] was only a sham and the vilest grade of hypocrisy. They had just as well sail under their own banner (that of the antichrist) and never again disgrace the worthy name of our Lord and Savior Jesus Christ by trying to hide under His name. This is a time for Satan.

Millions of souls are driven by the cruel war lash into the slaughter-pens of hell. This, however, is probably no worse in God's sight than the hypocritical absurdity of much so-called christianity [sic] that prevails in both North and South America as well as the other countries of the world.[30]

"LOYALTY AND PERSEVERANCE," 1916

There is surely nothing more beautiful than real loyalty to Christ. It is counted patriotic for one to be loyal to his country. It is surely more than patriotism for one to be loyal to our Lord and King.

One may love his country and be obedient to its laws, and love it so well that he will die on the battlefield in its defense, and still be disloyal to God. And on the other hand one may be loyal to Christ and be disloyal to his country, because the laws of the country often conflict with the laws of Christ. Acts 4:19, Acts 5:29.

When this is found to be the case, then it becomes our part to decide which of the two we will obey. Then we have to decide whether we will be loyal to Christ and break the laws of the country, or obey the laws of the country and be disloyal to Christ.[31]

---

30. Tomlinson, "The Present Situation," 1. Excerpt.

31. Tomlinson, "Loyalty and Perseverance," 1. Excerpt.

"The Awful World War," 1917

While Jesus said that there would be wars, there is no statement nor inference whatever that shows He endorsed or favored war. His teaching is altogether to the contrary. Better suffer wrong than to do wrong, is the spirit of Christ. At one time He said, "If my kingdom were of this world, then would my servants fight." John 18:36. But as His kingdom is not of this world. He teaches us to resist not evil, (Math. 5:39) but rather if they smite you on one cheek turn the other also.

Our attitude toward war can be no other way than that taught by our Lord. If we are of the world so we can take part in the wars then we are not of His kingdom. We cannot be of the world and of the Lord at the same time. . . . As for me I cannot fight Germany, nor lend my influence in that direction and support such a movement. I can be imposed upon, but I cannot fight.

No doubt many of our people are wondering what do to in case our country gets into war. Shall we enlist in the governmental service and fight for our rights? Can we shoulder a gun and march out to the battle front and point our gun toward our enemy and fire into his ranks and send his soul to hell, when Jesus, our King, tells us to love our enemies? Math. 5:44.

There is scarcely any use for me to instruct our people about going to war, because the Holy Ghost, if given perfect right of way, will teach every soul to have the spirit of the Master. And it is plainly shown in the Book [Bible] that it is not the spirit of the Master to fight.

Jesus loves the world. This takes in Germany as well as America. If we are Christ's, then we love the world too, and our love is not limited to our own native country. If Jesus fought because His rights were trampled upon, then we should do the same. But where do we see Him slaying the multitudes because they were trampling upon His rights? It is pride and selfishness usually that leads to war.

It is not my purpose to discuss war from the world standpoint. It is only my part to show that the Lord's children are citizens of another country. "Not of the world," says Jesus, "even as I am not of the world." Jno. 17:16. "For our citizenship (R.V.) is in heaven." Philippians 3:20. The War in which we are engaged is of far more importance than the world wars being waged. Ours is a spiritual warfare, that seeks to save souls from hell instead of sending them there by flashing steel into their vitals.

. . . If War is declared on our country, much pressure will be brought to bear to influence our young men to volunteer. Enthusiasm will run high. The appeal to arms to support our country will catch like wild fire. No body [sic] will want to be called a coward at such a time and away they will go, and alas many, many, will never return. It may be easy for our own church boys to be caught by the spell. We must have them prepared to say, no, and stay as far away from the influence as possible.[32]

"Teachings," 1917 (Church of God, Cleveland, TN)

Against members going to war—Ex. 20:13, 1 Chron. 28:3, Psalm 120:7, Math. 5:38–48; 6:14, 15; 26:50–56, Luke 22:49–52, John 18:10, 11, 36; Rom. 12:19.[33]

CHURCH OF GOD (HUNTSVILLE, ALABAMA)
[War Budget], 1970

One of the first steps in the kingdom of the saints would be the boldest, to change the world from a program of war to a program of peace. This would take the form of transposing the war budget of the United States, for example, to the building up of peoples in less fortunate circumstances both at home and abroad . . .

We expect the people of God to do exploits for Peace on Earth as daring and risky as do men of war. Let our nation risk its neck for Peace like we call on our finest youth for war! Yes, that is my proposal, that with pure faith in God, we beat our swords into plowshares, and learn war no more.[34]

CHURCH OF GOD IN CHRIST
"Article IX of Magistrates and Civil Governments," 1911

We believe that civil magistrates are ordained for the peace, safety, and good of the people. That it is our duty to pray for

32. Tomlinson, "The Awful World War," 1. Excerpt.

33. "Teachings," in *Church of God General Assembly Minutes*, 65.

34. *The Book of Doctrines: 1903–1970*, 157–158. Quoted in Beaman, *Pentecostal Pacifism*, 93.

154 PENTECOSTAL AND HOLINESS STATEMENTS ON WAR AND PEACE

them, and obey them in all things which is not contrary to the word of God, and that does not take authority over, or force the conscience in matters of bearing arms or going to war. That it is our duty to honor them, pay tribute, to respect them in all lawful requirements of civil government.[35]

"Article 17" [Political Governments], 1917

We believe that governments are God-given institutions for the benefit of mankind. We admonish and exhort our members to honor magistrates, and the powers to be, to respect and obey the civil laws.

We hereby and herewith declare our loyalty to the President and the Constitution of the United States, and pledge fidelity to the flag for which the Republic stands, but as a God-fearing, peace-loving, and law-abiding people, we claim only our inheritance as American citizens, namely: to worship God according to the dictates of our own conscience.

We believe the shedding of human blood, or the taking of human life, is contrary to the teachings of Our Lord and Savior, Jesus Christ, and as a body, we are adverse to War in all its various forms.

We herewith offer our services to the President for any service that will not conflict with our conscientious scruples in this respect, with love to all, malice toward none, and with due respect to all who differ from us in our interpretation of the Scriptures.[36]

Wesley Feltus (b. 1897), COGIC Conscientious Objector, 1918

Honorable Board of Exemption for the County of [—] In the State of —

---

35. *Official Manual of the Church of God in Christ*, 24. The Church of God in Christ is perhaps one of a few Pentecostal denominations of any size that is currently officially on record against members participating in war. The movement's doctrinal position is almost identical to the Church of God (Cleveland, Tennessee) and the Pentecostal Holiness Church.

36. "Article 17," *53rd–54th Annual Convention 1960–61 Yearbook of the Church of God in Christ*; Cornelius, "What the Church Believes," 68. See also Bishop Mason, *Official Manual of the Church of God in Christ*, 24.

GREETINGS:—We your petitioners would most respectfully show to your Honorable Board that we as General officers of a regularly and duly Organized Church and have been for many years recognized by all Railroad Bureaus, By the Name of the Church of God in Christ. This church is in operation throughout the United States and it has been ever since 1895. We would respectfully show to your Honorable Board:

That the Creed of our Church is now and has been ever since its organization in the City of Jackson, Miss. adverse to war and blood shed. This our Creed was reaffirmed in 1907 in Memphis, Tenn. our New Head Quarters.

We have from the beginning, taught the members and ministers of our Church to follow peace with all men and Holiness without which no man shall see the Lord. Heb. 12:14 against retaliations, Matt. 5:38–39.

We have taught against Domestic Disobedience which breeds strife, Eph. 6:5–6; Coll. [sic] 3:23. The Members of said church are not allowed to carry arms or to shed the blood of any man and still be members of said church. Because those things are forbidden in the scriptures, Matt. 5:38–42. In the scriptures we are commanded not to resist evil, Rom. 12:17, I Thess. 5:15, Heb. 10:30 Vengeance belongs to God. Whoso sheddeth man's blood, by man shall his blood be shed, Gen. 9:6 Rev. 13:10. Not only so but we have taught all of the cardinal doctrines of Christianity. We would show to your Honorable Board that your applicant Wesly Feltus for exemption is a full fledged baptized member of the above named church, or a regular ordained minister of our faith and order in charge of our Churches at Grainsville, La.

We would show to your Honorable Board that this form of petition was adopted by our General Assembly at its last regular session on Nov. 22, 1917 at Memphis, Tenn. That Assembly was composed of eight hundred delegates representing about fifteen thousand adherents. We as General officers of the church of God in Christ, join the application of this well known Bro. Wesley Feltus for exemption Whose conscientious and religious scruples are adverse to war and the shedding of human blood.

Elder C. H. Mason, General Overseer [sic],

R. E. Hart.

State Overseers.

156 PENTECOSTAL AND HOLINESS STATEMENTS ON WAR AND PEACE

E. M. Pace, Jeff Lewis, D. Bostick, E. Reece, Henry Feltus, S. T. Samuel, E. R. Driver, Samuel Riley, D. J. Young, Elder Holt, and Others.

Affidavit:
State of _____ County of _____
Mr. _____ et al affirms that the statements of the foregoing petitions are true of their own knowledge except to the matters therein stated to be on information and belief and these matters they believe to be true. Affirmed and subscribed before me ____ this day _____.
Signed:
Eld. Henry Feltus State Overseer.[37]

[Members Seeking Conscientious Objection], 1918

My name is C. H. Mason; I am General Overseer of the church of God in Christ. Along last summer I sent out the certificates of membership to the various pastors of my Church and the Overseers. A copy of the certificate of membership which was sent out to be issued to the members reads as follows:

Faith of the Church
of God in Christ
Born in the Mind
of its believers 1895

Its Belief is in God the father, and Jesus Christ the Lord. Its creed is the New Testament, it holds for peace and good will toward all men as said in Heb. 12:14, which is as follows: Follow Peace with all men and Holiness, without which no man shall see the Lord. It believes in true Holiness unto God. Ephesians 4:22.

The members of said church are not allowed to carry arms, to shed the blood of any man, and still be members of said church.

---

37. In July 1918, John Wesley Feltus, the son of Henry Feltus, COGIC State Overseer for Mississippi, was drafted. He submitted the following affidavit to his draft board, which was then given to agents of the Bureau of Investigation and placed in an evidentiary file against him. See "Feltus," *Investigative Case Files of the Bureau of Investigation.* Our copy was transcribed by a government agent, probably introducing some errors. In the fourth line below "GREETINGS," we have changed Crred to Creed rather than use the notation [*sic*]. We have changed "captized" to "baptized," "were are" to "we are," and hyphens to underscores in the form as we assume this reflects the original. Emphasis in original, and improper capitalization in original.

Scriptures that forbid them in their creed: Matt. 5:38–42: there the Lord says resist not evil. Rom. 12:17, I Thess., 5:15, Heb. 10:30. Vengeance belongs to God. Whoso sheddeth man's blood, by man shall his blood be shed. Gen. 9:6, Rev. 13:10.

This is to Certify that Bro. _____ is a member of the Church of God in Christ at _____

    State _____

    Pastor_____

    Deacons_____

    Scribe_____.[38]

Elder David A. Hall, Sr. COGIC, 2004

Conscientious objection runs deep in my family. My father, Elder Cleophas Hall, Sr., was drafted into the army in 1942 and went to the Pacific Theater, where he faced battle on the front lines without a gun. Bishop Mason taught that saints did not take life, and my dad went through World War II without a gun. . . . It takes courage to serve in the military, and it takes another type of courage to stand on the principles of peace. I made the choice and selected a course of open defiance to the War in Vietnam . . .[39]

Gilbert E. Patterson, Former Presiding Bishop of the COGIC, 2000–2007

[Bishop G. E. Patterson] revealed that as a youth he declared his conscientious objector status and was called before his draft board. There, he defended the tenets of the faith and teachings of

38. This statement was sent by C. H. Mason to COGIC leaders in July 1917 to give members seeking conscientious objector status to be given to the draft board. The form was entered in testimony from C. H. Mason at trial in Austin, Texas, in 1918. C. H. Mason's testimony dates the document transcribed here as originating the previous summer, 1917. See McCaleb, "United States versus Henry Kirven." Improper capitalization in original.

39. Hall, "What the Church Teaches about War," 193–4. Hall is a PCPJ member and pastor of the Temple Church of God in South Memphis, Tennessee, the church founded by C. H. Mason in 1907. Hall is also the bishop elect of the Tennessee Headquarters Jurisdiction, overseeing forty-one churches. He is CEO of COGIC Publishing and editor of *The Whole Truth* Magazine and Newspaper.

158   PENTECOSTAL AND HOLINESS STATEMENTS ON WAR AND PEACE

C. H. Mason. He made clear his willingness to serve his country, but only as our [COGIC] faith would allow.[40]

"COGIC Endorses Human Rights Statement at The Hague," Netherlands, 2008

Peace and security are essential conditions for the enjoyment of human rights and fundamental freedoms. Whilst States are entrusted to guarantee the peace and security of their societies and their citizens, this should not lead to curtailing basic human rights. We denounce the development of security measures and means that endanger human life rather than protect it, for example the tremendous worldwide expenditures on weapons. This life-threatening devastating power makes it imperative to look for peaceful means of resolving tensions.

The prevalence of violence within the international and national communities remains a source of serious concern and impedes the realisation of human rights. We call on all concerned to pursue all peaceful means of redress and to refrain from a misuse of violence. In addition, we wish to highlight the problem of structural violence within society and of domestic violence in particular. It is of utmost importance to counter this and to save by so doing the lives of the most vulnerable among us.[41]

CHURCH OF GOD IN CHRIST, CONGREGATIONAL
[Founders Oppose War], 1932

In 1932 Elder J. Bowe, a founding member of the Church of God in Christ, was forced to leave its fellowship because of his belief that the proper form of church government is congregational, not episcopal [sic]. He then established the Church of God in Christ, Congregational. Two years later George Slack, who had

---

40. Ibid.

41. See Pipkin, "COGIC Endorses Human Rights in The Hague," 5. Excerpt from human rights statement endorsed, not written, by COGIC. The entire statement can be found in the spring 2009 *Pax Pneuma*. Bishop Charles E. Blake was one of the ten world religious leaders invited to sign the Faith in Human Rights statement on December 10, 2008. Blake's ambassador, Rev. David Hall, CEO of the COGIC publishing house and member of Pentecostals and Charismatics for Peace and Justice (PCPJ), signed the Human Rights statement for Blake at The Hague, Netherlands.

been excommunicated by the parent body for teaching that tithing is not a New Testament doctrine, joined the church. In addition to the convictions of Bowe and Slack, the new body espoused conscientious objection to war. Otherwise its teachings remained identical to the original body, to which Bowe returned in 1945.[42]

CHURCH OF GOD (STANBERRY, MISSOURI)
From *The Bible Advocate*, 1917

We are forever opposed to war, we hereby forbid our members haveing [*sic*] in their possession any weapon for killing, we are opposed to our members training or in any way preparing to kill, we refuse to be trained or drilled for cambatant [*sic*] military service in any nation, Heartily Approved.[43]

From the Federal Bureau of Investigation, 1917

Jose M. Rodrigues stated that they are not opposed to any thing against the Government they are in favor of the Government, but he said that The Church of God with Headquarters in Stanberry, Mo. A. N. Dugger, Principal, has made an agreement with the United States Government to Exempt all the members of this Church in the Conscription age from going to war.

and [*sic*] to that efect [*sic*] they have an article in *The Bible Advocate* [emphasis mine] published in Stanberry, Mo. June 19, 1917 which reads as follows.

["]Church Membership cards will be issued to young men now Belonging to the Church of God, who wish to show their Church affiliation for military Exemption, upon their application to this office accompanied with evidence of their identity, when not personally known.["][44]

42. Jones, *Black Holiness*, 109.

43.. Statement quoted in Sorola, "Distributeing [*sic*] Cerculars [*sic*] for Meetings," 3. This statement comes from *The Bible Advocate*, Stanberry, MO: Church of God, 1917, and was cited during an FBI interview with Jose M. Rodrigues, church treasurer, from San Antonio, Texas, on August 7, 1917. The report was made by Manuel Sorola [Sorela?]

44. Ibid. Improper capitalization in original.

160   PENTECOSTAL AND HOLINESS STATEMENTS ON WAR AND PEACE

CHURCH OF THE LIVING GOD (BERKELEY, CALIFORNIA), 1917

[Court Proceedings, re: Joshua Sykes], 1919

. . . that the said congregation should always take the position that they were not citizens of the United States; that they were subservient only to the laws of the Kingdom of Heaven and that they therefore should not assist in the conduct of war between the United States and Germany in any manner that would assist the United States and Germany in any manner that would assist the United States in winning the said war; that if they, the said congregation, or any one of them were forced into the army of the United States, they should bare their breasts and be shot rather than serve the country.

. . . Joshua Sykes spoke, that all of the members of his church should spread the doctrines which he had taught them; that his congregation should not display the flag of the United States in their homes or elsewhere and instructed the said congregation not to visit homes where the flag of the United States was displayed; and also instructed the said congregation . . . that if the national hymn were sung, none of the said congregation was to stand in recognition of said national hymn[,] . . . that the men belonging to his church should not participate in the building and manufacture of ships that would be used by the United States in the war against Germany, and that all members of his congregation who would invest in Liberty Bonds or exhibited flags or Red Cross banners in their homes would be cut out of the Kingdom of Heaven and perish[,] . . . that all members of their congregation and their Church should not register under and in pursuance to the rules and regulations provided for the registration of alien enemies, but that they should register as citizens of the Kingdom of Heaven . . .[45]

CHURCH OF THE LORD JESUS CHRIST OF THE APOSTOLIC FAITH

"Apostolic Standard on Conscientious Objection," n.d.

The Church of the Lord Jesus Christ is conscientiously opposed to participation in combat and non-combat service in any form.

---

45. "U.S. vs Joshua Sykes." Sykes, who was part of the Azusa Revival, and a number of others were prosecuted and imprisoned in Rykers Island, Washington. See Cecil M. Robeck, *The Azusa Street Mission*, 189, 282–83.

Pentecostal Statements   161

It is further opposed to the wearing of military and naval uniforms, taking oaths, pledging allegiance to any national state or flag. We do not involve ourselves in international political conflict. While we encourage all of the members of the Church of the Lord Jesus Christ to be loyal to the sovereign national state to which they have residence, we believe that there is an eternal law which supersedes any law of a given society, this being the Holy Scriptures. We take this position since we believe ourselves to be only pilgrims and strangers journeying in a strange land, having heavenly citizenship. We look for a better land and a better day when there will be no more wars nor personal conflict.

"For the weapons of our warfare are not carnal, but mightly through God to the pulling down of strongholds" (II Cor. 10:4).[46]

"Maltreatment," n.d.

In time of persecution or ill treatment at the hands of an enemy, we should not avenge ourselves but rather give place to wrath; for it is written, "Vengeance is mine; I will repay, saith the Lord." (Rom. 12:19; Deut. 32:35). Neither shall we take up any weapon of destruction to slay another, whether in our defense or in the defense of others, for it is written, do violence to no man. (Luke 3:14; Matt. 26:52; John 18:36; John 15:18–19). We should rather suffer wrong than to do wrong.[47]

"Civil Government," n.d.

All Civil magistrates are ordained of God for peace, safety and the welfare of all people. (Rom. 13:1–10). Therefore it is our duty to be in obedience to all requirements of the laws that are not contrary to the word of God and that do not force one to violation of the sixth commandment by bearing arms and going to war. It is our duty to honor them, pay tribute or such taxation as may be required without murmuring. (Matt. 17:24–27, 22:17–21) and show respect to them in all lawful requirements of the civil government.[48]

---

46. Perry, *Words of Conscience*, 45.

47. Ibid. See also Johnson, *Is Jesus Christ the Son of God Now?*

48. Perry, *Words of Conscience*, 45–46.

162 PENTECOSTAL AND HOLINESS STATEMENTS ON WAR AND PEACE

Raymond Washington, Conscientious Objector, 1968

Local Board 104
St. Louis, Missouri
Dear Local Board:

This will advise you that Raymond Washington is a conscientious objector, and a member of the Church of the Lord Jesus Christ of the Apostolic Faith which teaches conscientious objection.

We understand he has received orders to report for induction in the Armed Forces, and he has asked us for assistance, as he is conscientiously opposed to going. We have advised him of the form 150 to fill in, which he did not know about.

It is our request, on his behalf, that you reopen his classification to consider his stand, and grant him a personal hearing.

Your attention to this situation, will be very gratefully appreciated.

Sincerely,
S. McDowell Shelton
Bishop and General Overseer[49]

CHURCHES OF GOD OF THE ORIGINAL MOUNTAIN ASSEMBLY INCORPORATED

"Artickles [sic] of Faith," 1916

We believe that salvation is fully tought [sic] in the Newtestament [sic].

We believe that man must repent or perish.

We believe in regeneration through faith in Christ Jesus.

We believe in sanctification and holiness and that we should live holy and pure both of heart and life.

We believe in the gifts promised to the church (1st. Cor. 12) [sic] and, also, the signs that should follow the believer, such as speaking in other tongues healing the sick and observing all the scriptural teachings such as regeneration, water baptism by emersion and resurrection of the dead both of the just and the unjust and that there is eternal happiness for the righteous and eternal punishment for the wicked after death.

---

49. Shelton, *Church of the Lord Jesus Christ of the Apostolic Faith.*

We believe in following peace with all men and holiness without which no man shall see the Lord (Heb. 12–14) [sic].

We believe it to be wrong for christians [sic] to take up war arms and go to war, for Jesus said thou shall not kill, therefore, we forbid that any of our members engage in war.

The New Testament is our faith and our creed, therefore we stand for its teachings both to the good and the bad.

We believe in keeping the Sabbath holy.

We re-affirm and establish the principles and doctrines of the said church of God herein from the date of its organization the 24th day of August 1907 down to the present date.

We believe in the millennial reign in accordance as the scriptures referd [sic] too. Rev. 5:9–10, Rev. 20:4–6. Rev. 11:15. Jso. 24:23. 2 Tim. 2:12.[50]

"Teachings," 1967

We believe it to be wrong for Christians to take up arms and go to war. For Jesus said, "thou shalt not kill." (Ex. 20:13).[51]

"Teachings," 1970

26. The Church of God, Mountain Assembly takes the position that Abortion [sic] is homicide, which God's Holy Word condemns (Ex. 20:13; Matt. 19:18); therefore, we are against abortion, except in the case when the mother's life is diagnosed to be in danger, and abortion is prescribed to protect her life.

27. The Church of God, Mountain Assembly, Incorporated believes that nations can and should settle their differences without going to war. However, in the event of war, if a member engages in combatant service, it will not affect his status with the Church. In case a member is called into military service who has

50. "Artickles [sic] of Faith."

51. Minutes of the Churches of God of the Original Mountain Assembly, 26–27. This publication also pays tribute to the Rev. Kim Moses, who was a Pentecostal World War I religious objector (ibid., 28).

CONGREGATIONAL HOLINESS CHURCH
Concerning War, 1966

While we believe that government is ordained of God, and that God's children should be "subject unto the higher powers," according to Rom. 13:1–7, yet as the Word of God admonishes us to "Follow peace with all men," to "Love our enemies," to "Resist not evil," we believe war to be at variance with the principles of the Gospel, and that God's children should not take up arms against their fellowman. Matt. 5:39–48; Heb. 12:14.[53]

FILIPINO ASSEMBLIES OF THE FIRST-BORN, INCORPORATED
Article XII [on] Military Service, 1954

Inasmuch as our main purpose is to preach and propagate the gospel of peace through Christ and we know that War is against the carrying out of our main purpose we therefore declare ourselves as against going to war.

As followers of the Lord Jesus Christ, the Prince of Peace, we believe in implicit obedience to the divine commands and precepts which instructs us to follow peace with all men. Heb. 12:14; Thou shalt not kill; Exodus 20:13; Resist not evil; Mat. 5:39; Love your enemies; Matt. 5:44; these and the other scriptures have always been accepted and interpreted by our churches as prohibiting Christians from shedding of blood or taking human lives. While proposing to fulfill all obligations of loyal citizenship, we are constrained to declare that we cannot conscientiously participate in the actual destruction of human lives which is contrary to the basis of our faith.

However, we declare our unswerving loyalty and faithfulness to the governments of the United States and of the Philippines

---

52. "Teachings," in *Standard Resolutions of the Church of God Mountain Assembly*, 4; *History of the Church of God Mountain Assembly*, 116.

53. *The Gospel Messenger*, 10. This statement is exactly the same as the International Pentecostal Assemblies.

and will serve in any capacity outside of taking up arms if required to do so.[54]

HOMESTEAD HERITAGE (WACO, TEXAS) [ANABAPTIST-PENTECOSTAL HYBRID], 1970S
What We Believe, 2012

No human being can make guarantees about anything they do as enduring for all eternity, not, at least, in any positive sense. But within the constant flux of human life we believe a truth and Spirit from the God who defines Himself as "love" should be present and not just represented; and we believe that this truth, Spirit and love will endure forever, never to be lost. This presence of God we see as redemptive love. Only this, it seems, can ever ensure that the changes we make along life's way constitute progress toward the eternal and not regression and dissolution toward decay and death.

All these values have seemed to providentially point us to return to the enduring truths of the traditional way. In fact, I think that way may have chosen us. This would be true whether in craftsmanship, farming and vocations or in marriage, family, community relationships and social mores. This traditional approach says that love, truth, dreams, hopes, families and so on did not begin with us and hopefully will not end with us. It confesses that, beyond living in the past or in the future, there are some permanent things that remain the same forever because they are of enduring worth. So we have also tried to return to the enduring way of the eternal Word (Matt. 24:35). This is true whether in our Christian experience, beliefs or values, all of which we seek to bring together into a coherent and relational whole.

To those who might insist that a growing sense of convenience or comfort or ease defines progress, we would admit that in our daily lifestyle we may have sacrificed some of those hallmarks of "progress" in order to find fulfillment. If we do so, it is because we also believe that nothing of lasting worth comes easily and that people express how much they value something by the sacrifice and suffering they're willing to make to find and

---

54. *Constitution and By-Laws* [of the] *The Filipino Assemblies*, 11.

keep it. Perhaps some of the "cross bearing" that the Anabaptists have been historically noted for comes through here.

In any case, what we value is, simply put, living. To put it a bit more complexly, we value living relationships with God, people and land; and we are willing to sacrifice some conveniences and comforts in order to live the full life, the good life, in relation to all three. To us, this ultimately means the "eternal life," and so the "good life" becomes synonymous with the "good news" of a new creation, of a new rule of nonresistant love that at the cross triumphs over all the powers of brute force and greed.

Here on our farm, then, a principle guides us: we believe in participating as fully and relationally as possible in those things *essential* for this life of love's rule—growing our own food, giving birth to and rearing our own children, taking care of our own elderly, worshipping God in freedom of conscience as well as in Spirit and truth. We call this life lived under the rule of love "the kingdom of God."[55]

---

55. Adams, *What We Believe*, 2–3; *Homestead Heritage*. Excerpt. Emphasis in original. Homestead Heritage, composed of approximately forty-three families and 900 community members, living together on a private 500-acre farm in north Waco, Texas, is a Christian communal agricultural and crafts community that has uniquely blended elements of "Pentecostal fervor with Anabaptist simplicity and accountability." The group, which goes by the name of Brazos de Dios—a name derived after the river that runs through their property—are not technically Amish or Mennonite, despite having close relationships with traditional Anabaptists. They are, however, Christians from many different walks of life "engaged together in a modern-day experiment in radical discipleship." The name, "Homestead Heritage," is the umbrella organization under which the group carries out their public work. One such work, organizing a yearly farm festival, gives outsiders who flock to the festivals a glimpse into their "pre-Industrial Revolution world." Their beginnings can be traced to an inner-city mission in New York City. By the 1970s and 1980s, it "evolved into an experiment in community living, moving to a Colorado farm and then to Texas. Along the way, changes came about and an Anabaptist influence surfaced. While some elders come from Oneness Pentecostal backgrounds, the present community defies easy categorization." They do not use the word "Trinity" when teaching about the Godhead, and are hesitant to affirm the language of Nicene orthodoxy. While they do not exhibit aberrant teachings about God, their "impulse is to stick closely to biblical language." Summary and quotes taken from Olson, "Where Community is No Cliché."

Pentecostal Statements 167

IGLESIA CRISTIANA EVANGELICA MEXICANA
"Gobierno Civil," n.d.

Creemos que el gobierno es ordenado por Dios y todos los cristianos deben estar sujetos a las leyes de la tierra, excepto aquellas que sean contrarias a la voluntad revelada de Dios. Prometemos lealtad y respaldo moral y espiritual a nuestro país; en tiempos de guerra, la participación del individuo en combates donde se arrebata la vida al semejante será asunto dentro del gobierno de su propia conciencia. Referencias Bíblicas: Romanos 13:1–7; Hechos 5:29; Mateo 5:39–48; Hebreos 12:14.[56]

INTERNATIONAL CHURCH OF THE FOURSQUARE GOSPEL
"XVII Civil Government," 1923

We believe that civil government is of divine appointment, for the interests and good order of human society; and that governors and rulers should be prayed for, obeyed, and upheld, at all times except only in things opposed to the will of our Lord Jesus Christ, who is the ruler of the conscience of His people, the King of Kings, and the Lord of Lords.

Scripture References Where Taught: The powers that be are ordained of God. . . . For rulers are not a terror to good works, but to the evil. Rom. 13:1, 3. (Also Deut. 16:18; II Sam. 23:3; Ex. 18:21–23; Jer. 30:21.)

We ought to obey God rather than man. Acts 5:29. Fear not them which kill the body, but are able to kill the soul. Matt. 10:28. (Also Dan. 3:15–18; 6:7–10; Acts 4:18–20.)

One is your Master, even Christ. Matt. 23:10. And he hath on His vesture and on His thigh a name written, KING OF KINGS, AND LORD OF LORDS. Rev. 19:16. (Also Ps. 72:11; 2; Rom. 14:9–13.)[57]

---

56. *Articulos de Fé de la Iglesia Cristiana Evangelica Mexicana*, 7.

57. McPherson, *Declaration of Faith*, 23–24. Emphasis in original. While McPherson's 1923 *Declaration of Faith* has remained consistent since its creation, the 1936 Foursquare Yearbook, which publishes Foursquare creedal statements, omits civil disobedience to authority if government "opposed the will of our Lord Jesus Christ," as McPherson's more radical commentary clearly expresses. This represents a possible change of attitude. In 1936, for example, thirteen years after McPherson wrote her *Declaration of Faith*, and with McPherson at the height of her celebrity status, the

168 PENTECOSTAL AND HOLINESS STATEMENTS ON WAR AND PEACE

Aimee Semple McPherson (1890–1944), ICFG Founder

From "The Coming Prince of Peace," 1920

Every dog of war was on the leash, every modern invention of war was put into use to destroy men, women and little children and baptize them in their own blood.[58]

"Do You Believe That Religion Can Prevent War?" 1930s [Answered by McPherson]

True religion or Christianity can prevent war because the very embodiment of Christ's teaching of the Sermon on the Mount is opposed to war. There is something appalling in the distinction which society makes between the killing of a man in the heat of anger, and the organized slaying of millions.

Christ said that HATRED was MURDER. War is not the triumph of righteousness. It is the triumph of brute force. The mere existence of the prophecy "they shall learn war no more" is a sentence of condemnation on war.

Between converting a man and killing him lies a considerable distance. To love your neighbor as yourself and then to stick a bayonet through his heart is contrary to the principles of Christianity.

War could be prevented if the nations would heed the command of the Prince of Peace when he said, "Love your ENEMIES, bless those that curse you and pray for them that despitefully use you." So that these indescribable wars fulfill not the law of love, but the law of pride and hatred.[59]

Foursquare's creedal statement on civil government reads, without any qualification, "We believe in obedience to civil government." See *Report of the Annual Convention*, 3. Furthermore, McPherson, while advocating civil disobedience for things opposed to the will of God, failed to clarify what constitutes disobedience for her followers. Other denominational statements in this book, for example, specify what requires disobedience, such as bearing arms. While McPherson made room, biblically, for resisting authority, she did not lay out the terms of what justified noncooperation with authority.

58. McPherson, "The Coming Prince of Peace," 11.

59. McPherson, "Questionnaire from the N.Y.N.A." Emphasis in original. This document was a type-written questions and answers that was submitted to McPherson. She wrote out her responses and likely returned the original to the N.Y.N.A. The document I have is a carbon copy of her responses provided by ICFG headquarters. She also told the reporter, in contrast to soldiering, that, "Every true minister who occupies the pulpit is indeed a messenger of peace, and a promoter of international good-will." McPherson's position on War is paradoxical. Although she believed it was contrary

"In Your Opinion, Is a World Conflict Pending?" 1930s [Answered by McPherson]

I believe in an impending world conflict because of the over-increasing racial hatred, for HATRED spells WAR. . . . The insane armament competition, the greed for more land and expansion of colonies, the zealous ambitions of the dictators for military supremacy, and the secret pacts and alliances of certain nations, will eventually plunge the world into another bloody conflict.

Instead of swords "beaten into plowshares" (Isaiah 2:2,4), it is just the reverse. Rather, it is, "Beat your plowshares into swords, and your pruning hooks into spears" (Joel 3:9, 10). So, instead of the precious ore being diverted into channels of blessing, it is being melted in the furnace by the gods of war for the purpose of destroying humanity.[60]

---

to Christianity to kill, she admitted, in case of American participation in war, she would not inaugurate a campaign protesting U.S. involvement—if the enemy came to American shores. She did, however, oppose American military participation in *foreign* wars. Regarding McPherson's possible attraction to Christian pacifist principles, it is virtually impossible to make her view on peace and war consistent. She was not entirely consistent, and for good reason. Her context varied as widely as her travels. Her answer to the N.Y.N.A. reporter, however, was exceptionally clear. She believed participation in war contradicted the elementary principles of Christianity; namely, the Sermon on the Mount. As a Christian, she upheld Jesus' nonviolent example. As an American, she upheld patriotism and soldier heroism. She endorsed these two mutually contradictory belief systems: retribution and pacifism, without feeling the need to reconcile. Furthermore, she not only pushed gender and social activism boundaries, but she rhetorically encouraged her people toward biblical nonviolence, while not self-identifying as a "pacifist." By World War II, her peacetime pacifism gave way to selective pacifism when nonviolence became too controversial and radical during national crisis. Furthermore, contrary to popular scholarship, the portrait of her early movement challenges the present-day assumption that she simply accommodated and compromised herself and her movement to mainstream conservative political and religious values. By 1940, however, she did, indeed, relax her attraction to biblical nonviolence and repudiated the pacifistic orientation of first-generation Pentecostals, choosing instead a mainstream approach to war that has come to define contemporary American Pentecostalism. Summary taken from Pipkin, "The Foursquare Church and Pacifism." See also Sutton's *Aimee Semple McPherson and the Resurrection of Christian America.*

60. Ibid.

"The Way to Disarm IS TO DISARM," 1932

Something is stupefying in the spectacle of great nations whose people have not a thing in the world against each other being taxed to the verge of starvation to build great military machines.

And for what?

If the nations would stop building warship and equipping armies we would be all but overwhelmed with prosperity. The world would have more money and more happiness than at any time in history.

The pity and hideousness of it is that no one wants war. Not even the soldiers.

Don't imagine for a minute that a gentle little shoemaker from Bavaria wanted to leave his family and go out to plunge a bayonet into the heart of the father of a little family in the grape vineyards of Normandy. They had to be goaded into it. Boys had to be poisoned with hatred, with tales of atrocity to make them fight.

. . . The nations protest that they want peace; but they have to shout these protestations above the din of the cannon makers.

. . . The Sermon on the Mount was the soundest diplomacy, the sanest business ethics, the most practical rule for success and happiness every written or spoken in the whole history of the world.

Christ said it all. Those few, simple words contain the whole lesson of life. And that which He stated was the Inexorable Law.

There is no way to get around it. It can't be tinkered with; or evaded or compromised. The Master gave the Law to the world in gentle, loving words—simple words that the smallest child could understand. But those words were final and inexorable. Try to disobey that Law and see what you will get. Try to substitute hatred and double dealing and trickery for brotherly love and see where you will land . . .

In war, no nation can annihilate another nation without suffering annihilation itself.

Oh, the sorrows and the tragedies that would have been saved to this poor old world had we but believed that Jesus Christ knew what He was talking about and meant what He said.

This disarmament conference will result in nothing; they never do. One nation will slip over a sixteen-inch gun on a careless rival and will find that a new kind of poison gas has been slipped over in return.

Pentecostal Statements   171

If civilization is to be saved, the world must cry "Stop"—and stop.

The only way to disarm is to disarm.[61]

"AIMEE MAKES PEACE PLEA TO MUSSOLINI," 1935 [NEWSPAPER REPORTER]

Aimee Semple McPherson sent a second message to Benito Mussolini today, urging prevention of war between Italy and Ethiopia. Addressed to the Italian dictator, whom she met on a recent world tour, the message said: "Countless Foursquare members are praying that God may direct your impending decision in order that the sword of war shall not again be plunged into the world's already bleeding heart." It was signed by the officers of the Foursquare Church in convention here.[62]

"OPPOSED TO WAR," 1935 [NEWSPAPER REPORTER]

Aimee did not exactly say that she disliked Mussolini, but she was not exactly in favor of him. "I do not believe in war," she said. She added that the Four-Square Gospel was opposed to war. I then asked if, since the Four-Square Gospel was so disposed, it would not be practicable for the group to enter politics

---

61. McPherson Hutton, "The Way to Disarm IS TO DISARM," J3. Article not quoted in entirety. Here, McPherson is speaking about the Disarmament Conference held in Geneva in 1932, and her criticism of War is directed at European nations. She typically, when criticizing war, gave immunity to the U.S. The Sermon on the Mount, for example, is rarely used as a moral standard to criticize the U.S. government. After all, she believed everything the U.S. did was for "peace" because America was a Christian nation. So criticisms of the U.S. military rarely entered her antiwar discourse. Evidently McPherson was an antiwar activist. She, like other peace advocates of her time, was influenced by the 1930s antiwar movement. McPherson did not conclude, however, that either disarmament or the elimination of weapons of mass destruction would bring real peace. True peace, individual or national, according to her, could only be accomplished by following the "Prince of Peace." Any means toward achieving peace without Jesus was, for McPherson, superfluous and premature, which, in the end, led to McPherson publicly protesting the double-talk of the liberal class and international peace conferences. See Pipkin, "The Foursquare Church and Pacifism."

62. "Aimee Makes Peace Plea to Mussolini," 11. Not only did McPherson personally "not believe in war," and regardless of her ambiguity on bearing arms, she was nevertheless active in protesting war. In multiple ways, through newspaper, letters, and her radio station, she reached out to her political enemy, fascist leader Mussolini, pleading that war be abandoned.

172 PENTECOSTAL AND HOLINESS STATEMENTS ON WAR AND PEACE

and implement the doctrines for which they stood. "That doesn't seem to be the tendency," said Aimee. "We believe that we can do better work by remaining out of politics. We shall use our vote as best we can in line with our broader view, but I think its better that we stop there."[63]

"Editorial Comments [on] War," 1937

Get this: the men who really MAKE war and inflame people to a point of patriotic fervor are NOT the men who go to the struggle. How many Congressmen, Diplomats or Premiers bore arms or smelled the smoke of battle in the last war? To the author's personal knowledge, NOT ONE. As long as they can protect their own devoted hides and send the OTHER fellow to the front, they clamour for war, especially when those manufacturing munitions and other war materials make it worth their while to promote the war spirit. As long as the conflict is on another's soil and they can stay at home and run their factories and other enterprises, that FLOURISH on war, they are for it.[64]

"Editorial Comments," 1937

If any man is qualified to give a definition of war, [General] Sherman is that man. He had seen it in all its phases; from defensive tactics and filed attacks to his devastating march across Georgia. His verdict is summed up in three words: "War is Hell!"

War IS hell! and no sane person can advocate it—especially in its modern destructive form. One can not [sic] escape the conclusion that Satan himself must "sit in" at all the councils of war today. There must be war-mad demons perched on the shoulders of every military commander and riding in the cockpit of every bombing plane.[65]

63. Bouchette, "Sister Aimee Shies at Politics," 3. Article not quoted in its entirety. Here, McPherson, on behalf of the Foursquare Gospel, publicly goes on record opposing war.

64. McPherson, "Editorial Comments War," 2. Emphasis in original.

65. McPherson, "Editorial Comments," 2. Emphasis in original.

Pentecostal Statements   173

Foursquare "Article XVII on Military Service," 1937

WHEREAS our Convention Assembly has manifested by voice of opinion pro and con on the subject of Military Service in the event of war; and

WHEREAS there are Ministers and Laymen who are pacifists and have conscientious convictions not to take up arms to kill their fellow-men, according to their interpretations of the Scriptures, and in so doing feel they would endanger their souls into an eternal and everlasting Hell of fire and brimstone by incurring the wrath of God; and

WHEREAS there are those among our ministers and laymen who feel they are obligated to the government of the United States of America and would take up arms to resist invasion of our country and they interpret the Scriptures to teach entire obedience to human government and that only the rulers are responsible to God for commanding to take up arms to kill humanity; and

WHEREAS, because of this divided opinion, the General Assembly and Board of Directors are hereby appealed to;

NOW THEREFORE, BE IT RESOLVED: That there be inserted in our Constitution and By-Laws a clause for the benefit and protection of conscientious objectors in this organization who, when drafted into the Military service of the United States of America and its possessions, and brought before the examining Boards, may be exempt from combatant service.

RESOLVED FURTHER: That the International Church of the Foursquare Gospel, a regular accredited organization and incorporated Church Body, does hereby appeal to the President of the United States of America in such emergencies when any of its members, because of conscientious convictions, cannot take up arms, that they be delegated to noncombatant service.

RESOLVED FURTHER: That we hereby recommend that every minister and layman in this organization render service in some form to the United States Government in time of war.[66]

66. "Article XVII on Military Service." Emphasis in original. While The Foursquare Church did not officially go on record as accepting or opposing Christian pacifism, Foursquare documents, as well as the Foursquare Military Service bylaw, reveal that a vocal group of Foursquare pacifists existed within the early movement (1930s). This pacifist sect, while not necessarily using the term "pacifism" to describe their opposition to war, and despite the seemingly overwhelming articles praising military heroism, believed it was morally and biblically wrong for Christians to take life. Furthermore,

174 PENTECOSTAL AND HOLINESS STATEMENTS ON WAR AND PEACE

The *Foursquare Crusader*, 1938

SHOULD A CHRISTIAN TAKE UP ARMS IN TIME OF WAR

PASTOR C. W. PHILLEO, MANAGING EDITOR OF THE *FOURSQUARE CRUSADER*, 1938

The question is perhaps, a little late. It already has been answered—IN THE BIBLE. Until the Ten Commandments are repealed the Christian has no alternative but to stay aloof from war and its consequent destruction of human life.

Should one be drafted? Well, prayer changes things. And the God who saved Noah from the flood, and preserved Daniel in the lions' den and his brethren in the fiery furnace, surely can "handle" so inconsequential a thing as a little draft-board.

Prayer, wisdom and the proof of patriotic loyalty on our part, coupled with a willingness to serve our country in NON-COMBATANT service should turn the trick for any obedient child of God.[67]

---

many pastors and leaders within the early movement, including McPherson, demonstrated similar rationales in promoting Christian nonviolence as did early Pentecostal pacifists. On July 5, 1934, leaders from the Foursquare Northwest District sent a letter to the Foursquare headquarters asking denominational executives to pass a resolution protecting their members who were opposed to bearing arms in case of war. The appeal was successful, and on January 11, 1937, The Foursquare Church officially adopted and passed a broad resolution granting protecting for their pacifist members. The resolution, while not written to disclose the organizations official stance for or against Christian participation in war, was drafted simply to acknowledge the diversity of opinions on the topic and to pledge denominational support for members who opposed combatant service. On June 19, 1942, five years after the passage of the pacifist clause, and soon after U.S. entry into World War II, Foursquare executive leaders and pastors unanimously voted to delete the military service bylaw. See Pipkin, "The Foursquare Church and Pacifism" and Pipkin, "The Foursquare Conscientious Objector: 1917–1943."

67. "Should a Christian Take up Arms in Time of War?" 1–2. Emphasis in original.

Pastor Myron Sackett, 1938

I personally am very patriotic. I think that Old Glory is the greatest flag in the world and I would rather live under the Stars and Stripes, than any flag I know of. I am very eager to defend our flag, but as a Christian I could not conscientiously kill anybody, and still think that I was doing what the Lord wanted me to do, neither could I advise anybody else to do so. I am confident that if everybody in the world was a Christian, we would not have war. However, if war broke out in our country I would want to go and do my part to defend our flag, but I would not want to take up arms and kill anyone. I cannot give life and I do not feel I have any right to take life.[68]

Pastor R. J. Turner, 1938

Jesus taught that we should render unto Caesar the things that are Caesar's and unto God the things that are God's. At once this brings us to the fact of two kingdoms—The Kingdom of the world, and the Kingdom of God. To which does the Christian belong? John 18:36—"Jesus said, my kingdom is not of this world; if my kingdom were of this world then would my servants fight."

In the light of the Scripture the Christian cannot destroy life for in Luke 9:56, "For the Son of Man is not come to destroy men's lives, but to save them."

Every Christian should conscientiously protest combatant military service but be willing to render non-combatant service in time of war.[69]

68. Ibid.
69. Ibid.

176 PENTECOSTAL AND HOLINESS STATEMENTS ON WAR AND PEACE

Charles Wm. Walkem, Foursquare Leader

REV. CHARLES W. WALKEM

You will never have to love your enemies very long. The process will kill them.[70]

The religion that makes you feel like fighting . . . never came from your Father.[71]

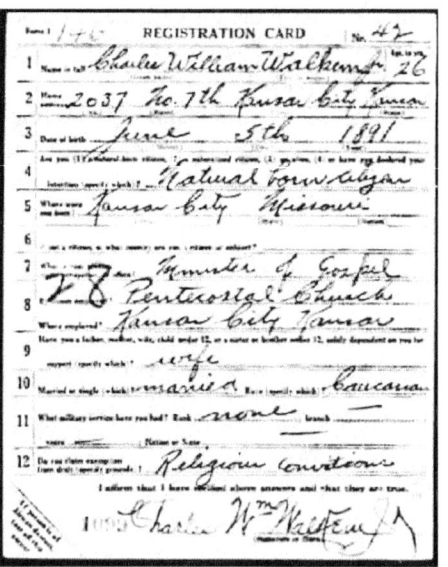

70. Walkem, "Gems of Truth," 24.

71. Ibid.

Here is the World War I draft card for Charles Walkem. He claimed religious exemption during his tenure as an Assemblies of God minister in Kansas City, Missouri. Sometime later he associated with The Foursquare Church, working closely with Aimee Semple McPherson at her Temple. He served as a Foursquare pastor and manager of the Foursquare radio station (KFSG). He was a frequent writer in her church's official publication. On line 12, he wrote, "Religious conviction" as reason for exemption.

Walkem frequently responded to inquires in a column titled, "The Question Box." Here, he answered a question regarding war by borrowing Aimee McPherson's earlier antiwar statement during an interview with a reporter from the N.Y.N.A. (See "Do you believe religion can prevent war?" Answered by McPherson.) For unknown reasons, McPherson published her opposition to killing under Walkem's column, thus associating his name in her periodical with antiwar opinion. Walkem, however, likely agreed with her perspective given he was a religious objector to war. This statement, too, may have served as the movement's official talking point on war given it was used by McPherson and repeated word-for-word by Walkem in their religious publication.[72]

The Question Box

By Rev. Chas. Wm. Walkem, D.D.

Question No. 38 — Do you believe that religion can prevent war?

TRUE religion can prevent war because the very embodiment of Christ's teaching of the Sermon on the Mount is opposed to war. There is something appalling in the distinction which society makes between the killing of a man in the heat of anger, and the organized slaying of millions.

Christ said that HATRED was MURDER. War is not the triumph of righteousness. It is the triumph of brute force. The mere existence of the prophecy "They shall learn war no more" is a sentence of condemnation on war.

Between converting a man, and killing him, lies a considerable distance. To love your neighbor as yourself, and then to stick a bayonet through his heart, is contrary to the principles of Christianity.

War could be prevented if the nations would only heed the command of the Prince of Peace when He said, "Love your ENEMIES; bless those that curse you and pray for them that despitefully use you." So that those indescribably horrible wars fulfill not the law of love, but the law of pride and hatred.

"The Greatest of All" by Rolf McPherson, Second Foursquare President, 1954

Kingdoms, today, are measured by their wealth, by the material they are able to produce in time of

72. Walkem, "The Question Box," 5.

war, by their army, navy and air-force. In recent years, the comparison is made between the stock-piles of atomic and hydrogen bombs. How different the words of Jesus, "By this ye shall know that ye are my disciples, if ye have love one to other." What a contrast are the disciples of Christ's kingdom from the disciples of the kingdoms of this earth. . . . God says, "Return good for evil." Jesus said, "Love your enemies"—even those who persecute you. Oh, the magnificence of Calvary, as we hear our Savior say, "Father, forgive them! They know not what they do."

We are to follow His example; for He was a true king. And yet, a king without an army. Yes, a king without even a sword. His kingdom was one of love. . . . Jesus said: "My kingdom is not of this world, else would my servants fight for me." His kingdom could never be established by force. All the armies of the world could never establish His love in the hearts of women. The sword could never bring conviction and love into the hearts and lives of men. No number of chariots and horses could accomplish this task for which He came. These can not [sic] usher in peace. Nations rise against nations; there are wars and rumors of war, and so it goes on. I believe it is time to go forth to "bomb" the world with the Word of God. God's Word is a powerful weapon, a great battle for righteousness can be won. I believe it is time to raise up an army to "fight the good fight of faith," not with carnal weapons, not with weapons of the world, but with the weapons of love. Christ refused to use the powers of this world to save Himself; for the proof of our love is not in slaying our enemies but in dying for our enemies. . . . In the garden of Gethsemane He said to Peter, "Put thy sword again into its place; they who take the sword will perish by the sword." . . . Christ has not put His sword into the hands of His disciples to fight the battle; but He gives us the Word of His love, and that "Word is quick and powerful and sharper than any two-edged sword."[73]

---

73. McPherson, "The Greatest of All," 4–6. Excerpt. The insertion of this sermon is merely to show that Rolf, like his mother, Aimee McPherson, were both active in the promotion of Jesus' way of peace, while both simultaneously remained committed to supporting the U.S. Armed Forces.

Pentecostal Statements   179

INTERNATIONAL PENTECOSTAL ASSEMBLIES, FOUNDED 1936
"Concerning War," n.d.

While we believe that government is ordained of God, and that God's children should be "Subject unto the higher powers" according to Rom. 13:1–7, yet, as the Word of God admonishes us to "Follow peace with all men," to "Love our enemies," and to "Resist not evil," we believe war to be at variance with the principles of the Gospel, and that God's children should not take up arms against their fellowmen. Matt. 5:39–48; Heb. 12:14.[74]

LA IGLESIA DE DIOS PENTECOSTAL, INCORPORADA
"Articulo V—Servicio Militar," 1954

Mientras reconocemos el Gobierno Humano como una ordenación divina y afirmamos nuestra fiel lealtad al Gobierno de nuestra nación, a la vez creemos preciso declarar nuestra posición referente a la destrucción de la vida humana:

Por canto somos seguidores de nuestro Señor Jesucristo, el Principe de Paz, creemos en la implícita obediencia a los divinos mandamientos y preceptos que nos instruyen, tales como: "Seguid la paz con todos" (Hebreos 14:14) [sic] [Hebreos 12:14]; "No mataras (Exodo 20:13); "No resistais al mal (Mateo 5:39); "Amad a vuestros enemigos (Mateo 5:44), etc.; y,

Por cuanto estas y otras Escrituras han sido siempre aceptadas e interpretadas por nuestra Iglesia como prohibiendo a los cristianos derramar sangre ye quitar vidas humanas; y,

Por cuanto nosotros, como un cuerpo de cristianos, mientras intentamos cumplir las obligaciones de la ciudadania, somos constreñidos a declarar que nuestra conciencia no nos permite participar en guerras y resistencia armada, lo cual envuelve la destrucción de la vida humana, siendo esto contrario a nuestras convicciones relacionadas con la Palabra de Dios, que es nuestra unica regal de fe; por consiguiente:

---

74. *General Principles of the International Pentecostal Assemblies*, 8. This statement is exactly the same as the Congregational Holiness Church. The International Pentecostal Assemblies, successor to the Association of Pentecostal Assemblies, founded March 14, 1921, by Elizabeth A. Sexton, Hattie M. Barth and Paul T. Barth, and the National and International Pentecostal Missionary Union founded in 1914 by Dr. Philip Wittich.

180   PENTECOSTAL AND HOLINESS STATEMENTS ON WAR AND PEACE

Resuélvase que esta Iglesia, no obstante lo expresado, declara fiel lealtad a nuestro Gobierno y al Jefe del Ejecutivo, y que sostendremos nuestro firme propósito de ayudar en todas las formas posibles, convenientes a nuestra fe.[75]

MOUNT SINAI HOLY CHURCH OF AMERICA, INC.
"Secret Societies and War," 1947

Any society requiring an oath, affirmation or promise of secrecy as a condition of membership, is held to be a secret society and any member joining or continuing in such violate his covenant obligations and should in due form be excluded from the church.

There has been much comment on the subject concerning Saints [sic] going to war. We admit that this is a very difficult question to deal with when we consider it in the light of us being law abiding Citizens [sic], but when we consider it as a strict command from God's word which says "Thou shalt not Kill" then we take a firm stand against war. As the Old and New Testament says the same, and we know that War is for the destruction of humanity, and to gratify the selfish wishes and ambitions of one people over another. Scripture references are as follows, Rev. 13:10, St. Mark 10:19, Exodus 20:13, James 4:1–2.[76]

OLAZABAL COUNCIL OF LATIN-AMERICAN CHURCHES
"Constitution and Bylaws," 1953

As our main purpose is the preaching and propagation of the Gospel of peace through our Lord Jesus Christ, and as we know that War is in contraposition with our main purpose, we declare that we do not favor the taking up of arms to participate in war.

As followers of our Lord Jesus Christ, the Prince of Peace, we believe in implicit obedience to the divine commandments and precepts as given in the Word of God which instruct us to follow peace with all men.

---

75. *Constitucion Y Reglamento De La Iglesia De Dios Pentecostal Incorporanda*, 21–22.

76. *Manual of Mount Sinai Holy Church of America*, 21–22.

Pentecostal Statements 181

Hebrews 12:14. To refrain from killing, Exodus 20:13. Not to resist evil, St. Matthew 5:39. To love our enemies, St. Matthew 5:44. This and other Scriptures have been accepted and interpreted by our churches as the basis upon which a Christian is forbidden to shed blood or to take part in the act of taking away the life of our fellow men.

While we propose to comply with the obligations of loyal citizenship, we are constrained to declare that conscientiously we are unable to participate in the actual destruction of human lives, which is contrary to the basis of our faith.

Nevertheless, we declare our loyalty, faithfulness and submission to the Government of the United States or to whatever country we happen to reside, providing that in all this it will not violate our conscience and religious convictions, in the adoration of God and His service.[77]

OPEN BIBLE STANDARD CHURCHES, INC.
"Civil Government," 1940 and 1967

The two images below are taken from the 1940[78] and 1967 *Policies and Principles of the Open Bible Standard Churches.*[79] Here you can clearly see

77. "Constitution and Bylaws," in *Statements of Religious Bodies on the Conscientious Objector*, 47.

78. *Policies and Principles of the Open Bible Standard Churches Inc.*, Des Moines, IA, June 1940, 48. Document provided by Linda Dixon, Executive Assistant to Teri Beyer, Secretary-Treasurer, Open Bible Churches, and Aaron Friesen, Director of Distance Education, New Hope Christian College. The Open Bible Standard Churches, formerly the Bible Standard Conference, dates back to 1919, when their founders withdrew from Florence Crawford's Apostolic Faith Church in Portland, Oregon, over divorce and remarriage issues. In 1935, the Bible Standard Conference, led by Fred Hornshuh, an Apostolic Faith Portland pastor, merged with the Open Bible Evangelistic Association in Des Moines, a Foursquare Church offshoot, to form the Open Bible Standard Churches. Following the merge, and seeking to reaffirm their Apostolic Faith pacifist heritage, leaders created and passed a bylaw on civil government. While the wording is different from Crawford's statement on peace, their commitment to nonviolence was nevertheless motivated by her movement. With U.S. involvement in World War II approaching, and seeking to publicly reaffirm their allegiance to Jesus-inspired peace, they adopted a hybrid statement representing both movements. The first paragraph, reminiscent of the Foursquare part of the group, strongly resembles, with minor variants, the *Declaration of Faith* written by Aimee Semple McPherson, The Foursquare Church's founder. The second paragraph, which reaffirmed their nonviolent convictions, represented Hornshuh's group, and is virtually a replica of the International Pentecostal Assemblies (1936) and the Congregational Holiness Church (1966).

79. *Articles of Faith of the Open Bible Standard Churches; Minister's Manual*

182 PENTECOSTAL AND HOLINESS STATEMENTS ON WAR AND PEACE

the handwritten editorial notes, "change in entirety," that frame the Open Bible Standard's 1967 change from their original 1940 affirmation on peace and nonviolence. This image serves as the archetype of the great reversal of Pentecostal pacifism and signifies: 1) a U-turn from their past devotion to the gospel's radical emphasis on pacifism; 2) a symbolic change of the larger Pentecostal movement, whom, when abandoning their pacifist roots, did so behind the scenes, sometimes without comment; 3) the way these deletions were handled; typically a mere footnote, eliciting little or no response.[80]

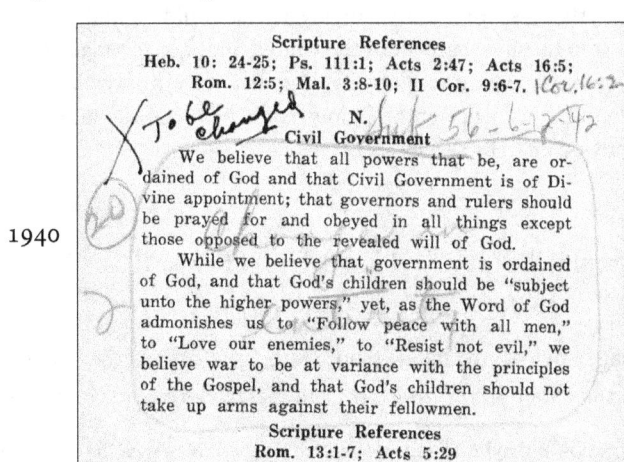

Containing the Policies and Principles of the Open Bible Standard Churches, 47.

80. The Open Bible Standard Churches, Assemblies of God, and The Foursquare Church, represent how some Pentecostal groups modified their prohibitions against killing by either altering their statements in a less threatening way or by retraction. To deal with the radical nature of nonviolence in a country that has come to rely on war-making, these institutions used either deletion, denial, or diversion as a means to mitigate antiwar controversy. The Open Bible Standard Churches, without comment, used the process of deletion to erase their previous antiwar interpretation of the Gospels while retaining (footnoting) pacifist scripture references. The Assemblies of God, in a possible attempt to rebrand the organization in the interest of American hegemony,

ORIGINAL PENTECOSTAL CHURCH OF GOD
[Against Bearing Arms], 1970

As for war, the Government gives an individual the right to be a Conscientious Objector. We claim that right. We will serve in the armed forces, and give aid to our country, but will not take up arms.[81]

PENTECOSTAL ASSEMBLIES OF THE WORLD (PAW)

World War I draft card of Andrew Leon Coleman, African-American member of PAW. He claimed "religion" as reason for exemption.[82]

---

not only removed all nonviolent scripture passages, but denied such a transformation constituted any real change. By falsifying their history and suppressing the reality of what they previously affirmed, they framed their 1967 revision as a continuation of their earlier tradition, while it is an obvious denial of their 1917 antiwar declaration. Consequently, to reflect tolerable opinion and to market themselves as less radical, the supposedly statist Paul was substituted for Jesus in framing their response to war. Since the selective use of Paul's words (Rom 13) has historically been quoted as the quintessential model of Christian obedience to power, he was naturally the better candidate to move the organization forward in their alliance with the status quo. Furthermore, this change shows that Pentecostal hermeneutical developments were likely related to their accommodation to power, force, and wealth. Because of this new alliance, denominational theologians adjusted their reading of the Bible to support the existing social establishment which they benefited. The Foursquare Church, in good public relations fashion, deleted their pacifist clause by diverting attention away from their disapproval of pacifist sentiment by using the *Selective Training and Service Act of 1940*. Since this law provided exemption to any person who opposed War in any form regardless of whether that belief was part of their denominational creed, leaders felt it redundant and unnecessary to maintain a bylaw on behalf of their religious objectors. In this context, diversion served two functions. First, it saved church officials the personal embarrassment of abandoning pacifist members by using the law as a pretext to delete. Second, leaders were able to divert bad press away from the movement that comes with pacifist association. Therefore, these brief examples show how some Pentecostal groups did a coordinated and intentional change, at different times, and either did by deleting without comment (The Open Bible Standard Churches) or denying a change took place (Assemblies of God) or using diversion to warrant deletion (The Foursquare Church). For an analysis of the Assemblies of God change, see Beaman, *Pentecostal Pacifism*, 113–21. For a review of the history of Foursquare's relationship to pacifism, see Pipkin, "The Foursquare Church and Pacifism."

81. James Oakley Brown to Arthur Carl Piepkorn [Personal letter].

82. This image reprinted by permission of Ancestry.com. To view additional family history records, please visit www.ancestry.com.

184 PENTECOSTAL AND HOLINESS STATEMENTS ON WAR AND PEACE

From "Minute Book and Ministerial Record," 1917–1918

Our chief aim is to glorify God our Savior, even Jesus Christ, who gave himself for us, that He might redeem us from all iniquity, and purify unto Himself a peculiar people, zealous of good works; that we should show forth the praises of Him who hath called us out of darkness into His marvelous light; and that we may be blameless and harmless, the sons of God, without rebuke, in the midst of a crooked and perverse nation, among whom we shine as light in the world, holding forth the Word of Life, to give light to them that sit in darkness and in the shadow of death, to guide their feet into the way of peace. See Tit. 2:13, 14; I Pet. 2:9; Phil. 2:15, 16; Lu. 1:79.

Our duty is to lift up the fallen, visit the sick, strengthen the weak, encourage the faint-hearted, comfort the feeble-minded, point the lost to the way of salvation, and urge all believers to seek a spirit-filled life (Eph. 5:18; Acts 19:1–16) and prepare for the coming of the Lord (Jas. 1:27; I Thes. 5:14; Mar. 16:15–18; Matt. 25:1–13.)

Moreover it is our indispensable duty, as partakers of the "royal priesthood" (I Pet. 2:9; Rev. 1:6; 5:10), to offer supplications, prayers, intercessions, and giving thanks for all men; for kings, presidents, governors, magistrates and all that are in authority; that we may lead a quiet and peaceable life in all godliness and honesty. (I Tim. 2:1–4; Rom. 13:1–7). And to submit ourselves "to every ordinance of man for the Lord's sake; whether it be to the king, as supreme, or unto governors, as unto them that are sent by him for the punishment of evildoers, and for the praise of them that do well," so long as these ordinances to not infringe upon the liberty of service towards God according to the dictation of the heart or conscience. (See I Pet. 2:13–17; Tit. 3:1, 2; Mat. 22:21.)[83]

"Article XII Mal Treatment," 1917–1918

In time of persecution, or ill-treatment at the hands of an enemy, we should not "avenge ourselves," but rather give place to wrath; for it is written "Vengeance is mine; I will repay, saith the Lord." (Ro. 12:19; Deut. 32:35.) Neither shall we take up any weapon of

---

83. *Minute Book and Ministerial Record of Pentecostal Assemblies of the World*, 3–4; *Minute Book of the Pentecostal Assemblies of the World*, 11. Excerpt.

destruction to slay another, whether in our own defense, or in the defense of others, for it is written, "Do violence to no man." (See Lu. 3:14; Mat. 26:52; John 18:36; 15:18, 19.) We should rather suffer wrong than to do wrong.[84]

"Article XIII Civil Government," 1917–1918

All civil magistrates are ordained of God for peace, safety, and the welfare of all people (Rom. 13:1–10), therefore, it is our duty to be in obedience to all requirements of the laws that are not contrary to the word of God, and that does not force one to the violation of the sixth commandment by bearing arms, or going to war. It is our duty to honor them, pay tribute, or such taxation as may be required without murmuring (Mat. 17:24–27; 22:17–21), and show respect to them in all lawful requirements of the civil government.[85]

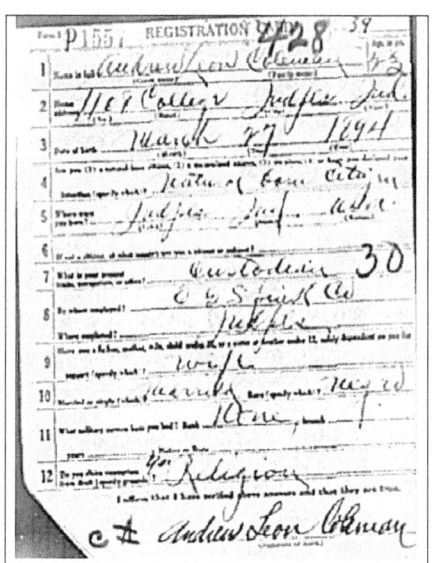

"Our Boys in Time of War," 1919

The Pentecostal Church . . . opposes to its members participating in warfare in any capacity. But in case our government is drawn into a struggle with an enemy threatening or making an invasion

---

84. *Minute Book and Ministerial Record of Pentecostal Assemblies of the World*, 6.
85. Ibid.

186 PENTECOSTAL AND HOLINESS STATEMENTS ON WAR AND PEACE

on our country, we stand for loyalty to our government and our flag. We would ask for non-combatant service in some capacity that does not require the Christian to bear arms, which would force him to participate in shedding blood and taking human life. We recognize the institution of human government as being of divine ordination and in doing so, affirm unswerving loyalty to the government of the United State: [*sic*] however, we take a definite position regarding the bearing of arms or taking human life.[86]

PENTECOSTALS AND CHARISMATICS FOR PEACE AND JUSTICE

Paul Nathan Alexander, PCPJ Founder

"WHY A PENTECOSTAL PEACE FELLOWSHIP IS NEEDED," 2001

My critique of Pentecostal approval of war and other forms of violence and oppression is not unique. Various lay people, pastors, and scholars reveal concern on various occasions in various ways. But these efforts are random and not well organized, an article here, a proposal there, or an occasional chapter in a book . . .

Thousands of people are being educated around the world in Pentecostal institutions and are not being given the theological resources with which to critique nationalism, patriotism, war, and other divisive issues. A Pentecostal peace fellowship would be able to encourage teaching on the significance of peacemaking as an essential element of the Spirit-filled life.[87]

---

86. McClain, "Our Boys in Time of War," 4. Quoted in Barba, *Wars and Rumors of Wars*, 8.

87. Alexander, "Spirit Empowered Peacemaking." This is an excerpt from Alexander's paper which first suggested the need for a Pentecostal peace and justice fellowship. The paper was presented in July, 2001 at the European Pentecostal Charismatic Research Association conference at the University of Leuven in Belgium. In March, 2002, at a Society for Pentecostal Studies conference in Florida, roughly thirty Pentecostals signed on. PCPJ, formerly Pentecostal Peace Fellowship (2001–2005) then Pentecostal Charismatic Peace Fellowship (2005–2006), is a non-profit 501(c)3 organization. Like other Christian peace networks, they work within their own heritages to advocate the peace and justice of Jesus, while cooperating with believers from other parts of the world and traditions. The network has members in more than twenty denominations, fifteen countries, and forty educational institutions. See Alexander, "Pentecostal Charismatic Peace Fellowship." See too the PCPJ website (www.pcpj.org). PCPJ members are also active in creating and endorsing many statements such as nuclear disarmament (www.

Pentecostal Statements   187

FROM "SPEAKING IN THE TONGUES OF NONVIOLENCE," 2007

Nationalism and the body of God form a lethal combination. It leads me to think of one of the most violent games ever invented, and one of my favorites, an entertainment that unites emperor and clergy, military and peasantry in an attempt to defeat the enemy and perpetuate one's own kingdom. The game, of course, is chess. The bishops, the representatives of the people of God, stand closest to the king and queen. They are even closer than the calvary (the knights) or the siege towers (the rocks). The church entangled in the empire, seeking first its kingdom, striking at an angle for the color of its national kin. Chess is a great game, but it portrays a rather unfaithful theology and practice.[88] The chess set often lacks Spirit empowered prophets who protest and provide an alternative to nationalistic and violent civil religion. Yet many first generation pentecostals believed that God had poured out the Spirit to create just such a community to speak truth to power.[89]

FROM "TOWARD PARTICULAR DECLARATIONS OF HUMAN GIFTS," 2008

Atheism is the best thing that ever happened to my faith in God, for I was a Jesus-lovin', tongue-talkin', gun-totin', American-flag-wavin' Pentecostal Christian farm boy from Kansas. I was a Christian who cheered as the missiles flew and enthusiastically sang [to the Beach Boys tune 'Barbara Ann'] "Bomb, bomb, bomb . . . bomb, bomb, Iraq" in January 1991. I told racist jokes, was a hardcore Christian Zionist, and supported torture.

All in the name of God; in the name of Jesus specifically. But I quit believing in that God, any God actually, for several years and I journeyed along as a convinced atheist. Along the way I discovered nonviolent peacemaking and restorative justice seeking in my religious heritage and I slowly journeyed my way back to Christian faith.

Pentecostals are (if you allow me a loose comparison) the Sufis, the dervishes, the Hasidic, mystical version of Christianity.

---

matthew5project.org), open letters to U.S. officials, policy advocacy, and a film documentary called "With Love From Palestine." This documentary shares the stories of Palestinian Pentecostal-evangelicals in the West Bank and Israel.

88. Alexander, "Speaking in Tongues of Nonviolence," 1.

89. Ibid., 2.

188   PENTECOSTAL AND HOLINESS STATEMENTS ON WAR AND PEACE

Most Pentecostals dance and sing with enthusiasm and believe in healing, hope, and miracles; it's a religion of signs and wonders—and the world needs healing, hope, miracles, signs, and wonders. I am painfully and intimately aware of the failures, greed, nationalism, and violence perpetrated by my Pentecostal Christian family. Pat Robertson, an internationally known Pentecostal with millions of television viewers, called for the assassination of Venezuela's President Hugo Chavez . . .

What can religious leaders do to promote human rights? Don't get in bed with warmongers when they co-opt human rights language to promote war and invasion—we will not have peace, justice, and enhanced human rights through violent regime changes. Religious leaders must stand against this and provide creative and wise alternatives.[90]

"PCPJ Purpose Statement," 2003

Whereas, the way of God as revealed in Jesus Christ is the way of peace and forgiveness, and;

Whereas, the life and teachings of Jesus and his disciples exemplified reconciliation, forgiveness, and nonviolence as integral to the Good News, and;

Whereas, the Holy Spirit empowered the disciples to suffer and die as they represented the way of the Kingdom of God rather than prospering and killing for any earthly kingdoms, and;

---

90. Alexander, "Toward Particular Declarations of Human Gifts." Excerpt. Paper presented at The Hague, Netherlands, June 2–4, 2008. A copy of Alexander's speech was provided to us by Alexander. Used with permission. The longer version of his speech is found in Alexander, *Christ at the Checkpoint*. Alexander's peacemaking stance contributed to his teaching contract not being renewed at Southwestern Assemblies of God University (Waxahachie, Texas) in 2006. His example exemplifies the consequences and sacrifices required from taking Jesus' example on nonviolence seriously in a country that relies so much on violence. Alexander notes the school "finally had enough of my quiet, yet consistent, questioning of nationalism and war." Because of his antiwar stance, some faculty refused to talk to him while others tried to get him fired. Five years after coming out as a peacemaker, Alexander was told that his faculty contract would not be renewed because of his "political and theological views." His inspiration, he said, came in part from reading early Pentecostal statements on war and peace. See Alexander, *Peace to War*, 345, 348, 349, 350. Alexander is now co-director of Evangelicals for Social Action and professor of social ethics at Palmer Theological Seminary of Eastern University (King of Prussia, Pennsylvania). He has written many Pentecostal and activist related books such as *Pentecostals and Nonviolence*, *Christ at the Checkpoint*, *Peace to War*, and *Signs and Wonders*.

Whereas, the church did not participate in state sanctioned violence (except as the recipients of it) for the first two centuries after Jesus Christ, and;

Whereas, numerous early twentieth century Pentecostals recognized that the missionary message of the Good News necessitated nonviolence and racial reconciliation at local, national, and international levels of society, and;

Whereas, the dehumanization and abuse of people, whether because of ethnicity, nationality, gender, age, religion, etc., are directly contrary to the unifying power of the Spirit of Christ, and;

Whereas, Pentecostals and Charismatics are called to be and speak God's new language in the world, a language of forgiveness, transformation, justice, and peace;

Therefore, be it resolved, that Pentecostals & Charismatics for Peace & Justice be established

to educate the hundreds of millions of Pentecostals and Charismatics in the world regarding their nonviolent and reconciliation focused Biblical and Pentecostal heritage, and

to educate us in the practices of nonviolence, and

to inform us of national and international issues regarding injustice, oppression, and exploitation, and

to facilitate action that brings about peace through writing, speaking, demonstrating, civil disobedience, and other nonviolent methods of affecting positive change, and

to serve as an association of Spirit-filled and Spirit-empowered followers of Jesus that allows and promotes discussions of war, capital punishment, human rights, racism, immigration, nationalism, and oppression, discrimination, or violence of any type, and

to cooperate with other peace fellowships and organizations to build peace and work for justice.[91]

"PCPJ: Our Mission"

Our mission is to encourage, enable, and sustain peacemaking and justice-seeking as authentic and integral aspect of Pentecostal & Charismatic Christianity, witnessing to the conviction that Jesus Christ is relevant to all tensions, crises, and brokenness in the world. PCPJ seeks to show that address-

91. "PCPJ Purpose Statement."

190 PENTECOSTAL AND HOLINESS STATEMENTS ON WAR AND PEACE

ing injustice and making peace as Jesus and his followers did is theologically sound, biblically commanded, and realistically possible. We invite you to participate with us in the way of Jesus-shaped Spirit-empowered peace with justice.[92]

"PCPJ Guiding Principles," 2007

Unity and Consensus

Members and coordinators will seek guidance / counsel from others within the group before making decisions that affect the operation of the fellowship. We believe in multiple leaders and decision making by consensus. We believe in open, honest, and nonviolent communication and conflict transformation. PCPJ practices consensus decision-making and servant leadership (Acts 2:42–47).

Diversity

PCPJ will demonstrate concern for the holistic well-being of all others with whom it comes into contact. We believe in gender, ethnic / racial, and denominational diversity in leadership. We believe the baptism of the Holy Spirit overcomes class, racial, and gender divisions (Acts 2:14–21). People are gifted differently for Spirit-filled peace and justice work, but PCPJ is a community of opportunity to share gifts, and creates spaces for people to operate in their gifts (1 Cor. 12:1–13).

Jesus-Shaped & Spirit-Empowered

We believe our priorities and decisions should be Jesus centered / shaped (Christocentric / Christomorphic). We believe in the present ministry of gifts and graces of the Holy Spirit (Acts 2:39). We believe the anointing of the Holy Spirit calls us to ministry as it called Jesus (Luke 4:18). Spirit-filled peacemaking and justice seeking is contrary to the way of the world, but Jesus is with us! (John 16:33)

Roots in Pentecost

We believe interest and action go together. As Spirit-filled peacemakers and justice seekers we wed communal commitment and Christ-confirmed actions with our convictions (1 Cor 5:18–19). We believe that peacemaking and justice seeking is part of New Testament and classical Pentecostal Christianity and a growing, healthy church (Acts 9:31). PCPJ is a network of persons in-

92. "PCPJ: Our Mission."

tentional about reclaiming our New Testament and Pentecostal peace with justice heritage (Romans 15:13). PCPJ witnesses first to our church traditions then to the wider church and finally to the world (Acts 1:8).[93]

PENTECOSTAL EVANGELICAL CHURCH
[Relation to War], 1967

Our young men shall serve our Country [sic] as they choose, preferably in the best places according to their skill, we do believe that the Word of God is true and we are not to take a life (thou shalt not kill) however they shall do all to help the wounded and dying, even in the Front Lines [sic] as in non-combat service.[94]

PENTECOSTAL FIRE-BAPTIZED HOLINESS CHURCH
From *Discipline of the Pentecostal Fire–Baptized Holiness Church,* 1961

We as the Pentecostal Fire-Baptized Holiness Church are opposed to war and forbid any of our members participating in same.[95]

PENTECOSTAL HOLINESS CHURCH
Daniel P. Awrey's (1869–1913) Nonresistance, 1910

From Springdale, Awrey moved to Atlanta, Texas. He held a meeting in a schoolhouse at nearby O'Farrell where about 15 were saved. But some evil reports began to spread, and one man threatened to run him out of town. A few days later, as he was returning from the post office, a man ran up and said, "When are you going to leave this town?" Awrey told him that he lived there and did not intend to leave.

93. "PCPJ Guiding Principles." Adopted on April 28, 2007.
94. Rev. Ernest Beroth to Arthur Carl Piepkorn [Personal letter].
95. *Discipline and General Rule of the Pentecostal Fire-Baptized Holiness Church,* 7.

With that, the man grabbed an old board left over from a picket fence and broke it over Awrey's head. He took other boards and beat him about the shoulders and back. Then he knocked Awrey's head against a telephone pole.

A prayer arose in Awrey's heart, "Father forgive him, for he knows not what he does." The man proceeded to hit him with a stick, and by this time a crowd had gathered. An old blacksmith went to get his gun, and the assailant fled.

During the time of beating, Awrey had not uttered a word. Once the ordeal was over, he praised and shouted "Glory to God" for protecting him. Awrey reported that the Lord kept him in such perfect peace and so filled with love, that he didn't even feel any pain in his body.

Afterwards the mayor called on him, and Awrey had the opportunity to share what great things the Lord had done for him. The man who had assaulted him was fined $17.00.

Later the man learned that the report he had heard, which had caused the beating, was untrue. Awrey tried to make friends, but the man refused.

Another time, after coming home from prayer meeting he heard a rap at the door. Awrey sensed that someone meant him harm. He looked out and saw a man with a large club under his coat. He said he wanted Awrey to visit a sick family and pray with them. Awrey replied that he was no doctor and shut the door. The man came back again, this time with a mob. He said that Awrey just had to come. In answer, he said he would go in the morning. Then Awrey and his family sneaked over to the mayor's house and stayed there all night.

On July 4, 1896, some men with pistols threatened to kill him. They took him to the railroad track and asked if he wanted to be hung to a telegraph pole or to be whipped. The men cut some switches and began to beat his bare back. They made several propositions to him, but he would not agree, so they continued to strike him unmercilessly. Afterwards, without malice he preached to them under the power of the Spirit and said, "Goodbye, we will meet at the judgment." Although his back was raw, and a friend wrote a letter to the authorities that Awrey "was the worst treated white man he had ever seen," he was so full of God that he hardly felt any pain.

The newspapers reported, "The charge preferred against him is that he preaches the sanctification doctrine, and it was leading their friends astray."

Pentecostal Statements   193

As Awrey prayed about this incident and other similar times of testing, several scriptures came to mind, including, "But when they persecute you in this city, flee ye into another" (Matt. 10:23). It was time to move on.[96]

[PHC on Military Service], 1921

Motion was introduced to state that The Pentecostal Holiness Church is opposed to military service or bearing arms. Objection made to the consideration of the question, and the objection prevailed.[97]

[PHC on Military Service], 1929

On motion, the following adopted: "Realizing that there are some people in our Church who are conscientiously opposed to the taking of human life while in military service, and feeling that we should help those who are thus minded, we make a motion that this General Conference instruct the General Board to take up said question with the Department of War of the Government of the United States of America in Washington, D.C., and secure such compromise on the above subject as is possible."[98]

Rev. J. Vinson Ellenberg, 1943

On August 18, 1943, the Rev. J. Vinson Ellenberg was examined and recommended for the chaplaincy and soon thereafter was sent to the Chaplain's School at Harvard, after which he was given an assignment. For some reason Mr. Ellenberg was unable to adjust himself to Army life, and stated that he had a feeling he was violating his personal convictions in performing the duties

---

96. Daniel Awrey wrote this while he was affiliated with The Fire Baptized Holiness Church before it merged with the Pentecostal Holiness Church. See Awrey, "Life Sketches," 16. Quoted in Gohr, "Telling the Lord's Secrets," 25–6.

97. "Minutes of the Fourth General Conference of the Pentecostal Holiness Church," 25.

98. "Minutes of the Sixth General Conference of the Pentecostal Holiness Church," 32.

required of him. He was finally given a discharge before he went overseas.[99]

From "Report of Committee For Service Men's Commission," 1945

The Pentecostal Holiness Church, while decrying the evils of war, yet in the defense of our Country, and in appreciation for religious and other liberties, essential to civilization as enjoyed under the Government of the United States of America, pledges its support to this government so long as said government provides such liberties. However, at the same time, the Pentecostal Holiness Church will support and defend any individual member whose personal convictions concerning war make him a Conscientious Objector, either with a A–1–0 classification or a 4–CO classification.

We believe the National Board for Religious Objectors is doing a good work in protecting the rights of individual citizens, and we hereby recommend that moral and financial consideration be given this organization by our annual Conferences.[100]

At the last General Cnference, [sic] four years ago, our country was not at war, but since then we have engaged in the most gigantic struggle in the history of the world, on the side of the Allied Forces. Our position as a Church is quite clear, that, while we abhor and decry the evils of war, yet we do not hesitate to rise in defense of our country, especially when attacked as we were at Pearl Harbor by one of the Axis powers.

More than 7,000 of our boys, together with several hundreds of our girls from Pentecostal Holiness homes have engaged themselves, many of them as volunteers in every section of operations and in every branch of our Armed Forces with heroic courage and high honors. To those who have died, (the present number being 123,) [sic] we pay tribute in a full minute of silent, sacred prayer, followed with a prayer of thanksgiving for victory in Europe and for an early and final victory elsewhere, with the establishing of a righteous peace over all the world. This prayer to be offered by our presiding Bishop.

99. Campbell, *The Pentecostal Holiness Church*, 408.

100. "Minutes of the Tenth General Conference of the Pentecostal Holiness Church," 47. The National Board for Religious Objectors is now http://www.centeronconscience. org/.

Pentecostal Statements   195

We extend our sincere sympathy to all of our bereaved families and our warmest and most heartfelt welcome to those of our boys returning home. To our Chaplains who are yet ministering, to our doctors and nurses yet serving, and to our boys who are yet fighting, we pledge our unceasing prayers for their protection and safe return. We pray for the salvation of the unsaved ones and for God to return all of them to us with a desire and a determination to help us carry on the glorious work of sending forth the Gospel of Christ into all the world, until every creature, of all nations, race, kindred, tribe, and tongue shall have heard the good news of our Savior's love.[101]

[World War I], referencing 1918

As in other denominations, some Pentecostal Holiness members were ardent pacifists and sought to expound their views even at the cost of members in their parent organization. Some persons apparently felt it their duty to warn people not to cooperate with the government since it was controlled, in their opinion, by forces of evil.[102]

---

101. Ibid., 49–50.

102. Paul, "The Religious Frontier in Oklahoma," 141. The Pentecostal Holiness Church (PHC) is almost exceptional for early Pentecostal groups leaving very little written evidence of official pacifism. Still, the group did have to address the issue of pacifism, given the established pacifist trend among Pentecostals. This incident reinforces the sense of how widespread the pacifism was held across the Pentecostal movement, with few official exceptions. Significantly, two early groups which formed by leaving the PHC in 1918 and 1920 were explicitly pacifist. The Pentecostal Fire-Baptized Holiness Church, founded in August 1918 during World War I was pacifist. Also, Watson Sorrow founded the Congregational Holiness Church in 1920, pulling out of the PHC, and immediately went on the record as being pacifist. (See statements for Congregational Holiness Church and Pentecostal Fire-Baptized Holiness Church.) Thus, it seems likely, that a pacifist group, although marginal, existed within the PHC from the beginning, albeit silenced, which may have motivated some to form their own pacifist denominations. One other group which came out of the PHC in 1921, The Association of Pentecostal Assemblies, was likely pacifist. It was formed under the leadership of Paul Theodore Barth and his mother-in-law, Elizabeth Sexton. Barth was a PHC minister in 1917. See *Minutes of the Third Session of the General Convention of the Pentecostal Holiness Church*, 3. According to Piepkorn, *Profiles in Belief*, 122, the denomination founded by P. T. Barth, The Association of Pentecostal Assemblies, merged with another to form the International Pentecostal Assemblies (IPA) in 1936. The IPA had a statement on pacifism, "Concerning War," which was precisely the same as that of the Congregational Holiness Church, which came out of the PHC in 1920. One other example of pacifism in the PHC was that of Gustave Sigwalt, a popular PHC evangelist

196   PENTECOSTAL AND HOLINESS STATEMENTS ON WAR AND PEACE

[World War II], referencing 1940

Another case was more embarrassing and not so easily handled. A minister, who was a member of the Oklahoma Conference and the father of seven children, became suddenly convinced that he should not register for the draft on conscientious grounds. Conference officials tried to reason with this minister and then turned the case to Bishop Muse when they were unable to shake his convictions. Muse was interested in the man and his family, but he was also interested in the reputation of the Church. He was determined not to permit the impression to get abroad that this small denomination was disloyal to the country and its leaders. After all other steps had failed, Muse advised in a letter:

. . . that the Board in conjunction with myself sign a statement declaring the attitude of the Church based upon the General Conference Minutes . . . and that one of the Board members take this in person to the Federal Attorney so that he will know the stand of the Church. I think our signed statement disavowing Golden's attitude and affirming the church's loyalty and willingness to serve will stand to be a buffer or cushion to soften any publicity that might arise from this fanatical stand.

Even if the registration was for actual military selectees, it would be tomfoolery for even a conscientious objector to refuse to register. I fear he is in a delusion fancying he will be a martyr, when in reality God will be dishonored or rather His cause dishonored. I seriously doubt if he changes his mind at the last minute. However, the Federal Attorney informed him if he had any business affairs to straighten up he had better take care of it before Monday night. So if you note any publicity, you can know that we have declared the church's stand for loyalty and service.

Pray for God to jar this man loose from his fool-hardy stunt.[103]

[World War II], referencing 1940

As World War II broke out in Europe in late 1939, and continued on into 1940 and 1941, the church took a marked stand favor-

---

in Florida. Sigwalt was imprisoned in 1918 for speaking against the war. See Beaman, forthcoming. These five cases illustrate that although the pacifism in the PHC was not official, and was likely squelched, it "came out," sometimes in a new denomination.

103. Ibid.

ing isolation. The Advocate, in 1940, warned the nation and the church against succumbing to "allied propaganda" and "pulling the chesnuts" of England and France out of the fire. "Let our annual conferences pass resolutions this year calling upon our national government to keep the fathers and sons of the country out of Europe's brawls," intoned the editor of the official organ. When the General Conference of 1941 convened in Franklin Springs, Georgia, the nation was on the brink of war, but the church continued to hold strongly for peace; although official statements called for "Unqualified opposition to unprovoked and aggressive warfare" and pledging "allegiance to the government of the United States." The conference further warned the church against "the danger of becoming affected by war hysteria as well as subversive propaganda." Clearly the church wanted no part in another world war. Yet when the war came, the church gave total support to the war effort.[104]

ROMANIAN APOSTOLIC PENTECOSTAL CHURCH OF GOD
[Relation to Government], 1972

Obedience to civil authorities insofar as they do not interfere with our Faith, Religious Practices and Conscience.[105]

SEVENTH DAY PENTECOSTAL CHURCH OF THE LIVING GOD
[War], 1969

We are against violence to your brother or neighbor. It is our intention to have an amendment added to our charter stating this, if God's People have to go to war, it should be in a non-violent capacity. The Scriptures state, "Thou shall not Kill." Ex. 20–13.[106]

104. Synan, *The Old-Time Power*, 206.
105. Romanian Apostolic Pentecostal Church to Arthur Carl Piepkorn.
106. Bishop Theron B. Johnson to Arthur Carl Piepkorn.

PENTECOSTAL AND HOLINESS STATEMENTS ON WAR AND PEACE

THE COMEOUTER [PENTECOSTAL PERIODICAL]

The Comeouter

Come out of her, my people, that ye be not partakers of her sins, and that ye receive not of her plagues.

VOL. 1   HIGHLAND PARK, KY., MARCH 1, 1918.   NO. 1

"The Patriotic Harlot," by Elbert Carlton Backus, 1918

There is no better example of the inconsistency of churchianity in general than its attitude towards that which the world calls patriotism,—no better example of its morbid ideals and of its faulty interpretation of Christianity.

The common conception of patriotism is accepted by the church without question. And why not? For 1600 years it has been the one great moulder of human ideals. Now in what it is pleased to term the highly enlightened and civilized 20th century shall it begin to disown that which it has been hundreds of years in bringing to pass? The leopard may change his spots and water may turn and run up hill, but apostasism will never lose its characteristics. Never will it cease to point with pride to its achievements. Never will it cease to excuse and to defend its inconsistencies and its narrowness, nor to assert its holiness and infallibility. But even if the popular conception of patriotism had sprung from some other source and the church doubted its legitimacy ever so much, the conservative, suave, compromising, insidious proselyter would surely adhere to its age old custom of following the lines of least resistance, the broad road to good favor and wealth and force its conscience to yield before public opinion.

Church patriotism, like the church itself, is outwardly beautiful but inwardly full of dead men's bones and of all uncleanness. The idea of noble self sacrifice stands out boldly, so boldly in

Pentecostal Statements   199

fact that all the disgusting, inhuman things connected with his profession are forgotten, or ignored, and the ideal patriot is glorified as one who has stood the supreme test and has laid down his life for others,—for his country. Certainly such self sacrifice, if prompted solely by Christian love, is sublimely beautiful and eminently Christlike; for "Greater love hath no man than this, that a man lay down his life for his friends." But let us pause just here to reflect that no love can possibly be Christian which is not universal in its scope. Christ loved ALL mankind, Christ died for ALL mankind, and although, in life, he was the champion of a great and just cause and waged a fierce warfare, when he at last was ushered roughly into the presence of the Father, not one drop of blood stained his hands save what was all his own. From the dying Christ and his compassionate prayer: "Father forgive them," turn to the uniformed idol of Christendom, sloshing heedlessly through the blood of his brethren, fighting like a demon until he himself is stricken; see HIS dying eyes burn with the bitter hatred of his soul even after his palsied hands refuse to move, and hear HIS last breath come hissing through clenched teeth, laden with a horrible curse upon the foe. Ah, who has failed to note that behind the beautiful veil of martyrdom covering church patriotism there lurks another idea so repellent that no soul untainted by the virus of hell could fail to turn shuddering away from the hateful thing. Who has failed to note the significant fact that the ordinary person does not think of patriotism apart from flags, marching soldiers, and the roar of battle. Who does not realize that the popular patriot in addition to all his seemingly good, Christ-like qualities must also be a murderer!

War is intensely barbarous; the favorite medium through which the demon of hate gluts its hellish appetite with tears, blood, and human carrion. Yet wars would not, could not be fought against the will of professed apostles of love and peace. The Williams, Georges, Nicholases and Wilsons together with most of their subjects and supporters are "Christians," At [sic] least, they are members of "God's" church, rulers by divine right, etc; yet they have rushed together, these brethren of God's family, in the most senseless and awful fratricidal butcheries the world has ever known. Then while these Christian rulers recklessly pour out the God given resources of earth and destroy the flower of the human race, think of the hundreds and thousands of flag decorated churches where the sanctimonious servants of

the devil congregate on the holy Sabbath and offer up their sac-
rilegious prayers, beseeching the Prince of Peace to throw his
influence and power into the balance on the side of Catholics,
Methodists and Baptists who are trying to kill their brother
Catholics, Methodists and Baptists who are so unfortunate as
to live just across some imaginary national boundary line. Then
think of these prayer mumbling, psalm singing hypocrites calling upon God with their next breath to bless the millions they
are giving and the hundreds of missionaries they are sending to
preach the gospel of Christ to the heathen. Oh, God!

Falling heir, as we have, to the false teachings of the past and
to their resulting false conceptions which have been drilled into
and fastened upon us by every conceivable agency, it is hard
for us to realize just what sort of world ours would be today,
if instead of teaching patriotism, with its narrow clannishness,
selfish nationalities and deadly strife the church had risen high
enough in the scale of Christianity to at least teach the doctrine
of the despised infidel who declared the world was his country
and his religion was to do good. Certain it is that the earth, after
so many centuries of such teaching, would not now be war torn
as it is, and the church would not stand responsible, as it surely
does, for the present world war and for numberless other wars
which have preceded [sic].

Oh, the bloody harlot, Apostasism! Born just outside the
Garden of Eden, and thriving today as never before upon the
errors, inconsistencies and corruption of the modern church, it
has never ceased since the days of Cain to follow off after its
Baals, its Mohammeds, its Fathers and its Reverends; all the
while offering up religiously its imperfect and unacceptable sacrifices to God. It has always been devilishly aggressive, this old
harlot, compassing land and sea to make one proselyte, compromising, adulterating, nullifying and even forcibly suppressing genuine Christianity, substituting its filth[,] malice and hate
for righteousness and love of the religion represented by Abel,
Moses and the Christ.

The apostle, John, looking far down through the centuries
to come saw apostasism with all its idolatrous sects of every
description and denomination represented by a lewd woman,
drunken upon the blood of those who loved the plain, pure
truth. After the Philistine and the Jew, the Christian and the
Mohammedan, the Catholic and the Protestant had all fought
their "Holy Wars;" after the sanctified Methodists had returned

the hate of the "grace" endowed Baptists; after false religion had done its perfect work and had set every man against every other man, and the world had become one seething mass of suspicion, enmity and strife, John saw the source of German "Kulture" and hell on earth.

The thing he saw was inconsistent churchdom; the American branch of which, as a Christian institution, had observed nationally a day of prayer for the cessation of human slaughter and then in a few months, as a patriotic institution, observed another day of prayer for bloody victory. The thing he saw was all false religion of all time which had deceived the nations and with which the war lords of earth had committed fornication. "And in her was found the blood of all that were slain upon the earth."[107]

THE FULL GOSPEL CHURCH ASSOCIATION (ARMARILLO, TEXAS)
"Civil Government," 1958

We teach that all Christians should be subject to the laws of the land, except those contrary to the revealed will of God; and pledge Allegiance [sic] and moral and spiritual support to the UNITED STATES OF AMERICA. In times of war the individual's participation in actual combat and taking of life shall be governed by his own conscience.[108]

---

107. Backus, "The Patriotic Harlot," 4–7. Emphasis in original. Backus was formerly a Methodist and a lay preacher for at least a year, but was removed a few years from the ministerial rolls. By 1918 he seems to have transitioned to a Pentecostal faith, loosely called "Holiness Mission," or "Holy Roller." It is possible that in transition from Methodist to Pentecostal he had espoused a form of socialism. Sometime later, he returned to the Methodist Church. Backus and a close colleague, Lon Echols, led a congregation that met in a barn in Highland Park, Kentucky. Both were indicted by a U.S. Grand Jury in Louisville, Kentucky, in July 1918 for espionage, for this publication among others, for their efforts to disrupt the war. The periodical states: "The paper [The Comeouter] has absolutely no financial support besides what the editors are able to furnish; and they are both poor men, dependent for a livelihood upon their daily labor" (p. 7).

108. Thorn, The Full Gospel Church Association. Emphasis in original.

202 PENTECOSTAL AND HOLINESS STATEMENTS ON WAR AND PEACE

THE GENERAL ASSEMBLY AND CHURCH OF THE FIRSTBORN[109]

From *Articles of Faith of the Church,* 1967

[Scripture]

We believe the Bible to be the Word of God, and we must live by every word of it as recorded in the New Testament, judgement to the line, and righteousness to the plummet.[110]

[Bearing Arms]

We believe in being subject to Kings, Presidents, Rulers and Magistrates in obeying, honoring and sustaining the Law as far as it harmonizes with the Divine Law. We teach our young men to serve their country in War in any capacity except to bear arms, for Jesus says, "Thou Shalt Not Kill," and He also said, "All they that take the sword shall perish with the sword." Luke, 3–14: "Soldier, do violence to no man."[111]

[Peaceful Living in Society]

We believe in being honest, true, chaste, benevolent, virtuous and in doing good to all men. Indeed we may say we follow the admonition of Paul. We believe in all things. We have endured many things, and hope to be able to endure all things to the glory of God.

Therefore, we believe according to our Articles of Faith, we should have the right to lead a quiet and peaceful life and worship God according to the dictates of our conscience, none molesting or making afraid, as the Constitution allows.[112]

---

109. Also known as "The Followers of Christ."

110. *Articles of Faith of the Church; The General Assembly and Church of the Firstborn.*

111. Ibid.

112. Ibid.

[RELIGIOUS LIBERTY]

We claim the privilege of worshipping Almighty God according to the dictates of our conscience and allow all men the same privilege; let them worship how, when and what they may.[113]

THE PENTECOSTAL CHURCH OF GOD OF AMERICA
"Relation to War," 1966

Whereas, we believe that our government is ordained of God, and whereas, we are thankful to the government of the United States of America for the freedom to worship God according to the dictates of our conscience, and

Whereas, there are those within our church organization who conscientiously object to the bearing of arms in the time of war, be it resolved that we as a church organization affirm their respective right to this conviction as they offer their respective services to our government in any way consistent with non-combative service.[114]

TRIUMPH THE CHURCH
[Triumph Church verses Church Militant], n.d.

Q. Was there another Church in the earth before Triumph?

A. Yes. Church Militant.

Q. Is there any difference between the Triumph Church and Church Militant?

A. Yes. Church Militant is a Church of warfare, and Triumph is a Church of Peace.

---

113. Ibid.

114. *General Constitution and By-Laws of the Pentecostal Church of God of America*, 22. See also McNeill, *As of a Rushing Mighty Wind*, 67–68. Noel McNeill notes this group "actively supports" the government in time of war and "encourages its members to serve in any way consistent with non-combative service." The movement, he writes, "leans towards Christian Pacifism."

204 PENTECOSTAL AND HOLINESS STATEMENTS ON WAR AND PEACE

Q. What happened to Church Militant when Triumph was revealed?

A. God turned it upside down and emptied His Spirit into Triumph.

Q. Is Triumph just a Church only?

A. No. It has a kingdom with it.[115]

"Article 85–Triumph Belief on War," 1959

Triumph the Church and the Kingdom of God in Christ does not believe in fighting war or murdering in any form from an individual divine standpoint. We believe it is wrong to kill, according to the Scripture: Exodus 14:14; Joshua 23:10; I Sam. 25:28; Matt. 26:52; II Cor. 10; I Peter 2:21; Rev. 13:10. We believe we ought to obey God's word as Christians.

We believe in the Divine Guidance of God individually, collectively, and Nationally [*sic*]. We feel that it is against God's will to kill or to fight; because of the consecrated life that is ordered through the Bible, according to Scriptures outline. We do not object to the defense of our country when it is being demoralized by the enemy. We sustain defense by finance and labor. We hold that our subjects who have the principle of our teaching instilled in them, should be exempt from natural COMBATANCE. We sustain the system of governmental force, but reserve the rights to support it by legitimate ways and means to prove American citizens.[116]

UNITED PENTECOSTAL CHURCH
"Holiness," 1930

Godly living should characterize the life of every child of the Lord, and we should live according to the pattern and example given in the Word of God. "For the grace of God that bringeth salvation hath appeared to all men, teaching us that, denying

---

115. Hollenweger, *Pentecostals* 45–46; citing *Triumph the Church and Kingdom of God in Christ, Junior Guide and Easy Lessons*, 15.

116. *Constitution and General Rules of Triumph The Church*, 72–73. Emphasis in original. This booklet gives tribute to "Bishop Elias Dempsy Smith, Founder, Chief Apostle, Priest and King" (ibid., 7).

ungodliness and worldly lusts, we should live soberly, righteously, and Godly, in this present world" (Titus 2:11, 12). "For even hereunto were ye called: because Christ also suffered for us, leaving us an example, that ye should follow His steps: who did no sin, neither was guile found in His mouth: who, when He was reviled, reviled not again; when He suffered, He threatened not; but committed Himself to Him that judgeth righteously" (1 Peter 2:21–23).

"Follow peace with all men, and holiness, without which no man shall see the Lord" (Heb. 12:14).

"But as He which hath called you is holy, so be ye holy in all manner of conversation; because it is written, be ye holy; for I am holy. And if ye call on the Father, who without respect of persons judgeth according to every man's work, pass the time of your sojourning here in fear: forasmuch as ye know that ye were not redeemed with corruptible things, as silver and gold, from your vain conversation received by tradition from your fathers; but with the precious blood of Christ, as of a lamb without blemish and without spot" (1 Peter 1:15–19).

We wholeheartedly disapprove of our people indulging in any activities which are not conducive to good Christianity and Godly living, such as theaters, dances, mixed bathing, women cutting their hair, make-up, any apparel that immodestly exposes the body, all worldly sports and amusements, and unwholesome radio programs and music. Furthermore, because of the display of all of these evils on television, we disapprove of any of our people having television sets in their homes. We admonish all of our people to refrain from any of these practices in the interest of spiritual progress and the soon coming of the Lord for His church.[117]

"Conscientious Scruples," 1930

We recognize the institution of human government as being of divine ordination, and, in so doing, affirm unswerving loyalty to our Government; however, we take a definite position regarding the bearing of arms or the taking of human life.

As followers of the Lord Jesus Christ, the Prince of Peace, we believe in implicit obedience to His commands and precepts, which instruct us as follows: ". . . that ye resist not evil . . ." (Matt.

117. *Articles of Faith of the United Pentecostal Church*, 9–10.

5:39): "Follow peace with all men . . ." (Heb. 12:14). (See also Matt. 26:52; Rom. 12:19; James 5:6; Revelation 13:10). These we believe and interpret to mean Christians should not shed blood nor take human life.

Therefore, we propose to fulfill all the obligations of loyal citizens, but are constrained to declare against participating in combatant service in war, armed insurrection, property destruction, aiding or abetting in the actual destruction of human life.[118]

"Conscientious Scruples," 1940

. . . We regret the false impression created by some groups of so-called "conscientious objectors" that to obey the Bible is to have a contempt for law or magistrates, to be disloyal to our Government and in sympathy with our enemies, or to be unwilling to sacrifice for the preservation of our commonwealth. This attitude would be as contemptible to us as to any patriot. The Word of God commands us to do violence to no man. It also commands us that first of all we are to pray for rulers of our country. We, therefore, exhort our members to freely and willingly respond to the call of our Government except in the matter of bearing arms. When we say service, we mean service—no matter how hard or dangerous. The true church has no more place for cowards than has the nation. First of all, however, let us earnestly pray that we will with honor be kept out of war.

We believe that we can be consistent in serving our government in certain noncombatant capacities, but not in the bearing of arms.[119]

"Resolution 6," 2011

Whereas, Our position in the Articles of Faith concerning Conscientious Scruples causes concern and has mixed support from the ministerial constituency and does not therefore accurately represent our corporate identity, and

118. Ibid., 11–12.

119. *Manual* [of the] *United Pentecostal Church*, 22. The 1930 and 1940 statements were republished in the 1966 manual. Their 2012 manual reiterates their historic position against war with the addition of one sentence: "We further believe that our military personnel must live in a manner consistent with the Articles of Faith." See *Manual [of the] United Pentecostal Church International*, 38.

Whereas, Many of our pastors are ministering to members in combat positions, and

Whereas, Many of our churches are ministering near military bases and serving the needs of many members in the military and aggressively reaching the lost serving in the ranks of the military, and

Whereas, Some of our military personnel have faced the difficult decisions of military service and some have chosen combat positions and have a shadow cast over them by our present position, and

Whereas, A recent UPCI publication highlighted the story of a man in combat position on the cover of its magazine, and

Whereas, The present position leaves no room for individual choice of a minister offering counsel to a member who is making military choices, and

Whereas, We have taken no written position on the involvement of a United Pentecostal Church member serving as a Police Officer or Security Agent, thus carrying a weapon with the possible use of force, and

Whereas, We have not addressed the equally difficult decisions concerning personal home and family protection in the event of a confrontation with a violent attacker, and

Whereas, In signing ministerial applications and affirmation statements, many ministers are not in agreement with our stand on Conscientious Objector Status and are consequently endangering their personal integrity, and

Whereas, This deep and complicated issue merits the value of individual deliberation and heartfelt consideration, and

Whereas, This deep and complicated issue merits the value of individual deliberation and heartfelt consideration, and

Whereas, A restating of position will in no way limit a local church pastor from teaching to refrain from active combat in the military, and

Whereas, A new approach to this sensitive subject will not limit the child of God from declaring a conscientious objector status if their conscience so dictates; therefore

Resolved, That the Article of Faith entitled, "Conscientious Scruples" contained in the Articles of Faith of the United Pentecostal Church International, as set forth on page 35 of the Manual of the United Pentecostal Church International, 2011 Edition, be amended to read as follows:

Mankind is God's earthly image bearer as stated in Genesis 1:27. "So God created man in his own image, in the image of God created he him." As reflectors of this divine image, human life has been invested with the highest level of intrinsic value. The whole idea of taking of human life is complicated with a wide variety of complexities (Exodus 20:13; Genesis 4:8–10; Numbers 35:6, 12). We recognize the deep and difficult deliberation required in these decisions. We therefore support our members in prayerfully and scripturally exploring their individual responsibility to God in these matters. We therefore honor the right of our members to serve as conscientious objectors and not bear arms. We also encourage those who serve according to their conscience, in any and all capacities, to express courages loyalty to country while serving in appropriate roles working "heartily, as to the Lord" (Col. 3:23).[120]

"An Open Letter to UPCI Ministers: A Historical Perspective on Our Conscientious Scruples" by L. Danny Barba, 2012

The recent discussion about the altering of the principles of UPCI's articles on conscientious scruples marks a monumental shift in our theology. Have you ever wondered what the founders of the Oneness-Pentecostal movement would say about issues we vote on today? Yes, those very same founders who received the Oneness revelation and practiced Jesus' name baptism. This is a historical question I took up over a year ago in my PhD history seminar at the University of Michigan. As a very committed member of the UPCI for over half my life now, a life-long citizen and patriot of the US, and now a trained-historian, I wondered how our founders understood their relationship and commitment to the US when our country required them to take up arms with the possibility of taking human life.

Various records clearly show what Pentecostal pioneers *did*, not just *said*, when faced with such moral dilemmas about involvement and bearing arms in war. The record overwhelmingly points to pacifism as rooted in the bible as was the Oneness

---

120. *United Pentecostal Church International 2011–2012 Annual Report*, XVII–XIX. During the general conference business session held on October 12, 2011, the motion to delete pacifism was approved, but still needed a two-thirds vote of the district conferences. On August 29, 2012, the general superintendent reported that the amendment received a 79 percent approval rate. The new statement is now part of their Articles of Faith. See *General Superintendent Update*.

Pentecostal Statements 209

understanding of the Godhead. Although he declined to join any church body, Azusa Street eyewitness evangelist Frank Bartleman decried the wholesale slaughter of human life and the premature consigning to hell of millions of soldiers.

In fact, a vigorous pacifism, together with the expulsion of Oneness ministers from the Assemblies of God, propelled the need for organization. Looming global war sent early Pentecostal pioneers rushing to form a religious body in order to be granted conscientious objector status. Oneness Pentecostal organization founder Sam McClain, who received the Holy Ghost in 1912 and was of age to serve, recounts the tumultuous time "the United States was preparing to enter World War I and as we had so recently organized, we could not get noncombatant service for our young men in the draft." Did they refuse to serve out of sheer cowardice? God forbid. A deep conviction against the possibility of taking human life kept them from serving. In 1919 McClain published an early Oneness position on War in the *Apostolic Herald* stating: "The Pentecostal Church . . . opposes to its members participating in warfare in any capacity. But in case our government is drawn into a struggle with an enemy threatening or making an invasion on our country, we stand for loyalty to our government and our flag. We would ask for non-combatant service in some capacity that does not require the Christian to bear arms, which would force him to participate in shedding blood and taking human life."

Writing in 1919 as a leader of the Pentecostal Assemblies of the World (PAW), McClain likely knew about the treatment of conscientious objectors (those who refused to fight) in World War I America. Numerous Oneness-Pentecostal pastors and elders served time behind bars for their pacifist position. One record shows that out of nineteen conscientious objectors detained at Disciplinary Barracks, Ft. Leavenworth, Kansas (1919), all identified as "Pentecostals." Among them were members of the PAW, the antecedent of the UPCI. Here are a few of the many specific examples of how earnestly our founders were willing to stand up for their belief in pacifism: Elder Morton of the Detroit area was incarcerated at Kingston Penitentiary; according to the roster of US Disciplinary Barracks, Ft. Leavenworth, Kansas, William Smith of Illinois was sentenced to ten years behind bars; according to the *Sacramento Bee*, upon the apprehension of Pastor William Reid of Sacramento California for charges of "acts unbecoming of an American" and "remarks that were of seditious nature" the Sacramento Chief of Police spitefully upbraided Reid, "you should be lined up against a wall and shot." Even worse than all these cases, many were sent to federal penitentiaries where they met a firing squad who had hoped to change the minds of pacifists. When some refused to recant they were fired upon with empty guns in an act of intimidation and violation of their First Amendment rights to coerce them to recant." Others were tarred and feathered, run out of town; and most despicably, viewed as expendable and thus used as cannon fodder. Dr. Talmadge French has shown how Bureau of Investigation (now called the FBI) authorities even covertly joined churches, and were baptized in Jesus' name, in order to investigate the PAW's stance on War. In that same church in Santa Fe, NM, federal authorities arrested two preachers. Later, because of his pacifist stance, federal authorities sought to ban Garfield T. Haywood's theological publication, *The Voice in the Wilderness*, but accidentally banned another publication by a similar title, *A Voice in the Wilderness* instead.

Why would Oneness Pentecostals have taken such a stance knowing that their members had suffered such persecution? I propose that *their holiness convictions remained stronger than their political convictions.* These holiness-minded pioneers believed that shedding blood on behalf of their country was unholy, unjust, and unlike Jesus.

Holiness minded pioneers took holiness seriously. The divine injunction, "Be ye holy for I am holy" took precedence over political or national affiliation. When will we like Paul understand that our citizenship (*Politeuma*) is in heaven (Philippians 3:20), and it is that citizenship that should take precedence citizenship to any country, U.S., Canada, or otherwise? Are the principles of peace in Jesus' Sermon on the Mount an example of cowardly theology? If we move to sanction the killing of individuals, even if in the name of the nation-state, we choose to not only reject the words of the founding fathers of Oneness-Pentecostalism, but also the words of Jesus, our Heavenly Father.

Why this gradual loss of our founders' beliefs in sticking to the words of Jesus? Historians have noted that the reason leaders of Assemblies of God largely caved in to bearing arms in war and later changed its articles of faith was due to the participation of their boys in the military and their desire to gain acceptance among the rising National Association of Evangelicals. In other words, being Pentecostal took the back seat to being American and accepted by evangelicals. Are we giving in to the same social pressure? Is our theology of nonviolence now weaker because we love America so much? Do we not owe it to our much-vaunted non-US constituencies and sister churches throughout the world to stay the hand of US military power that may result in their destruction and loss of life. Lest we find ourselves on the same moral trajectory as other American church groups who feel at ease in Zion, let us reevaluate the motion at hand.

While it is not unknown to the UPCI to reverse and revise the positions of our earliest founders with regards to salient doctrinal issues, by hastily voting for this new article we nevertheless run the risk of being carried about by every wind of patriotic doctrine. Our Pentecostal history offers us a rich understanding of how Holy-Ghost-filled people ought to view and maintain their relationship to their country. It is my belief that if we do not look closely enough at this issue because of being blinded by our political convictions that we should march in lock-step with, we run the risk of putting something before our God. Thus, putting the commandment of America before the commandment of God Almighty is nothing short of (patriotic) idolatry. Finally, consider how would we respond to this issue if it were being discussed in our churches around the world, especially in communist countries? What makes it permissible to shed blood for one country but not for another? Last time I checked, God's commandments transcend every people, kindred, tongue, and nation.[121]

"An Open Letter to UPCI Ministers: A Biblical Examination of the Current and Proposed Resolution to the UPCI Articles of Faith on Conscientious Scruples" by Donald W. Whitt, III, 2012

Recently, members within the UPCI have proposed a revision to the article on Conscientious Scruples. The proposal calls for an amendment to the current article which would allow more space for members and clergy not only to enter into the Armed Services, but also to take human life. This is a letter in response to the proposed revisions to the current article. I have organized my letter by comparing the current article on Conscientious Scruples and the proposed resolution. I compare how each letter

121. Barba, "An Open Letter to UPCI Ministers." Paper used with permission. Email correspondence with Barba, January 18, 2013, personal files of Brian Pipkin.

uses loyalty, what loyalty means to national identity, and how the bible verses they reference add or detract from the respective articles.

I am a youth pastor for a UPCI church. I do not currently hold a license; however, I have hopes and aspirations of joining the ranks of licensed UPCI ministers in the future. I find the current discussion and possible revisions to the Conscientious Scruples article to be deeply disturbing. To further add to the issue, depending on how you slice the pie, I would not consider myself a pacifist.

Professionally, I am a public servant in law enforcement. I grew up in a UPCI church and I hold a master's degree specializing in politics and religion. As a result of my profession, this is a matter that I continually struggle with and meditate on with much consternation. I know this is an extremely complex matter that directly impacts our holiness, Christian identity, and national identity. It is a matter which calls for rigorous introspection and healthy discussion while considering the complexities involved with taking a human life. The complexities need to be tackled, examined and nuanced through the lenses of biblical understanding while avoiding hypothetical situations and anecdotes.

The two articles share a theme of loyalty. Loyalty is a fundamental part of our national identity and the expression of that loyalty may be described as patriotism. The first paragraph "affirm[s] unswerving loyalty" to the government because "the institution of the human government" is of "divine ordination." The third paragraph recommends that Christians should "fulfill all the obligations of loyal citizens" and the fifth paragraph condemns groups which use scripture to justify disloyalty or to argue that there is no need to lay down one's life "for the preservation of our commonwealth." The current article describes loyalty as unswerving and suggests that loyalty is expressed by fulfilling the obligations of a loyal citizen; it condemns disloyalty, gives space for the expression of loyalty by laying down one's life, and justifies loyalty to a government because government is divinely ordained. The current article suggests that our Christian and national identities are founded in theological concepts of loyalty.

The proposed 2011 resolution only speaks to loyalty in the latter portion of the last sentence, "[w]e also encourage those . . . to express courageous loyalty to a country while serving in appropriate roles working 'heartily, as to the Lord' (Colossians

3:23)." The current article encourages *unswerving* loyalty while the proposed resolution encourages Christians to have *courageous* loyalty. The difference is more than splitting hairs; the proposed resolution encourages courageous loyalty without any of the context the current article provides. The current article condemns disloyalty while the proposed resolution has no such condemnation. The current article suggests that loyalty is expressed by laying down one's life and fulfilling the obligations of the citizen while the proposed resolution suggests that loyalty is expressed by taking the life of another human being. The proposed resolution, if endorsed by the UPCI, would seem to suggest that our patriotism is expressed not by fulfilling the obligations of the law, and defending the country with our own life, but by taking the life of another human.

Furthermore, the use of Colossians 3 in the proposed resolution is perplexing as Colossians 3 establishes that a Christian's principle identity is based upon our redemption in Christ and is thus an inappropriate selection of scripture to provide biblical support for taking a human life. The overarching chapter addresses the putting off the former sins of the "old man" and putting on the "new man" (Colossians 3:9–10) and verses 10 and 11 imply that our *principle* identity upon redemption is established in Christ, with other Christians, regardless of *national* identity or status: "And [you] have put on the new man, which is renewed in the knowledge after the image of him that created him: Where there is neither Greek nor Jew, circumcision nor uncircumcision, Barbarian, Scythian, bond nor free: but Christ is all, and in all." Colossians 3:15 declares that the peace of God should rule in our hearts as we are all called into one body, and again, establishes a spiritual identity amongst Christians which supersedes any national identity. It is unclear how Colossians 3:23 or an expanded look at Colossians 3 is even relevant to the issue of loyalty and taking human life as a courageous expression of that loyalty. The reference is used completely out of context. Colossians 3:23 deals with slaves and their masters and cannot be used to justify Christians bearing arms in service to their country.

The current article invokes a series of biblical scriptures that speak to holiness, avoiding violent confrontations, consequences of a violent lifestyle, condemnation of unjust killing, and the Lord's justice. They reference turning the other cheek, (Matthew 5:39); following peace with all men and holiness, without which no man shall see the Lord (Hebrews 12:14); those who live by the sword will die by the sword (Matthew 26:52, Revelation 13:10); vengeance is the Lord's (Romans 12:19), and the unlawful killing of the just (James 5:6). The use of scriptures in the original article appears to be one of pacifism (Matthew 5:39) with strong admonition for those who use violence (Matthew 26:52, Revelation 13:10), and the exercise of peace is an expression of holiness (Hebrews 12:14). The current article lays a basis of scriptures that are consistent with and support the theme of pacifism.

The proposed resolution invokes a series of biblical scriptures that condemn murder, yet declares that the "taking of human life is complicated with a wide variety of complexities." The resolution references the commandment "thou shalt not kill" (Exodus 20:13), the murder of Abel at the hands of Cain (Genesis 4:8–10), and cities of refuge (Numbers 35:6, 12). Exodus 20 and Genesis 4 are quite clear on the matter of murder and Numbers 35 discusses cities of refuge in which murderers can retreat from an avenger while they await judgment. These references are clear on the matter of murder and do not support the resolution's assertion that taking human life is a complex matter. The proposed resolution does not offer *any* scripture to support the taking of human life in the name of the nation.

Thus, to replace the current article with the 2011 proposal would be, in my opinion, premature at best. It dismisses the scriptures cited in the Conscientious Scruples article, the discussion of loyalty and martyrdom, and offers no scriptural basis to add to the subject it proposes, while indicating that taking human life is an expression of patriotism. The resolution's declaration regarding the taking of human life is irresponsible in that it neglects to offer sound scripture supporting such a declaration and casually dismisses the matter of taking human life as simply too complex to resolve.

I do not consider myself a pacifist, but I cannot support this 2011 revision in its current form. As a young man viewing the process from the outside, the process of changing this article is very important to me. I hope the proposal will not quickly pass without deep introspection and much revision to the proposed resolution. I would like to see a theological examination of the greater context of the scriptures cited in the original article. Minimally, I would like to see an examination of and a reconciliation of Brother Bernard's chapter on the "Sanctity of Human

Pentecostal Statements 215

Life" in his book *Practical Holiness*. He introduces a hearty and compelling argument to abstain from any violent action whatsoever. We need to diligently examine what other Apostolic theologians, like pioneering oneness leader Frank Bartleman, amongst others, have to say about this issue.

In addition to the material at hand by Brother Bernard and other authors, we should understand how the Bible speaks to the myriad of issues that this subject presents: holiness, righteousness, national identity, spiritual identity, and our involvement in the execution of secular government—including its defense, and its offensive campaigns. Furthermore, we need to consider what can learn from the Old Testament about this subject. David wasn't allowed to build the temple of God because he was a warring king—incidentally, wars which were sanctioned by God. If we are the temple of God, how does taking life affect *our* righteousness? Would God no longer want to dwell in *us*? However, the law allowed for war, self defense, and capital punishment, which would almost certainly require taking the life of a subject. How does that inform our decision? We should examine how Romans 12 and 13 inform us about the subject of public service and the execution of a secular government. To what extent are we willing to execute and establish justice and equality? How does the bible differentiate between murder and the taking of life?

I know that the UPCI has had vigorous, wide-ranging debates over the years about many lessor subjects. Surely this subject deserves a robust and hearty discussion regarding the "wide variety of complexities" involved with taking human life. An organization that has the courage to fearlessly tackle the legal, sociological, historical, moral, ethical, philosophical, theological, and above all, the biblical conditions involved here, is one I would like to join. While there may not be a strong consensus regarding the outcome of the Conscientious Scruples article, I can handle a sincere conclusion that falls within the range of possibilities represented by either article. I'm less sure I can respect a collective indifference.[122]

122. Whitt, "An Open Letter to UPCI Ministers." Used with permission. Email correspondence with Lloyd Barba, January 19, 2013, personal files of Brian Pipkin. Barba reported a significant amount of resistance from ministers who did not known them. However, pastors who conversed with Barba and Whitt, even those they thought would strongly oppose them, ended up supporting their cause. Some even helped distribute these letters among the UPCI constituency. Barba reported that a UPCI minister, a veteran, supported their cause to protect and preserve the Conscientious Scruples article.

WESTGATE CHAPEL [INDEPENDENT ASSEMBLIES OF GOD]
"Article XII Concerning War," 1962

Members Bearing Arms (a) This Assembly recognizes that Government is ordained of God, and that its members should be subject to the "Higher Powers," as the Word of God admonishes us, and also that the ruler "beareth not the sword in vain." Romans 13:1–7. (b) The Assemblies gives full recognition and accords the privileges of full communion to those of its members who bear arms.

Conscientious Objectors (a) This Church does not advocate general conscientious objection. (b) It recognizes that a person may be a conscientious objector because of religious convictions based on Scripture, such as, "all they that take the sword shall perish with the sword." Matt. 26:52. Such a member believes war to be at variance with the principles of the Gospel, and in his case, the Church believes that he should not, contrary to his conscience, take up arms against his fellowmen. (c) The Assembly gives full recognition and accords the privileges of full communion to those of its members who are conscientious objectors.[123]

---

123. *Articles of Incorporation and By-Laws of Westgate Chapel.* Westgate Chapel is part of the Independent Assemblies of God.

6

International Holiness and Pentecostal Statements

INTRODUCTION

In 1917 the Assemblies of God (USA) published an article titled "The Pentecostal Movement and the Conscription Law" in the *Weekly Evangel*. Here, they laid out the responses of British Pentecostals to the Great War taking place in Europe, years before U.S. entry into the war.

> From its very inception, the Pentecostal Movement has been a movement of evangelism, studiously avoiding any principles or actions which thwart it in its great purpose. All the wings of the movement, which have grown out of the work that originated in the Southwestern States and the Pacific Coast are a unit in this respect.
>
> From the very beginning, the movement has been characterized by Quaker principles. The laws of the Kingdom, laid down by our elder brother, Jesus Christ, in His Sermon on the Mount, have been unqualifiedly adopted, consequently the movement has found itself opposed to the spilling of the blood of any man, or of offering resistance to any aggression. Every branch of the movement, whether in the United States, Canada, Great Britain or Germany, has held to this principle. When the war first broke out in August of 1914, our Pentecostal brethren in Germany

found themselves in a peculiar position. Some of those who were called to the colors responded, but many were court marshaled and shot because they heartily subscribed to the principles of non-resistance. Great Britain has been more humane. Some of our British brethren have been given non-combatant service, and none have been shot down because of their faith.

It had not been seriously considered that the General Council of the Assemblies of God (one of the prominent branches of the Pentecostal Movement in the United States) would find it necessary to interpret its attitude toward war, until the war clouds gathered and actual war was declared. Neither the General Council, nor any other wing of the movement that we know of have ever written a creed, therefore it was found necessary for a number of the official members of the Executive Presbytery to assemble together and draw up a resolution interpreting the established principles or creed of all sections of the Pentecostal Movement, and especially that part represented by the General Council. A resolution was formulated, approved by the Executive and General Presbytery, and forwarded to President Wilson on April 28th, 1917.[1]

The author notes that Pentecostals as a whole were unified against going to war. It is here that these first-generation Pentecostals, unabashedly, claimed to follow "Quaker principles," based upon the teaching of Jesus in the Sermon on the Mount. This particular article highlights, internationally, that all Pentecostal affiliates, in the U.S., Canada, England, and Germany, opposed war, and that in England and German saints were being put to the test.

Furthermore, the author says that many conscientious objectors in Germany had been shot for their stance. It was not clear that any of those shot were Pentecostals, but it appears some German Pentecostals had done military service under duress, and others had been conscientious objectors. Some British Pentecostals were given noncombatant service. The article made clear that Pentecostals were completely against killing in war, but compromises had been made under compulsion in Europe. Still, it was American Pentecostal and Holiness groups, who upon reflecting the experiences of European Pentecostals in the Great War, framed

---

1. "The Pentecostal Movement and the Conscription Law," 6. This article claims to have promoted pacifism from its very beginning, as far back as 1914 (ibid., 7).

International Holiness and Pentecostal Statements   219

their own experience when the U.S. entered the war. Was this a kind of solidarity?

BAN THIS BOOK

Probably no one did more to promote Pacifism among Holiness and Pentecostal groups in the 1890s to World War I than the Booth-Clibborn's. Arthur and Catherine Booth-Clibborn were continental leaders of the Salvation Army and later Holiness evangelists. Arthur was a respected Pentecostal leader, and since several of their sons eventually became Pentecostal leaders, their vocal pacifism during the Anglo-Boer War was how they became major influencers of Christian-pacifism within the Pentecostal movement, especially in Europe. Arthur combined the Holiness emphasis on divine healing with promotion of pacifism. He believed that during the rule of Constantine the church lost the gift of healing as well as peacemaking. He believed that some of the gospel message and practice had been lost under the Roman ruler Constantine. The church, he believed, was being restored to a full-gospel in the modern era, and the full-gospel reintroduced healing and peacemaking. In an ironic style that anticipated Ghandi and Martin Luther King, Jr., Booth-Clibborn told the story of the disciple Peter cutting off the ear of the Roman soldier with a sword. Jesus told Peter to "put up thy sword," and healed the soldier. Booth-Clibborn, arguing that the Christian practice of violence is a form of communication that closes off hearing, wrote: "A Christianity which takes the sword will have but a one-eared humanity as its audience." Booth-Clibborn's influence was made around Europe, the British Isles, and very much in the U.S. Arthur's book entitled, *Blood Against Blood*, was banned in Britain during the Great War. No doubt, the pacifism of the Swiss Pentecostal Mission also owed much to the work of the Booth-Clibborn's.

BURN THIS TRACT

Most of this chapter gives examples of Holiness and Pentecostal pacifists in the British Isles, Canada, and Australia. Australian and Canadian examples are also included from the Assemblies of God. A Holiness group called, The Bible Holiness Mission, in Vancouver, B.C., has promoted pacifism down to the present. Pentecostalism spread to England and

Europe over the route already travelled by the Holiness movement. Since the Booth-Clibborn's were established leaders in those circles, their involvement in Pentecostal pacifism would carry forward in the same way.

Frank Bartleman, a Holiness evangelist who chronicled the Azusa Street revival from 1906–1907, made a trip through England and Germany during the outset of the Great War. He told of his direct work to spread pacifism on that trip among Pentecostal missions. Bartleman was controversial in both the U.S. and in Britain. In Britain, before the U.S. entered the war, Bartleman travelled to Germany and returned speaking highly of Germany and German culture, while he "spoke against the war spirit," in England, as he put it. Pentecostal missions with leadership out of the Church of England, were not amused. Later, back in America, leaders in the Assemblies of God who published Bartleman's tract, *Present Day Conditions*, called on their constituents to "destroy this tract."[2] Still, some young men of draft age in the British Isles were deeply influenced by the Booth-Clibborn's and by Bartleman.

Several young men who would later be leaders in the English Assemblies of God, John and Howard Carter and Donald Gee, became conscientious objectors. Their stories are briefly included here. The Carter brothers opposed war, with one receiving a prison sentence while the other was free to preach during the war. The latter, John Carter, had the luck of the draw to get a draft tribunal headed by a younger Neville Chamberlain who apparently was more liberal. In contrast, Howard Carter was asked by the judge if he would treat a wounded soldier. He was asked directly if he would let the soldier die rather than treat him so he could return to combat. Howard answered, "yes," he would let him die. He thought to himself, "Would I treat a viper and then release it?" He restrained himself and explained he would not treat a soldier who was to be returned to killing others. His brother, John, said nearly the same thing, but Howard went to prison.

Many Pentecostal young men suffered ill-treatment and isolation during the war, but used the occasion to find spiritual disciplines and study to become ministers. These men became Pentecostal leaders and their testimonies of conscientious objection were still being published in English Pentecostal circles in exemplary fashion in the 1970s. Others like F. B. Phillips of the Elim Foursquare Gospel Alliance promoted conscientious

2. "Destroy This Track," 4.

International Holiness and Pentecostal Statements   221

objection to war as late as 1939. In other cases, some Salvation Army members promoted pacifism into the late 1930s.

Within a different context, Pentecostal pacifism had taken root to some degree as a result of American Pentecostals taking pacifism to a much more hostile context. Let us introduce this with a riddle. Where did the first conscientious objection to the War in Afghanistan take place? When did it take place? It may have been among Pentecostals in Russia, known as the Siberian Seven. Among the complaints of the Russian Pentecostals who sought and gained asylum in the American Embassy in Moscow in the early 1980s, was that they had been persecuted severely for refusal of military service. If we remember that this was the time of the Russian War in Afghanistan, it may be that the first conscientious objectors to the "War in Afghanistan," not the current conflict, but the Russian one, were Pentecostals.

So, we know that Russian Pentecostals struggled to be pacifist from the 1920s to at least the 1980s. In Eastern Europe, Pentecostals promoting pacifism suffered much more severely and for a longer time. No doubt, there was already a great deal of Christian pacifism in Eastern Europe before Pentecostals arrived in the early twentieth century. Christian pacifism in the U.S. was fueled by Russian immigrants. However, Pentecostals did promote pacifism when they went to Eastern Europe from the U.S. Brother Voronaeff, for example, died at the hands of the Soviets, after compromising Russian Pentecostal pacifism by trying to work with the Soviets. This was one example among many.

In an example of how important pacifism was to American Pentecostals, we can see from these documents that American Pentecostals had difficulty empathizing with Brother Varonaeff because of the compromise he made. More recently, over one-hundred thousand Russian Pentecostals have come to America since the opening of immigration from the former Soviet Union. One of the social issues they raised with their American counterparts was the loss of American Pentecostal pacifist belief and practice.

Additionally, some Holiness and Pentecostal advocates were pulled toward the "good war" when they saw the possibility of what they interpreted as Bible prophecy being fulfilled by British occupation of Palestine during World War I. Frank Sandford is a case in point. He moved all the way from pacifism, which he had preached for two decades, to requiring all his male followers to join the army and fight on the side of Jesus in the coming Armageddon. Contemporary Pentecostals like John Hagee, pull upon the extreme edge of religious-political influence by pushing the American religious right to favor expansion of the state of Israel at the expense of Palestinians, all in the name of Bible prophecy.

In the testimony of the Awad family and the Holy Land Trust, we have a contemporary Pentecostal style witness to peace and the pursuit of justice for both Palestinians and Jewish Immigrants to Palestine from the past century. In the style of Martin Luther King, Jr., and Gandhi, the Holy Land Trust calls for nonviolent engagement in a tinderbox of conflict. Although many U.S. Pentecostals have forsaken the hard work of peacemaking, members of the Holy Land Trust and Bethlehem Bible College are wholeheartedly pursuing Jesus-inspired peace and justice. It is certainly a cause for joy to us to include this group as a way to end this book. Perhaps Christian accommodation to the ways of state violence will not be the last word. It is a hopeful sign.

Finally, mention should be made of the pacifism of some Pentecostals in South Africa as early as 1915. Sources for this could be the lasting influence of the Booth-Clibborn's, or the early inroads of John Alexander Dowie's followers in South Africa, but more likely was from some such as John G. Lake and others who came from the U.S. including those from the Assemblies of God. However, this cursory introduction to international Pentecostal pacifism begs more scrutiny.

Why was pacifism not a central part of the Pentecostal message in the African or South American contexts? Let us suggest two possibilities, and others can add light as they can. First, the most significant inroads of Pentecostalism in Africa and Latin America came later, and from sectors of Pentecostalism that were already somewhat institutionalized and beyond their active pacifist phase. Nevertheless, it is possible that some of the missionary movements of this later time were aligned with American power and interests in these places. However, it is also likely that there are stories of Pentecostal and Holiness pacifism from these places that have yet to resurface. These are stories we long to hear.

Moreover, as American Pentecostal and Holiness heirs to faith today reflect upon post-Soviet émigrés to the U.S. whose pacifism seems perhaps "out of time," or as we reflect upon Palestinian Christians who suffer under U.S. policies in the Middle East that have been framed by an eschatology that requires a violent solution to conflict, or as American Pentecostals and Holiness folks show solidarity with brothers and sisters

International Holiness and Pentecostal Statements   223

in Latin America or Africa now, how are we informed by their experience
to become peacemakers in the world?

AUSTRALIA

Assemblies of God

"ARTICLE 23," 1943

Shane Clifton, in Global Pentecostal and Charismatic Studies, writes regarding the Assemblies of God (Australia), that, "Pentecostals were note-
worthy for their stance as conscientious pacifists. During the creation of
their constitution, Article 23 was given to the question of military service,
and declared that obedience to Christ, the Prince of Peace, and His prohibition against the shedding of blood meant that:

> We, as a body of Christians while purposing to fulfill all the
> obligations of loyal citizenship, are nevertheless constrained to
> declare we cannot conscientiously participate in war and armed
> resistance which involves the actual destruction of human life,
> since this is contrary to our view of the clear teachings of the
> inspired Word of God which is the sole basis of our faith.[3]

BRITAIN

"Maranatha" by H. Musgrave Reade,[4] 1912

> We are on the eve of one of the greatest upheavals in Europe that
> the world has ever seen; the bloodiest battles, with the most ter-
> rific carnage both on land and sea, will take place very shortly,
> engaging almost all the great powers of this continent, when
> prophecy will be fulfilled to the very letter. Europe at the pres-
> ent moment may be likened to a vast armed camp, with four-
> teen million soldiers enrolled and ready for a terrible butchery
> of each other. Every deadly instrument which modern science
> and human ingenuity can devise has been adopted for this hell-
> ish purpose of the destruction of human life. On every sea,
> also, are crowded those ugly, infernal engines of death called

3. Clifton, *Global Pentecostal and Charismatic Studies*, 3. Clifton quotes from
"United Constitution, Article 23," 1943.

4. Reade was a founding member of the Labour Party in England and pastor of the
Apostolic Faith Church in Winton, Bournemouth, England.

224 PENTECOSTAL AND HOLINESS STATEMENTS ON WAR AND PEACE

Dreadnoughts, ready to vomit forth death and destruction upon each other, and to send hundreds of souls to eternity in a few moments.[5]

"The Spirit of the Age" by H. Musgrave Reade, 1917

The "national spirit" tends to make men see everything through a distorted medium, and is a great enemy to a healthy conscience towards God. (Conscience *towards God* is the only conscience acceptable to Christ). This world spirit—the same spirit as urged the Jewish patriots and religionists to hurry the Son of God to Calvary—has hurried even true believers into committing themselves, in a most solemn way, to a business which is out of accord with the mind of their Divine Master.

Hypnotized by the spirit, high-placed ecclesiastics on both sides have made the vindication of the national cause identical with triumph of the kingdom of God!

And national sectarianism is responsible for the sentimental blasphemy that death in battle saves the soul?

This evil spirit is first aroused, and then played upon by inflammatory articles in the unscrupulous press. The deliberate suppression of "the other side of the case" is repugnant to elementary honesty; and yet there are souls whose bible is their pet newspaper, and imagine that what they read in the popular press of the country, where the accident of birth has put them, is an adequate or honest statement of the facts, "He that will lie for the good of the 'cause' will lie as to the case being good for which he lies." And today we see the phenomenon of each of the belligerent nations claiming to be morally in the right, and its enemy morally in the wrong, while their respective rulers denounce each other as transparent hypocrites!"

It has been remarked during the present war that after all, the only religion which the average Englishman ever took kindly to

---

5. "Maranatha," 15. Excerpt. Reade was one of the founding members of the British Labour Party before distancing himself from socialism. He wrote this article prior to his conversion to Pentecostalism. He was pastor of the Apostolic Faith Church in Winton, Bournemouth, England. See Reade, *Christ or Socialism?*; *The Latter Rain Evangel* (April, 1912), 15, describes Mr. Reade as one "who was for many years a leading socialist but wonderfully converted to Christ . . ." Reade's journey took him from socialism to conversion to Christ (1900), Keswick revivalism (1903), to being a missionary for the same in India (1904), to being a Pentecostal pastor before 1909. At that point, he was also a colleague with Welch coal miner, Evan Roberts. See *Christ or Socialism?* 24–25, 33, 83.

is patriotism. Man is not merely an animal. He feels his need of
an ideal. God's ideal for man is Christianity; but Satan is using
the national spirit as an ideal to displace God's.

What an appalling sight confronts men today. Having rejected the Gospel of Christ, Christendom has adopted a new religion, national sectarianism, which leads to—mutual slaughter!

It is a remarkable phenomenon that each of the belligerent
nations claims to be fighting for an ethical ideal superior to that
of its enemy—a belief that makes the "will to slaughter" by each
of the combatants all the more determined. In this way the great
deceiver and murderer seeks to *conceal* the sordid beastliness of
the battlefield.

There are some who say that this war will end war. What a
pathetic delusion! As if Satan would cast out Satan! . . . War is a
game from which all parties rise [?] the losers.

The world's hope is a delusion. And why? Because it rests on
a false foundation. Man's hope rests on man, and man is himself
ruined by sin. . . . . Unlike the world's rulers, He [Jesus] never
debates what part of the truth to conceal in order to remain
popular with His people. In Him there are no narrow limits of
nationality, for He is the Son of *man*. He does not command
His people to kill or to be killed: He died Himself to save His
people from their sins. Devotion to Him does not involve injury to other men; on the contrary, His servants seek the eternal
blessing of others. Unlike the world, He never deceives, and He
always satisfies.

True Christianity can never be popular. The believer is no
longer a devotee of the spirit of the age. In contrast to the world's
weapons of violence and fraud, he is to wield the forces of faith,
and prayer and truth. He has renounced the idols of godless conscience, cultured unbelief and national sectarianism.[6]

Rev. Albert E. Saxby, 1912–1914

During World War I, the congregation in Harringay, led by A. E. Saxby
(1873–1960), where Donald Gee, early British Pentecostal leader and conscientious objector was a member, stated: "Let it be known that, as followers of Christ, its members could not participate in war and bloodshed."[7]

---

6. Reade, "The Spirit of the Age," 13–15. Excerpt. Emphasis in original.

7. Carter, *Donald Gee: Pentecostal Statesman*, 17–18.

226   PENTECOSTAL AND HOLINESS STATEMENTS ON WAR AND PEACE

Frank Bartleman at A. E. Saxby's Church, 1912–1914

Frank Bartleman (1871–1936), an American Pentecostal leader, toured Europe from 1912 to 1914, meeting many fellow Pentecostals in Russia, Germany, and England. Bartleman reported that Saxby gave a favorable response to his anti-war sermon:

> I spoke at Pastor Saxby's Mission Sunday morning. Here God gave me a strong message against the war spirit also. But it was very differently received. The leader thanked me warmly. He had come into Pentecost, with his congregation, from the Baptist Church. The other mission was really Church of England. They had never severed their connection fully with the State Church System.[8]

Central Pentecostal Mission (London), 1912–1914

In contrast to the warm reception Bartleman received at Saxby's church, Bartleman, when speaking at the Central Pentecostal Mission, found himself in the midst of a militarized Pentecostal group. While his promotion of pacifism was met with resistance, he also reported some success.

> The Lord gave me a strong message against the war spirit in Christians. The leader said if he were a young man he would enlist himself. They were opening their meetings with a "War Hymn." The Conscription Act had not yet passed. My message dropped like a bomb in the camp. But some thanked me for it later, especially some of the missionary student young men, members of the P.M.U [Pentecostal Missionary Union] . . .[9]

Alexander A. Boddy, British Pentecostal Leader[10]
"The War," 1914[11]

We British Pentecostal people should pray very earnestly that "Militarism" may come to an end through this war; that our Empire should learn its lessons soon through humiliation and

8. Beaman, *Pentecostal Pacifism*, 56.

9. Ibid.

10. Alexander A. Boddy (1854–1930) was a Church of England Minister and early British Pentecostal leader.

11. Boddy, "The War," 191. Quoted in Lenz, "Visions on the Battlefields," 288.

International Holiness and Pentecostal Statements 227

penitence, and come out refined and purified to serve the cause
of Christ more loyally than before. We should acknowledge our
sins, and earnest prayer meetings should be held, asking God to
uphold the right and give decisive victories, if it be His will.

I am quite sympathetic with those who are genuinely exercised as to whether or not a Christian man should go to war; but
let us remember that the laws which govern the Church of God
as such, don't govern the Nations of the earth as such. It is not
the Church of God that has gone to war, but the British Empire,
and both are fulfilling divine purposes, though those purposes
are not the same. Let us also remember that every Christian is a
citizen of some State; shares in the benefits of that State, and has
obligations to discharge in relation to it. When a man becomes a
Christian, he does not shake off the State, neither is he lifted out
of it. If a widespread riot took place in this town, I would be very
glad of the protection of the police. If State machinery, which
is the Law, was to break up, not a life in Christendom would be
safe. The State is of God, and is truly so in this dispensation as
in the last (Rom. xiii., 1–7. 1 Tim., ii., 1–2. 1 Pet. ii., 12–17); and
if we as Christians share the advantages of it, we must share its
responsibilities also. The work of the Church of God as such,
is to preach the Gospel, to make Christ known as Saviour and
Lord, both by word and life. But in addition to that it is the duty
of Christians as citizens to suppress intemperance, to wage war
against immorality, to protect children, to provide for the aged
and helpless, and to prevent wanton cruelty to animals. The securing of these things will not save the souls of those who com-
pose the nation, but it may save the nation as such, and secure
for it an honourable place among the nations of the earth.[12]

12. Ibid., 206. Excerpt. Quoted in Lenz, "Visions on the Battlefields," 291–92.
Donald Gee, British Pentecostal leader in the Assemblies of God, writing in 1980, attributed Boddy's decline in ministry to his embrace of British Nationalism. He wrote,
"The first World War brought a surge of national patriotism, and as a State Church
clergyman A. A. Boddy was caught up in the tide. Even Pentecostal meetings were
closed with the singing of the National Anthem. At the close of hostilities in 1918 an
attempt was made in London to recommence the annual Whitsuntide Convention. But
Alexander Boddy, although still loved and respected by old Pentecostal friends, had
lost the Fire. The glory had somehow departed, and he was only a shadow of the former
master of assemblies. In 1922 he resigned from All Saints,' and died in the pastorate of
the little village church of Piddington, near Durham, in 1930." See Gee, *These Men I
Knew*, 22. Quoted in Lenz, "Visions on the Battlefields," 298.

Lenz, in commenting about Gee's interpretation of Boddy's national loyalty, observed that Gee "incorrectly interpreted Boddy's loyalty to Great Britain as 'national

228   PENTECOSTAL AND HOLINESS STATEMENTS ON WAR AND PEACE

Pentecostal Missionary Union (PMU) [Letters to Missionaries]

T. H. Mundell, PMU Secretary, to Miss F. E. Jenner, Yunnan, W. W. China, 1915

So far as I can see the Christians have only one attitude towards this war which is clearly set out in our Lord's teaching. "My kingdom is not of this world else would my servants fight." "They are not of the world even as I am not of the world." This War is essentially of this world and I hold that no Christian ought on any account take part in actually destroying and killing his fellow men. This is undoubtedly one of God's Judgements [*sic*] upon the nations, England included, and I feel that we are on the very verge of the Coming of the Lord and that prophecy is being rapidly fulfilled. Many believe that evolving out of this terrible conflict will be the setting up, of the Anti-Christ when Daniel 7 and Rev. 13 will have quick fulfillment.[13]

T. H. Mundell to Rev. W. S. Norwood, Abbotabad, India, 1915

So many are realizing that the Christians attitude towards this war should not on any account be to take any part in the fighting lines except in the way of prayer and practical deeds to help

---

patriotism' primarily because of his own stance as a conscientious objector during the First World War." Furthermore, despite Boddy's justifications for supporting the Allied war, he simultaneously remained "sympathetic to the plight of Pentecostal pacifists and even promoted Arthur Sydney Booth-Clibborn's popular anti-war book, *Blood Against Blood*, to the readers of Confidence." With the introduction of conscription during World War I, copies of *Blood Against Blood* were confiscated and banned in Britain. Furthermore, although Alexander Boddy promoted Booth-Clibborn's book, it was not clearly endorsed by Boddy. See Anderson, *Spreading Fires*, 225.

13. T.H. Mundell to Miss F. E. Jenner, Yunnan. The PMU, the first Pentecostal mission agency, created in January 1909, was formed in Great Britain under the leadership of C. Polhill. For more information about the PMU, see Hocken, "Pentecostal Missionary Union," 970–71. In the PMU's last years, Hocken observed a "widening gap between the educated Anglican patriots, Polhill and Boddy, and the rank-and-file working-class Pentecostals, who included many conscientious objectors to military service (ibid., 971). While Mundell took a strong position against war, advocating Christian-pacifism, Polhill, like Boddy, took a stand in favor of "just war" ideology. Allen Anderson writes that despite Polhill's views on war, the PMU council, in 1918, made the "unanimous decision" that if their missionaries volunteered for war service, they would have "entirely severed their connection with the PMU." Quoted in Allan Anderson's, *Spreading Fires*, 227–28.

International Holiness and Pentecostal Statements 229

those in need. Our Lord's teaching is so clear on this point that "My Kingdom is not of this world else would my servants fight" and "they are not of the World even as I am not of the world." I personally strongly hold that just as Christ if He had been on earth today would not on any account have taken part in the fighting, no more should the Christian think of doing so.[14]

T. H. Mundell to Mr. F. D. Johnstone, Africa, 1915

We are looking forward to having a good Convention in London instead of at Sunderland this year. The war news, so far as one can tell, is most satisfactory to England although we cannot see any prospect of an early [end] determined as it is to fight to the bitter end.

I was much struck in reading today Romans 12, which is a real threat upon the duty, life and experience of every living Christian and how contrary it is to all the warfare and turmoil, hatred and destruction which is now going on in the world from the beginning to the end. The first verse, setting out the requirements of presenting our bodies a living sacrifice, holy, acceptable unto God and not being conformed to this world,—and ending with—if your enemy is hunger, [sic] feed him; if he thirst, give him drink—vengeance belongeth unto God and avenge not yourself. For anyone to take and [sic] this and preach it in all its fullness at the presence [sic] time he might incur the possibility of being mobbed or imprisoned although many Christians at the present time are seeing that they cannot take part in the war as there is no single text of scripture in the New Testament warranting them doing so.[15]

T. H. Mundell to Mr. A. A. Swift, China, 1915

Well my dear Brother it is true, it is not, that we fight against flesh and blood but against spiritual wickedness in heavenly places. How different to this awful war-spirit would be the experience of every Christian if they would carry out the commands and injunctions in Romans 12 (Read the whole chapter.) and instead of presenting their bodies to ungodly men to be slaughtered or for the purpose of slaughtering others, to give themselves absolutely

14. T. H. Mundell to Rev. W. S. Norwood.
15. T. H. Mundell to Mr. F. D. Johnstone.

230　PENTECOSTAL AND HOLINESS STATEMENTS ON WAR AND PEACE

to God as a living sacrifices etc then they would have the joy as many of your dear Missionaries are proving "what is that good and acceptable and perfect will of God."[16]

The Pacifism of Howard Carter and John Carter, British Assemblies of God Leaders

FROM HOWARD CARTER'S DIARY, 1916

9 March 1916. I received a notice to be at the Council House Birmingham by 3:30 & arrived at that time. After waiting till it was past 5 o' clock, I heard my name called so I took my place before the table round which was gathered a number of men and also a woman. After sundry enquiries concerning the Pentecostal movement by the President, I was asked by a man on his left if I would help a wonderful soldier if I saw one—to which I answered after hesitating a while that I could not help him recover, to the end that he should destroy life. The man then said, "By that do you mean you would let him die?" To which I answered in a rather doubtful tone, "Yes." He advised me in a friendly way to reconsider what I had said as a Christian, for he was sure I would change views. It came into my mind to say that I could not nurse a viper to health again as I should but be reviving him to sting again, but through fear of being misunderstood, I kept silence.[17]

HOWARD CARTER—MAN OF THE SPIRIT BY JOHN CARTER, 1971

The Great War was raging and many lives had been sacrificed upon the fields of Flanders. Men were acutely needed and in 1916 a bill authorising Conscription was passed in Parliament. The Act provided for the hearing by Tribunals of objectors to military service.

---

16. T. H. Mundell to Mr. A. A. Swift.

17. Howard Carter, "Diary," March 9, 1916. Quoted in Bundy, "Howard Carter," 12. Howard Cater (1891–1971) appealed but was unsuccessful, and on January 24, 1917, he was notified to report for military service. According to Carter, the authorities refused to recognize him as a minister of a legit organization, and on March 16, he was escorted by the military to Wormwood Scrubbs Prison. Continued failure to cooperate with authorities (putting on a khaki uniform) resulted in him being sentenced to 112 days hard labor.

International Holiness and Pentecostal Statements   231

Both of us [John and Howard Carter] had a conscientious objection on religious grounds to participating in war and bloodshed, and we filed our applications for exemption at the same time. Nevertheless we were not called for hearing at the same tribunal. I received notification before my brother and attended the appointed tribunal for the hearing of my grounds for objection. The Chairman was Neville Chamberlain who later became Prime Minister. At that time I was employed at Lloyds Bank, Head Office, Birmingham. To everyone's great surprise I was granted absolute exemption on conscientious grounds, something that was scarcely known at that time.

A little later Howard, at another tribunal was granted exemption conditional upon undertaking medical service. He said he was prepared to do this work provided that any men he nursed back to health were not returned to the fighting lines. As this was an impossible request his application was about to be dismissed when reference was made to the fact that he was a full-time Minister of Religion, being a pastor of the church at Duddeston.

It was felt this presented a case for the civil court so a hearing was arranged before a judge as, under the Act. Ministers of Religion were exempt from military service. Many questions were asked and it appeared that the Court was at the point of coming to a decision in his favour when the judge asked to what denomination his church belonged. When it was learned that the church at Duddeston was unattached and quite undenominational, the case was dismissed on the grounds that he was not a recognised Minister. The newspapers the following morning bore the head-lines "Minister to Serve. Not a Minister of a recognised Denomination."

The anomalous position was that I was as free as though no war was raging, whilst my brother now awaited arrest by the military police. One morning we traveled together to the City, shook hands and parted. I to follow my usual job as cashier and Howard to report for custody and imprisonment.

He was escorted to Wormwood Scrubbs Prison, London, where his hair was cropped very short, he was dressed in prison clothes, and put into a cell by himself. As the door shut with a clang and the key turned in the lock, Howard sat on the edge of the bed and began to tremble from had to foot. Temperamentally he was highly-strung, and all he had passed through at the two hearings coupled with the arrest and solitary confinement so wrought upon his sensitive nature that he began to wonder whether he might lose his reason.

Violently trembling he felt he must ring for the prison doctor. He rose to press the bell that would summon assistance, and then fell back on the bed remembering that he had preached how God could meet one's need whatever the circumstance. He heard a nearby prisoner screaming and he himself felt the temptation to do likewise, but he took a grip upon himself and resisted.

. . . Upon my brother's [Howard Carter] removal to prison, the oversight of the work at Duddeston fell upon my shoulders. My exemption from military service allowed me to continue with my daily occupation at the Bank, and to devote my spare time to the study of the Word and the ministry at the Assembly. The War was now producing such a drain upon the country's manpower that more soldiers were needed for the front, so the Government decided that all exemptions should be reviewed.

I had therefore to appear before another Tribunal, resulting in the cancellation of my total exemption given on conscientious grounds. They informed me I must do work of national importance, and I was sent as a "labourer" (such was the designation upon my official card) to a farm in Lancashire for the purpose of milking cows.

Mr. T. J. Jones had been called up but was totally rejected on medical grounds as it was discovered that he had a heart murmur. He therefore became responsible for the two assemblies— at Saltley and Duddeston.

Towards the end of 1918 I learned that Howard had been released from Dartmoor Prison and had been transferred to a Farm Training Colony in Berkshire. The purpose of the Colony was to train teen-age boys, who had been in trouble with the police, to become good citizens. When I learned that he was out of prison and working in this Institution, I was naturally anxious to see him again after our long separation, so I made application for a transfer from the dairy farm, and this was granted. It was a great joy to us both to be reunited and we had much to discuss.

The "brothers" on the Colony were each placed in charge of these unruly boys and certain manual tasks were allotted each day—cutting down trees, chopping wood, market-garden work, etc. Strict discipline was the rule. A certain religious atmosphere was maintained by the Superintendent, and it is to be hoped that

International Holiness and Pentecostal Statements   233

some lasting good was wrought in the characters of these unfortunate lads.[18]

"Conscientious Objector by John Carter," 1979

As the demand for man-power became acute owing to the carnage of war, this led to the introduction of Conscription in 1916. Many Pentecostal young men felt constrained to take their stand as conscientious objectors, so tribunals were set up to try such cases.[19]

"Compulsory Military Service: An English Conscientious Objector's Testimony," 1917

Early in March, 1916, compulsory military service was forced upon the country and I at once put in an application for total exemption from military service as a conscientious objector. I had been thus minded ever since the war started and wondered what I should do if compulsion actually came. I had prayed very much and my parents and brothers had been praying too, for we all had the same attitude towards war, believing that from New Testament teaching that a Christian should not go to war.

To my surprise, I found that the Military Service Bill contained a clause which allowed anyone who had a conscientious objection to war to appeal and either get non-combatant work or total exemption. So I appeared as the act allowed me to, and about the end of April a paper came warning me to appear at the Tribunal Court.

I went up and appealed on Christian grounds. I stuck to the Scriptures and gave my objection from a Scriptural standpoint. They questioned me very closely and I answered their questions by quoting Scripture. They told me that they did not want me to preach to them but to simply answer questions. They all hung their heads as I gave my objections. At last one of them asked what I would do if an enemy came to my home and was about to kill my mother. I told him I would pray. However, they proved

18. Carter, *Howard Carter: Man of the Spirit*, 39, 40, 45–46.

19. Carter, *A Full Life*, 36. Excerpt. John Carter (1893–1981), founding member of the Assemblies of God in Britain and Ireland, was born in Birmingham and was a member of the Elim Evangelistic Band (now Elim Pentecostal Church). See Cartwright, "Carter, John. H," 456.

234   PENTECOSTAL AND HOLINESS STATEMENTS ON WAR AND PEACE

that my objection was sincere, and that I did not give various foolish reasons as many of the Socialist and others had done, but stood on solid ground, so they granted me exemption from combatant service and put me in the non-combatant corps.[20]

"War, the Bible, and the Christian" by Donald Gee, 1930

The nominal churches of Christendom today prove by a thousand utterances and actions everywhere what they feel *ought* to be the attitude of the church of Jesus Christ towards war. . . . There is an admitted and instinctive feeling that opposition to the war spirit is the only possible attitude consistent with the spirit and teaching of Jesus Christ. . . . Yet we feel reluctantly compelled to affirm that the churches as a whole miserably failed in the last, as in almost every preceding War in this matter of a firm and united stand against militarism. Patriotism surged over everything: its virtues were represented as the truest expression of the Christian life, and its sacrifices were upheld as evidencing the very spirit of Calvary. Different sections of the church, resident in different nations fighting each other to the death, invoked the blessing of God upon contending causes, and upon the most hellish means which those causes could devise to bring victory. Some churches became little better than recruiting stations.

. . . The attitude of the churches in the last war was little short of a tragedy. . . . It is probably safe to say that, however passionately patriotism may overwhelm everything else in time of war, the world certainly *expects* the Christian church to take a stand against war, and it is deeply disappointed at heart when that stand is not taken, however much it may persecute for the time the "conscientious objector."[21]

[The Old Testament] Immediately we find war of the bloodiest kind, wars of exterminations, engaged in by God's chosen people, at God's express command, and with God's special blessing. Joshua 8; 1 Samuel 15; 2 Samuel 5:24; etc. This seems in

20. "Compulsory Military Service," 7. Excerpt. This letter was courtesy of Bro. James Harvey who received this letter from a friend. The article was published in the *Weekly Evangel* with the hope of encouraging other Pentecostal young men toward conscientious objection. The end of the article states the reason for publication: "We publish it, believing it will help many of our young men in the stand they will take at this time."

21. Gee, "War, the Bible, and the Christian," 6. Excerpt. Emphasis in original. Donald Gee (1891–1966) was an early British Assemblies of God leader.

International Holiness and Pentecostal Statements   235

strange contradiction to the teaching of the New Testament at
first sight. A moment's consideration will make us remember,
however, that the divine government differs with the progress-
ing dispensations, and the Old Testament is never the ultimate
ground for the Christian to base his actions upon. It's history
comprises "times of ignorance" at which God winked (Acts
17:30); its spiritual dynamic was a law written on tables of stone,
and enforced by heavy physical penalties on every hand (e.g.
Leviticus 26, etc.); the very bringing in with Christ of a New
Covenant of which the keynote is the word "better" (Heb. 8:6,
etc.) was a proof of its temporary character.[22]

[Render unto Caesar] When the clash is between the law of
God and the law of man, then the only answer for the Christian
is contained in the immortal words of Peter. "We ought to obey
God rather than men." Acts 5:29. Conscientious objection then
becomes the only possible course, however serious the consequences. The Bible puts clear before us the magnificent example
of Daniel and the three Hebrews. Daniel 3 and 6. He who said,
"Render unto Caesar the things that are Caesar's" also said, "But
unto God the things that are God's." The two are to be combined
to the last possible limit, but when further combination of allegiance becomes impossible—then *God* must come first.

The Christian's true citizenship is in heaven, Phil. 3:20., R.V.
He obeys the laws of his earthly country in exactly the same way
as an alien passing through. His ultimate allegiance is always to
his heavenly King.[23]

DONALD GEE: PENTECOSTAL STATESMAN BY JOHN CARTER, 1975

By this time the Great War had been in existence for eighteen
months and was growing in intensity. The Assembly at Harringay,
which was the spiritual home of the Gees, let it be know that, as
followers of Christ, its members could not participate in war and
bloodshed. With the introduction of conscription, Mr. Gee filed
his application for exemption from military service on conscientious grounds. The tribunal allowed his appeal on condition that
he performed work of national service, and this took the form
of agricultural employment, an occupation for which he had no
aptitude or knowledge or inclination. Let him describe in his

22. Ibid., 7.

23. Gee, "War, the Bible, and the Christian" [Part II], 2. Excerpt. Emphasis in
original.

own words the Lord's dealings with him as he and his wife came to what he calls "our crossroads," as he faced the momentous personal decision that no other course was open but to become a conscientious objector, not knowing all that this might entail.

[Gee wrote] "After a protracted trial at the tribunal the last question hurled at me was, 'Would you be willing to be a missionary?' Needless to say I answered a prompt 'Yes.' The judges retired for quite ten minutes to consider their verdict (a most uncommon thing with a 'C.O.'), and I sat there in the Court with my eyes shut, praying hard. I had a wife and a newly born babe at home. They amazed me with the verdict—'total exemption from military service on condition that you take up work of national importance to our satisfaction within fourteen days.' I had expected nothing less than imprisonment, and almost staggered out of the Court with joyous surprise."[24]

Pentecostal Pilgrimage by Donald Gee, n.d.

[Gee's written experience as a Pentecostal conscientious objector.] It was the social suffering as a hated "conchie" that went deeper however. Except for some fellow-Christians I soon found that I was a complete social outcast. Boys delighted to throw stones and dirt at me along the road: men and women vented their spite in venomous words and open threats. Sometimes at night they would stand outside our cottage and shout their taunts after we had retired for the night. I welcomed work on the more secluded parts of the farm, especially if I could be all alone. As an only child from birth I had grown up with a deep inward sensitiveness and shyness that few realised. Unfriendly treatment that others would have taken little notice of was mental torture to me. Often I was inclined to envy my friends who had been sent to prison. To my imagination they were passing through a more sheltered ordeal than my own in a village. And I suppose that they, in their turn, were tempted to envy me.

Only God knows what I suffered in my soul at that time. Yet I now know that He used it to put some needed iron into my character. Both physically and spiritually I gained at least some measure of manliness under that stern curriculum. Neither could I blame my persecutors. They were mostly the kind of folk who could have no kind of appreciation of the grounds on which I

24. Carter, *Donald Gee*, 17–18.

International Holiness and Pentecostal Statements   237

based my conscientious objection to military service. Their own sons, and husbands, and fathers were all away in the filth and constant danger of the trenches at the various fronts. The casualty lists after the battles on the Western Front were appalling. Moreover in the war of 1914–1918 the civilian population in England dwelt in comparative safety. There were only a few Zeppelin raids. All that my neighbours in Buckinghamshire saw in me was a young man, perfectly fit, who was escaping the perils and sufferings of their own loved ones. No wonder they hated the sight of me. I could not but appreciate their point of view, though it made my mental suffering all the harder.[25]

Elim Pentecostal Church,[26] 1915

"Resolution on the Christian's Attitude to War," 1935

That while this General Conference of the Elim Foursquare Gospel Alliance affirms its loyalty to His Majesty the King and to the government of our land, it believes that the Church of Jesus Christ which is called out from the world to preach the Gospel of salvation and peace to all men is based on spiritual principals which are incompatible with the Christian's participation in war. It considers, however, that this is a matter which every believer should settle for himself in the light of the Word of God.[27]

Is War Christian? by F. B. Phillips, Elim Foursquare Church Press Manager, 1937

. . . The outstanding characteristic of the Christian should be sacrificial love. This love should be meted out to all, whether they be friend or enemy, whether they be nice and kindly dis-

25. Massey, *Another Springtime*, 27–28. Excerpt.

26. George Jeffreys (1889–1962) founded the Elim Evangelistic Band in 1915. The movement later changed its name to Elim Foursquare Gospel Alliance and then later to Elim Pentecostal Church. This movement is not to be confused with The Foursquare Church, founded by Aimee Semple McPherson.

27. Email correspondence with Desmond Cartwright, July 19, 2011, personal files of Brian Pipkin. Cartwright, Elim Pentecostal Church historian, notes that Elim passed a resolution on "The Christian's Attitude to War" on October 31, 1935. One-hundred people voted in favor, with two opposing and one abstaining. The two opposing were John Leech K.C. and James McWhirter with George Jeffreys, founder of the Elim Gospel Church, abstaining.

posed of us, rich and generous, or whether they be horrid and even brutal, poor and mean. Do you say, impossible? Granted, in the natural, but remember we are writing about the life of a Christian who has been miraculously made a new creature.[28]

. . . Although one hears so much talk of sacrifice and the laying down of one's lie for the King and country in war time, I must remind you that this is not the object war. On the contrary[,] . . . the object of War is not only to take life, but to take as many lives as possible in a short a time as possible, with the least possible expense. How different is this from Calvary. It is written, "Christ came not to destroy men's lives, but to save." Then again we read, "While we were yet sinners (or enemies by wicked works) Christ died for us." Hatred is the spirit of war, while love is the spirit of Calvary.[29]

. . . Most assuredly the fruit of Christianity in the world is peace, and not strife. But just as our Lord and Master was hated and persecuted so surely will the world hate and persecute us if we follow in His steps (see John xv. 18–21).[30]

[Re: Where Duty Calls] We now have arrived at a point in this book where I trust I am not presumptuous in thinking that we have seen enough scriptural arguments to convince us that it is absolutely wrong for a Christian in any circumstances to participate in war. This being so, I must write in this chapter a little about what the Christian's duty is in time of war.

His duty, as we shall see, is by no means easy, but rather the path is strewn with hardships, losses, scorn, imprisonments, cruelty, and may be even death, if he will be true to His Lord. But what matters all this, for has not our Master Himself been this way, and as we follow Him, will He not abide with us and be our El Shaddai?

In the last war the Government has a little consideration for the man with a conscientious objection to fighting, and set up Tribunals all over the country to which the conscientious objectors could appeal. If they were able to convince these Tribunals

28. Phillips, *Is War Christian?*, 10. Regarding Phillips, Desmond Cartwright wrote: "Phillips [1896–1979] was a printer by trade and it was his own press that printed the first *Elim Evangel* in 1919. He was pastor of a small Pentecostal Mission in Tamworth, Staffordshire. When the Elim work in Ireland transferred to London in 1923/1924, he moved with them and opened their new press of which he became the manager." Email correspondence with Desmond Cartwright, July 22, 2011, personal files of Jay Beaman.

29. Ibid., 30–31.

30. Ibid., 56.

International Holiness and Pentecostal Statements   239

of their sincerity the Tribunals were empowered to grant the applicants exemption from military service.

This sounds very simple and easy I know, but it did not always work out so well. Naturally a good deal depended upon the type of men that were sitting on the Tribunal. . . . And now with regard to munitions, what is the Christian duty? Just as it is inconsistent for a Christian to fight so it must also be inconsistent for a Christian to manufacture munitions or implements used for fighting. And so also is it just as inconsistent for a Christian to loan his money for the making of munitions.

"If you believe that War is wrong, you aren't entitled to do anything that will help other people engage in it. If you believe that War is of the Devil, and you hold shares in an armament firm, then the dividends which you draw are the Devil's dividends. And if you are employed in a munitions factory, then the wages which you draw are the Devil's wages." . . . Regarding any so-called non-combatant service in the army, I strongly advise Christians to leave this alone. In the last war many men who had enlisted in this way were, in emergencies, called upon to fight in the trenches.

There is one other thing which may be a problem to some, and that is in reference to work of national importance. In the last war many of the Tribunals offered work of national importance to the conscientious objectors. This work varied considerably in its kind, and also the circumstances under which it was offered varied, too. In my opinion if such work is harmless, and the one who accepts it is not thereby releasing someone else from combatant service, then he is justified in accepting. Some may disagree with me on this point, but personally I fail to see in what way this is wrong. In fact I go further than this and say that according to the Word of God I believe he is doing the right thing. For does not the Scripture say, "if it be possible, as much as lieth in you, live peaceably with all men"? (Rom. xii. 18).

If, however, to accept the work offered means that another man goes to war, then I would emphatically say "go to prison rather than take it."[31]

All who are in Christ Jesus are brothers and sisters, no matter of what tongue or nationality. No country or cause therefore has any right to demand that man shed his brother's blood.[32]

31. Ibid., 64–69.
32. Ibid., 84.

PENTECOSTAL AND HOLINESS STATEMENTS ON WAR AND PEACE

Salvation Army, 1939
W. Bram Weaver, WW II Pacifist, From His Application to Tribunal

My objections to any form of Military Service are based on the following:

1. War is definitely irreconcilable with the life and teaching of Jesus Christ of whom I am a follower.

2. Being the son of Salvation Army officers I have been brought up in close association with the SA, an international organisation which propagates the Gospel in All countries and is NON-POLITICAL. As a lifelong Salvationist my conscience will not permit me to be identified with the military machine whose object is the destruction of life.

3. I consider it more important for the Kingdom of Jesus Christ to be established than the mere preservation or extension of ANY nation or empire.

4. War is no real and lasting remedy for existing evils and civilisation needs a method different from the senseless and barbaric murder of countless lives.

5. The above-mentioned convictions which have been rooted and grounded in me for many years make it impossible for me to participate in war.[33]

"Divine Healing Vs. War" by Arthur and Catherine Booth-Clibborn, 1892

Life-giving and death-giving war

During recent years in Holland—standing between the Dutch and the English races engaged in bloody conflict—I discovered in the course of study that war only came into the Christian Church when healing went out. Now healing comes in and war must go out.

But it is a narrow way which leads to this fuller Life. Let no one imagine it can be easy. Let no one follow who is not ready for calumny persecution or death. "Ye shall be hated of all men for my sake, but he that endureth unto the end the same shall be saved."

---

33. Clifton, "The Salvation Army's Actions and Attitudes in Wartime," 377. Emphasis in original. While the SA was never on record as a pacifist denomination, there were strong elements tending towards pacifism, and by World War II there was a group of identifiable pacifists in the denomination, especially in England.

International Holiness and Pentecostal Statements   241

The right war can alone drive out the wrong war. To enroll in the full war of divine life can alone keep christians [sic] from the war of death.

Christ said: "I came not to destroy men's lives but to save them." It is when we work with Him to do the latter with the passion of love in the war of redemption, that we can be delivered from the former war and the passion of hate. "To save men's lives" means the salvation of the body, soul and spirit by the full gospel.

When Christ places the "saving" and "destroying" as opposites then divine healing must be the natural opposite to war. These two must therefore exclude each other.

Sword-bearing Christians have a one-eared humanity for audience

The lurid light of the Anglo-Boer war will not be lost, if it enables English and Dutch Christians to read afresh the New Testament, which they were the first to translate into the vernacular and give to the world. It will read *red* for them it is true in that awful light, but they can then learn the meaning of Calvary and the death of the King, who allowed his blood to be shed in order to stop all blood-shedding by His subjects.

Peter's sword cut off the ear of one of the men he was sent to evangelize. Christ healed the ear and said: "put up thy sword." War and Healing are thus eternal opposites. A Christianity which takes the sword will have but a one-eared humanity as its audience. But when healing comes the sword will be put up, the ear will be healed and mankind will respect such Christianity as that, and listen with two ears.

How my heart has bled in realising this in Holland, as an Englishman the last two years. It is to be wondered that I broke all bonds which prevented me preaching the whole gospel, and that one of my last acts before taking off my uniform was to help a young Dutchman to desert to Christ, and cross the frontier rather than touch a sword any more.

Christians will never learn the efficacy of the blood of Christ for healing, until they give up shedding that of their fellow Christians. Then will they learn that "by His stripes we are healed"—and that by christian [sic] war, strife, and stripes, soul-saving work is wounded and often destroyed.

I do not say a Christian cannot be really converted who is a soldier, or that many Christians have not done great good

242 PENTECOSTAL AND HOLINESS STATEMENTS ON WAR AND PEACE

among their barrack mates. But I am deeply convinced that with a higher degree of the light and life of full Christianity, and the Sermon on the Mount, he would, like the early Christians lay down his arms. My books upon war (see last page) set forth what I believe to be the truth in this respect, and adduce in support of it, many examples from the acts of the early Christians.[34]

"War and the Gospel" by Arthur and Catherine Booth-Clibborn, 1892

The progress of the world can wait for no human being and no institution. War is Anti-Christian. It has got to go out of every truly Christian circle. The noble young follower of Christ, who feels he can no longer bear arms, must not hear the trumpet of the Church of God give an uncertain sound, and to be left to struggle alone because it is afraid to share his cross and loss. To protest against War in a general moralistic way, but yet to refuse public association in word and deed with one who becomes a true soldier of Christ, in refusing to be a soldier of the world, is for the Christian Church to be unfaithful to the highest duty God has laid upon it, namely to help and stand by the solitary and helpless ones of the flock.

True Christianity legislates for minorities—apostate Christianity legislates for majorities.

True Christianity works with the thick end of the wedge,— the false works with the thin end.

From his first sermon at Nazareth, for which He was cast out of the Synagogue, Christ spoke the highest, the most fearless, the most complete and most disagreeable truth. When individuals or Churches fear the consequences to themselves of preaching the whole truth they are apostate.

True Christianity acts upon principle alone—false Christianity allows itself to be influenced or guided by considerations of policy.

True Christianity always moves, like light, in straight lines, regardless of consequences. False Christianity takes the crooked road to avoid the cross and the loss. All straight lines lead to Calvary, all crooked lines to Rome. The pagan Rome of Carnal

---

34. Booth-Clibborn, *For the Word of God and the Testimony of Jesus*, 64–65. The Booth-Clibborn's, European Holiness leaders, and major influencers of Pentecostal pacifism, claimed this document was written in 1892 and copyrighted in the U.S. in 1892.

International Holiness and Pentecostal Statements   243

power, or the apostate Rome of Bible-despising, faith-killing principles of carnal wisdom is the end of all such paths. It is thus that carnal war and militarism have ever been associated with dead religion, and not with living, with world religion and now with unworldly, and both are seen together in the Revelation in the vivid picture of the Harlot seated on the Beast. Such is all Protestant religion which does not reject beast power, and which approves these anti-christian "Christian" armies. It is in some degree or other a daughter of the "mother of harlots" scarlet Rome. (Rev. XVII. 5).

It is better to be silent and give no testimony against war, or else give a full and clear testimony. Better let the trumpet be silent than to give an uncertain sound.

All so called "Christian testimony against war" which does not definitely encourage every Christian soldier to lay down his arms even if he be imprisoned or shot for it, and which refuses to suffer publicity with him is either false and hypocritical or else culpably ignorant.

Hence last summer I unhesitatingly engaged to help a young Dutchman to do so, as I saw his spiritual experience as on a level with his Bible knowledge on this point, and would carry him through.

Our Continental Mission fearlessly inscribes these truths on its banner—come what may.

Carnal War is something so definitely from above or below that it is better to be either against it or for it, honestly and completely.

I foresaw for years that the great truths advocated in this statement as parts of the full gospel, were just those needed to maintain the power and success of the Army if accepted by it, by enabling it to follow the normal upward and onward development of gospel truth, so that it might keep step with the needs of the age.

I saw in them the natural god-given counteractant to the Socialistic tendencies of the age which can side-track God's work, so that inferior things get a superior place, as well as to excess in the use of means, which can become a great snare in the extreme development of external attractions and demonstrations, to the determent of the interior life.

It was with the truest devotion of the [Salvation] Army[35] that we kept on hoping against hope. But I now see that the law of

35. Booth-Clibborn was a Quaker-turned Salvation Army Leader. He married the

systems cannot be altered. I recognize that the Army cannot accept these truths in its present form: but that nevertheless God will go on blessing the effort of every Holy Ghost man and woman in its ranks, according to their faith.

Every thoughtful Christian will recognise the following truths.

—That on this armed continent no half measures can be adopted as regards militarism. Christians must be for or against it—and on evangelical grounds alone—for they know no other.

—That Divine Healing is the natural counteractant to the war spirit.

—That the doctrine of the second coming of Christ, so intimately associated with that of the coming marriage of Christ and His Bride, is the divinely appointed counteractant (Ephesians V) to all anti-christian [*sic*] errors concerning marriage and the home, just as was the reopening of the Bible the natural counteractant in the days of the Reformation to the enforced celibacy of the minister of religion, male or female, and all such godless fanatical customs which had been adopted in the supposed interest of "the Church of God."

Those who give the Word of God its true place in life and home and work are naturally accustomed to see *in it alone* (not in human wisdom or policy) the one source of safety and success, the one counteractant to all errors and deviations, and the one guide, under the illumination of the Spirit, leading safely upward and onward into the fuller and deeper and wider experience of divine truth, which the Christian Church is called to make, as we approach the end of the age.

. . . In considering the two questions of divine healing and war during recent years, a conviction has arisen and gradually taken shape in my mind, till it now shines forth as a harmonious, a complete truth. It is this. No association of christians, [*sic*] no Church will be able to deal effectually with the *question of the anti-christian* [*sic*] *character of war*, except one clothed with the

---

daughter of the Salvation Army founder, William Booth, and took Catherine's last name. Both Arthur and Catherine Booth-Clibborn, Continental leaders of the Salvation Army, tried to move the Salvation Army to promote divine healing and pacifism. In this they were unsuccessful, and this in part contributed to their break with the Salvation Army. It is the Salvation Army referred to here as "the Army." So, the Booth-Clibborn's promoted another kind of Army (like the Salvation Army) that would fight for what they saw as the full-gospel—fighting against war.

International Holiness and Pentecostal Statements   245

spiritual and physical strength which comes through *the experience and teaching of Divine Healing.*

To fight with success that highest expression of all that is negative: death-dealing war, men require to be endued with all the powers which belong to that highest expression of all that is *positive*: life-giving war.

All the gifts of the Spirit are included in that necessary equipment. This cannot be denied. They are all in the legacy,—the Testament of Christ. They are still at our disposal in the Holy Spirit who has never been withdrawn, but still remains *"given"* to the Church of God on earth. It remains therefore for some Church to rise and claim them.

Every faithful Christian must now realize that the hour has come for war to be put out of Christianity, in order for the Christian religion to become once more authentic. This fact alone proves that the hour has come for the restoration of the gifts of the Spirit, for they alone can bring about this result.

It is not only useless but it is disloyal for the Church of God to war against war on merely humanitarian grounds. It is worse still for it to do so on a unitarian [*sic*] basis like that of Tolstoyism however noble and true a man Tolstoy may be on a human place. It must do so on Gospel grounds alone. But it cannot do this till it recognizes war as being Anti-Christian, gospel-killing thing. It will never have full light and strength for this till it recognizes that the Gospel and Christianity are not complete without divine healing, that saving *positive* which alone can, must and will drive out the dark wounding, killing *negative*.

Would it not be therefore desirable for Christians who oppose war as a matter of moral principle, to call a halt and examine whether they possess the Apostolic credentials necessary to such a campaign. The spirit of carnal war could not live in the spiritual atmosphere of the primitive Church. Should not Christians before all else seek to get back that atmosphere.

No philosophical, humanitarian, self-complacent, arm-chair advocating of peace principles will be of much use in this age. It will do more harm than good. It will mislead people by getting them to seek the effect without seeking first the cause.

It will bring Christians to unite with Turks and Chinese, as at the Peace Conference, or at the Parliament of religions (those hideous betrayals and denials of the Gospel) to bring peace and goodwill among men on merely moralistic humanitarian grounds.

246 PENTECOSTAL AND HOLINESS STATEMENTS ON WAR AND PEACE

Let every true lover of peace principles rejoice therefore that divine healing is coming back. Let him learn to see in it the natural antidote to war. Let him recognize the full import of this blessed sign of the times. Let him get thus a true idea of the programme which is now before the Church. Let him thus be a "man of the times," "up to date," in the true sense, a faithful, God-instructed "servant of his century" and then he will not be long before he too will rejoice that "The Lord hath founded Zion."[36]

CANADA

Pentecostal Assemblies of Canada

"The Pentecostal Movement and War," 1939

WHEREAS, We have accepted the Word of God as our rule of conduct and purpose to be governed by its Divine principles, and as our Assemblies for the past twelve years or more have always accepted and interpreted the New Testament teaching and principles as prohibiting Christians from shedding blood or taking human life.

RESOLVED, That in time of persecution or ill treatment at the hands of the enemy, we should not "avenge ourselves," but rather give place to wrath; for it is written, "Vengeance is mine; I will repay, saith the Lord." (Rom. 12:19; Deut. 32:35). Neither shall (we) take up any weapon of destruction to slay another, whether in our own defence or in the defence of others, for it is written, "Do no violence to no man" [sic]. (See Luke 3:14; Matt. 26:52; John 18:36; 15–18, 19). We should rather suffer wrong than do wrong.

RESOLVED, That all civil magistrates are ordained of God for peace, safety, and for the welfare of the people (Romans 13:1–10). Therefore it is our duty to be in obedience to all requirements of the Law that are not contrary to the Word of God. It is our duty to honor them, pay tribute, or such taxation as may be required, without murmuring (Matthew 17:24–27), and show respect to them in all lawful requirements of the Civil Government.[37]

---

36. Ibid., 108–10. Emphasis in original. We capitalized Protestant, Christian, and Christianity.

37. "The Pentecostal Movement and War," 3. Quoted in Althouse, "Canadian

International Holiness and Pentecostal Statements   247

Apostolic Pentecostal Church of Canada

"DUTIES OF CIVIL GOVERNMENT," 1965

That all civil magistrates are ordained of God for peace, safety
and the welfare of all people. (Rom. 13:1–10). Therefore it is our
duty to be in obedience to all requirements of the laws that are
not contrary to the Word of God. It is our duty to honor them,
pay tribute or such taxation as may be required, without murmuring (Matt. 17:24–27, 22:19–21), and show respect to them
in all lawful requirements of the civil government.[38]

The Bible Holiness Mission (Vancouver, British Columbia)

[STATEMENTS], 1971

War: we are noncombatants similar to the Mennonites.

Racism: we are against racial discrimination and segregation.

Abortion: we regard as a form of murder.

Divorce: we do not recognize remarriage while partner lives.

Planned Parenthood: is left to the individual conscience.

Alcoholic Beverages: we practice and encourage total abstinence.

Economy: many of our members are active in the credit union
and cooperative movement.

Labour: we encourage the formation of membership in Christian
labour guilds or associations.

Education: attendance at Christian schools is encouraged, or
failing that, extra training in the house using Christian school
textbooks.[39]

PALESTINE

The Awad family—Alex, Bishara, and Sami—are an activist-oriented
family committed to peace and justice in Palestine and Israel with ties
to the Pentecostal tradition. While the they may not self-identify as

---

Pentecostal Pacifism," 32–33. Emphasis in original.

38. *General Bylaws of Apostolic Church of Pentecost of Canada*, 15.

39. Wesley H. Wakefield to Arthur Carl Piepkorn.

248 PENTECOSTAL AND HOLINESS STATEMENTS ON WAR AND PEACE

Pentecostal in title, they have links to Pentecostalism through heritage (Pentecostal mother), affiliation (Pentecostal education), and, in the case of Sami, experience (speaking in tongues).[40]

Alex and Bishara grew up in a Pentecostal home. In his book, *Palestinian Memories*, Alex shares the story of his Pentecostal mother, Huda Awad, who attended an Assemblies of God school and later affiliated with the Church of God (Cleveland, Tennessee).[41] Alex's brother, Bishara Awad, founded the Bethlehem Bible College (BBC), a small evangelical-Pentecostal institution for Palestinian Christians.[42] Bishara, now retired college president, who self-identifies as a Pentecostal Christian[43], notes that BBC has a strong heritage of nonviolent practice and belief.[44] The schools mission is to "follow Jesus' way of creative justice and mercy."[45]

In 2010 the BBC arranged and oversaw a conference entitled "Christ at the Checkpoint: Theology in Service of Justice and Peace." This evangelical-ecumenical meeting brought together peace activists, ethicists, students, pastors, and theologians to discuss justice, peace, and reconciliation in the Palestinian/Israeli context. Out of the conference emerged the Bethlehem Affirmation—a strong statement in support of peacemaking and nonviolence. The Awads were among the primary conference organizers.[46] Many of the papers presented at the 2010 conference can be accessed in the book, *Christ at the Checkpoint: Theology in the Service*

---

40. Although there are Palestinian Christian evangelicals who do not self-identify as Pentecostal, there are many in practice. Some prefer a hyphen such as evangelical-Pentecostal. Whatever the title, there are Palestinian Christians that openly embody the Pentecostal experience. For a firsthand account of a Palestinian Pentecostal experience, see Harris, *Speaking in Tongues in Palestine*.

41. See Awad, *Palestinian Memories*.

42. *Bethlehem Bible College*. The school was established in 1979 and serves an average of 125 students each year.

43. John Harris, member of Pentecostals and Charismatics for Peace and Justice (PCPJ), met Bishara during a PCPJ trip to Palestine in 2007 where Bishara identified himself as a Pentecostal Christian. Harris noted that the BBC is an evangelical and Pentecostal institution. See Harris, *Palestinian Pentecostals*.

44. Bishara confirmed the college believes and practices nonviolence, although they do not have an official peace statement. Email correspondence with Bishara Awad, January 2, 2013, personal files of Brian Pipkin.

45. *Bethlehem Bible College Mission*.

46. Conference organizers who endorsed the manifesto are John Angle, Alex Awad, Bishara Awad, Sami Awad, Steve Haas, Munther Isaac, Yohanna Katanacho, Manfred Kohl, Salim Munayer, and Jack Sara.

International Holiness and Pentecostal Statements   249

of Justice and Peace.[47] The success of the 2010 conference inspired the Palestinian evangelical-Pentecostal community to host a second international conference in 2012 in Bethlehem—"Christ at the Checkpoint: Hope in the Midst of Conflict." A third "Christ at the Checkpoint" conference is scheduled for March 2014.

Rev. Alex Awad, Bishara's brother, teaches at BBC and is a Methodist missionary pastoring a Baptist church in East Jerusalem. Among Alex's many graduate degrees, one was completed at Lee University, a Pentecostal affiliated university (Church of God, Cleveland, Tennessee).[48] Bishara's son, Sami, founded the Holy Land Trust, a non-profit humanitarian organization assisting Palestinian families.[49] The Holy Land Trust has a strong commitment to nonviolence. Sami, who earned his master's degree specializing in peace and conflict resolution, shared his commitment to nonviolent doctrine. He also shared his experience of speaking in tongues during his keynote address—"Spirit Empowerment, U.S. Christians, and Hope for the Land of Pentecost"—at the 2012 Society for Pentecostal Studies conference at Regent University in Virginia Beach, Virginia.[50]

Other Palestinian Christians who have been influenced by or participate in Pentecostalism include Rev. Jack Sara (president of Bethlehem Bible College since 2012 and former pastor of the Evangelical Alliance Church in the Old City of Jerusalem), Yohanna and Dina Katanacho (faculty at Bethlehem Bible College), Rev. Nihad Salman (pastor of Immanuel Evangelical Church in Bethelehem), and Rev. Munir and Sharon Kakish (pastor of Ramallah Local Church and director of an orphanage in Ramallah).[51]

The following statements reflect a family with Pentecostal roots and experience, seeking to integrate their peace and justice faith in the

47. Alexander, *Christ at the Checkpoint.*

48. *Alex Awad.*

49. *Holy Land Trust.*

50. Email correspondence with Paul Alexander, January 7, 2013, personal files of Brian Pipkin. Sami refers to himself as a Palestinian Christian evangelical, although he practices Pentecostal experience such as speaking in tongues. See Awad, "A Palestinian Christian Evangelical Response to the Holocaust." See also Harris, "Are Christian Zionism and Social Justice Compatible?"

51. For a more detailed description of the peace and justice work of these and other Palestinian Christians, see Alexander and Welsh, "Exemplars of Godly Justice," 67–86.

250 PENTECOSTAL AND HOLINESS STATEMENTS ON WAR AND PEACE

Palestinian context. While some self-identify as Pentecostal in title, others are Pentecostal in practice.

Bethlehem Bible College, 2013

Bethlehem Bible College seeks to prepare Christian leaders to serve Arab churches and society. We train our students to model Christ-centered-ness, Godly humility, and biblical wholeness. As life-long learners, our graduates follow Jesus' way of creative justice and mercy in both their personal and professional lives.[52]

"The Bethlehem Evangelical Affirmation," 2010

We affirm the foundational truth that God loves everyone (John 3:16).

We affirm that as followers of Jesus Christ we are called to do justice and love mercy (Micah 6:8), to be ministers of reconciliation (2 Corinthians 5:11–21), and to be peacemakers (Matthew 5:9).

We affirm that the Holy Spirit empowers followers of Jesus to speak and live humbly and prophetically (Acts 1:8).

We recognize that this is the time to resolve the Israel-Palestinian conflict.

Therefore, we are convinced that the Holy Spirit is leading us at such a time as this to unite as Christians throughout the world in order to pray and work for a just peace in Israel and Palestine.

To this end, we commit to reconnect with the local Palestinian church and to listen and learn from all those who follow Jesus in the Holy Land and to share their stories with our own faith communities.

We further commit to work together to advocate changes in public policy and so achieve a just and lasting resolution to conflict. Our vision and our hope is that Israelis and Palestinians will live in justice and peace in the land of the Holy One.[53]

---

52. *Bethlehem Bible College Mission.*

53. *Bethlehem Affirmation.* Although many drafted and endorsed the affirmation, it is a statement agreed to by the conference organizers and endorsed by the planning committee. Several members of the Awad family were on the drafting committee.

International Holiness and Pentecostal Statements   251

"Christ at the Checkpoint Manifesto," 2012

The Kingdom of God has come. Evangelicals must reclaim the prophetic role in bringing peace, justice and reconciliation in Palestine and Israel.

Reconciliation recognizes God's image in one another.

Racial ethnicity alone does not guarantee the benefits of the Abrahamic Covenant.

The Church in the land of the Holy One, has born witness to Christ since the days of Pentecost. It must be empowered to continue to be light and salt in the region, if there is to be hope in the midst of conflict.

Any exclusive claim to land of the Bible in the name of God is not in line with the teaching of Scripture.

All forms of violence must be refuted unequivocally.

Palestinian Christians must not lose the capacity to self-criticism if they wish to remain prophetic.

There are real injustices taking place in the Palestinian territories and the suffering of the Palestinian people can no longer be ignored. Any solution must respect the equity and rights of Israel and Palestinian communities.

For Palestinian Christians, the occupation is the core issue of the conflict.

Any challenge of the injustices taking place in the Holy Land must be done in Christian love. Criticism of Israel and the occupation cannot be confused with anti-Semitism and the delegitimization of the State of Israel.

Respectful dialogue between Palestinian and Messianic believers must continue. Though we may disagree on secondary matters of theology, the Gospel of Jesus and his ethical teaching take precedence.

Christians must understand the global context for the rise of extremist Islam. We challenge stereotyping of all faith forms that betray God's commandment to love our neighbors and enemies.[54]

---

54. *Christ at the Checkpoint.* Christ at the Checkpoint (www.christatthecheckpoint. com) emerged as an action of BBC. The conference is organized by the BBC and its partner organization, Holy Land Trust. The statement was agreed on and endorsed by conference organizers. Among them were professors of BBC. Alex Awad, Bishara Awad, Sami Awad were on the drafting committee.

252 PENTECOSTAL AND HOLINESS STATEMENTS ON WAR AND PEACE

Holy Land Trust, 1998

"Mission"

Through a commitment to the principles of nonviolence, Holy Land Trust aspires to strengthen and empower the peoples of the Holy Land to engage in spiritual, pragmatic and strategic paths that will end all forms of oppression. We create the space for the healing of the historic wounds in order to transform communities and build a future that makes the Holy Land a global model for understanding, respect, justice, equality and peace.

While Holy Land Trust is not a religious organization, we aspire to learn from the spiritual teachings of all faiths that bring unity to the human family and closeness to the Creator of all things. We seek to deepen our knowledge and understanding of the teachings of Jesus Christ, a man who brought a message of peace, goodwill and hope to the land where we live. We believe that, as Martin Luther King Jr. said, Jesus Christ in his teachings, compassion and interactions "was an extremist for love, truth and goodness." We seek this extremism in our work and mission.[55]

"Nonviolent Project"

Nonviolence is at the heart of Holy Land Trust's work and is incorporated into everything we do and strive for. Beyond abstaining from using violence, our nonviolence trainings provide participants with direct action tools and assists in developing strategies to involve the greater community. While we may not have the solutions to end the occupation or violence that human beings face in their daily lives, HLT engages by creating a sense of belonging through the application of nonviolence as a means to empower ourselves, as well as our communities. We believe the nonviolence movement should arise from and belong to the people.[56]

Sami Awad (Founder of Holy Land Trust), 2010

"Love"

Engage in continuous acts of love to your oppressor. For it is *not* a choice we have as followers of Jesus to love the other and the

---

55. *Holy Land Trust Mission.*

56. *Holy Land Trust Nonviolence Project.*

International Holiness and Pentecostal Statements 253

enemy, but it is a commandment that we are to abide in. I will not accept any argument that says that engaging in actions of expressing God's love to the other undermines or underestimates our goal and aspirations as Palestinians or that it makes us look at if we are weak or vulnerable. It is only in strength that you can express love.[57]

"Nonviolence"

And for me I do interpret these acts of love through my involvement in nonviolence and nonviolent action, and in speaking words that allow for this deep healing to take place. We must love and must forgive and must engage in opening real opportunities for others to also love and engage and forgive. Too many apologies, too much compensation, and too much guilt have been spread. And not enough forgiveness and closure have happened.[58]

Immanuel Evangelical Church, 2013

We believe all people, no matter where they live, have the responsibility to defend individual rights. When defending rights, however, we believe a Christian response should always be consistent with the way of Jesus, the Prince of Peace, who modeled nonviolent resistance. We believe violence will never achieve peace and justice. Violence only inspires more violence—it is cyclical; it always comes back to you. We also believe when Jesus said, "Deny yourself," he did not intend for us to deny our individual rights when people want to oppress us. Instead, we believe denying yourself applies to our relationship with Jesus, our King and master. We deny unto Jesus; not to institutions or individuals who wish to subjugate us. Therefore, we believe preaching the gospel of peace and standing up for our rights, is our duty under any political establishment on this earth.[59]

57. Quoted in Alexander, *Christ at the Checkpoint*, 28. This statement was given at the Christ at the Checkpoint Conference, March 5–9, 2010.

58. Ibid.

59. Email correspondence with Nihad Salman, February 7, 2013, personal files of Brian Pipkin. Salman is the pastor of the Immanuel Evangelical Church, a Pentecostal congregation in Bethlehem, Palestine.

PERU

Darío A. López Rodríguez, Church of God (Cleveland, Tennessee)

[Pentecostal Eschatology], 2007

Los pentecostales necesitan comprender que proclamar que Cristo viene, no les tiene que hacer ciudadanos irresponsables o los tiene que convertir en sujetos enajenados de la realidad social y política en la que viven, sino que los tiene que insertar en esa realidad como embajadores de la reconciliación, artesanos de la paz, defensores de la verdad en un mundo de mentiras y de medias verdades, y en profetas de la justicia de Dios. En otras palabras, tienen que ser misioneros responsables que se preocupen por todas las necesidades humanas, entendiendo que el prójimo necesita comer pan y necesita salir de las condiciones infrahumanas en las que se encuentra.

[English translation] Pentecostals need to understand that proclaiming Jesus' return does not make irresponsible citizens or alienated individuals of the social and political reality in which they live, but it does place them in this reality as ambassadors of reconciliation, craft-workers of peace, defenders of truth to a world of lies and half-truths, and prophets of God's justice.[60]

"Subversive Memory," 2009

If the Church of God wants to be faithful to her "subversive memory," she must also remember that in her origins she was a movement of religious reform in which poor country folk, the rag-tag and outcasts of the world all found room. It was in the world of the poor and oppressed where the Pentecostal five-fold Gospel (Jesus Saves, Heals, Sanctifies, Baptizes in the Holy Spirit, and is Coming King) found room and flowered in the midst of the social and political storms in a world that was quickly being transformed. To be faithful to this "subversive memory," the Church of God must be on the side and by the side of the vic-

---

60. Email correspondence with Dario Lopez, 2007, personal files of Brian Pipkin. Interview questions translated by Sheila Ventura, Los Angeles, California, 2008. Rodriguez is a Church of God (Cleveland, TN) pastor in Lima, Peru. He also serves as the president of the National Evangelical Council of Peru, and is Bishop of the Lima Region of the Church of God of Peru. He is also a PCPJ member and author of multiple works on Pentecostalism and social justice. In his 2012 book, *The Liberating Mission of Jesus*, Rodriguez focuses on a sociopolitical reading of the Gospel of Luke, highlighting the subversive and radical context of Jesus' liberating message to the poor and powerless of society.

tims of the many kinds of violence, and must walk together with the millions of crucified ones of these times, situating herself on the "other side" of history and "showing up" on behalf of the defenseless ones of this world who are cast aside by the system as if they were disposable objects. To continue on the missionary path, a path that was opened up by her founders and which never should have been abandoned, requires the understanding that life in the Spirit demands that we love and defend the life of all human beings as an invaluable gift from the God of Life, especially the life of those who live in subhuman conditions without anyone to defend them simply because they have been condemned to live in the "dungheap" of history.

The tireless quest for integral peace, the vocation and practice of peacemaking, and opposition to all violence which disfigures and distorts the purpose of God, must be another way in which the Church of God can recover her "subversive memory." Here, it must be remembered that in her origins and early years of existence, the Church of God had a calling to and a practice of peacemaking and non-violence which ran against the current of the dominant society. If this is her historical legacy and counter cultural heritage, in order to be faithful to her dawning years of history and to her Pentecostal identity, she must cast her lot for peace and publicly denounce those who are guilty of killing hundreds of human beings with impunity. She will not be able, then, to justify, in the name of religion, the political and military actions of today's empire but must understand that no human empire, military force, economic power, or religious system can or shall ever attain the stature of the Kingdom of God.

. . . To keep from following the current of global capitalism and the culture which it promotes, the Church of God must see herself as an alternative society which is capable of reflecting the values of the Kingdom of God and its justice in her internal life and public face. In other words, instead of becoming the "official voice" of the predominant empire and the religious legitimizer of its military actions, she must carry the voice of those who have no voice and become a church which makes things uncomfortable for those who believe that the Gospel of the Kingdom of God can be whitewashed, adulterated, bartered, sequestered, or silenced.[61]

---

61. Rodríguez, "From Alternative Religion to Established Religion," 62–3.

256   PENTECOSTAL AND HOLINESS STATEMENTS ON WAR AND PEACE

RUSSIA

During the Revolution, the Russian Pentecostals maintained a position of pacifism. This changed during a time of extreme persecution from Soviet authorities in 1927 to a position of "admonishing members to participate in military service." This was no small matter with the Assemblies of God in the U.S. who were sponsoring this word, and they seriously considered withdrawing support over this issue.[62]

J. E. Varonaeff, First Pentecostal Missionary to Russia, 1884–1937

Varonaeff, as a young man, under his birth name, before he claimed conscientious objector (CO) status under the Tzar, was forced into exile using another Christian brother's passport. Upon his return to the Soviet Union, believing the claims of the revolutionary government to grant religious freedom, he came under severe persecution. One of the points of contention was the Assemblies of God teaching of religious objection to war. Varonaeff compromised with the Soviet authorities under extreme pressure (prison) and his European brethren were in great opposition to his position that Pentecostals must do military service if drafted.

The American Assemblies of God, sponsoring organization, was also greatly concerned, both for their stated belief against war and for the welfare of Varonaeff. He and his wife were both imprisoned in Siberia for many years. He was rumored to have been brutally killed, and later it was confirmed he was dead. His wife was released and immigrated to the U.S.. The following documents illustrate the pacifism of the Pentecostals in the Soviet Union and their satellite states early on, as well as the extreme pressure they were subjected to under Stalin's government.[63]

---

62. Quoted in Beaman, *Pentecostal Pacifism*, 33.

63. John Efimovich Varonaeff (1884–1937) also known as Ivan E. Voronaeff, was the pastor at the Russian Baptist Church in Manhatan, New York. He was the first Pentecostal missionary to Russia, and at his death, there were 80,000 Pentecostals in Russia. See "Letter: Verifying Voronaeff's death on 5 November 1937 by order of Soviet authorities," and Varonaeff's Draft Registration Card, World War I, 1918.

"Conscientious Objectors are Not Tolerated by Voronaeff,"[64] September 21, 1928

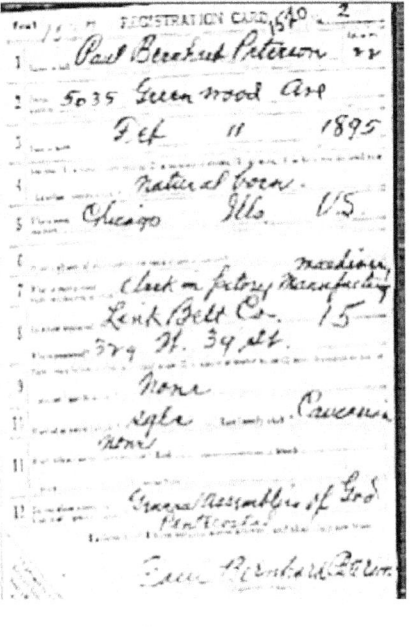

Paul Peterson, Russian and Eastern European Mission (REEM) General Secretary, World War I draft registration card. Peterson was a religious objector, affiliated with the Assemblies of God, and later associated with the Russian Bible Institute in Philadelphia and with REEM.

> . . . We have not written to Brother Voronaeff on the subject as we have no jurisdiction over him and leave it to you to deal with him. Present indications are that we shall take no action concerning our thirteen workers in that country, who are all working under Brother Voronaeff, until you have made disposition of his case. The writer of the article, M. A. Galcak, [?] is one of the workers Brother Voronaeff has had with him from the beginning and one of our missionaries. Very likely he was asked by Brother Voronaeff to write this report of the convention and he voices the opinion and makes clear the position of the assemblies of God in U.S.S.R. toward the question of military service.
>
> The position they assume is exactly opposite to that of the Assemblies of God in the U.S.A. The matter is very serious, as

---

64. This quote is taken from a letter from Paul B. Peterson, REEM General Secretary, to Noel Perkins, Assembly of God Minister (USA) regarding Voronaeff.

258   PENTECOSTAL AND HOLINESS STATEMENTS ON WAR AND PEACE

you will quickly see, because it is clearly stated that unless you approve of military service by Christians you cannot be a member of the Assemblies of God in U.S.S.R. This is wrong no matter how many verses of Scriptures they may quote to ease their conscience in assuming this position.

I might explain that the question of military service is one of the burning questions among the Russian believers in all the countries of Eastern Europe. We assume that Brother I.S. Prokhanoff, President of the All-Russian Evangelical Christian Union, when in a Soviet dungeon five or six years ago was compelled at the point of a revolver to sign a document to the effect that there would be no further opposition to military service in his Union. We know he was in prison, that after some time he was set free and that his Union has advocated military service for several years, which was a complete reversal of their original attitude. The All-Russian Baptist Union have agreed to the same policy, and now Brother Voronaeff and the leaders of the Pentecostal work in U.S.S.R. have also lined up with the government rather than to go to prison or suffer a worse fate. There are individuals among the Baptists that I am acquainted with who are now in exile because they would not accept the decision of the Baptist Union. Russian believers as a whole have always been against military service. Our opinion is that the Evangelical Christians and Baptists (the two strongest Protestant groups in the U.S.S.R.) have in their anger toward Brother Voronaeff because of the inroads he has been making upon their people with the teaching of the baptism of the Holy Spirit, reported him to the Soviet government as being against military service in the hope of putting him out of the way and that government agents have compelled him to take this stand. We gather this from the wording of the article referred to, as you will note that brethren were reprimanded for their interpretation of a resolution passed at a previous convention. We have an idea that the brethren stood together as opposed to military service and that their resolution was carefully worded. When asked for an interpretation the less cautious and wise frankly told where they stood and so now the Union has had to come out in the open with a declaration that every one can understand, and especially the government.

This action on the part of the brethren in the U.S.S.R. has saddened us, and we are fervently praying that God will somehow intervene and reveal to them the seriousness of their compromise. Their stand is absolutely unchristian, for certainly

International Holiness and Pentecostal Statements 259

no demand by the Soviet government of this nature should be made the condition for uniting the Assemblies of God. It pains us to think about it. May God help them and have mercy upon them . . .

P.S.—I might add that when the Russian brethren in the eastern part of Poland read the article in "The Evangelist" which we are sending you, they returned all copies of the magazine to Brother Voronaeff, wrote him a denunciatory letter (according to Brother G. H. Schmidt, who has reported this to us) and asked never to send them the magazine again.[65]

[Paul B. Peterson to Noel Perkins, July 12, 1929] In regard to Brother Voronaeff and the situation in Soviet Russia, we wish to advise that we have the published statement of the attitude assumed by the Assemblies of God in U.S.S.R. relative to disfellowshipping members who fail to enter military service or as preachers of the Gospel fail to encourage this among the believers. This statement appeared in the second issue of "The Evangelist."[66] The magazine was published in Soviet Russia for several months until a recent shortage of paper. It was this published article with caused the Russian Union in the East and ourselves to get in touch with Brother Voronaeff regarding their stand. If the brethren in U.S.S.R. would sign a declaration of the kind you mention this should settle the matter. But to do this would mean the rescinding of the resolution they passed in October, 1927, if they were to live up to the by-laws of the General Council and the R.E.E.M.

In spite of Brother Voronaeff's admonition not to discuss this matter by correspondence any further, we felt that we could write him without causing him embarrassment or danger and under date of June 14th wrote him as follows:

65. "Verifying Voronaeff's death by order of Soviet authorities." Emphasis in original.

66. We were unable to locate the second issue of *The Evangelist* magazine which records the official published statement on the military service matter. However, the first issue, 1928, is located at the Flower Pentecostal Heritage Center and was edited by Voranaeff himself. It does not, however, speak to this issue. Additionally, World Outreach International claims to be the successor organization to REEM. Unfortunately, they, too, do not have any archived information pre-1965. The founder of the work of World Outreach, Len Jones, did not pass on any historical materials to the successor organization. They also do not have any record of a magazine called *The Evangelist*. Email correspondence with John Bell of World Outreach, UK, March 20, 2012, personal files of Brian Pipkin.

260 PENTECOSTAL AND HOLINESS STATEMENTS ON WAR AND PEACE

"We thank God for all the good news about the work, but are frank in saying that we are not at all pleased with your reply to the vital question we have had under consideration for some time. . . . Every man has a right to freedom of conscience and we certainly cannot excommunicate people from the church of the living God because they exercise freedom of conscience and still are faithful to the Lord and His Word. This is walking on dangerous ground and we don't want to be found there . . ."

[Voronaeff replied] "As for the question concerning the military service, we have already answered you and answer once more, that our brotherhood in U.S.S.R. in its meeting in the year of 1927, has recognized and recognizes the military service equal to all citizens. We have for this a good ground in the word of God. If our Russian brothers, living in American and Poland do not recognize military service equal to all citizens, we have nothing against them. It is their own business. Apostle Paul says: 'Let every man be fully persuaded in his own mind' (Rom. 14:5; 13:1–7). Upon this question we must be free one from the other. In America and Poland there are some customs and laws, and by us in U.S.S.R. we have others. You submit to the Government and laws of your country and we submit to the laws and Government of our Union S.S.R., not transgressing of course the laws and teaching of our Lord Jesus Christ. (I Cor. 9:20–23 [?])."

Voronaeff stated in one of the letters we received from him a short time ago and the contents of which we passed on to you that if they change their attitude all the work they have done during the last seven years will come to naught. On our part we believe that if they are going to maintain their stand on excommunicating from the assemblies people who act according to the dictates of their conscience in this matter this will prove disastrous to their work. They have become slaves of the Soviet State in surrendering to the demands of that government. They are no longer free Christians but are tools in the hands of the Bolsheviks. The Soviets have cleverly won them, and instead of possible imprisonment, exile, or death they have chosen the line of least resistance and have failed to take into consideration the Lord's approval or disapproval of their attitude. There have been martyrs in Russia in the past and in other parts of the world as well because the Christians stood for principles that they considered most important in their worship of God . . ."[67]

67. Ibid.

International Holiness and Pentecostal Statements   261

"Voronaeff's stand to disfellowship preacher-members who refuse to perform military service in the USSR,"[68] June 13, 1929

. . . You will recall that when you were in the office on Tuesday, April 23rd, I showed you a letter received that morning from Brother Voronaeff. In this communication he referred to a letter which had been sent us on February 5th and which dealt with the subject of excommunication of members from assemblies in Russia who would not submit to military service or would not preach adherence to the Soviet law of all men serving in the army. I immediately wrote him to send us another copy of this letter and it was received last Friday. Below I give you everything in this letter concerning the point in question, and we are not changing a single word but verbatim in order that we may not pass on to you any interpretation that we may place upon the wording used. He writes as follows:

"As for brothers C. Alekciouk and S. Makcimoff, for already about two years they are exiled in Solovetsky island, they are sent there for three years and in one year they will be free. Makcimoff was a preacher in Smolensk and was arrested there, after him, brother Alekciouk was also a preacher in Smolensk, he was also arrested and both were sent together to Solovetsky islands. Makcimoff was a bachelor and Alekciouk has left a wife and a daughter one year old. They were sent for having, it is said, transgressed the Soviet laws of our country. The New York Russian assembly sends monthly to brother Alekciouk for his wife and child ten dollars.

"As for brothers C. Alekciouk and S. Makcimoff, for already about two years they are exiled in Solovetsky Island, they are sent there for three years and in one year they will be free. Makcimoff was a preacher in Smolensk and was arrested there, after him, brother Alekciouk was also a preacher in Smolensk, he was also arrested and both were sent together to Solovetsky Islands. Makcimoff was a bachelor and Alekciouk has left a wife and a daughter one year old. They were sent for having, it is said, transgressed the Soviet laws of our country . . .

"As for your question in your letters, so we have given answers on them to the Russian brothers in New York, and we should ask you to leave part of this question, as we do not intend to lead about it any discussion by letters. Our Russian

___
68. Letter from Paul B. Peterson to Noel Perkins.

brother in New York, with brother Maticiouk at their head, has rudely and audaciously insulted us, but we forgive them, are [sic] they are people little experienced quite uninterested in governmental questions or citizens duties, which teaches us the word of God, but I am sure that the American brothers and your Administrative Council, are intellectual brothers understanding all the life circumstances. The apostle Paul says: 'When I was a child, I thought as a child and judged as a child, but when I became a husband so I left Childhood.'

"In America, you live under certain conditions and we in others. In your country predominates religious and in our country predominate antireligion and atheism, you respect the laws of your country, but we must not transgress the Soviet Power laws for otherwise all our work done during these seven years, will be put to an end, and the doors of the preachers (Mar. 16:13–18) will be closed. I warn you to be prudent with our Russian brothers in New York and their poor understandings. They are not aware of our conditions and do not inform about them. And if the Lord has given to our country, to make such a great revolution and give freedom to preach the full gospel of the Kingdom of God, so we must use this freedom and save the sinners. I beg you to write nothing about this, otherwise your letters may harm the business of God in our country. We hope you well [sic] understand us. If the American brothers love and esteem the laws of their country why our Russian brothers, should not esteem the Soviet Power laws?"

Since receiving this letter we have not had a meeting of the Trustees, but Brother Swanson and I have given some consideration to the matter. The question, of course, is a very delicate one and, while we wish to be charitable and take into consideration the difficulties and persecutions incident to opposing the Soviet Russian laws, we do not seem to be able to reconcile their attitude with God's Word on the point of excommunicating members fro the assemblies who will not serve in the army or urge obedience to the law regarding military service. It seems we have to decide which of two evils is the greater—to support the work in spite of the unbiblical attitude and actions of the brethren, or to withdraw our support and consequently have the work suffer. At this writing we really do not know what is wiser and more pleasing to the Lord, and we would greatly appreciate an expression from the Missionary Committee.[69]

69. Ibid.

International Holiness and Pentecostal Statements   263

"Siberian Seven Still in American Embassy in Moscow," 1980

Washington—Two years ago, June 27, 1978, seven Russian Pentecostal Christians forged their way past armed Soviet guards and took refuge in the American embassy in Moscow. They're still there today.

Believers of whatever faith—43 million Moslems, 40 million Russian Orthodox, 4 million Eastern Orthodox, 4 million Roman Catholics, 3 million Protestants and 2 million Jews—are subjected to persecution in the Soviet Union.

But on none does the Soviet yoke rest more heavily than on the necks of the country's 400,000 Pentecostal Protestants, whose beliefs compel them to contravene Russian law.

Pentecostals refuse to accept citizenship in an atheistic state, and will not carry internal passports because they are "children of the Lord." Their sons refuse military service, and hence automatically go to prison at age 18. They refuse to register their church as required by law, since this would compel them to accept government restrictions on missionary activity, religious education and the distribution of the gospels . . .[70]

SOUTH AFRICA

From *The Weekly Evangel*, 1915

Pray for the European work in South Africa, as we are standing clear cut on the issue of taking up arms against our fellows, and refuse to do it. There is no prospect of this being an immediate issue, as far as we can see, but we never can tell. In the beginning of the disturbances in South Africa, we were somewhat [unclear word] up, as there was danger of our action being misunderstood and interpreted to mean sympathy with the rebels. Now we praise God that those difficulties are past, we trust for good, and we can stand clear in the issue, according to the Word . . .[71]

70. "Siberian Seven Still in American Embassy in Moscow."

71. *The Weekly Evangel,* Oct 30, 1915, 4. Quoted in Allen Anderson, *Spreading Fire,* 226.

SWITZERLAND

Swiss Pentecostal Mission

[AGAINST WAR], N.D.

The Swiss Pentecostal Mission took an absolute stand against war "as an expression of violence, which is emotional and not godly."[72]

72. Walter Hollenweger quoted in Beaman, *Pentecostal Pacifism*, 33.

Appendix

MINUTE BOOK
AND
MINISTERIAL RECORD
OF

Pentecostal Assemblies of the World

PORTLAND, OREGON, U. S. A.
YEAR 1917-1918

THE PENTECOSTAL ASSEMBLIES OF THE WORLD

The "Pentecostal Assemblies of the World" is the continuation of the great revival that began at Jerusalem on the Day of Pentecost, A. D. 33, and is founded upon the foundation of the Apostles and the Prophets, Jesus Christ himself, being the Chief Corner Stone. Acts 2:1-42, Eph. 2:19, 20. Although the true followers have been little known yet from that time until now there has always been earnest contenders "for the faith for which was once delivered unto the saints." See Jude 3; I Kings 19:18.

At various intervals, throughout the past centuries, the followers of the apostolic faith and doctrines have become prominent through great revivals that have appeared in Great Britain, United States and Canada.

In the days of Tertullian (A. D. 207), Chrysostom (4th century), Christians of 13th century, the early Quakers, Wesley, Whitefield, and Irving the gifts and manifestations of the apostolic church were much in evidence as the revival spirit swept over the country.

In Kansas (1901) the revival broke forth and moved southward to Texas, being known locally only, but finally reaching Los Angeles, California (1906), from whence it spread throughout the whole earth, entering into nearly every nation under heaven, penetrating the heathen darkness of India, China, Africa and the Isles of the sea, fulfilling the commission of our Lord, "Go ye into all the world and preach the gospel to every creature." (Mar. 16:15-20; Matt. 28:18, 19; Lu. 24:47-49; Acts 1:4-11), and proclaiming the soon coming of the Lord.

So great was this awakening that in a few years in nearly every town of any size whatever there were witnesses to the pentecostal outpouring of the Spirit (Lu. 24:48; Acts 1:8; Acts 2:4), and soon there began to appear in different localities places of worship, wherein the gifts of the Spirit were manifested, designating themselves by such names as The Apostolic Faith Mission, Pentecostal Mission, Apostolic Faith Assembly, Full Gospel Assembly or Mission, Assembly of God, etc., their one common aim being to "earnestly contend for the faith which was once delivered unto the saints in the days of the apostles, taking the Bible as their creed, discipline, and rule of order and charter.

Our chief aim is to glorify God our Savior, even Jesus Christ, who gave himself for us, that He might redeem us from all iniquity, and purify unto Himself a peculiar people, zealous of good works; that we should show forth the praises of Him who hath called us out of darkness into His marvelous light; and that we may be blameless and harmless, the sons of God, without rebuke, in the midst of a crooked and perverse nation, among whom we shine as light in the world, holding forth the Word of Life, to give light to them that sit in darkness and in the shadow of death, to guide their feet into the way of peace. See Tit. 2:13, 14; I Pet. 2:9; Phil. 2:15, 16; Lu. 1:79.

Our duty is to lift up the fallen, visit the sick, strengthen the weak, encourage the faint-hearted, comfort the feeble-minded, point the lost to the way of salvation, and urge all believers to seek a spirit-filled life (Eph. 5:18; Acts 19:1-16) and prepare for the coming of the Lord (Jas. 1:27; I Thes. 5:14; Mar. 16:15-18; Matt. 25:1-13.)

Moreover it is our indispensable duty, as partakers of the "royal priesthood" (I Pet. 2:9; Rev. 1:6; 5:10), to offer supplications, prayers, intercessions, and giving of thanks for all men; for kings, presidents, governors, magistrates and all that are in authority; that we may lead a quiet and peaceable life in all godliness and honesty. (1 Tim. 2:1-4; Rom. 13:1-7). And to submit ourselves "to every ordinance of man for the Lord's sake; whether it be to the king, as supreme, or unto governors, as unto them that are sent by him for the punishment of evildoers, and for the praise of them that do well," so long as these ordinances do not infringe upon the liberty of service towards God according to the dictation of the heart or conscience. (See I Pet. 2:13-17; Tit. 3:1, 2; Mat. 22:21.)

APOSTOLIC DOCTRINE AND FELLOWSHIP.

Our Creed, Discipline, Rules of Order and Doctrine is the WORD of God as taught and revealed by the Holy Ghost. John 14:26; I Cor. 2:9-13.

All scripture is given by the inspiration of God, and is profitable for Doctrine, for Reproof, for correction, for instruction in righteousness; that the man of God may be perfect, thoroughly furnished unto all good works. II Tim. 3:16, 17.

ARTICLE I.

MEMBERSHIP—HOW OBTAINED.

As members of the body of Christ, which is the True Church (Eph. 1:22, 23), the Word of God declares but one way of entrance therein, and that is, "By one spirit are we all baptized into one Body," and that is a baptism of "water and spirit." 1 Cor. 12:12-27; Gal. 3:26-28; Rom. 6:3, 4; John 3:5; Acts 2:38.

ARTICLE II.

RECORD OF MEMBERSHIP.

The names of the members are kept on record in heaven. (Lu. 10:20.) For it is written, "The Lord shall count, when He writeth up the people, that this man was born there." (Psa. 87:5, 6.) All must be "born of water and spirit" in this dispensation, if they desire their names to be written in heaven. (See Hebrews 12:22-24.

ARTICLE III.

HOW NAMES ARE BLOTTED OUT.

We have nothing to do with that whatever, for thus saith the Lord, "whosoever hath sinned against me, him will I BLOT out of My book." Ex. 31:33 And again, "He that overcometh * * * I will not BLOT out his name out of the book of Life." Rev. 3:5.

ARTICLE IV.
GOD'S STANDARD OF SALVATION.

We earnestly contend for Gods' standard of Salvation. In the Word of God we can find nothing short of a Holy, Spirit-filled Life with SIGNS FOLLOWING as on the Day of Pentecost. Mark 16:16, 17; Acts 2:4; 8:14-17; 9:17, 18; 10:44-48; 19:1-6. See Rom. 12:1, 2; Heb. 12:14; Matt. 5:48; I Pet. 1:15, 16.

ARTICLE V.
REPENTANCE AND REMISSION OF SINS.

The only grounds upon which God will accept a sinner is Repentance from the heart for the sins that he has committed. A broken and contrite heart, He will not despise. (Psa. 51:17.) John preached Repentance. Jesus Proclaimed it, and before His ascension commanded that Repentance and Remission of Sins should be preached in His Name, beginning at Jerusalem. (Lu. 24:47.) And Peter fulfilled this command on the Day of Pentecost. See Acts 2:38.

ARTICLE VI.
DIVINE HEALING.

The Lord alone is our Healer. Ex. 15:26; Psa. 103:2, 3. The Lord made our bodies. Should it be thought a thing incredible that He can heal us? With His stripes we are healed. Isa. 53:4, 5, with Matt. 8:14-17. See John 14:12; Mar. 16:17; James 5:14.

ARTICLE VII.
THE LORD'S SUPPER.

Melchizedek, the Priest of the Most High God, gave the first Communion to our Father Abraham, consisting of Bread and Wine. (Gen. 14:18.) Christ, being come a High Priest "after the order of Melchizedek," evidently administered the same. (Heb. 6:24.) Water and Grape Juice are modern substitutes that have been invented by the formal Church of today, in which are many who have never been regenerated and born of the Spirit. (Matt. 26:26-29; I Cor. 11:23-32.)

ARTICLE VIII.
FEET WASHING.

This ordinance is as much a divine command as any other New Testament ordinance. Jesus gave us an example that we should do even as He had done. He said that we ought to wash one another's feet. And again, "If ye know these things, happy are ye if you do them." (John 13:4-17.) There is scriptural evidence that this was practiced by the Church in the days of the Apostle Paul (1 Tim. 5:10.)

ARTICLE IX.
THE COMING OF JESUS.

That Jesus is to come to earth again in person is a doctrine clearly set forth in apostolic times. Jesus taught it. The Apostles preached it. And the saints expected it. See Matt. 24:1. etc.; Acts 1:11; 3:19-21; I Cor. 1:7, 8; 11:26; Phil. 3:20, 21; I Thess. 4:14-17; Tit. 2:13, 14.

ARTICLE X.
OFFERINGS.

The old method of begging, rallying, giving socials, shows and concerts to carry on God's work is not God's plan. We believe that if the people of God would obey His word there would be plenty on hand to carry on His work without scheming and grafting. "Tithing and free-will offerings" is God's plan. Gen. 14:20; 28:22; Mal. 3:8-12. See Ex. 25:2; 35:5, 21, 29.

ARTICLE XI.
COLLECTIONS ON THE STREET.

Collecting money, or begging on the streets during street services, is a thing not pleasing to the Lord. It leaves an impression that the people of God are more engaged in getting money than for the salvation of the lost, and causes many to pass by, who otherwise should stop and hear the gospel. We should preach the gospel free, without charge (I Cor. 9:18), but if any feel disposed to give an offering at such times, let it be graciously received as from the Lord. See Isa. 55:1; I Cor. 10:33.

ARTICLE XII.
MAL TREATMENT.

In time of persecution, or ill-treatment at the hands of an enemy, we should not "avenge ourselves," but rather give place to wrath; for it is written "Vengeance is mine; I will repay, saith the Lord." (Ro. 12:19; Deut. 32:35.) Neither shall we take up any weapon of destruction to slay another, whether in our own defense, or in the defense of others, for it is written, "Do violence to no man." (See Lu. 3:14; Mat. 26:52; John 18:36; 15:18, 19.) We should rather suffer wrong than to do wrong.

ARTICLE XIII.
CIVIL GOVERNMENT.

All civil magistrates are ordained of God for peace, safety, and the welfare of all people (Rom. 13:1-10), therefore, it is our duty to be in obedience to all requirements of the laws that are not contrary to the word of God, and that does not force one to the violation of the sixth commandment by bearing arms, or going to war. It is our duty to honor them, pay tribute, or such taxation as may be required without murmuring (Mat. 17:24-27; 22:17-21), and show respect to them in all lawful requirements of the civil government.

ARTICLE XIV.
SECRET SOCIETIES, ETC.

According to the word of God we firmly believe and hold that the people of God should have no connection whatever with labor unions, secret societies, or any other organization or body wherein there is a fellowship with unbelievers, bound by an oath. Jas. 5: (3-) 7; II Cor. 6:14-18. We are exhorted by the word of God to "be content with such things as we have," and "be content with our wages." I Tim. 6:8; Heb. 13:5; Lu. 3:14.

ARTICLE XV.

TRANSLATION OF SAINT.

We believe that the time draweth near for the coming of the Lord to make a change in the present order of things, and at that time all the righteous dead shall arise from their graves, and we that are alive and living righteous before God shall be translated or "caught up" to meet the Lord in the air. Mat. 24:36-42; Lu. 17:20-37; I Cor. 15:51-54; Phil. 3:20, 21; I Thes. 4:13-17.

ARTICLE XVI.

THE MILLENNIUM.

Moreover, we believe that the distress upon the earth is the "beginning of sorrows" and will become more intense until there "shall be a time of trouble such as there never was since there was a nation even to that same time" (Mat. 24:3-8; Dan. 12:1), and that that period of "tribulation" will be followed by the dawn of a better day on earth. And that for one thousand years there shall be "peace on earth and good will toward men." (Rev. 20:1-5; Isa. 65:17-25; Mat. 5:5; Dan. 7:27; Mic. 4:1, 2; Hab. 2:14; Rom. 11:25-27.)

ARTICLE XVII.

FINAL JUDGMENT.

When the thousand years are finished there shall be a resurrection of all the dead, who shall be summoned before the Great White Throne for their final judgment, and all whose names are not found written in the Book of Life shall be cast into the Lake of Fire, burning with brimstone, which God hath prepared for the devil and his angels, Satan being cast in first. Rev. 20:7-15; Mat. 25:41-46; Rev. 21:8.

ARTICLE XVIII.

WHOLLY SANCTIFIED LIFE.

We believe that in order to escape the judgment of God and to have the hope of enjoying the glory of life eternal, one must be thoroughly saved from their sins, wholly sanctified unto God and filled with the Holy Ghost. And that a wholly sanctified life is the only true standard of a Christian Life. Heb 12:14; I Pet. 1:15-17.

BRIEF RECORD OF MINUTES 1907-1917.

The first ministerial meeting of the different Pentecostal Assemblies met in general assembly for the transaction of business at Los Angeles, California, October 27, 1907.

Bro. Pendleton was elected chairman, pro tem.

Bro. Clark was elected secretary, pro tem.

The purpose and desires were and are still, that the Pentecostal Assemblies might be governed according to the Word of God; and with willing and unanimous consent chose the BIBLE as their Charter, Constitution and By-Laws.

The chairman was authorized to appoint a committee to see about publishing a paper. There being no further business a motion was made to adjourn. Carried.

Bibliography

Adams, Blair. *What We Believe: A Synopsis of the Vision, Spiritual Roots and Cultural Position of Heritage Ministries*. n.p.: n.d.

"Aimee Makes Peace Plea to Mussolini." *Berkeley Daily Gazette*, August 28, 1935, 11.

Alex Awad. No Pages. Online: http://www.alexawad.org/about.php.

Alexander, Paul, and Robert Welsh. "Exemplars of Godly Justice: Peacemaking and Justice Seeking in Dangerous Contexts." *PentecoStudies* 11.1 (2012) 67–86.

Alexander, Paul. *Christ at the Checkpoint: Theology in the Service of Justice and Peace*. Eugene, OR: Pickwick, 2012.

———. *Peace to War: Shifting Allegiances in the Assemblies of God*. Telford, PA: Cascadia, 2009.

———. "Pentecostal Charismatic Peace Fellowship." In *Encyclopedia of Pentecostal and Charismatic Christianity* edited by Stanley Burgess, 351–55. New York, NY: Routledge, 2006.

———. *Signs and Wonders: Why Pentecostalism is the World's Fastest Growing Faith*. San Francisco, CA: Jossey-Bass, 2009.

———. "Speaking in the Tongues of Nonviolence." *Evangelical Review of Society & Politics* 1.2 (2007) 1–19.

———. "Spirit Empowered Peacemaking: Toward a Pentecostal Peace Fellowship." Paper provided by Paul Alexander to Brian Pipkin.

Althouse, Peter. "Canadian Pentecostal Pacifism." *European Journal of Pentecostal Theology* 4.2, (1990) 32–33.

The American Flag, Pledge of Allegiance. The Third Way Café. No pages. Online: http://www.thirdway.com/peace/?Page=1843|Pledge+of+Allegiance.

Anderson, Allan. *Spreading Fires: The Missionary Nature of Early Pentecostalism*. Maryknoll, NY: Orbis, 2007.

Anderson, Robert Mapes. *Vision of the Disinherited*. New York: Oxford University Press, 1979.

Annual Minutes 1914. Microfilm in Oral Roberts University Library, Pentecostal Archives.

Annual Minutes, 1916. Microfilm in Oral Roberts University Library, Pentecostal Archives.

272   Bibliography

Annual Minutes, 1917. Microfilm in Oral Roberts University Library, Pentecostal Archives.

The Apostolic Church, Doctrine and Discipline. Bay City, TX: Apostolic, n.d. The Arthur Carl Piepkorn: Profiles in Belief Collection, Graduate Theological Union Archives, Berkeley, CA.

Apostolic Faith (Portland, Oregon). (n.p.; n.d) 2. The Apostolic Faith Headquarters, Portland, Oregon.

Apostolic Faith 1.2 (1912) 2. See Online: http://originalapostolicfaith.org/archives,_apostolic_faith_report.htm.

"Artickles [sic] of Faith." In *Minutes of the Tenth Annual Session of the Mountain Assembly of the Churches of God held with the Lower Elk Valley Church,* n.p. Jellico, TN: Churches of God, August 6–7–8 [sic], 1916. The Arthur Carl Piepkorn: *Profiles in Belief* Collection, Graduate Theological Union Archives, Berkley, CA. For some reason it reads CollectioBeamann.

"Articles of Faith of the Assemblies of the Lord Jesus Christ." In *Constitution, Rules, Articles of Faith,* 14. Memphis, TN: Apostolic, 1965. The Arthur Carl Piepkorn: *Profiles in Belief* Collection, Graduate Theological Union Archives, Berkeley, CA.

Articles of Faith of the Bethel Baptist Assembly Inc. Evansville, IN: Bethel Baptist Assembly, n.d. The Arthur Carl Piepkorn: *Profiles in Belief* Collection, Graduate Theological Union Archives, Berkeley, CA.

Articles of Faith of the Church. Letter to Arthur Carl Piepkorn. (February 6, 1965) The Arthur Carl Piepkorn: *Profiles in Belief* Collection, Graduate Theological Union Archives, Berkeley, CA.

The Articles of Faith of the General Conference of The Church of God of the Apostolic Faith. Tulsa, OK: The Church of God of the Apostolic Faith, 1966. The Arthur Carl Piepkorn: *Profiles in Belief* Collection, Graduate Theological Union Archives, Berkeley, CA.

Articles of Faith of the Open Bible Standard Churches, Inc. Des Moines, IA: Open Bible Standard Churches, n.d. The Arthur Carl Piepkorn: *Profiles in Belief* Collection, Graduate Theological Union Archives, Berkeley, CA.

Articles of Faith of the United Pentecostal Church. St. Louis, MO: United Pentecostal Church, n.d. The Arthur Carl Piepkorn: *Profiles in Belief* Collection, Graduate Theological Union Archives, Berkeley, CA.

Articles of Faith Rules and By-Laws, The Fire Baptized Holiness Church. [Labette, KS] n.p., 1963. The Arthur Carl Piepkorn: *Profiles in Belief* Collection, Graduate Theological Union Archives, Berkeley, CA.

Articles of Incorporation and By-Laws of Westgate Chapel. Edmonds, Washington: Westgate Chapel, n.d. [1962?] The Arthur Carl Piepkorn: *Profiles in Belief* Collection, Graduate Theological Union Archives, Berkeley, CA.

"Article 7." In *Minutes of the General Conferences of Brethren in Christ (River Brethren) from 1871–1904,* 55. Harrisburg, PA: Brethren in Christ, 1889. The Brethren in Christ Historical Library and Archives, Grantham, PA.

"Article 17." In *53rd–54th Annual Convention 1960–61 Yearbook of the Church of God in Christ.* Memphis, TN: Church of God in Christ, 1960–61.

"Article 32." In *Minutes of General Conference,* 55. Harrisburg, PA: Brethren in Christ Church, 1913. Document provided by Glen Pierce, Director, Brethren in Christ Historical Library and Archives of Messiah College, Grantham, PA.

"Article XVII on Military Service." In *Minutes of Corporate Session, Fourteenth Annual Convention, 11 January 1937,* n.p. ICFG corporate document.

Bibliography 273

"Article XXIII Examining Board Report." In *Minutes of the General Conference.* Harrisburg, PA: Brethren in Christ Church, 1948. The Brethren in Christ Historical Library and Archives, Grantham, PA.

Articulos de Fé de la Iglesia Cristiana Evangelica Mexicana. CD. Reynosa, Tamaulipas, Mexico: Iglesia Cristiana Evangelica Mexicana, n.d. The Arthur Carl Piepkorn: *Profiles in Belief* Collection, Graduate Theological Union Archives, Berkeley, CA.

Ashcroft, John. "Let the Eagle Soar." YouTube. Online: http://www.youtube.com/watch?v=woLQI8X2R6Y.

Awad, Alex. *Palestinian Memories: The Story of a Palestinian Mother and Her People.* 2nd ed. Bethlehem: Bethlehem Bible College, 2012.

Awad, Sami. "A Palestinian Christian Evangelical Response to the Holocaust." In *Christ at the Checkpoint*, edited by Paul N. Alexander, 23–29. Eugene OR: Pickwick, 2012.

Awrey, Daniel. "Life Sketches: 'Beaten With Many Stripes.'" *The Latter Rain Evangel* 2.7 (1910) 16.

Backus, Elbert Carlton. "The Patriotic Harlot." *The Comeouter*, March 1, 1918, 4–7. In Investigative Case Files of the Bureau of Investigation 1908–1922. The National Archives Research Administration, Publication Number M1085, Series Old German Files, 1909–1921, Case Number 210390, 16.

Bailey, Wilma Ann. *"You Shall Not Kill Or You Shall Not Murder?": The Assault on the Biblical Text.* Collegeville, MN: Liturgical, 2005.

Barba, Lloyd D. "An Open Letter to UPCI Ministers: A Biblical Examination of the Current and Proposed Resolution to the UPCI Articles of Faith on Conscientious Scruples." January, 2012. Personal files of Brian Pipkin. No Pages. Online: http://cdnclipper.wordpress.com/2012/01/16/an-open-letter-to-upci-ministers/.

———. *"Wars and Rumors of Wars: Oneness Pentecostal Pacifism and Patriotism from WWI—WWII."* Paper presented at the Society for Pentecostal Studies, Regent University, VA, March 2012.

Barclay, Robert. "The Quaker Peace Testimony." Online: http://www.quaker.org/minnfm/peace/Robert%20Barclay%20%201678.htm.

Bartleman, Frank. "Christian Citizenship." Los Angeles: published by the author, n.d. From iFPHC (iFPHC.org).

———. "In the Last Days." *Word and Work*, September 1916, 393–94. Document courtesy of Cecil M. Robeck.

———. *War and the Christian.* Los Angeles: published for the author, n.d. From iFPHC (iFPHC.org).

———. "What Will the Harvest Be?" *The Weekly Evangel*, August 7, 1915. From iFPHC (iFPHC.org).

Beaman, Jay. *Pentecostal Pacifism: The Origin, Development, and Rejection of Pacific Belief among the Pentecostals.* 1989. Reprint. Eugene, OR: Wipf & Stock, 2009.

Bell, E. N. "Questions and Answers." *The Weekly Evangel*, April 14, 1917, 9. From iFPHC (iFPHC.org).

———. "Questions and Answers." *The Christian Evangel*, October 19, 1918, 5. From iFPHC (iFPHC.org).

Beroth, Rev. Ernest (General Bishop of the Pentecostal Evangelical Church), to Arthur Carl Piepkorn. Personal letter. August 17, 1967. The Arthur Carl Piepkorn: *Profiles in Belief* Collection, Graduate Theological Union Archives, Berkeley, CA.

Bethlehem Affirmation. No Pages. Online: http://www.bethlehemaffirmation.com.

Bethlehem Bible College Mission. No Pages. Online: http://www.bethbc.org/welcome/about-us/mission.

Bethlehem Bible College. No Pages. Online: http://www.bethbc.org.

274   Bibliography

Black, J. H. "Birthday Anniversary." *Apostolic Faith* 1.3 (1912) 12. See Online: http://originalapostolicfaith.org/archives,_apostolic_faith_report.htm.

Boddy, Alexander A. "The War." *Confidence* 7.10 (1914) 191.

———. "The War." *Confidence* 7.11 (1914) 206.

The Book of Doctrines: 1903–1970. Huntsville, AL: Church of God Publishing House, 1970.

Booth-Clibborn, Arthur Sydney, and Catherine Booth-Clibborn. *For the Word of God and the Testimony of Jesus*. London: Arthur Booth-Clibborn, 1902. From iFPHC (iFPHC.org).

Booth-Clibborn, Arthur Sydney. *Blood Against Blood*. New York: Cook, n.d.

Booth, Catherine Mumford. *Popular Christianity: A Series of Lectures Delivered in Princes Hall, Piccadilly*. Boston: McDonald, Gills and Co., 1887.

Booth, Herbert. *The Saint and the Sword: A Series of Addresses on the Anti-Christian Nature of War*. New York: Doran, 1923.

Bouchette, Bob. "Sister Aimee Shies at Politics." *The Vancouver Sun*, October 28, 1935, 3.

Brown, James Oakley, to Arthur Carl Piepkorn. Personal letter. June 4, 1970. The Arthur Carl Piepkorn: *Profiles in Belief* Collection, Graduate Theological Union Archives, Berkeley, CA.

Bundy, David. "Howard Carter, Pentecostal Warrior." *Assembly of God Heritage* 19.1 (1999) 12. From iFPHC (iFPHC.org).

———. "Thomas Cogswell Upham and the Establishment of a Tradition of Ethical Reflection." *Encounter* 59 (1998) 23–40.

Bursell, H. R., to J. W. Welch. Letter. 30 May 1917. From iFPHC (iFPHC.org).

Bursell, H.R., to J. W. Welch. Letter. 13 May 1917. From iFPHC (iFPHC.org).

Cameron, Richard. *Methodism and Society in Historical Perspective*. New York: Abingdon, 1961.

Campbell, Joseph E. *The Pentecostal Holiness Church 1898–1948*. Franklin Springs, GA: Publishing House of the Pentecostal Holiness Church, 1951.

Carter, John. *Donald Gee: Pentecostal Statesman*. Nottingham, UK: Assemblies of God Publishing House, 1975.

———. *A Full Life: The Autobiography of a Pentecostal Pioneer*. Nottingham, UK: Assemblies of God in Great Britain and Ireland, 1979.

———. *Howard Carter: Man of the Spirit*. Nottingham, UK: Assemblies of God, 1971.

Cartwright, D. W. "Carter, John H." In *International Dictionary of Pentecostal and Charismatic Movements*, edited by Stanley M. Burgess and Eduard M. Van Der Maas, 456–57. Grand Rapids: Zondervan, 2003.

Change of Command. Produced by Mennonite Central Committee. 3.35 min., 1998. Online: http://www.mcc.org/stories/videos/change-command.

Christ at the Checkpoint. No Pages. Online: http://www.christatthecheckpoint.com/index.php/about-us/2012-press-release.

"Church of God and Military Service." No pages. Online: http://www.chog.org/church-god-and-military-service.

Clifton, Albert Shaw. "The Salvation Army's Actions and Attitudes in Wartime: 1899–1945." PhD thesis, King's College London, 1989.

Clifton, Shane. *Global Pentecostal and Charismatic Studies, Volume 3: Pentecostal Churches in Transition: Analysing the Developing Ecclesiology of the Assemblies of God in Australia*. Leuven: Brill, 2009.

Collins, Harry J. Jr., and Floyd L. Hagan, Sr., (with editorial Assistance by Doug Herkovich and Linda Robuck). *History of Christ's Sanctified Holy Church*. Zebulon,

NC: Davis Sons, 2005. Citing Dan Bonner's biography. No pages. Online: http://www.cshc.com/ message.php?topicID=27574&.

"Compulsory Military Service: An English Conscientious Objector's Testimony." *The Weekly Evangel*, April 28, 1917, 7.

Constitucion Y Reglamento De La Iglesia De Dios Pentecostal Incorporanda. n.p.: 1954. The Arthur Carl Piepkorn: *Profiles in Belief* Collection, Graduate Theological Union Archives, Berkeley, CA.

"Constitution and Bylaws." In *Statements of Religious Bodies on the Conscientious Objector: Compiled by the National Service Board For Religious Objectors*, 47. Washington, DC: National Service Board for Religious Objectors, 1953.

Constitution and By-Laws of the California Evangelistic Association. Long Beach, CA: California Evangelistic Association, February 20, 1939. The Arthur Carl Piepkorn: *Profiles in Belief* Collection, Graduate Theological Union Archives, Berkeley, CA.

Constitution and By-Laws [of the] *The Filipino Assemblies of the First-born, Incorporated.* Delano, CA: The Filipino Assemblies of the First–Born Incorporated, 1954. The Arthur Carl Piepkorn: *Profiles in Belief* Collection, Graduate Theological Union Archives, Berkeley, CA.

Constitution and General Conference By-Laws of The Missionary Church Association. Fort Wayne, IN: Bible Truth, 1956. The Arthur Carl Piepkorn: *Profiles in Belief* Collection, Graduate Theological Union Archives, Berkeley, CA.

Constitution and General Rules of Triumph The Church and Kingdom of God in Christ. Atlanta: Triumph The Church, January 20, 1902–July 20, 1959. The Arthur Carl Piepkorn: *Profiles in Belief* Collection, Graduate Theological Union Archives, Berkeley, CA.

Constitution of The Missionary Church Association [source 1956] *and The United Missionary Church* [merger 1966]. n.p.: n.d. The Arthur Carl Piepkorn: *Profiles in Belief* Collection, Graduate Theological Union Archives, Berkeley, CA.

"Convention Minutes." In *The Church Advocate and Holiness Banner*, October 22, 1914. Quoted in Clarence Cowen, "A History of the Church of God (Holiness)." PhD diss., University of Missouri, 1948.

Cornelius, Lucille J. "What the Church Believes and Teaches: Messages from the Chief Apostle: Political Governments." In *The Pioneer: History of the Church of God in Christ*, 68. No publisher, 1975.

Dayton, Donald W. *Theological Roots of Pentecostalism.* Grand Rapids: Zondervan, 1987.

Dayton, Donald, and Lucille S[ider] Dayton. "An Historical Survey of Attitudes toward War and Peace within the American Holiness Movement." Unpublished paper read to the Seminar on Christian Holiness and the Issues of War and Peace. Winona Lake, IN, June 7–9, 1973.

Dayton, Donald, and Lucille S. Dayton. "An Historical Survey of Attitudes towards War and Peace within the American Holiness Movement." In *Perfect Love and War: A Dialogue on Christian Holiness and the Issues of War and Peace*, 7–89. Nappanee, IN: Evangel, 1974.

"Destroy This Track." *Christian Evangel*, August 24, 1918, 4. From iFPHC (iFPHC.org).

Discipline and General Rules of the Pentecostal Fire-Baptized Holiness Church. Toccoa, GA: Pentecostal Fire-Baptized Holiness Church, 1961. The Arthur Carl Piepkorn: *Profiles in Belief* Collection, Graduate Theological Union Archives, Berkeley, CA.

Discipline of God's Missionary Church. Privately published, 1971. The Arthur Carl Piepkorn: *Profiles in Belief* Collection, Graduate Theological Union Archives, Berkeley, CA.

276   Bibliography

Discipline of Indiana Yearly Meeting of Friends. Richmond, IN: n.p., 1887 and 1905.

Discipline of Oregon Yearly Meeting of the Friends Church. n.p.: 1924. Document located at George Fox University, Northwest Yearly Meeting of Friends Archives.

Discipline of the Church of God (Apostolic), Inc. Beckley, WV: Church of God [Apostolic], n.d. [after 1943]. The Arthur Carl Piepkorn: *Profiles in Belief* Collection, Graduate Theological Union Archives, Berkeley, CA.

Discipline of the Emmanuel Holiness Church. Privately published, 1963. The Arthur Carl Piepkorn: *Profiles in Belief* Collection, Graduate Theological Union Archives, Berkeley, CA.

Discipline of the United Holiness Church of North America. Privately printed, 1969. The Arthur Carl Piepkorn: *Profiles in Belief* Collection, Graduate Theological Union Archives, Berkeley, CA.

The Doctrines and Discipline of the Holiness Christian Church of the United States of America, Incorporated. n.p., 1948. The Arthur Carl Piepkorn: *Profiles in Belief* Collection, Graduate Theological Union Archives, Berkeley, CA.

The Doctrines and Discipline of the Mennonite Brethren in Christ Church. New Carlisle, OH: General Conference Executive Committee, 1924. Manuscript courtesy of Kevin Blowers, Bethel College Library, Mishawaka, IN.

Douglas, Cecelia Luelf, and Ruth Smith Taylor. *The History of the Bible Holiness Church.* Independence, KS: Whispering Pines, 2011.

Dresser, Amos. *The Bible Against War.* Oberlin, OH: James M. Fitch Printer, 1849. Online: http://www.nonresistance.org/docs_pdf/Bible_Against_War.pdf.

Emmanuel's Fellowship Statement of Faith. Privately published, October 1966. The Arthur Carl Piepkorn: *Profiles in Belief* Collection, Graduate Theological Union Archives, Berkeley, CA.

"Feltus, Wesley." In *Investigative Case Files of the Bureau of Investigation 1908–1922.* The National Archives Research Administration, Publication Number M1085, Series Old German Files, 1909–1921, Case Number 239489.

"Force or Power?" *Time Magazine* 42.15, October 11, 1943, 48.

Ford, Jack. *In the Steps of John Wesley: The Church of the Nazarene in Britain.* Kansas City, MO: Nazarene, 1968.

Fox, George. "The Quaker Peace Testimony." Online: http://www.kimopress.com/early.htm# .

Gee, Donald. *These Men I Knew: Personal Memories of Our Pioneers.* Nottingham, UK: Assemblies of God, 1980.

———. "War, the Bible, and the Christian." *The Pentecostal Evangel,* November 8, 1930, 6–7.

———. "War, the Bible, and the Christian" [Part II]. *The Pentecostal Evangel,* November 15, 1930, 2.

The General Assembly and Church of the First Born: Who We Are and What We Believe. n.p. (3-page pamphlet distributed in 1967). The Arthur Carl Piepkorn: *Profiles in Belief* Collection, Graduate Theological Union Archives, Berkeley, CA.

General Bylaws of Apostolic Church of Pentecost of Canada, Incorporated. Saskatoon, Saskatchewan: Apostolic Church of Pentecost of Canada, 1965. The Arthur Carl Piepkorn: *Profiles in Belief* Collection, Graduate Theological Union Archives, Berkeley, CA.

General Constitution and By-Laws of The Pentecostal Church of God of America. n.p.: n.d. The Arthur Carl Piepkorn: *Profiles in Belief* Collection, Graduate Theological Union Archives, Berkeley, CA.

Bibliography   277

General Principles of the International Pentecostal Assemblies. Atlanta: International Pentecostal Assemblies, n.d. The Arthur Carl Piepkorn: *Profiles in Belief* Collection, Graduate Theological Union Archives, Berkeley, CA.

General Superintendent Update. United Pentecostal Church International. August 29, 2012. No Pages. Online: http://www.upci.org/news/126-general-superintendent-update-08292012.

The GI Rights Hotline. The Civilian Public Service Story: Living Peace in a Time of War. No pages. Online: http://civilianpublicservice.org/storycontinues/hotline.

Goff, J. R., Jr. "Charles Fox Parham." In *International Dictionary of Pentecostal and Charismatic Movements,* edited by Stanley M. Burgess and Eduard M. Van Der Maas, 955–57. Grand Rapids: Zondervan, 2003.

Gohr, Glenn. "Telling the Lord's Secrets." *Assemblies of God Heritage* 20.4 (2000–2001) 25–26.

The Gospel Messenger Official Organ of the Congregational Holiness Church. n.p., 1966.

The Guidebook of the Emmanuel Association. Rev. ed. Colorado Springs, CO: Emmanuel Association, 1966. The Arthur Carl Piepkorn: *Profiles in Belief* Collection, Graduate Theological Union Archives, Berkeley, CA.

Hall, David. "What the Church Teaches about War." In *Pentecostals and Nonviolence,* edited by Paul N. Alexander, 193–94. Eugene, OR: Pickwick, 2013.

Hamm, Thomas D., Margaret Marconi, Gretchen Kleinhen Salina, and Benjamin Whitman. "The Decline of Quaker Pacifism in the Twentieth Century: Indiana Yearly Meeting of Friends as a Case Study." *Indiana Magazine of History* 96, March 1, 2000, 50.

Harris, John. "Are Christian Zionism and Social Justice Compatible." *Middle East Experience.* July 2, 2012. No Pages. Online: http://www.middleeastexperience. com/are-christian-zionism-and-social-justice- compatible/#.UOZA5qVgPoc.

———. *Palestinian Pentecostals in The West Bank—Following Jesus and Working for Peace.* Pentecostals and Charismatics for Peace and Justice, 2007. No Pages. Online: http:// www.pcpj.org/index.php/resources-topmenu-45/75-middle-east-studies/413- palestinian-pentecostals-in-the-west-bank-following-jesus-and-working-for -peace.

———. *Speaking In Tongues in Palestine.* Pentecostals and Charismatics for Peace and Justice, 2007. No Pages. Online: http://www.pcpj.org/index.php/resources- topmenu-45/75-middle-east-studies/495-speaking-in-tongues-in-palestine.

Healing Evangelists, 1881–1957, CD. Springfield, MO: Gospel, 2008.

Hershberger, Guy, Ernst Crous, and John R. Burkholder. "Nonresistance." In *Global Anabaptist Mennonite Encyclopedia,* 1989. No pages. Online: http://www.gameo. org/encyclopedia/contents/N656ME.html.

Hiebert, Clarence. *The Holdeman People: The Church of God in Christ, Mennonite, 1859–1969.* Pasadena, CA: William Cary Library, 1973.

History of the Church of God Mountain Assembly. Williamsburg, KY: Churches of God of the Original Mountain Assembly 1906–1970. The Arthur Carl Piepkorn: *Profiles in Belief* Collection, Graduate Theological Union Archives, Berkeley, CA and iFPHC.

Hocken, P. D. "Pentecostal Missionary Union." In *International Dictionary of Pentecostal and Charismatic Movements,* edited by Stanley M. Burgess and Eduard M. Van Der Maas, 970–71. Grand Rapids: Zondervan, 2003.

Hollenweger, Walter J. *The Pentecostals: The Charismatic Movement in the Churches.* Minneapolis: Augsburg, 1972.

Holy Land Trust. No Pages. Online: http://www.holylandtrust.org.

278   Bibliography

Holy Land Trust Mission. Holy Land Trust. No Pages. Online: http://www.holylandtrust. org/index.php/about.

Holy Land Trust Nonviolence Project. No Pages. Online: http://www.holylandtrust.org/ index.php/nonviolence-project.

"Homestead Heritage." No pages. Online: http://www.homesteadheritage.com/.

Hostetler, Paul. *Perfect Love and War: A Dialogue on Christian Holiness and the Issues of War and Peace.* Nappanee, IN: Evangel, 1974.

"In Re: Reverend Harry Hays, German Activities." In *Investigative Case Files of the Bureau of Investigation 1908-1922.* Investigative Case Files of the Bureau of Investigation 1908 to 1922. FBI Old German Files, Case #124307, 17 Jan. 1918. Washington, DC: National Archives Research Administration.

Johnson, Bishop Theron B.(General Overseer, The Seventh Day Pentecostal Church of the Living God), to Arthur Carl Piepkorn. Personal letter. 27 January 1969. The Arthur Carl Piepkorn: *Profiles in Belief* Collection, Graduate Theological Union Archives, Berkeley, CA.

Johnson, Sherrod C. *Is Jesus Christ the Son of God Now?* Philadelphia, PA: Church of the Lord Jesus Christ of the Apostolic Faith, n.d. [Eight-page pamphlet] The Arthur Carl Piepkorn: *Profiles in Belief* Collection, Graduate Theological Union Archives, Berkeley, CA.

Jones, Charles Edwin. *Black Holiness: A Guide to the Study of Black Participation in the Wesleyan Perfectionist and Glossolalic Pentecostal Movements.* Metuchen, NJ: Scarecrow, 1987.

Jolley, Edgar Otis. "Christians May Now Go to War." *The Repairer* XXII.4, April 1918, 2-3. *Investigative Case Files of the Bureau of Investigation 1908-1922.* FBI Old German Files, Case #209513, 217799. Washington, DC: National Archives Research Administration.

Keith, Jeanette. *Rich Man's War, Poor Man's Fight: Race, Class, and Power in the Rural South During the First World War.* Chapel Hill, NC: University of North Carolina Press, 2004.

Kelley, Martin. "The Quaker Peace Testimony: Living in the Power, Reclaiming the Source." In *Quaker Ranter Blog about Friends, Life & Religion.* Online: http:// www. quakerranter.org/2005/01/the_quaker_peace_testimony_liv/.

Kellogg, Walter Guest. *The Conscientious Objector.* New York: Boni and Liveright, 1919.

Kiergan, A. M. "War—What For?" *The Church Advocate and Holiness Banner,* March 16, 1915, 1. The Kansas Historical Society.

Kostlevy, William. "The Church of God (Guthrie, Oklahoma)." In *Historical Dictionary of the Holiness Movement,* edited by William C. Kostlevy and Gari-Anne Patzwald, 54. Lanham: MD, Scarecrow, 2001.

———. *Holy Jumpers: Evangelicals and Radicals in Progressive Era America.* New York: Oxford University Press, 2010.

———. "Jernigan, C. B." In *Historical Dictionary of the Holiness Movement,* edited by William C. Kostlevy and Gari-Anne Patzwald, 143. Lanham, MD: Scarecrow, 2001.

Kraybill, Donald B. *The Upside Down Kingdom.* Scottdale, PA: Herald, 1990.

Laleff, Michael. *From Atheism to Christ: A Challenge to Skeptics.* San Diego, CA: Royal B. Churchill, n.d.

Leaves of Healing VI. March 31, 1900.

———. *VIII.* 1901.

———. *XI.* May 17, 1902.

Lenz, Darin D. "Visions on the Battlefields": Alexander A. Boddy, Early British Pentecostalism, and the First World War, 1914–1918." *Journal of Religious History* 32.3 (2008) 288–98.

"Letter: Verifying Voronaeff's death on 5 November 1937 by order of Soviet authorities." Personal Papers of John E. Varonaeff. From iFPHC (iFPHC.org).

Lindsay, Gordon. *John Alexander Dowie: A Life Story of Trials, Tragedies and Triumphs.* Dallas: Christ for the Nations, 1980.

Lynch, Jos. B., and Sarah E. Collins, *The Doctrines and Disciplines of Christ's Sanctified Holy Church.* Virginia: n.p., 1893. The Arthur Carl Piepkorn: *Profiles in Belief* Collection, Graduate Theological Union Archives, Berkeley, CA.

Maguen, Shira, and Brett Litz. *Moral Injury in the Context of War.* United States Department of Veterans Affairs, 2011. No pages. Online: http://www.ptsd.va.gov/professional/pages/moral_injury_at_war.asp.

Manual of the Calvary Holiness Church. Privately printed, 1963. The Arthur Carl Piepkorn: *Profiles in Belief* Collection, Graduate Theological Union Archives, Berkeley, CA.

Manual of the Gospel Mission Corps, Inc. Cranbury, NJ: Gospel Mission Corps., n.d. The Arthur Carl Piepkorn: *Profiles in Belief* Collection, Graduate Theological Union Archives, Berkeley, CA.

Manual of Mount Sinai Holy Church of America. Philadelphia: PA: Mount Sinai Holy Church of America, 1947. The Arthur Carl Piepkorn: *Profiles in Belief* Collection, Graduate Theological Union Archives, Berkeley, CA.

Manual [of the] *United Pentecostal Church Articles of Faith.* St. Louis, Missouri: Pentecostal Publishing House, 1966. The Arthur Carl Piepkorn: *Profiles in Belief* Collection, Graduate Theological Union Archives, Berkeley, CA.

Manual [of the] United Pentecostal Church International. Hazelwood, Missouri, USA., 2012.

"Maranatha." *The Latter Rain Evangel,* April, 1912, 15.

Mason, Bishop C .H. *Official Manual of the Church of God in Christ, 7th Ed.* Published and authorized and approved by C. H. Mason, revised 1957.

Massey, Richard. *Another Springtime: The Life of Donald Gee, Pentecostal Leader and Teacher.* Guildford, UK: Highland, 1992.

McCaleb. "United States Vs. Henry Kirven, Austin, Texas: Violation Selective Draft." In *Investigative Case Files of the Bureau of Investigation 1908–1922.* The National Archives Research Administration, Publication Number M1085, Series Old German Files, 1909–1921, Case Number 245662. [July 15, 1918] 4.

McClain, Sam. "Our Boys in Time of War." *Apostolic Herald,* October 1919, 4.

McNeill, Noel. *As of a Rushing Mighty Wind: An Assessment of North America's Pentecostal Movements.* Unpublished paper, 1966. The Arthur Carl Piepkorn: *Profiles in Belief* Collection, Graduate Theological Union Archives, Berkeley, CA.

McPherson Hutton, Aimee. "The Way to Disarm IS TO DISARM." *Los Angeles Times,* February 14, 1932, J3.

McPherson, Aimee Semple. "The Coming Prince of Peace." *The Bridal Call* 3.8, January 1920, 11.

———. *Declaration of Faith.* Los Angeles: International Church of the Foursquare Gospel, 1923.

———. "Editorial Comments War." *Foursquare Crusader,* March 3, 1937, 2.

———. "Editorial Comments." *Foursquare Crusader,* November 3, 1937, 2.

———. "Questionnaire from the N.Y.N.A." [Questions answered by Aimee McPherson]. Personal papers of ASM. ICFG corporate documents.

Bibliography

McPherson, Rolf K. "The Greatest of All." *Foursquare Magazine* 27.1, January 1954, 4–6.

Minister's Manual Containing the Policies and Principles of the Open Bible Standard Churches, Inc. Des Moines, IA: Open Bible Standard Churches, February 1967. The Arthur Carl Piepkorn: *Profiles in Belief* Collection, Graduate Theological Union Archives, Berkeley, CA.

Minute Book and Ministerial Record of Pentecostal Assemblies of the World, Portland, Oregon, U.S. A., Year 1917–1918. In *Investigative Case Files of the Bureau of Investigation*, Old German Files, #57234.

Minute Book of the Pentecostal Assemblies of the World, Inc. Indianapolis, IN: Pentecostal Assemblies of the World, 1966. The Arthur Carl Piepkorn: *Profiles in Belief* Collection, Graduate Theological Union Archives, Berkeley, CA.

Minutes of General Conference of The Brethren in Christ (River Brethren) of U.S.A. and Canada. Abilene, KS: The Brethren in Christ, 1909. The Brethren in Christ Historical Library and Archives, Grantham, PA.

Minutes of the Churches of God of the Original Mountain Assembly, Incorporated 1967–1968. Williamsburg, KY: Churches of God of the Original Mountain Assembly, 1967. The Arthur Carl Piepkorn: *Profiles in Belief* Collection, Graduate Theological Union Archives, Berkeley, CA and IFPCH.

"Minutes of the Fourth General Conference of the Pentecostal Holiness Church 1921." In *General Conference Minutes 1911–2005*, 25. Oklahoma City, OK: Archives and Research Center, International Pentecostal Holiness Center, 2008.

"Minutes of the Sixth General Conference of the Pentecostal Holiness Church 1929." In *General Conference Minutes: 1911–2005*, 32. Oklahoma City, OK: Archives and Research Center, International Pentecostal Holiness Center, 2008.

"Minutes of the Tenth General Conference of the Pentecostal Holiness Church, 1945." In *General Conference Minutes: 1911–2005*, 47, 49–50. Oklahoma City, OK: Archives and Research Center, International Pentecostal Holiness Center, 2008.

"Minutes of the Third Session of the General Convention of the Pentecostal Holiness Church, Jan. 23–28, 1917." In *General Conference Minutes: 1911–2005*. Oklahoma City, OK: Archives & Research Center, IPHC, 2008.

Mittelstadt, Martin, and Matthew Paugh. "The Social Conscience of Stanley Horton." *AG Heritage* (2009) 15–16.

Mittelstadt, Martin. "My Life as a Mennocostal: A Personal and Theological Narrative." *Theodidaktos* 3.2 (2008) 10–17. From iFPHC (iFPHC.org).

Moore, Everett LeRoy. "Handbook of Pentecostal Denominations in the United States." M.A.R. thesis, Pasadena College, 1954. The Arthur Carl Piepkorn: *Profiles in Belief* Collection, Graduate Theological Union Archives, Berkeley, CA.

Moral Foundations. No pages. Online: http://faculty.virginia.edu/haidtlab/mft/index.php.

Mundell, T. H., to Miss F. E. Jenner, Yunnan, W. W. China. Letter. January 8, 1915. "Pentecostal Missionary Union." CD. From iFPHC (iFPHC.org).

———. to Mr. A. A. Swift, China. Letter. April 30, 1915. "Pentecostal Missionary Union." CD. From iFPHC (iFPHC.org).

———. to Mr. F. D. Johnstone, Kongo Inland Mission, Kongo, Belge, Central Africa. Letter. April 23, 1915. "Pentecostal Missionary Union." CD. From iFPHC (iFPHC.org).

———. to Rev. W. S. Norwood, Central Asian Pioneer Mission, Abbotabad, India. Letter. January 8, 1915. "Pentecostal Missionary Union." CD. From iFPHC (iFPHC.org).

Bibliography 281

Murray, Stuart. *Biblical Interpretation in the Anabaptist Tradition*. Kitchener, Ontario: Pandora, 2000.

———. *The Naked Anabaptist: The Bare Essentials of a Radical Faith*. Scottdale, PA: Herald, 2010.

"New Bylaws on Military Service Adopted by General Council." *Pentecostal Evangel*, October 8, 1967, 7. From iFPHC (iFPHC.org).

Official Manual of the Church of God in Christ, 7th Edition. Memphis, TN: The Church of God in Christ, 1957. The Arthur Carl Piepkorn: *Profiles in Belief* Collection, Graduate Theological Union Archives, Berkeley, CA.

Olson, Roger. "Where Community is No Cliché: Forty-three Families in Rural Texas Blend Pentecostal Fervor and Anabaptist Simplicity." *Christianity Today* 49.2, February 9, 2005.

Parham, Charles, F. "War! War! War!." In *Everlasting Gospel*. 1911. Reprint. n.p.: n.d.

Pastors Manual of the Kentucky Mountain Holiness Association. Jackson, KY: Kentucky Mountain Holiness Association, 1960. The Arthur Carl Piepkorn: *Profiles in Belief* Collection, Graduate Theological Union Archives, Berkeley, CA.

Paul, George Harold. "The Religious Frontier in Oklahoma: Dan T. Muse and the Pentecostal Holiness Church." PhD diss., University of Oklahoma, 1965.

"The Pentecostal Movement and the Conscription Law." *The Weekly Evangel*, August 4, 1917, 6.

"The Pentecostal Movement and War." *The Pentecostal Testimony*, October 1939, 3. From iFPHC (iFPHC.org).

"PCPJ Guiding Principles." No pages. Online: http://pcpj.org/index.php/about-us-mainmenu-44/who-we-are/529-pcpj-guiding- principles.

"PCPJ: Our Mission." No pages. Online: http://pcpj.org/index.php/about-us-mainmenu-44/who-we-are/146-the-goal-of-the -pentecostal-peace-fellowship.

"PCPJ Purpose Statement." No pages. Online: http://pcpj.org/index.php/about-us-mainmenu-44/who-we-are/116-purpose- statement.

"Peace." In *Declarations of Faith*. Richmond, Indiana: n.p., 1887 and 1905.

Peachey, Titus, and Linda Gehman Peachey. *Christ or Country, Seeking Peace*. Intercourse, PA: Good Books, 1991.

"Pentecostal Saints Opposed to War." *The Weekly Evangel*, June 10, 1915, 1. From iFPHC (iFPHC.org).

Perry, Shawn. *Words of Conscience: Religious Statements on Conscientious Objection*. Washington, DC: National Interreligious Service Board for Conscientious Objectors, 1980.

Phillips, Frederick B. *Is War Christian?* London: Victory, 1937.

Piepkorn, Arthur C. *Profiles in Belief: The Religious Bodies of the United States and Canada, Volume III (Holiness and Pentecostal) and Volume IV (Evangelical, Fundamentalist, and other Christian Bodies)*. San Francisco: Harper and Row, 1979.

Pipkin, Keith Brian. "COGIC Endorses Human Rights in The Hague." *Pax Pneuma* 5.1. (2009) 5–10.

———. "The Foursquare Conscientious Objector: 1917–1943." M.A.R. Thesis, Azusa Pacific University, 2009.

———. "The Foursquare Church and Pacifism." In *Pentecostals and Nonviolence*, edited by Paul N. Alexander, 64–120. Eugene, OR: Pickwick, 2013.

Policies and Principles of the Open Bible Standard Churches Inc., Des Moines, IA, June 1940. Document courtesy of the Open Bible Standard Headquarters.

282　Bibliography

Pruitt, Lawrence D. *The Christian Versus War*. Guthrie, OK: Faith, n.d. [12-page bi-fold booklet.] The Arthur Carl Piepkorn: *Profiles in Belief* Collection, Graduate Theological Union Archives, Berkeley, CA.

"Quakers Pledge Aid to a Nation in War." *New York Times*, May 29, 1917. ProQuest Historical Newspapers, *The New York Times* (1851–2003) 3.

Reade, H. Musgrave. *Christ or Socialism? A Human Autobiography*. London: Marshall [1909?]

————. "The Spirit of the Age." *Trust*, November 1917, 13–15.

Record Detail from World War I Conscientious Objectors Database. No pages. Online: http://130.58.64.153/fmi/xsl/SCPC_COWW1_detail.xsl?-recid=3787.

Redford, Maury, E. "History of the Church of the Nazarene in Tennessee." B.Div Thesis, Vanderbilt University, 1934.

Report of the Annual Convention. Los Angeles: International Church of the Foursquare Gospel, 1936.

"Resolution Concerning the Attitude of the General Council of the Assemblies of God toward Military Service Which Involves the Actual Participation in the Destruction of Human Life." *The Weekly Evangel*, August 4, 1917, 6. From iFPHC (iFPHC.org).

Robeck, Cecil.M. Jr. *The Azusa Street Mission and Revival*. Nashville, TN: Thomas Nelson, 2006.

————. "Frank Sandford." In *International Dictionary of Pentecostal and Charismatic Movements*, edited by Stanley M. Burgess and Eduard M. Van Der Maas, 1037–38. Grand Rapids: Zondervan, 2003.

Rodríguez, Darío López. "From Alternative Religion to Established Religion: The Deconstruction of the 'Subversive Memory' of the Church of God." *Pax Pneuma* 5.2 (2009) 62–63.

————. *The Liberating Mission of Jesus: The Message of the Gospel of Luke*. Eugene, OR: Pickwick Publications, 2012.

Romanian Apostolic Pentecostal Church of God of North America to Arthur Carl Piepkorn. Personal letter. (n.d.) The Arthur Carl Piepkorn: *Profiles in Belief* Collection, Graduate Theological Union Archives, Berkeley, CA.

Ruch, George. "Minutes of Business Meeting of the Pentecostal Assembly of God." Spokane, WA, May 8, 1917. From iFPHC (iFPHC.org).

Salter, Darius L. *Spirit and Intellect: Thomas Upham's Holiness Theology*. Metuchen, NJ: Scarecrow, 1986.

Sandford, Frank W. *Revelation*. No pages; No date. Online: http://pentecostalpacifism.com/Shiloh3.html.

Schell, William G. *The Better Testament; or, The Two Testaments Compared: Demonstrating the Superiority of the Gospel over Moses' Law according to the Epistles of Paul, Especially That Addressed to the Hebrews*. Moundsville, WV: Gospel Trumpet, 1899.

Schlabach, Theron F., and Richard T. Hughes, editors. *Proclaim Peace: Christian Pacifism from Unexpected Quarters*. Urbana, IL: University of Illinois Press, 1997.

Schrag, Martin H. *Oath and Nonresistance: Five Texts of the Earliest Brethren in Christ Confessions of Faith*. published ca. 1976. The Brethren in Christ Historical Library and Archives, Grantham, PA.

"Scriptural Statement of Fundamentals." In *Constitution and By-Laws of the Calvary Pentecostal Church, 16th edition*. Olympia, WA: Calvary Pentecostal Church, 1962. The Arthur Carl Piepkorn: *Profiles in Belief* Collection, Graduate Theological Union Archives, Berkeley, CA.

Seymour, William J. *The Doctrines and Discipline of Azusa Street Apostolic Faith Mission by William J. Seymour, The Complete Azusa Street Library, Vol. 7.* Edited by Larry Martin. Joplin, MO: Christian Life Books, 2000.

Shelton, McDowell S. *Church of the Lord Jesus Christ of the Apostolic Faith, Conscientious Objector (Vietnam: 1968).* Letter from Shelton, General Overseer, re: Conscientious Objector, Raymond Washington to St. Louis, MO, Draft Board. The Arthur Carl Piepkorn: *Profiles in Belief* Collection, Graduate Theological Union Archives, Berkeley, CA.

Shirley, Nelson. *Fair, Clear, and Terrible: The Story of Shiloh, Maine.* Latham, NY: British American, 1989.

Short History and Polity of the Christian Nation Church Incorporated A.D., 1896. n.p.: Christian National Church, Authorized by Congress of 1954. The Arthur Carl Piepkorn: *Profiles in Belief* Collection, Graduate Theological Union Archives, Berkeley, CA.

"Should a Christian Take up Arms in Time of War?" *Foursquare Crusader* 11.40, March 30, 1938, 1–2.

"Siberian Seven Still in American Embassy in Moscow." *The Washington Observer*, June 20, 1980.

Simons, Menno "Reply to False Accusations, III." In *The Complete Writings of Menno Simons: 1496–1561*, edited by John Wenger, 554. Scottdale, PA: Herald, 1966.

———. "Reply to Gellius Faber" In *The Complete Writings of Menno Simons: 1496–1561*, edited by John Wenger, 554–56. Scottdale, PA: Herald, 1966.

Smith, Christian. *The Bible Made Impossible: Why Biblicism is Not a Truly Evangelical Reading of Scripture.* Grand Rapids: Brazos, 2011.

Soldier's Heart. No pages. Online: http://www.soldiersheart.net.

Sorola, [Sorela?] Manuel. "The Church of God, Jose M. Rodrigues Treasurer—Distributeing [*sic*] Cerculars [*sic*] for Meetings and _____." In *Investigative Case Files of the Bureau of Investigation 1908-1922*, 3. The National Archives Research Administration, Publication Number M1085, Series Old German Files, 1909–1921, Case Number 27320.

Sorrow, Norman. Interview by Jay Beaman. Phone. Abbeville, SC. April 3, 2012.

"Statement of Christ's Sanctified Holy Church Concerning War." Letter from T. F. Barker or Joseph Clelland, West Columbia, SC, to Arthur C. Piepkorn, 1968. The Arthur Carl Piepkorn: *Profiles in Belief* Collection, Graduate Theological Union Archives, Berkeley, CA.

Stephens, Randall J. *The Fire Spreads: Holiness and Pentecostalism in the American South.* Cambridge: Harvard University Press, 2008.

Storms, Everek Richard. *History of the United Missionary Church.* Elkhart, IN: Bethel, 1958.

"Suspect Violation of Espionage Act." In *Investigative Case Files of the Bureau of Investigation 1908-1922.* The National Archives Research Administration, Publication Number M1085, Series Old German Files, 1909–1921, Case Number 170047, Roll number 568, 2.

Sutton, Matthew Avery. *Aimee Semple McPherson and the Resurrection of Christian America.* Cambridge: Harvard University Press, 2007.

Synan, Vinson. *The Holiness-Pentecostal Movement in the United States.* Grand Rapids: Eerdmans, 1971.

———. *The Old-Time Power.* Franklin Springs, GA: Advocate, 1973.

284   Bibliography

"Teachings." In *Church of God General Assembly Minutes: Roll of Churches & Ministers*, 65. Cleveland, TN: Church of God Publications, 1917. The Dixon Pentecostal Research Center, Cleveland, Tennessee, 2008.

"Teachings." In *Standard Resolutions of the Church of God Mountain Assembly, Constitutional Declaration and Bylaws*. Jellico, TN, n.d. The Arthur Carl Piepkorn: *Profiles in Belief* Collection, Graduate Theological Union Archives, Berkeley, CA and iFPHC.

Teachings and Practices of the Churches of God in North America. Columbia, IN: n.p., June 15, 1959. The Arthur Carl Piepkorn: *Profiles in Belief* Collection, Graduate Theological Union Archives, Berkeley, CA.

Teaching of the Church of God Concerning the Relationship of the Church to Civil Government, the Sacredness of Human Life and Our Attitude toward War. Anderson, IN: Church of God Anderson, n.d. *Investigative Case Files of the Bureau of Investigation 1908–1922*, FBI Old German Files, Case #136078, Roll Number 590. Washington, DC: National Archives Research Administration.

Teel, George M. *The New Testament Church*. Los Angeles: Pentecostal Printing House, 1901.

Thistlethwaite, Lillian. "Victory." *Apostolic Faith* 1.4, June, 1912, 1–3. See Online: http://originalapostolicfaith.org/archives,_apostolic_faith_report.htm.

Thorn, Dennis W. *The Full Gospel Church Association, Incorporated: Constitution, Faith and Teaching*. Amarillo, TX: The Full Gospel Church Association, Inc., 1958. The Arthur Carl Piepkorn: *Profiles in Belief* Collection, Graduate Theological Union Archives, Berkeley, CA.

Titus, W. A., and E. A. Buckles. *Minutes of Apostolic Faith or Church of God*. Mulberry, KA, February 18, 19, 20, 1918. The Arthur Carl Piepkorn: *Profiles in Belief* Collection, Graduate Theological Union Archives, Berkeley, CA and ifpch.

Tomlinson, A. J. "The Awful World War." *Church of God Evangel* 8.8, February 24, 1917, 1.

———. "Loyalty and Perseverance." *Church of God Evangel* 7.43, October 21, 1916, 1.

———. "The Present Situation." *Church of God Evangel* 6.10, March 6, 1915, 1.

Triumph the Church and Kingdom of God in Christ, Junior Guide and Easy Lessons (combined). n.p.: n.d.

United Pentecostal Church International 2011–2012 Annual Report. Hazelwood, MO: UPCI, 2012.

Upham, Thomas Cogswill. *The Manual of Peace: Exhibiting the Evils and Remedies of War*. Boston: American Peace Society, 1842.

"U.S. vs. Joshua Sykes, et al." U.S. District Court, Northern California, #7042, January 21, 1919.

Wacker, Grant. *Heaven Below: Early Pentecostals and American Culture*. Cambridge: Harvard University Press, 2003.

Wakefield, Wesley H., to Arthur Carl Piepkorn, February 2, 1971. Personal letter. The Arthur Carl Piepkorn: *Profiles in Belief* Collection, Graduate Theological Union Archives, Berkeley, CA.

Walkem, Charles. "Gems of Truth." *Foursquare Crusader*, August 7, 1935, 24.

———. "The Question Box." *Foursquare Crusader*, August 2, 1939, 5.

"War and Conscientious Objectors." No pages. Online: http://ag.org/top/Beliefs/topics/contempissues_11_war.cfm.

"The War Bonds You Hold Are Fighting Bonds!" Treasury Design No. 52, "Fighting Bonds." Gugler Lithographic Company War Mobilization Campaign Posters, [1944]. See Wisconsin Historical Society. No pages. Online: http://www.wisconsinhistory.org/whi/fullRecord.asp?id=66662.

Welch, J. W., to Brother Bursell. Letter. May 23, 1917. From iFPHC (iFPHC.org).

"What We Believe." No pages. Online: http://www.churchofgodinchristmennonite.net/node/5.

What We Believe: Doctrine and General Rules. Titusville, PA: The Allegheny Wesleyan Methodist Connection, n.d. The Arthur Carl Piepkorn: *Profiles in Belief* Collection, Graduate Theological Union Archives, Berkeley, CA.

Whitt, Donald W. III. "An Open Letter to UPCI Ministers: A Biblical Examination of the Current and Proposed Resolution to the UPCI Articles of Faith on Conscientious Scruples." January, 2012. Personal files of Brian Pipkin.

"Who We Are." No pages. Online: http://www.churchofgodinchristmennonite.net/node/12.

Williams, Ernest S. "The Conscientious Objector." *Pentecostal Evangel*, June 15, 1940, 4–5.

———. "Questions and Answers." *Pentecostal Evangel*, September 21, 1935, 5. From iFPHC (iFPHC.org).

Winebrenner, John. *History of all the Religious Denominations in the United States.* Harrisburg, PA: Privately published, 1848. The Arthur Carl Piepkorn: *Profiles in Belief* Collection, Graduate Theological Union Archives, Berkeley, CA.

Wolfram, A. L. "Two Swords—It Is Enough." *Pillar of Fire*, January 3, 1917, 3.

Woolman, John. *A Word of Remembrance and Caution to the Rich.* 1898. Reprint. London: The Fabian Society, 1987.

World War I Conscientious Objector Questionnaires A-B. Plowshares: A Peace Studies Collaborative of Earlham, Goshen and Manchester Colleges. No pages. Online: http://replica.palni.edu/cdm/compoundobject/collection/gopplow/id/3560/rec/2.

World War I Conscientious Objector Questionnaires, G Miller—J Plank. Record of George Samuel Miller. Plowshares: A Peace Studies Collaborative of Earlham, Goshen and Manchester Colleges. No pages. Online: http://replica.palni.edu/cdm/compoundobject/collection/gopplow/id/8098/rec/1.

World War I Conscientious Objectors Database. Swarthmore College Peace Collection. No pages. Online: http://130.58.64.153/fmi/xsl/SCPC_COWW1_ResultTable.xsl?-lay=web&-findall=&-sortfield.1=Camp&-sortorder.1=ascend.

Yoder, John Howard. *Christian Attitudes to War, Peace, and Revolution.* Edited by Theodore J. Koontz and Andy Alexis-Baker et al. Grand Rapids: Brazos, 2009.

Ziegler, Valarie H. *The Advocates of Peace in Antebellum America.* Macon, GA: Mercer University Press, 2001.

Name Index

Adams, Blair, 166
Alexander, Paul Nathan, 186–88
Asberry, Francis, 52
Awad, Sami, 252–3
Awrey, Daniel P., 191–93

Backus, Elbert Carlton, 198–201
Barba, L. Danny, 208–11
Barclay, Robert, 112
Barth, Hattie M., 179
Barth, Paul Theodore, 179, 195
Bartleman, Frank, 138–41, 226
Beckner, Ray Leonial, 142
Bell, Eudorus N., 144, 146
Black, J. H., 137
Boddy, Alexander A., 226–27
Booth, Catherine 118–19
Booth, Herbert, 119–23
Booth–Clibborn, Arthur and
        Catherine, 240–46
Bowe, J., 158
Buckles, E. A., 143
Bursell, H. R., 17–18

Carter, Howard, 230–33
Carter, John, 233
Chamberlain, Neville, 231
Crawford, Florence, 181

Dowie, John Alexander, 68–69
Dresser, Amos, 49

Dugger, A. N., 159

Echols, Lon, 201
Ellenberg, J. Vinson, 193–94

Feltus, Wesley, 154–56
Finney, Charles G., 47–48, 97
Fox, George, 111

Garrison, William Lloyd, 36
Gee, Donald, 234–37

Hall, David A. Sr., 157
Harms, Oscar C., 132
Haywood, Garfield T., 131
Holdeman, John, 44
Hornshuh, Fred, 181
Horton, Stanley M., 147

Jernigan, Charles Brougher, 93
Johnson, Theron B., 197
Jolley, Edgar Otis, 102–5

Kiergan, A. M., 70–71
King, Martin Luther Jr., 130

Laberge, Agnes Ozman and Philemon,
        19
Laleff, Michael, 9–11, 16
Lee, Jesse, 52

288 Name Index

Mason, C. H., 156–57
McPherson, Aimee Semple, 168–72
McPherson, Rolf, 177–78
Moses, Kim, 163
Mundell, T. H., 228–30

Opperman, Daniel C. O., 131
Ozman, Agnes, 19

Parham, Charles Fox, 134–35
Patterson, Gilbert E., 157–58
Peterson, Paul B., 257
Philleo, C. W., 174
Phillips, F. B., 237–39
Pruitt, Lawrence D., 87–92

Reade, H. Musgrave, 223–25
Richey, John R., 133
Rodrigues, Jose M., 159
Rodríguez, Darío A. López, 254–56

Sackett, Myron, 175
Salman, Nihad, 254
Sandford, Frank, 71–72
Saxby, Albert E., 225
Sexton, Elizabeth A., 179, 195
Seymour, William J., 137
Shelton, S. McDowell, 172
Siberian Seven, 263

Sigwalt, Gustave, 196
Simons, Menno, 43
Skyes, Joshua, 160
Sorrow, Fletcher Dolphus, 30
Sorrow, Watson, 30

Thistlethwaite, Lillian, 135–36
Titus, W. A., 143
Tomlinson, Ambrose Jessup, 150–53
Trueblood, D. Elton, 35, 38, 113
Turner, R. J., 175

Upham, Thomas C., 52–55

Varonaeff, J. E., 256–62

Wakefield, Wesley H., 247
Walkem, Charles Wm., 176–77
Washington, Raymond, 162
Weaver, W. Bram, 240
Welch, J. W., 15–19
Wesley, John, 51–52
Whitt, Donald W., 211–15
Williams, E. S., 146
Winebrenner, John, 45, 47, 50–51, 95
Winn, George and Carrie, 84–85
Wittich, Philip, 179
Wolfram, A. L., 110–11
Woolman, John, 112

Group Index

Allegheny Wesleyan Methodist
  Connection, 63–64
Apostolic Church (Bay City, Texas),
  133–34
Apostolic Faith (Baxter Springs,
  Kansas), 134–37
Apostolic Faith (Portland, Oregon),
  141–42
Apostolic Faith Mission, 137–41
Apostolic Faith/Church of God/
  Church of God of the Apostolic
  Faith, 143
Apostolic Pentecostal Church of
  Canada, 247
Assemblies of God, 143–47
Assemblies of the Lord Jesus Christ,
  147–48
Australia Assemblies of God, 223

Bethel Baptist Assembly, Inc., 148–49
Bethlehem Bible College, 250–51
Brazos de Dios. See Homestead
  Heritage, 166
Brethren in Christ, 64–68

California Evangelistic Association,
  149
Calvary Holiness Church, 68
Calvary Pentecostal Church, 149–50
Central Pentecostal Mission, 226
Christ at the Checkpoint, 251
Christ's Sanctified Holy Church, 72–74

Christian Catholic Apostolic Church,
  68
Christian Nation Church, 74
Church of God (Anderson, Indiana),
  74–84
Church of God (Cleveland,
  Tennessee), 150–53
Church of God (Fort Scott, Kansas),
  70
Church of God (Guthrie, Oklahoma),
  84
Church of God (Huntsville, Alabama),
  153
Church of God (Stanberry, Missouri),
  159
Church of God Apostolic, Inc., 84
Church of God in Christ, 153–58
Church of God in Christ,
  Congregational, 158–59
Church of God in Christ, Mennonite,
  43
Church of the Gospel, 93
Church of the Living God, 160
Church of the Living God, 71
Church of the Lord Jesus Christ of the
  Apostolic Faith, 160–62
Church of the Nazarene, 93
Churches of God in North America
  (Winebrenner), 50, 95–97
Churches of God of the Original
  Mountain Assembly
  Incorporated, 162–64

289

290   Group Index

Congregational Holiness Church, 164
Congregational: Broadway Tabernacle, 97

Elim Pentecostal Church, 237–39
Emmanuel Association, 98–99
Emmanuel Holiness Church, 98
Emmanuel's Fellowship, 99–100

Filipino Assemblies of the First–Born, Incorporated, 164–65
Followers of Christ, 202
Free Methodist Church, 100–102

God's Missionary Church, 106
Gospel Mission Corps, Inc., 106

Holiness Christian Church, 107
Holy Land Trust, 252–53
Homestead Heritage, 165–66

Iglesia Cristiana Evangelica Mexicana, 167
Immanuel Evangelical Church (Bethlehem, Palestine), 253–54
International Church of the Foursquare Gospel [The Foursquare Church], 167–78
International Pentecostal Assemblies, 179

Kentucky Mountain Holiness Association, 108

La Iglesia De Dios Pentecostal, Incorporada, 179–80

Mennonite Brethren in Christ / Later Missionary Church Association / United Missionary Church, 108–9
Mennonites, 43
Methodism and War, 52
Mount Sinai Holy Church of America, Inc., 180

Oberlin Holiness, 48, 97

Olazabal Council of Latin–American Churches, 180–81
Open Bible Evangelistic Association, 133
Open Bible Standard Churches, Inc., 181–82
Original Pentecostal Church of God, 183

Pentecostal Assemblies of Canada, 246–47
Pentecostal Assemblies of the World, 184–85, 265–70
Pentecostal Evangelical Church, 191
Pentecostal Fire–Baptized Holiness Church, 191
Pentecostal Holiness Church, 191–97
Pentecostal Missionary Union, 228
Pentecostals and Charismatics for Peace and Justice, 186–91
Pilgrim Holiness Church, 109–10
Pillar of Fire, 110

Religious Society of Friends, 111–15
Romanian Apostolic Pentecostal Church of God, 197

Seventh Day Pentecostal Church of the Living God, 197
Swiss Pentecostal Mission, 264

The Bethlehem Evangelical Affirmation, 250
The Bible Holiness Mission, 247
The Comeouter, 198
The Fire Baptized Holiness Church, 116
The Foursquare Church. See International Church of the Foursquare Gospel.
The Full Gospel Church Association, 201
The General Assembly and Church of the Firstborn, 202–3
The Missionary Church Association / The United Missionary Church, 116–18
The New Testament Church, 118

The Pentecostal Church of God of
America, 203
The Salvation Army, 118–24, 240–46
The Wesleyan Church, 124–25
Triumph The Church, 203–4

United Holiness Church of North
America, 125
United Pentecostal Church, 204–15

Westgate Chapel, 216

www.ingramcontent.com/pod-product-compliance
Lightning Source LLC
Chambersburg PA
CBHW061430300426
44114CB00014B/1621